All Bullshit and Lies?

All Bullshit and Lies?

Insincerity, Irresponsibility, and the Judgment of Untruthfulness

CHRIS HEFFER

OXFORD
UNIVERSITY PRESS

Oxford University Press is a department of the University of Oxford. It furthers
the University's objective of excellence in research, scholarship, and education
by publishing worldwide. Oxford is a registered trade mark of Oxford University
Press in the UK and certain other countries.

Published in the United States of America by Oxford University Press
198 Madison Avenue, New York, NY 10016, United States of America.

© Oxford University Press 2020

All rights reserved. No part of this publication may be reproduced, stored in
a retrieval system, or transmitted, in any form or by any means, without the
prior permission in writing of Oxford University Press, or as expressly permitted
by law, by license, or under terms agreed with the appropriate reproduction
rights organization. Inquiries concerning reproduction outside the scope of the
above should be sent to the Rights Department, Oxford University Press, at the
address above.

You must not circulate this work in any other form
and you must impose this same condition on any acquirer.

Library of Congress Cataloging-in-Publication Data
Names: Heffer, Chris, author.
Title: All bullshit and lies? : insincerity, irresponsibility and
the judgment of untruthfulness / Chris Heffer.
Description: New York : Oxford University Press, 2020. |
Includes bibliographical references and index.
Identifiers: LCCN 2020008750 (print) | LCCN 2020008751 (ebook) |
ISBN 9780190923280 (hardback) | ISBN 9780190923297 (paperback) |
ISBN 9780190923310 (epub)
Subjects: LCSH: Discourse analysis—Political aspects. | Rhetoric—Political aspects. |
Truthfulness and falsehood—Political aspects.
Classification: LCC P302.77 .H44 2020 (print) |
LCC P302.77 (ebook) | DDC 401/.41—dc23
LC record available at https://lccn.loc.gov/2020008750
LC ebook record available at https://lccn.loc.gov/2020008751

1 3 5 7 9 8 6 4 2

Paperback printed by Marquis, Canada
Hardback printed by Bridgeport National Bindery, Inc., United States of America

To My Mother
Who taught me not to lie (or bullshit)

Contents

Preface: On Epistemic Partisanship and Trust   ix
Acknowledgments   xiii

   Introduction   1

I. THEORETICAL UNDERPINNINGS

1. Trust, Cooperation, and Insincerity   27
2. Bullshit, Inquiry, and Irresponsibility   57

II. THE TRUST FRAMEWORK

3. Claims of and Evidence for Untruthfulness   87
4. Justified Untruthfulness   111
5. Insincere Discourse Strategies   138
6. Epistemically Irresponsible Discourse Pathologies   177
7. Culpability and Breach of Trust   211

III. CASE STUDIES

8. Discourse and Democracy: The TRUST Heuristic and Sample Analyses   233
9. Poisoning and Partisanship: An Analysis of the Salisbury Nerve Agent Attack   262

   Conclusion   284

References   297
Index   323

Preface: On Epistemic Partisanship and Trust

A number of extraordinary events over the past few years seem to have led to a destabilizing of our trust in those essential institutions (the media, government, science) on which we rely for truthful information: the UK vote to leave the European Union, the election of Donald Trump as US president, the Russian propaganda war on the Internet, the proliferation of fake news on social media, and many others. In a properly functioning informational state, we expect journalists, politicians, and lawyers to build their persuasive arguments on a foundation of established evidence. In adversarial trials, for example, opposing lawyers start with a set of "agreed facts" that are not in dispute, and the evidence they present regarding the remaining disputed facts has to pass through various forms of epistemic quality control such as admissibility, rules of evidence, and objections from the opposing lawyer. In a dysfunctional "post-truth" informational state, on the other hand, these epistemic quality controls are no longer perceived to be needed.

It is not that we have "gone beyond" truth, as the term "post-truth" would seem to suggest. As we make our way in life, we slip into rabbit holes and find ourselves in echo chambers: spaces in which messages are both amplified and insulated from rebuttal. In those epistemically protected spaces, we can develop partisan ideologies that go unchallenged and so become normalized. And as they become normalized, they begin to go beyond being views that are at least theoretically open to challenge and become "truths" that are beyond challenge. In this post-factual world, the assertions made by our favorite politician or paper are "true" not because they are grounded in evidence but because they say what we want to hear. We judge an assertion as factually true or false according to whether it conforms with our preexisting view. Roberts calls this "tribal epistemology":

> Information is evaluated based not on conformity to common standards of evidence or correspondence to a common understanding of the world, but on whether it supports the tribe's values and goals and is vouchsafed by tribal leaders. "Good for our side" and "true" begin to blur into one. (Roberts 2017, n.p.)

"Tribal epistemology" is a rather unfortunate term since it can refer to the (unbiased) anthropological study of indigenous worldviews (Wautischer 1998). I prefer to coin the term *epistemic partisanship*, which focuses on the bending of knowledge itself to one's partisan interests. Indigenous tribes, when they come into contact with outsiders, may adapt or abandon their worldview in favor of the new one they have been exposed to. If someone is *epistemically partisan*, on the other hand, she is *impervious* to other perspectives. A claim is *true* only to the extent that it is held by or supports one's ideological party and is *false* to the extent that it fails to align with the party perspective.[1] For example, the US right-wing commentator Rush Limbaugh once declared:

> We live in two universes. One universe is a lie. One universe is an entire lie. Everything run, dominated, and controlled by the left here and around the world is a lie. The other universe is where we are, and that's where reality reigns supreme and we deal with it. And seldom do these two universes ever overlap. (Roberts 2017, n.p.)

If you are epistemically partisan, there is no point in being presented with counter-evidence because you already *know* the truth.

Epistemic partisanship is a significant threat to social and political stability. It can lead to a dangerous disdain for expertise and evidence. During the EU referendum in the United Kingdom in 2016, Justice Secretary Michael Gove, when asked in an interview to name one economist who backed Britain's exit from the EU, infamously replied that "people in this country have had enough of experts" (Mance 2016), while the biggest donor to the Leave.eu campaign, Arron Banks, explained immediately after the referendum that the Remain campaign lost the vote because "they featured fact, fact, fact, fact, fact" (Booth et al. 2016, n.p.). Expertise and facts were "irrelevant" to the campaign because there was just one overriding and unquestionable "truth": the need to "take back control." Epistemic partisanship can also lead to greater tolerance of malicious lying and bullshit. In the past, politicians would lose all credibility (and usually their posts) if they were found to have lied. Now, confirmed liars like Donald Trump in the United States and Boris Johnson in the United Kingdom seem impervious to accusations of lying. Their confirmed lies are considered as "irrelevant" by their

---

[1] Rini's (2017) "partisan epistemology" is weaker than this. She is referring to our tendency to trust media sources that reflect our partisan interests. But trusting one type of source more than another is not the same as holding a belief *solely* because it comes from a given partisan source. I trust the *Guardian* more than *Fox News*, but I do not trust everything written in the *Guardian* or distrust everything on *Fox News*. Someone who is *epistemically partisan* is not able to make this distinction: something is true *solely because* it was said by a given source.

supporters because of the one overriding and unquestionable "truth": that they were "making America/Britain great again."

The way to tackle this epistemic malaise is not to more vociferously call out lying on any and every occasion that a public figure might have been somewhat economical with the truth. To be called out for lying when you know you have not lied simply diminishes the credibility of the accuser. Instead, we need to develop a greater sensitivity to the economy of truthfulness and the role that epistemically partisan statements might play in that economy. Underlying the original approach to untruthfulness in this book is the surprisingly thorny question of how an epistemically partisan speaker can be untruthful. In traditional accounts we can only communicate untruthfully if we *believe* that what we say is false. Yet for Limbaugh, as for Trump's supporters, the truth matters. It is simply that the way one *accesses* truth differs from "common standards of evidence": it is not based on careful deliberation of the known evidence; it is more like religious faith. According to traditional accounts, if we sincerely believe that the *New York Times* and the BBC are "fake news," then we are being "truthful" in making that claim. If we sincerely believe that school massacres are staged by "crisis actors" trying to take our guns away, then we are being truthful if we make this claim. If we sincerely believe that British intelligence perpetrated the first ever nerve agent attack on British soil to deflect attention from the Brexit negotiations, then we are being truthful if we state this. This strikes me as a very impoverished view of truthfulness. Truthfulness cannot be just about honestly sharing what we believe, however unhinged that belief is. It must also involve some sort of personal *responsibility* to try to get facts right in the first place. In the framework developed in this book, untruthfulness encompasses both insincerity (a mismatch between belief and our conversational contribution) and epistemic irresponsibility (a failure to take care in establishing and conveying our beliefs). Anti-vaxxers, for example, may be perfectly sincere, but they are still untruthful because they have taken no appropriate care in forming their belief.

As a discourse analyst, what particularly concerns me is how we analyze untruthfulness in whatever context it occurs. My argument in this book is that the space between "truth" and "lie" is much more complex than is generally understood—it is *not* all bullshit and lies—and we have inadequate tools for analyzing untruthfulness in a post-factual world. If we restrict ourselves to language, we cannot analyze insincerity. If we restrict ourselves to deception, we cannot analyze sincerely held bullshit. We need to have a clear set of tools, though, to contribute to a fight-back against the harmful deceit and evidential quackery that is doing so much damage to our trust in people and institutions. We tend to commit both Type 1 (false positive) and Type 2 (false negative) errors. We all too easily call out lies when there is little if any evidence that the speaker believed that what he was saying was false. But we also often fail to call out epistemic irresponsibility when there is ample evidence that the speaker has not taken care in forming and conveying his beliefs.

The main purpose of the book is to develop a general theoretical framework for analyzing untruthfulness in discourse, independent of domain. In Chapter 8, I present a heuristic for applying the framework developed in earlier chapters to specific cases of putative untruthfulness in situated discourse. The framework can be applied to many different domains, from everyday conversation to testimonial perjury, from advocacy to advertising, from diplomacy to public relations. In the case study chapters I focus on the broad domain of public discourse, partly because the issue of the quality of information in the public sphere is so timely. It is certainly not the case, though, that these are the only domains of useful application of the framework I am proposing.

The book aims to have broad interdisciplinary appeal since the desire to judge untruthfulness in contemporary discourse can be found across a number of disciplines: philosophy, psychology, linguistics, communication studies, media studies, journalism, marketing, business studies, political science, sociology, anthropology, religious studies, and more. It draws heavily, as one might expect, on work in the pragmatics and philosophy of lying and deception (e.g., Carson 2010; Saul 2012; Meibauer 2014b; Dynel 2018; Stokke 2018; Meibauer 2019), but the domain addressed here is much broader, and so it also draws on such areas as the social psychology of lying and deception (e.g., DePaulo et al. 1996; McCornack et al. 2014), epistemology (e.g., Code 1987; Montmarquet 1993), semantics (e.g., Coleman and Kay 1981), discourse analysis (e.g., Galasiński 2000), sociology (e.g., Barnes 1994), and law (e.g., Shiffrin 2014). Given the intended interdisciplinary reach, I have tried not to get embroiled in "local" disciplinary disputes or to use disciplinary technicalisms or abbreviations.

Acknowledgments

This project has emerged through reflection and discussion over a considerable period of time. In terms of the genesis of ideas, I am particularly grateful to the late Bernard Williams, who first set me on the path of seeing untruthfulness in terms of both sincerity and responsibility. The linguistic pragmaticians Jocelyn Vincent Marrelli, Marta Dynel, and Jörg Meibauer ably paved the way in making untruthfulness a legitimate topic for linguists, though I fear I have gone well beyond what they might consider acceptable limits for a linguistic approach. Marta Dynel and Jörg Meibauer have also both provided assistance and encouragement. On the philosophy side, I am particularly indebted to Andreas Stokke, for his notion of insincerity as the disruption of inquiry, Thomas Carson, for his grounding of an ethical approach to deception in the Golden Rule, and the late Harry Frankfurt, for pioneering academic work on bullshit. Various aspects of the framework have been presented at conferences and workshops in Australia, China, Denmark, Finland, Germany and the United Kingdom, and I am very grateful for all the questions, comments and critique from members of the audience in each case. I am also grateful to several cohorts of MA and UG Research Experience students, who tested out aspects of the model and helped me conduct the informal survey reported in Chapter 4.

The writing of this book has benefitted from two semesters of paid School research leave in Spring 2016 and Spring 2019. Given the demands of a full-time position in a UK university in the 21st century, it would have been impossible to complete the book without these periods of leave. I appreciate the School's patience as I originally promised the book for the end of the first leave and I was still writing it at the end of the second. Given the almost equal demands of a young family, I am deeply grateful to my wife not only for "covering" for me more often than she should have but also for encouraging me to go on two strategically-timed writing retreat weekends away from the family, which helped me achieve a focus in the closing stages of the project which would not have been possible at home. At the same time, I often work best in noisy environments and I appreciate the forbearance of a number of cafés in Cardiff and Penarth where I occupied tables for long periods of time: notably the Penarth Pavilion Café and the Washington Café in Penarth and the café at the Royal Welsh College of Music and Drama in Cardiff.

I have always intended this book to have cross-disciplinary interest and so I have been very fortunate both to work in a multidisciplinary School and to have had a number of people from various disciplines read drafts of my work. Among my colleagues, I thank in particular: my Director of Research, the literary scholar Ann Heilmann, who read and commented enthusiastically on two very different versions of the book; my epistemologist colleague Alessandra Tanesini, who provided invaluable advice on at least two chapters and tried hard to make me avoid some of the most serious epistemological errors; and my visual communication colleague Lisa El Refaie, who was particularly helpful with diagram clarity. The harshest critic of my writing is my translation theorist wife, Cristina Marinetti, and I'm grateful to her in particular for pointing out a lack of clarity in early drafts of the Preface and Introduction. As a social constructionist, she has also been forbearing in listening to me talk "unquestioningly" of facts, evidence, truth and epistemic responsibility.

The book was also reviewed more formally both for the UK Government's Research Excellence Framework (REF) and for OUP. Both the internal REF reviewers (Ann Heilmann, Lisa El Refaie) and the external reviewer (Theo van Leeuwen) provided invaluable advice and encouragement on various states of revision. The OUP reviewers of both the book proposal and the complete manuscript were immensely helpful. Alan Durant waived his right to anonymity and provided exceptionally helpful comments. Chapter 9, "Poisoning and Partisanship," is a direct response to his request for more exemplification. Often the harshest critics are ultimately the most useful ones and the other OUP reviewer of a very unpolished manuscript led me to substantially revise the book and try to make sure that the originality did not come at the expense of scholarship and clarity. The originality remains but the book hopefully makes better connections with existing work particularly in the philosophy of deception. The scope of the book is too broad, and the focus too different, to be described as a work in the philosophy or pragmatics of deception as such, but I would like philosophers and pragmaticians working in this area to be able to get something from it and so I hope that the remaining lacunae and misconstruals are not too egregious. Naturally, any remaining errors are entirely my fault and I would appreciate readers pointing them out to me.

The publication process with OUP New York has been smooth and professional. The project has been overseen by two editors. Hayley Stebbins was very encouraging, patient and supportive during the proposal and initial manuscript phases. Meredith Keffer took over during the revision phase and has been supportive and efficient during the publication process. Prabhu Chinnasamy has been an efficient and reliable project manager and done well to keep the project to schedule despite the developing Covid 19 pandemic. Dorothy Bauhoff has been an acute and attentive copy editor picking up on my epistemically irresponsible mistakes. Macey Fairchild was a supportive editorial assistant and particularly helpful with the cover art. And I am appreciative of the fact that whoever translated the text into General American did not claim, as has happened in the past, that my British spellings were mistakes.

Finally, and most importantly, I am immensely grateful for the love and support of my family: my wife Cristina, who was particularly tolerant of time taken away from the family and herself, and my daughters Isabella, who is bemused that I have written a book with "Bullshit" in the title, and Valentina, who still believes in Santa and has never known a time when I was not writing this book.

Introduction

I.1. Analyzing Untruthfulness

This book develops a comprehensive framework for analyzing and judging untruthfulness in discursive practice. The TRUST (Trust-Related Untruthfulness in Situated Text) framework represents a radical reconceptualization of our understanding and analysis of untruthfulness, one that addresses the practical need both to analyze real cases of discursive untruthfulness in social and political life and to form ethical judgments about those cases. In the Preface I staked my claim to the timeliness and significance of this project. In this Introduction, I discuss the key theoretical and analytical challenges the framework tries to meet, and then set out the series of propositions that respond to those challenges and that constitute the key elements of the framework to be explored in the remainder of the book.

What is required for a detailed theoretical framework for analyzing the language and ethics of untruthfulness in situated text? First, the *scope of untruthfulness* needs to be broad enough to cover perceived actual cases of discursive untruthfulness in our current social and political world without being so broad that it ceases to have analytical purpose. And we need to be able to define clear categories and subcategories that will work within the defined domain of untruthfulness. There is little point in having a framework that cannot be applied effectively where we want to apply it. Second, we need a means of judging the *ethical value* of the act of untruthfulness. Is the act justified in the circumstances? If so, why? If not, what is it that makes it unethical? And having judged that the act is indeed unethical, how do we judge the speaker's degree of culpability? Many in the social sciences steer clear of ethical judgment altogether, but if unethical untruthfulness is perceived as a problem in society, it will not be solved by excising ethics. Finally, we need to be able to *judge* acts of untruthfulness in the full complexity of their *situated context*. Untruthfulness necessarily involves complex relations between word, mind, and world that are not easily accessible to the analytical observer. This means that analytical compromises need to be made and neither a purely philosophical approach based on intuition nor a purely linguistic approach based on empirical observation is going to be sufficient. The project will necessarily be interdisciplinary.

In the following sections I shall take up the challenges of scope, ethical value, and situated context and indicate how these are addressed in the book.

I.2. The Scope of Untruthfulness

The TRUST framework focuses on "untruthfulness" rather than the more common themes of "deception," "lying," and "insincerity." In this section, I discuss why deception and lying are not good starting points for the framework (I.2.1), why the concept of insincerity needs to be extended (I.2.2), why we need to further extend the analysis to epistemic irresponsibility (I.2.3), and why the concept of untruthfulness makes the best starting point for analysis (I.2.4).

I.2.1. Deception and Lying

While there is considerable terminological and definitional variation, there is some consensus within linguistic pragmatics and philosophy of language on the basic meaning of the terms "deception" and "lying."

Deception is intentionally causing the hearer to hold, or continue or cease to hold, a false belief; if the hearer is deceived, she comes to believe as true something the speaker knows to be false (Chisholm and Feehan 1977). Deception can be achieved through many different verbal, nonverbal, and visual means. Lying is the most well-known among many means of verbal deception. Nonverbal deception includes such means as the use of rising pitch conveying surprise to deceive the hearer about the speaker's prior knowledge of the proposition. Visual deception includes such means as camouflage, which deceives the viewer either by hiding an entity or disguising it as something else. Deception is the primary concern of psychologists interested in the processes of interpersonal communication (e.g., Burgoon et al. 1996; McCornack et al. 2014). It is also the focus of the major interdisciplinary field of "lie" detection (e.g., Vrij 2008; Ekman 2009), though this research tends to work with a rather superficial conception of lying and deception consisting in a binary lie/not lie paradigm (McCornack et al. 2014).

In distinguishing *lying* from deception, it is important to separate the *means* from the *goal*. As a discursive category, there is a general consensus in pragmatics and philosophy of language that, whatever else it might be, lying is stating what you believe to be false in a context where you are expected to be telling the truth (e.g., in judging but not joking). Lying thus lends itself very well as a *means* for achieving the immediate *goal* of deception. The means and goal, though, have traditionally been conflated. There is a very long tradition of including an *intent to deceive* the hearer as a necessary element of lying (e.g., Augustine 1961; Isenberg 1964; Chisholm and Feehan 1977; Bok 1978; Simpson 1992; Adler 1997; Williams 2002; Frankfurt 2005; Faulkner 2007; Dynel 2015; Meibauer 2018).[1] However, a number of philosophers have recently identified several types of "bald-faced lies"[2] that do not involve an intent to deceive (e.g., Carson 2006, 2010; Sorensen 2007, 2010; Fallis 2009; Saul 2012; Stokke 2013; Stokke and Fallis 2017). While lying with intent to deceive is the most common form of lying, the identification of non-deceptive lying helps distinguish verbal categories from rhetorical goals. This, in turn, can help identify the immediate discursive aim of lying not as deception but as disrupting inquiry (Stalnaker 1984, 2002; Roberts 2004; Stokke 2018). Indeed, I shall argue in Chapters 1 and 2 that the disruption or closing off of inquiry is the discursive aim of all forms of ethically engaged untruthfulness.

Deception is not a key category in the TRUST framework, partly to avoid the conflation of verbal means and rhetorical goal. Being untruthful (e.g., in hyperbole) does not necessarily mean wanting to deceive others, and being deceptive (e.g., making lying compliments) does not necessarily mean being deceitful in the moral sense. But deception is also backgrounded as a category in the TRUST framework because doing so shifts the focus from *hearer* belief, which is ultimately beyond the will of the speaker, to *speaker* belief, which is open to ethical choice. Whether or not a hearer is actually taken in by an act of untruthfulness is, to a great extent, ethically irrelevant. The fact that many in the United States and the United Kingdom will not trust a word that Trump or Johnson says, because both have established clear reputations as blatant liars and bullshitters, does not make a Trump/Johnson lie or bullshit any the less unethical.

Lying, on the other hand, is a major category in TRUST, but as a subcategory of insincerity rather than deception.

I.2.2. Insincerity

Insincerity is a lack of congruence between what a speaker *believes* and what he conversationally *contributes*. However, just as there has been a tendency to conflate deception with lying, there has been a similar tendency to conflate

---

[1] While the deceit is usually about the truth of what is stated, it is also possible for the deceit to be solely about the speaker's belief, as when a spy boss, knowing that one of his audience is a double agent, says, "Thank God there are no traitors in my section!" (Chisholm and Feehan 1977: 153; Fallis 2010: 9).

[2] This term is used quite differently in the fields of deception production and detection, where it is used to mean what linguists and pragmaticists would call a "straightforward" deceptive lie (McCornack et al. 2014).

insincerity with lying. Insincerity is often conceived, after Searle's account of it in the speech act of assertion (Searle 1969), in the restricted sense of saying what you do not believe. This also corresponds to Grice's First Maxim of Quality in his Cooperative Principle: "Do not say what you believe to be false" (Grice 1975). Knowingly stating a false belief, though, is generally considered to be lying.

Lying is certainly a key form of insincerity, but it is not even the most common form for at least two reasons. First, we not only *state* what we believe is false, but also *imply* and *presuppose* it. Stokke (2014, 2018, 2019b), in particular, has extended insincerity to indirect meaning such as false implicature (implying something false), false presupposition (intentionally presupposing something false), and false irony (pretending to be ironic). The distinction between what is said directly and what is meant indirectly has led to a binary distinction between "lying" as the "paradigmatic case of insincerity in speech" (Stokke 2014: 496) and more "problematic" indirect insincerity, which Stokke calls *misleading*. Second, we do not only state, imply, or presuppose what is false, but we *conceal* what we believe to be true, knowing that we should reveal it, either by deliberately omitting it from our account, by evading it (if questioned), or by blocking others from discovering or revealing it. The psychologist Ekman (2009: 28) notes that "concealing" is the preferred option of "liars" because it is easier to perform, easier to hide, and is often considered less reprehensible than what he calls "falsifying."[3] Accordingly, we can assume that there will be more cases of concealing in situated text than falsifying. Furthermore, even comparatively overt strategies of concealment, such as the artful dodging of questions in political interviews, can lead speakers to successfully deceive audiences (Rogers and Norton 2011). Indeed, artful dodging of uncomfortable truths through evasion and misleading was, until recently, the mainstay of politicians' rhetorical armory at interview. The artful dodger carefully navigates the space between truth and lie while managing to dodge the truth or the lie.

We certainly do not want to restrict the scope of untruthfulness, then, to *utterance insincerity*, or saying what you do not believe, but to extend it to the insincere speaker's strategies of artful dodging, which I shall call *withholding* (e.g., Webber 2013). An account of this extended notion of *discursive insincerity* is provided in Chapter 1, while details of the insincerity framework are teased out in Chapter 5. However, even discursive insincerity is still not sufficiently broad as a starting point for the TRUST framework.

---

[3] Ekman's use of "falsifying" for "lying" is somewhat idiosyncratic and there are good grounds for maintaining a threefold distinction between lying ("falsifying"), misleading, and withholding (both "concealing" in Ekman). I shall subsequently argue that lying, misleading, and withholding all serve the purpose of concealing the truth.

I.2.3. Epistemic Irresponsibility

There is a further type of insincerity not yet mentioned: we can also be insincere not by stating what is false or concealing what is true, but by failing to reveal that we do not actually know. Frankfurt (2005) introduced this type of insincerity through his philosophical account of "bullshit," or speech showing a "lack of connection to a concern with truth" (2005: 33). For Frankfurt, while lying deceives the hearer about what is said (the speaker says one thing but believes another), bullshitting deceives the hearer about the speaker's knowledge of what is said (the hearer falsely assumes that the speaker knows what she is talking about) (2005: 13). It might be said that the bullshit artist is insincere not by conveying a false belief, but by conveying a false warrant: by making an assertion, she is warranting the truth of what she says, but she conceals the fact that she has no grounds for that warrant. Accordingly, Frankfurt's "bullshit," better called "bullshitting," combines insincerity with a sense of epistemic irresponsibility: the speaker does not *care* about the truth of what she is saying. Bullshitting will be discussed in Chapters 2 and 6.

Whether withholding, misleading, lying, or bullshitting, insincere speakers are aware of what they are doing, and we have no difficulty in assigning responsibility for the insincerity when that insincerity is not justified. But what of the speaker who produces falsehoods while sincerely believing that she is telling the truth? Consider the case of Credulous Leader, who has for years been informing himself of current affairs almost exclusively through conspiracy websites such as Gateway Pundit (http://www.thegatewaypundit.com/) and InfoWars (https://www.infowars.com/) and has accordingly developed a very distorted view of the world which he now sincerely passes on to his supporters. In the absence of deliberate deception, analysts would traditionally have to fall back on the category of "careless mistake" (Sweetser 1987: 53), which tends to excuse the epistemic behavior. This seems like an implausible reaction, though, from those who know that Credulous Leader is spouting conspiracy theories. The reason we are unforgiving in such cases is because we can hold adults responsible for the way they establish, maintain, and convey their beliefs; in other words, we can hold them *epistemically responsible* for what they say (Code 1987). Furthermore, if that adult is in a position of responsibility toward others, as in the case of Credulous Leader, then there is an even greater obligation to be epistemically responsible. So if we are to account for much untruthfulness in the media and on social media, in advertising and in political campaigns, in academia and in the law, we need to hold speakers accountable to more than just their sincerity, but also to their responsibility in establishing, conveying, and retaining their beliefs. And while it is easiest to understand epistemic responsibility in the context of professional duties, this does not mean that we do not expect it in other contexts. The framework of epistemic responsibility will be teased out in Chapters 2 and 6.

In conclusion, then, we need to extend the *scope* of untruthfulness both from utterance insincerity (lying and misleading) to discursive insincerity (withholding), and from intentional insincerity to epistemic irresponsibility.

I.2.4. Untruthfulness

The TRUST framework takes *untruthfulness* as its umbrella term since it can cover the broadest spectrum of truth-defying behavior in situated discourse. A few linguistic pragmaticians (e.g., Vincent Marrelli 2004, 2006; Dynel 2018) and at least one philosopher (Williams 2002) have recognized the broader area of untruthfulness. Untruthfulness is not confined to a claim about the epistemic status of a belief in a speaker's mind (as in lying) or a claim about the speaker's intended communicative goal (as in deception). It can certainly be *covert*, as in lying and misleading, but it can also be *overt*, as in irony and hyperbole, and so need not involve either lying or deception (Dynel 2018). Accordingly, "untruthfulness" is more ethically agnostic than the morally inflected terms "lying" and "deception." Judging that an utterance or a piece of discourse is untruthful does not mean that it is *unethically* untruthful. Much more analysis needs to come into play to make that judgment.

Untruthfulness can be seen as a subset of general *misrepresentation* in discourse (Fraser 1994). Vincent Marrelli (2006: 16–22) divides misrepresentation (which she calls "non-truthfulness") into "unintentional" and "not unintentional" forms. Unintentional forms include unwitting untruths due to ignorance or distraction, miscommunication, or performance infelicities (Austin 1962), or misperception by the hearer. "Not unintentional" forms include "neutral" forms, where either it is not clear whether or not there is an intention to deceive or the speaker is being intentionally non-deceptive (i.e., overtly untruthful), and "intentional forms," which are the intentionally deceptive covertly untruthful forms such as lying, misleading, and withholding. It might be tempting, given these categories, to distinguish between unintentional "non-truthfulness" and intentional "untruthfulness," with the former not relevant to a study of unethical untruthfulness. However, while distraction, miscommunication, misperception, and performance infelicities can most often be excluded, I have claimed earlier and will argue more explicitly in Chapter 7 that ignorance may be *culpable* and thus belong to the realm of ethically engaged untruthfulness. It is also for this reason that untruthfulness cannot be confined to lying, deception, or insincerity, all of which must be intentional.

It should be noted from the start that what I am developing in this book is an *analytical framework* for judging others' acts of untruthfulness. It does not claim to be an account of how people happen to use words relating to untruthfulness (for which it would be better to undertake an analysis of large corpora of the language) or how people perceive the meaning of such words (for which it would be better to undertake surveys). Nevertheless, there is prima facie linguistic evidence that untruthfulness is not restricted to lying, insincerity, or deception. The word *untruthful* falls into three semantic fields in the Concise Roget's Thesaurus: *dishonest, erroneous, false* (Kirkpatrick 2000: 789). *Dishonest* and *erroneous* clearly fall into the insincere and irresponsible sides of untruthfulness, while *false* in Roget falls across the sincerity/responsibility divide (Kirkpatrick 2000: 526). Similarly, "telling the truth" can be used idiomatically as a synonym of "being honest," but it can also be used literally to mean "saying what is the case," as in the oath's "tell the whole truth," which does require evidential grounding. So, there are good semantic reasons for thinking that, in everyday understanding, untruthfulness involves not only insincerity but also (epistemic) irresponsibility. This prima facie evidence is not intended to be conclusive in any way. It is quite possible, for example, that detailed corpus analyses would reveal meanings distinctive to "untruthfulness." The point at this stage, though, is simply to rule out the superficial objection that a framework for untruthfulness encompassing both insincerity and epistemic irresponsibility in no way reflects the way we talk about untruthfulness in everyday life.

I.3. The Ethical Value of Untruthfulness

The second major challenge in developing an analytical framework concerns the *ethical value* that is to be ascribed to a given discursive act of untruthfulness. First, there is the question of *whether* we can ascribe ethical value at all (I.3.1). Next there is the question of *wherein* that value lies; I suggest it lies in relations of trust (I.3.2). Then there is the question of *who* is ethically responsible, the speaker or the hearer (I.3.3). Finally, there is the question of how we can *weigh up* the ethical import of an act of discursive untruthfulness (I.3.4).

I.3.1. Ethical Value and its Excision

Throughout the long history of philosophical and pragmatic reflection on truthfulness, it has always been recognized that being untruthful does not necessarily amount to being unethical (e.g., Augustine 1961; Bok 1978; Sweetser

1987; Saul 2012; Dynel 2018). However, while moral philosophers have tried to tease out the line between ethical and unethical untruthfulness, social scientists have often tried to excise ethics altogether. Saussure's linguistic value does not include ethical value (Saussure 1983[1916]). Similarly, Coleman and Kay, in their seminal analysis of the prototype meaning of "lie," noted with regard to their putative "lying" stories the "unfortunate" fact that judgments by their "subjects" regarding motives, good and ill, entered into their thinking about how to score the stories (1981: 35). The researchers saw this ethical consideration as something to "control for," to bracket out. As a discourse analyst, I want to be able to extricate discursive and pragmatic issues from ethical ones (lying is an insincere discourse strategy but not always a reprehensible one). The ethics, though, cannot simply be bracketed out and need to be part of the full account.

Ethics can be excised not only in the name of science, but also because a researcher rejects the scientific acceptance of reality. For example, in Fuller's (2006) anti-realist approach to bullshit, calling out bullshit is always and only a rhetorical strategy of privileging one's own partial perspective over another's: "The bullshit detector believes not only that there is truth but also that her own access to it is sufficiently reliable and general to serve as a standard by which others may be held accountable" (2006: 246). In short, one cannot categorize a claim as "bullshit" since there is no way of distinguishing "truth" from bullshit. This leads, though, to an ethically impoverished view of bullshit, as seen in a recent sociological theory of the concept (Wakeham 2017). Following Fuller's (2006) anti-realist line, Wakeham proposes categories of bullshit that have nothing to do with the truth status of a message but only with when speakers use the term "bullshit" to criticize others ("bullshit as criticism") or to refer to their own speech behavior ("self-described bullshitters"), or when hearers frame a speech context as a "bullshitting" one so that they can lower their expectations of truthfulness ("contextualized bullshitting"). Even "self-professed bullshitters" apparently do not make an ethical judgment of their speech behavior in a given context but simply "*communicate their savvy*[4] in terms of understanding the difference between what is required of them (typically by some authority) and what is real or true (at least in their minds)" (Wakeham 2017: 30). In short, an anti-realist approach to untruthfulness, as discussed in Chapter 3, leads to an extremely impoverished view of bullshit and of untruthfulness in general.

---

[4] All emphases in quotes are mine unless indicated as "original." This reverses standard practice, but far more of the emphases are mine than original, so this choice is more parsimonious.

I.3.2. Trust-Related Untruthfulness

If ethics are going to be included in the framework, the next question is wherein that ethical value lies. In ascribing ethical value to untruthfulness, philosophers have tended to overvalue linguistic units and undervalue interpersonal relations (e.g., Bok 1978; Kant 2012; Saul 2012). For example, there is a strong philosophical tradition of linking untruthful *speech form* with ethical evaluation. Famously, Kant (2012) saw lying as always wrong, so that one could not even lie to a murderer at the door. Such a belief depended on a linguistic ideology of speech in which *saying* what you believe is false offended the "true" nature of communication and, as such, offended God. The concept of the "mental reservation," in which one could save one's soul by telling the truth in one's mind to God while lying to one's interlocutor, is one of the absurd extremes to which this linguistic ideology could go (Bok 1978: 35–37). We see the same privileging of linguistic form or context over interpersonal relations in many accounts of justified untruthfulness (Chapter 4). Thus justified untruthfulness has been linked to properties of the speech act (only assertions are considered to warrant the truth [e.g., Austin 1962; Searle 1969]) or the speech situation (e.g., "Truth Relevant contexts" [Sweetser 1987]) or simply in terms of "exemptions" and "excuses" for breaking a discursive rule (Pettit 2015). However, justification is never so definitive that it can come down to a simple question of formally defining the speech act or event. For example, the moral permissibility of polite lies varies enormously not only across cultures but also among social groups and even among individuals. Turning to interpersonal relations, ethical value has often been located, either explicitly or implicitly, in an "intent to deceive." But deception can be a red herring. Not only are bald-faced lies often blameworthy (e.g., Sorensen 2007; Carson 2010; Arico and Fallis 2013), but there are also many cases, particularly in politeness, where speakers intend to deceive but their deceptiveness is not considered blameworthy. Furthermore, epistemic irresponsibility is often unethical even when there is no clear intent to deceive.

The TRUST framework locates the ethical value of untruthfulness in relations of trust between speakers. The crucial importance of *trust* in the ethical evaluation of lying and untruthfulness has been recognized and explained by a number of philosophers (e.g., Williams 2002; Faulkner 2007). However, the role of trust in the demarcation between ethical and unethical forms of untruthfulness and in determining the ethical culpability of a discursive act of untruthfulness has not been explored systematically. The TRUST framework attempts to provide a systematic account of the *ethical value* of untruthfulness in situated discourse. This process starts at the beginning of Chapter 1 and permeates all chapters, but with a particular focus in Chapters 4 (on justified untruthfulness) and 7 (on culpability). This introduces a normative aspect to the framework that is highly controversial from a linguistic or social scientific perspective. The modifier "trust-related" in the TRUST acronym, then, indicates a focus that includes ethical as well as linguistic considerations, but it should not be read as narrowing the scope of the framework to unethical forms of untruthfulness. The framework captures ethically positive or neutral forms of untruthfulness that either enhance relations of trust (as in politeness), or do not engage them (as in privacy), as well as the ethically negative forms that breach interpersonal or institutional trust.

I.3.3. Ethical Responsibility and Caveat Auditor

One significant problem with excising the ethical dimension from acts of untruthfulness is that responsibility for harm done can unwittingly shift from the dishonest speaker to the duped hearer. Researchers can inadvertently shift focus from the speaker's moral agency in being untruthful to the hearer's cognitive capacity to discern credible testimony, their *epistemic vigilance* (Sperber et al. 2010). Thus, it is implied that if hearers are deceived it is not because the speaker has willfully set out to deceive them, but because they have been insufficiently vigilant in assessing what the speaker has said. This is rather like blaming the theft of an old lady's handbag not on the thief who has done the stealing, but on the old lady for not being more careful in watching out for thieves.

The *caveat auditor* problem makes us aware of three ethical issues that need to be taken into account in developing a framework for analyzing untruthfulness. First, we need a framework that will focus on the *speaker's commitment to truthfulness* rather than the hearer's epistemic vigilance when assessing a speaker's utterances. Second, the framework must be able to distinguish between those many cultural contexts (e.g., fiction, irony, play, privacy, politeness, and protection) where it may be *justifiable* for speakers to suspend their commitment to truthfulness and those contexts such as professional dishonesty where the speakers are being unethically untruthful even if many hearers have learned not to trust those speakers (as indicated earlier with respect to Trump and Johnson). Finally, the framework must be flexible enough to accommodate the cultural and individual heterogeneity that characterizes most contemporary societies. We need to be able to consider not only whether suspension of a speaker's commitment to truthfulness is *typically* justifiable in a given speech context but whether it is *justified* considering all the circumstances of the specific speech situation. These issues are discussed in Chapter 4.

I.3.4. Weighing Ethical Value

One consequence of the formalist fallacy, which locates the moral wrong in a formal linguistic unit, is that discursive acts tend to be conceived in binary terms as either wrong or not wrong. But there are arguably many degrees of moral culpability in unethical acts of untruthfulness. The TRUST framework recognizes three levels of ethical engagement that respond to the following questions:

(1) Is the act of untruthfulness *justified* in the context and therefore *not wrong*?
(2) Is the speaker *blameworthy* for the wrongness of the act of untruthfulness?
(3) How *culpable* is the speaker for the act of untruthfulness?

First, categorizing an utterance as insincere or epistemically irresponsible does not in itself have ethical value: a polite lie is insincere but usually not wrong; bullshit banter is epistemically irresponsible but not wrong if participants are aware of what they are doing. Chapter 4 explores the conditions under which an act of untruthfulness may be considered *justified*, and thus not morally wrong. Second, speakers become morally blameworthy when they can be considered *willfully* insincere or epistemically *negligent*. Willful insincerity and epistemic negligence will be explored in Chapters 5 and 6. Third, though, there is a very significant range of culpability that depends mainly on dimensions relating to the breach of trust that aggravate or mitigate the act of willful insincerity or epistemic negligence. These dimensions, along with further aggravating and mitigating circumstances, are explored in Chapter 7.

I.4. The Analysis of Untruthfulness in Situated Discourse

In addition to the challenges of scope and ethical value, a third major challenge for the TRUST framework concerns a lack of practical tools for *analyzing* untruthfulness in *situated discourse*. There has been little attempt to provide a systematic *practical* framework for analyzing untruthfulness in situated contexts (I.4.1). One of the major hurdles is that we generally do not have access to the intentions or beliefs of the speaker, on which a judgment of insincerity depends (I.4.2). Linguists have tried to solve the problem by removing speaker intention from the equation, but this either distorts the concept of untruthfulness or severely restricts the application of the framework (I.4.3). Finally, though, if we accept the inclusion of mind and world, there is the problem of what constitutes evidence of untruthfulness (I.4.4).

I.4.1. A Systematic Practical Framework

The vast majority of work on aspects of untruthfulness (though mainly lying) has been conducted through discussion of hypothetical scenarios. Even when linguistic pragmaticians (e.g., Meibauer 2014b; Dynel 2018) and semanticists (e.g., Coleman and Kay 1981; Hardin 2010) work on lying and other forms of untruthfulness, they tend to do so mostly through invented examples. A few philosophers (e.g., Bok 1978; Carson 2010) have examined authentic examples of lying and deception in various domains. Carson (2010), for example, applies a moral theory based on his version of the Golden Rule to case studies of deception in such domains as advertising, negotiation, sales, and politics. These are insightful ethical analyses and I borrow Carson's version of the Golden Rule in my own analysis in Chapter 4. However, from a discourse analytical perspective, the analysis of authentic examples is often very brief. For example:

> Listerine mouthwash was long advertised as a strong (bad tasting) mouthwash "that kills millions of germs which can cause colds on contact." This ad was deceptive. Listerine does kill bacteria, but bacteria do not cause colds (colds are caused by viruses). These ads harmed many consumers. (Carson 2010: 183)

As a moral philosopher, Carson is interested in what makes advertising deceptive and morally wrong, and he uses a range of different examples to illustrate his argument. The point of TRUST, on the other hand, is to provide a systematic framework for analyzing any particular case of putative untruthfulness in situated discourse. It is intended to work with naturally occurring text that is contextually embedded, or "situated," in a given communicative event: the gossip's tweet; the opinion-maker's blog; the journalist's article; the reader's comment; the campaigner's slogan; the politician's interview; the defendant's cross-examination; the CEO's speech; the public relations message; and so on. It is designed to make sure that analysts consider and weigh up as many different elements of the situated discourse as possible and that the approach they take to different cases is as systematic as possible. In this sense it is a *discourse* analytical rather than *moral* analytical approach, even if it draws heavily on philosophy and goes well beyond the bounds of current discourse analytical methods.

Accordingly, a TRUST analysis of the Listerine ad would require a number of individual steps:

(1) CLAIM: Is this the type of claim that can be subject to an analysis of untruthfulness? Is it factually significant? Is it falsifiable? A researcher will naturally select examples that are suited to analysis, but many actual claims of untruthfulness are not, so this step is necessary when judging claims of untruthfulness. The analysis of claims is discussed in Chapter 3.

(2) EVIDENCE: Is there evidence that the claim is false? Carson provides straightforward evidence[5] from a landmark 1976 appeals case, but analyses of evidence can be much more complex than this. The analysis of Evidence (and indeed the not self-evident reason for requiring evidence of falsity in the first place) is also discussed in Chapter 3.

(3) SUSPENSIONS: Are the advertisers justified in suspending their commitment to truthfulness? No, this is not a conventional case of puffery ("washes whiter than white") but is clearly warranting the truth and no justification can be found for deceiving customers in this case. However, the justifiability of suspensions of truthfulness, discussed in Chapter 4, can be much more complex than this.

(4) SINCERITY: For the claim to be insincere, we need evidence that the advertisers believed it was false. If they did, then this is a lie rather than misleading (Carson's "deceptive") because we have a defining relative clause restricting the scope of "germs" (i.e., "germs which can cause colds on contact"). Since those particular germs are viral and the ones Listerine kills are bacterial, there is no equivocation of the sort there would be if the advertisement claimed, for example, "Germs cause colds; Listerine kills millions of germs." If believed false, the claim is *willfully* insincere. The analysis of insincerity and willfulness is discussed in Chapter 5.

(5) RESPONSIBILITY: Even if the advertisers were not aware of the different types of germs and the ineffectiveness of Listerine on the ones that cause colds, they have clearly been epistemically irresponsible in making this claim since they could easily have checked their claim with scientists. Furthermore, the conditions hold for judging this act of epistemic irresponsibility as *negligent*. The analysis of epistemic irresponsibility and the conditions for negligence are discussed in Chapter 6.

(6) CULPABILITY: Given that Carson is applying a utilitarian moral theory, he goes on to detail the ways in which consumers will be harmed. The analysis of culpability in Chapter 7, though, indicates a number of different dimensions of culpability, of which harm is only one.

There have been very few discourse analytical studies of forms of untruthfulness and, for reasons explained in the following, these have tended to be confined to a narrow range of phenomena such as textual distortions and taking words out of context (Galasiński 2000). Habermas's (1998) "discourse ethics" might look initially promising, but rather than being an account of the ethics of discourse, it is a theory of ethics that provides a form of moral dialogism

---

[5] It is perhaps not clear from the explanation that germs include both viruses and bacteria, but Listerine only kills surface bacteria in the mouth and not the viruses that cause colds.

in which one should seek others' reasonable agreement before forming one's moral conscience. There is also an established subfield of communication studies called "Communication Ethics." However, while there is considerable discussion of "truth" and "truthfulness" in this work, there is only fleeting reference to "untruthfulness," "lying," or "bullshit" in three of the seminal edited collections in the field (Christians and Traber 1997; Keeble 2008; Cheney et al. 2011) and there are no attempts to create systematic frameworks for analyzing untruthfulness.

There have been many categorizations of *types of deception*, which will be discussed in Chapter 5, but these only cover step 4 in the preceding sketch of the TRUST heuristic, and even then not directly since they focus on deception rather than insincerity. There has also been some work on types of bullshit, discussed in Chapter 6. However, there has been no previous systematic attempt to take the discourse analyst from identification of a putative case of untruthfulness, through consideration of whether the untruthfulness is justified, to the categories of untruthfulness involved, and finally to an assessment of the culpability of the breach of trust. The lack of such a framework may be due to what might be called the "Word-Mind-World" problem of untruthfulness.

I.4.2. The Word-Mind-World Problem

My central claim about the *situated analysis* of untruthfulness is that TRUST can be applied to specific putatively untruthful claims made in situated text or discourse. However, given the cognitive nature of sincerity (based on speaker belief) and the empirical nature of epistemic responsibility (based partly on available evidence), it is particularly difficult to judge untruthfulness in discourse. A lie that is not detectable as a lie is textually indistinguishable from a "felicitous assertion" in speech act pragmatics (Austin 1962), and factual falsity is neither necessary nor sufficient for untruthfulness: we can lie while telling the truth, and we all make innocent factual mistakes.[6] Untruthfulness, then, needs to be seen in the context of the full speech situation (Hymes 1974) or the "total speech act in the total speech situation" (Austin 1962: 148), including the genre, the surrounding discourse, intertextuality, and the common ground between speaker and hearer. However, untruthfulness cannot be detected in the words themselves. There must always be a relation between word and mind (discursive insincerity) or word, mind, and world (epistemic irresponsibility).

---

[6] Though see discussion in Chapter 4 of Turri and Turri (2015), who attempt to prove otherwise.

This very real analytical problem of getting from objective falsity to subjective untruthfulness is often missed because we take mental shortcuts. The fundamental attribution error (Ross 1977), which leads us to attribute intentionality to others' actions whereas we would often put them down to circumstances when judging our own behavior, leads us to be quick to move, in many contexts, from factual falsity to lying when judging others' discursive behavior. Parents know only too well how quickly children make this link ("You said you were going to pick me up—you lied!") but adults equally engage in this "fast thinking" (Kahneman 2013). In this respect, the fact-checking organization PolitiFact's alethic categories are revealing: "True," "Mostly True," "Half True," "Mostly False," "False," and "Pants on Fire." The first five clearly concern objective truth and falsity. The last, jocular category is defined as "the statement is not accurate and makes a ridiculous claim" (Drobnic Holan and Qiu 2015). While ridiculousness is certainly a subjective evaluation, it is not one that points necessarily to false belief: intelligent design is far from scientifically accurate and certainly makes ridiculous claims, but those claims are sincerely believed as true by very many people. So, the rhyming implication of "Pants on Fire" is actually quite misleading: simply because a claim is "ridiculous" does not make it into a lie. However "unhampered by accuracy" (Drobnic Holan and Qiu 2015) Trump may be, he is not necessarily always lying, though we have many attested cases of him doing so.

The solution to this problem in the TRUST framework is to focus on epistemic irresponsibility when there is no clear evidence of insincerity. For this reason, in the TRUST heuristic (see Chapter 8), the analysis of sincerity precedes the analysis of epistemic responsibility. We would want to judge a speaker as being insincere where the evidence permits this. However, where there is no clear evidence of insincerity, there is often clearer evidence of irresponsibility.

I.4.3. Discourse Analysis and the Word-Mind-World Problem

This necessary link beyond the text to mind and/or world, though, has made linguists and discourse analysts reluctant to tackle the topic of untruthfulness despite long recognizing the fundamental social significance of lying and the need to tackle untruthful discourse in the form of propaganda (Weinrich 2005[1965]) and obfuscating jargon (Bolinger 1973: 542). Both Weinrich (2005[1965]) and Bolinger (1973) tried to avoid the mind/world problem by attempting to locate "lying," for analytical purposes, in the linguistic forms themselves. Bolinger tried to extricate lying from speaker intentionality to make it more accessible to text analysis: "[W]hen two parties are in communication, anything that may be used which clogs the channel, and is not the result of accident, is a lie. I am trying to paint the lie as black as I can by not requiring that it be intentional" (Bolinger 1973: 542). Yet the line between "accidental" and "non-intentional" "clogging of the channel" seems very fine indeed. One might consider this to be the domain of "bullshit," but then Bolinger is losing the important distinction between lying and bullshit teased out in Chapters 2 and 6.

Weinrich (2005[1965]) went further and, in an article entitled "The Linguistics of Lying," argued that collocations such as *Blut und Boden* ("Blood and soil"), which was used by the Nazis to justify both purity of race and territorial expansion through *Lebensraum* ("living space"), can become "lying words": "Words thought of without contextual determination cannot lie. But all it takes is a little context, like a connection with *and*, for words to lie" (Weinrich 2005[1965]: 36). Again, this is a very odd use of *lie* where there is no human agency behind the lying. But if the agency is implied (one lies through lying words), then again this does not work since there have always been people who sincerely believe unsubstantiated or repugnant ideologies. This makes them ignorant or morally reprehensible, but it does not make them liars. Again, it might be possible to reinterpret *Blut und Boden* as bullshit: there was no empirical grounding for the Nazi claims relating to this collocation. However, in removing speaker intentionality and belief from their definitions of lying, Bolinger and Weinrich were ignoring both lay and expert understanding.

More recently, Galasiński (2000, 2019; Galasiński and Ziółkowska 2013), calling for "an 'all-linguistic' research into deception within discourse analysis," offers a typology of deception which "assumes that both the deceptive communication ('the lie') and the reality it misrepresents are linguistic" (Galasiński 2019: 521). For Galasiński, the "ideal data" for a discourse analysis of deception consists not in a contrast between word and world, between what is said and what we know is actually the case, but in the contrast between two linguistic representations of the world: the "initial description of reality" and the "misrepresentation of that description" (2019: 522). There is no need, in Galasiński's view, to consider the reality behind the claims at all. Accordingly, the application of his typology is restricted to the misrepresentation of the content or function of a previous linguistic utterance. Thus, the three types of deception he proposes are "falsifications" (lying about what was said), "distortions" (strengthening/generalizing or weakening/particularizing what was said), and "taking words out of context" (ascribing a different function to what was said). These are discourse analytical categories well worth studying in their own right, but they represent a very small slice of the untruthfulness pie: "falsifications" are a small subset of lying, "taking words out of context" is a significant element of misleading through framing (discussed in Chapter 5), while "distortions" are very common, but I shall argue in Chapter 6 that it is not at all clear that they are always deceptive.

Furthermore, even in so restricting the scope of inquiry, it is not at all clear that the problem of intentionality is avoided. While Galasiński (2000, 2019) accepts that the researcher still has no access to the speaker's intention to deceive, he considers that "on the assumption of the 'normality' of the world, one could argue that it is unlikely that person B would immediately forget what s/he had heard or that s/he would have misheard A, having heard everything else" (Galasiński 2019: 522). However, this view seems to assume an ideal communication process in which speaker A is eminently clear and unambiguous and able to make himself understood in his own terms (Heffer 2013b, 2017) and speaker B is consistently listening attentively with optimal hearing and is not subject to cognitive biases affecting what she actually hears (Arlinger et al. 2009).[7] It also ignores the fact that we are often busy processing what we are going to say and only half-listening to what our interlocutor is saying. Furthermore, while we usually do not *immediately* forget what we have consciously heard (numbers are a notable exception), there is a wealth of empirical evidence demonstrating that long-term memory is unreliable (e.g., Loftus 1992; Danziger 2008). Therefore, even confining oneself to discourse, one cannot make a completely "safe" attribution of lying or misleading.

Weinrich, Bolinger, and Galasiński, then, were not particularly successful in bringing lying/untruthfulness into the strict realm of linguistics and the analytical safety of textuality. However, the fact that the study of discursive untruthfulness cannot be confined to linguistics does not mean that linguistic analysis is not *necessary* in the analysis of discursive untruthfulness. The TRUST framework grounds analysis as far as possible in language and keeps discourse categorization distinct from ethical evaluation. For example, as indicated in Chapter 5, the three principal discourse strategies can be identified linguistically: lying involves explicit assertions, misleading is suggested linguistically (e.g., through lexical equivocation and false implicature), while withholding is marked by linguistic absence (though often cued). Yet any of the three can occur willfully or where the speaker's commitment to truthfulness has been justifiably suspended in the context. Furthermore, one of the key conditions for epistemic negligence, discussed in Chapter 6, is that the speaker has not hedged (epistemically attenuated) her claims in accordance with the availability of evidence.

In conclusion, we need to develop more subtly the links between word, mind, and world and how these relate to our ethical evaluation of untruthful discourse. To do this, we need to draw not only on linguistic pragmatics and discourse analysis, but also on epistemology, ethics, psychology, and the law.

---

[7] As a hearing-impaired father with a (often mumbling and imprecise) five-year-old daughter, this could not be further from my communicative reality.

I.4.4. Big Truth, Little Truths: The Evidential Enigma

Truthfulness, as will be argued in Chapter 1, is a thoroughly subjective notion: it concerns not the objective truth but the way one *engages attitudinally* with word and world. However, because of the cognitive access issue, Chapter 3 will argue that when analyzing situated discourse, it is mostly impractical not to start with a putatively false statement and the evidence for that falsity; in other words, with a "fact check." Furthermore, epistemic responsibility crucially involves (though is not confined to) trying to get one's facts right. This understandably discomfits not only anti-realists such as Fuller who believe that there is no independent reality, no "facts" as such, or no "reliable" ways of accessing those facts, but also those who subscribe to the social construction of belief, "the epistemic claim that the correct explanation for why we have some particular belief has to do with the role that that belief plays in our social lives, and not exclusively with the evidence adduced in its favor" (Boghossian 2001: 6).

The TRUST framework is agnostic with respect to the truth wars (Lynch 2004; Blackburn 2005) but, unlike Fuller (2006), it does assume that we can distinguish more from less reliable evidence. It is indubitably the case that people are often too quick to call out lies (in the absence of evidence of false belief) or bullshit (in the face of contrary opinion), but many claims do point to independently established states or events in the world that can be falsified. Other putative facts are not falsifiable and so fall into the realm of opinion. The political slogan "Let's take back control" seems to presuppose the dubious claim that we have lost control, but the notion of "losing control" is too nebulous to submit to an analysis of untruthfulness. This is an opinion to argue against, not a fact to check. We shall see in Chapter 3 what *is* required in terms of evidence for untruthfulness. TRUST generally requires analysts to consider the factual status of claims as a *precursor* to an analysis of untruthfulness, but this does not entail taking a naïve view of truth or an essentialist view of socially constructed phenomena.

I.5. The Central Theoretical Propositions of the TRUST Framework

Having introduced the challenges of scope, ethical value, and situated analysis of untruthfulness, it is now possible to set out the propositions advanced by the TRUST (Trust-Related Untruthfulness in Strategic Text) framework with respect to each of these challenges:

S: The Scope of Untruthfulness
The scope of untruthfulness in situated discourse needs to be attuned in two main ways:

S1 *Insincerity* needs to be extended from *utterance insincerity* (stating or suggesting what you believe to be false) to *discursive insincerity* (failing to disclose to the hearer what you believe should be disclosed). All forms of insincerity *conceal*[8] the truth. Some forms of concealment *verbally misrepresent* the truth. Some forms of verbal misrepresentation, in turn, also actively *falsify*. I propose the following more standard terms to refer to the different levels: *withholding* (concealing without verbally misrepresenting), *misleading* (verbally misrepresenting without falsifying), and *lying* (as the standard term for falsifying).

S2 *Untruthfulness* as a whole needs to be broadened from *discursive insincerity* to include the *epistemic irresponsibility* with which speakers act in forming, retaining, and/or conveying their beliefs. The central category of *dogma* (disregarding counter evidence) includes *distortion* (explicit linguistic misrepresentation) and *bullshit* (a reckless lack of grounding in evidence).

E: The **Ethical Value** of Untruthfulness
The ethical value of untruthfulness hinges on the notion of *trust* (thus the acronym TRUST), since we not only presume but trust that speakers will tell the truth. The central role of trust is manifested in three ways in the analysis of situated untruthfulness:

E1 There is no negative ethical value to untruthfulness when the speaker's commitment to truthfulness has been *justifiably suspended*: either there is no breach of trust (there is a mutual understanding that truth is not in play) or the interpersonal breach of trust is overridden by more pressing moral considerations (e.g., the right to privacy or preserving the hearer's face).

E2 Discursive insincerity and epistemic irresponsibility are considered to be *willful* or *negligent*, respectively, when there is an unjustified breach of trust. Epistemic irresponsibility breaches trust, and thus becomes negligent, only under certain conditions.

E3 The precise conditions of trust in place in a given discursive context, combined with further aggravating and mitigating circumstances, will determine the degree of *culpability* of the act of untruthfulness.

---

[8] I am using "conceal" loosely here as an antonym of "reveal." I note the distinction between passively withholding and actively concealing in Chapter 6.

D: The **Analysis** of Untruthfulness in **Situated Discourse**
It is possible to provide a systematic analysis of untruthfulness in situated discourse. The TRUST framework can be applied to specific, putatively untruthful claims made by real people in complex strategic contexts.

D1 Discursive insincerity can be analyzed in terms of a speaker's intentional *insincere discourse strategies* (withholding, misleading, and lying), which can be broken down into a number of sub-strategies and pragmatic tactics for achieving those strategies.

D2 Epistemic irresponsibility can be analyzed in terms of the discursive product: *irresponsible discourse pathologies* (dogma, distortion, and bullshit), which can be broken down into a number of *discursive symptoms*.

D3 The various forms of contextual, categorial, and ethical analysis required in TRUST can be combined into a simple *heuristic* that offers a clear set of sequential analytical steps which facilitate a comprehensive analysis of untruthfulness in situated discourse: CLAIM (analysis of the assertion and its falsifiability); EVIDENCE (for falsity and unreliability); SUSPENSIONS (whether a suspension of epistemic commitment is justified); SINCERITY (analysis of insincere discourse strategies and whether they are willful); RESPONSIBILITY (analysis of epistemically irresponsible discourse pathologies and whether they are negligent); CULPABILITY (analysis of the breach of trust along ethical dimensions and consideration of mitigating and aggravating circumstances); and a final JUDGMENT of the claim.

These theoretical propositions will be referred to throughout the book using the codes indicated in the preceding.

I.6. TRUST: An Overview

In a nutshell, then, the TRUST (Trust-Related Untruthfulness in Situated Text) framework aims to provide a comprehensive account of untruthfulness as encompassing both discursive insincerity (failing to disclose what you believe you should disclose) and epistemic irresponsibility (failing to establish, maintain, and convey one's beliefs with care).

Chapters 1 and 2 provide the theoretical grounding for the two central TRUST concepts of discursive insincerity and epistemic irresponsibility. Chapter 1 explores the theoretical underpinnings of the concept and ethics of insincerity, focusing on propositions S1 (insincerity) and E (ethical value). Starting with the ethics (E), I argue that to preserve trust in others, we not only presume truthfulness in our interlocutors, but that we have a concomitant ethical commitment to truthfulness. While deception breaches that interactional trust, not all cases of insincerity involve deception, and deception is not a requisite for breach of trust. The chapter then works toward an account of insincerity (S1). Grice's cooperative principle provides a good account of insincere implicature, but his maxim of sincerity is too narrow for our purposes. I then follow Stokke (2018) in seeing insincerity as a deliberate disruption of inquiry. However, I argue that Stokke does not go far enough and that we need an account of *discursive* insincerity.

Chapter 2 explores the theoretical underpinnings of the concept and ethics of epistemic irresponsibility, focusing on propositions S2 (epistemic irresponsibility) and E (ethical value). I begin by establishing the link between epistemic responsibility and trust and note how one can be responsibly wrong. I then discuss the concept of intentional bullshitting as a category bridging insincerity and irresponsibility. However, bullshit can also be unintentional while still being untruthful, and so we require a revised maxim of truthfulness that combines sincerity and epistemic responsibility. Since epistemic irresponsibility is generally not intentional, it manifests in discourse not in strategies but in *pathologies*. The umbrella discourse pathology is dogma, which closes off inquiry. Finally, I consider Saul's (2018) recent notion of "negligent falsehood" and compare it to the TRUST account of negligence.

Chapters 3–7 work through the steps of the TRUST heuristic (D3). Chapter 3 focuses on the first two steps: CLAIM and EVIDENCE. I begin by noting our four principal rational motives for calling out lies and bullshit (confession, detection, self-contradiction, and falsification), but point out that in the majority of cases we rely primarily on falsification. This is problematic because Chapters 1 and 2 stress that both discursive insincerity and epistemic irresponsibility are subjective rather than objective notions. Our reliance on falsification as a starting point for analysis restricts the application of the framework primarily to "factually significant" and "falsifiable" claims. Not all claims are clearly fact or opinion, and I make a distinction between "*salty*-type" statements that invite further investigation and "*tasty*-type" statements that invite agreement or disagreement but not further investigation. Only "*salty*-type" claims are open to analysis. Finally, I consider the challenge of anti-realism to the framework and argue that there is more consensus about evidence than the "truth wars" would suggest.

Chapter 4 outlines a systematic framework for analyzing the many discursive circumstances in which speakers may justifiably suspend their commitment to truthfulness (E1). I discuss three main types of suspension—conventional, consequential, and condonable—and consider the conditions under which they are both justifiable in principle and justified in practice. I note that there is no inevitable correlation between discourse context and trust, and that it is breach of trust that is the primary determinant of whether or not a speaker's suspension of her commitment to truthfulness is justifiable in principle. Moreover, suspensions that might be considered justifiable in principle (e.g., irony) are not always justified in practice (e.g., with vulnerable addressees).

Chapter 5 sets out a framework for analyzing insincere discourse strategies (D1). I argue that the underlying insincere discourse strategy is *withholding* (failing to disclose what you believe you should disclose), while *misleading* involves *linguistically* leading the interlocutor astray with regard to that concealed knowledge either by suggestion (*misleading without lying*) or explicit assertion (*lying*). The insincere discourse strategies may be realized through pragmatic tactics (e.g., equivocating and falsely implicating are pragmatic tactics used in the strategy of misleading). Insincere discourse becomes unethical when it is *willful* (i.e., breaching trust and not justifiably suspended) (E2).

Chapter 6 sets out a framework for analyzing epistemically irresponsible discourse pathologies (D2). I begin with the bridge category of insincere bullshitting. I then argue that the underlying discourse pathology is *dogma*, or closed-minded discourse that *disregards* counter-evidence. Dogma can then lead to the discourse pathology of *distortion* (e.g., overstatement), which *misrepresents* the evidence and/or the epistemic confidence we can justifiably have in it. Distortion, like misleading, is manifested linguistically and obfuscates the truth. Finally, *bullshit* is a form of radical distortion that misrepresents the evidence by appearing to ignore altogether the need for evidential grounding. Given that we are naturally prone to being epistemically irresponsible, the bar is set quite high for *epistemic negligence* (E2): the speaker must be performing a particular role that requires a duty of epistemic care; her investigation of the evidence must fall short of what one would expect given that role; and she must not have hedged her claims in proportion to the evidence.

Chapter 7 sets out a framework for analyzing the relative culpability of the breach of trust represented by willfully insincere and/or epistemically negligent discourse (E3). Given that blameworthiness is usually linked with intentionality, I need to argue in favor of culpable ignorance in order for epistemic irresponsibility to be ethically wrong. After illustrating why an analysis of culpability is necessary for the framework, I argue that we can best establish degree of culpability by considering the gravity of the breach of trust involved. I consequently propose nine contextually based trust-related dimensions (e.g., the vulnerability of the hearer, the institutional power of the speaker, and the perceived harm that might result from the untruthful discourse) and suggest that the ethical breach might be aggravated or attenuated accordingly. Finally, I consider further aggravating and mitigating circumstances that need to be taken into account when making a final ethical JUDGMENT of the discursive act of untruthfulness.

Chapters 8 and 9 apply the TRUST framework to specific examples of untruthfulness. In Chapter 8, I first review the six steps in the TRUST heuristic (D3) and then I apply that heuristic to high-profile cases of untruthfulness in public discourse: Trump's tweet about large-scale voter fraud; the Brexit "battle bus" claim that the United Kingdom sends £350 million a week to the European Union; and Tony Blair's assertions about Iraq possessing weapons of mass destruction. I trouble the simple attribution of lying in these cases and show how a TRUST analysis can lead to a deeper understanding of the types and ethical value of consequential untruthfulness.

In Chapter 9, I move from an analysis of specific texts to a much broader analysis of multiple untruthful claims connected with a single case: the poisoning of the Russian double agent Sergei Skripal. This represents a different way of applying the TRUST framework, working from the context of a news event to the many different types of discourse engaging with that event. The study also demonstrates how the framework can be used to confirm the truthfulness of claims as well as their untruthfulness. Finally, the danger of epistemic partisanship is seen very clearly in this study.

In the Conclusion, I discuss the implications, limitations, and directions of the three central claims in the TRUST framework and then discuss possible applications of the framework not only in the media, advertising, and the regulation of political campaigning, but also in explorations of intercultural (mis) communication and analyses of inter-group and inter-individual variation.

PART I
THEORETICAL UNDERPINNINGS

The first part of the book establishes the theoretical grounding for the two faces of untruthfulness: discursive insincerity and epistemic irresponsibility. Chapter 1 grounds sincerity in an indispensable need for trust and cooperation and notes how insincerity can breach trust. It argues that insincerity should be rooted not in deception but in the disruption of inquiry. It also draws on a psychological account of how untruthfulness works in situated discursive practice to argue that insincerity needs to be extended to the extremely common cases where speakers "edit out" truthful information from their speech production.

Chapter 2 argues that while the growing work on *bullshitting* and *bullshit* enriches our understanding of epistemically irresponsible discourse, the focus on relating bullshitting to lying and insincerity prevents us from seeing bullshit as deriving from a distinct aspect of untruthfulness. Instead, taking dogma rather than bullshit as a point of departure opens up this aspect of untruthfulness to broader epistemic concerns.

1
Trust, Cooperation, and Insincerity

> *No liar preserves faith in that about which he lies. He wishes that he to whom he lies have faith in him, but he does not preserve this faith by lying to him.*
>
> —Augustine (1950: 57)

1.1. Introduction

Underlying the TRUST framework is a broadened conception of the *scope* of truthfulness (S) that encompasses two different but connected aspects of the way in which we make communicative contributions: the *sincerity* with which we share our beliefs and the *responsibility* to take care in forming and conveying those beliefs. This chapter provides theoretical groundwork for the insincerity aspect of a broadened conception of untruthfulness. It begins by grounding truthfulness in an indispensable human need for trust and cooperation (1.2). In order to cooperate successfully, we need to presume that others are talking truthfully, but since we cannot read others' minds, we must *trust* that they are being truthful. When a speaker intends to deceive a hearer, though, that trust is betrayed and we may feel resentment. This might be the beginning of an established account of the link between truthfulness, trust, and deception and thus responds to my claims relating to *ethical value* (E). However, I trouble that account in the following section (1.3), where I argue that the central focus of an untruthfulness framework should not in fact be deception since not all cases of insincerity involve deception; deception is not a requisite for breach of trust; and the other face of untruthfulness, epistemic irresponsibility, does not involve a conscious intent to deceive. Instead, I argue that we should focus on communicative cooperation and the nature of inquiry. First, I explore the link between cooperation and insincerity through Grice's Cooperative Principle (1.4). I note how a certain type of indirect speaker meaning (implicature) can only be understood against a background of conversational presumptions, and I consider attempts to explain lying in terms of Grice's sincerity maxim. However, this sincerity maxim effectively only covers lying, excluding other forms of insincerity covered by deception. Second, then, and after Stokke (2013, 2018), I move the focus to ongoing communicative inquiry. A first step in extending the scope of sincerity to communicative inquiry is to move from a focus on what is linguistically *asserted* to a focus on what is *contributed* to the ongoing inquiry (1.5). This will cover cases of misleading such as false implicature, where what is asserted is true but what is contributed is false. But it still leaves out the most common form of deception: deliberate omission of problematic information. In the final section (1.6), then, I turn to the analysis of *situated discourse* (D) and sketch out a notion of *discursive insincerity* rooted in what we know of the process of deceptive communication. The notion of discursive insincerity then becomes an umbrella concept for understanding the nesting of lying within misleading and misleading within withholding, which underlies the categories of insincerity discussed in Chapter 5.

1.2. Truthfulness, Trust, and Cooperation

Human society is built around cooperation, and one of the principal means by which we cooperate is through language. For language to contribute successfully to our cooperative enterprises, we must be cooperative in the way we use language. This means we must be able to trust that others are being truthful (1.2.1). Yet if we want others to be truthful, we must be willing to reciprocate, and thus there is motivation for an evolutionary development of an ethical commitment to truthfulness (1.2.2). An intent to deceive, then, betrays our trust that the speaker is committed to being truthful (1.2.3).

1.2.1. Trust and the Presumption of Truthfulness

There is a very considerable philosophical (e.g., Grice 1975, 1989; Lewis 2002; Williams 2002; Carson 2010; Pettit 2015) and psychological (e.g., Gilbert 1991; Levine et al. 2010; Levine 2014) literature effectively establishing that we work in interaction with a default presumption that, all things being equal, the speaker will be truthful. Terminology varies widely across sources. For example, the presumption is called a "truth bias" in psychology (e.g., Buller and Burgoon 1996),[1] a "Maxim of Quality" by Grice (1975, 1989) and a "warranty of truth" by Carson (2010: 26). However, theorists seem to be referring to broadly the same concept, and there are good grounds for calling this a "presumption" and relating it to

---

[1] Arguably this is because psychologists tend not to be concerned with the distinction between truth and truthfulness. From an individual psychological perspective, everything is necessarily subjective.

subjective truthfulness rather than objective truth.[2] The notion of presumption (an experience-based inference that guides action) is useful because it conveys the idea that a certain assumption holds *unless and until* it is *overturned* by new evidence (Walton 2014). We can start with the presumption that people will be truthful but then overturn this presumption in the light of the context (e.g., fiction or irony) or if we perceive evidence of abuse (such as lying) or abnormal conditions (such as a cognitively impaired interlocutor). Thus, Carson notes that

> [i]n our linguistic community ... there is a *presumption* that the warranty of truth is in force in any situation. *Convention* dictates that one warrants the truth of one's statements in the absence of special contexts, special signals, or cues to the contrary. (Carson 2010: 26; original emphasis)

Furthermore, there is empirical evidence that this presumption or bias is overturned in contexts where it is perceived as less likely to hold, such as in judging the honesty of salespeople (DePaulo and DePaulo 1989). In these contexts, normal spontaneous judgment of truthfulness shifts to "reflective judgement" (Faulkner 2014b: 192). When we perceive, on reflection, that an interlocutor tends to be untruthful, we reduce our trust in that interlocutor, who in turn becomes perceived as less *trustworthy* (DePaulo and DePaulo 1989).

The most convincing evolutionary and social psychological explanation for this presumption of truthfulness is our need to trust others and to be considered trustworthy in turn (Simpson 2007).[3] One can see how a "convention of truthfulness and trust" (Lewis 1983: 167) would develop evolutionarily. Once it is recognized that cooperation between individuals will lead to mutual benefit, there are instrumental advantages in being able to expect one's interlocutor to be truthful (Williams 2002: 58). If we are a prehistoric hunter and a companion observes a ferocious saber-tooth tiger behind us, we trust that our companion will reveal its presence to us. It can then be expected that I will reciprocate the favor in an analogous situation in the future. This is effectively a manifestation of Trivers's biological concept of "reciprocal altruism":

> Reciprocal altruism can ... be viewed as a symbiosis, each partner helping the other while he helps himself. The symbiosis has a time lag, however; one

---

[2] Sweetser (1987) argues, though, that our folk beliefs include a presumption of objective truth. See Chapter 4.

[3] Other explanations include Wilson's (1959) Principle of Charity, which requires us to interpret a speaker's statements as rational, Sweetser's Idealized Cognitive Model of helpfulness, with its maxim "Help, don't harm" (Sweetser 1987: 49) and Horn's precondition for interpreting other conversational maxims (Horn 2004: 7).

partner helps the other and must then wait a period of time before he is helped in turn. (Trivers 1971: 39)

The reason that trust is so inextricably linked to truthfulness is because we generally do not possess hard evidence that the speaker is in fact being truthful. Accordingly, we can only *trust* that the speaker is being truthful (Luhmann 1979; Hardin 2002). If it were almost always the case that speakers were being truthful, the need for trust would not be an issue. But we know that others are frequently not truthful. Therefore, trusting that someone is telling the truth inevitably involves taking risks (Luhmann 1979: 24): "Trust presumes a leap to commitment, a quality of 'faith' that is irreducible" (Giddens 1991: 19). Indeed, Fried argued that when we assert, we intend to "invite belief, and not belief based *on the evidence* of the statement so much as *on the faith* of the statement" (Fried 1978: 56). As a result, trust puts the trustor in a position of dependency, and dependency leads to vulnerability: if our prehistoric companion is lying, we get eaten. It has been demonstrated empirically that the more we trust, the less we worry about deception (e.g., Olekalns and Smith 2009). But the less we worry about deception, the more we are susceptible to being "duped and misled" (Goffman 1959: 65). At the same time, though, a strong reliance on trust is essential in everyday life since if we did not trust that the world will function "normally" on any given day we "would not even be able to get out of bed in the morning" (Luhmann 1979: 20). This trust of things extends to most of what we hear and read (Garfinkel 1963).

1.2.2. The Ethical Commitment to Truthfulness

There are evolutionary and social advantages, then, in presuming both that speakers are being truthful and that we can trust them to be truthful. Furthermore, in order to make sure that we can keep making that assumption and keep trusting our interlocutors, we need to reciprocate by being truthful and trustworthy ourselves. This instrumental stratagem of reciprocal altruism might be sufficient to ensure successful cooperation were it not for the problem of "freeloaders," or "individuals that take advantage of the more cooperative members of groups" (Avilés 2002: 14268). In order to keep the number of freeloaders down, there would be an evolutionary advantage in raising the presumption of truthfulness to a virtue. Williams (2002) argues that it would have been beneficial to all members of a community for instrumental stratagems of truthfulness and trust to become intrinsic virtues (i.e., not just what it is *expedient* to do, but what it is *right* to do). A virtue, unlike a simple prescription or norm, is a deeply entrenched character trait that "goes all the way down"; it is not a mere habit, but a disposition "to notice, expect, value, feel, desire, choose, act, and react in certain characteristic ways" (Hursthouse and Pettigrove 2016, n.p.). It is reasonable to think that raising truthfulness to a virtue would encourage adherence to this ethical norm in discourse (Williams 2002: 88–90).

We can see both historical and developmental evidence that truthfulness was raised to a virtue. Historically, the word "truth" originally meant not correspondence with the world but personal integrity or fidelity (to lie was a personal betrayal, or "treason"). It only came to mean conformity with facts and evidence when the centralization of power in Ricardian England led to a dependence on written documentation rather than oral affirmation (Green 1999). Developmentally, children first link lying with punitive sanctions but are gradually socialized into linking it with notions of trust and fairness (Peterson et al. 1983).

There is also clear contemporary evidence in our reaction to others that we take truthfulness as more than an expedient stratagem. We feel we are *wronged* both when we are not believed and when we are misled into believing others. We tend to take it as an affront if our belief is questioned: "It is an insult and it may be an injury not to be believed" (Anscombe 1979: 150). Faulkner points out that this tendency to affront has interpersonal consequences:

> The possibility of this affront engenders a susceptibility to resent any disbelief. This proneness to resentment places a demand on Y [the hearer] that Y believe X [the speaker] when X tells him that p. Belief is not subject to the will, so X cannot demand that Y believe that p, but the demand is rather that Y believe him, where this is a matter of trusting him for the truth. (Faulkner 2014a: 338)

At the same time, if we place firm trust in a speaker and subsequently discover that our trust in that speaker was misguided on a significant matter, this may not simply damage our assessment of her credibility and her trustworthiness, but may also harm our affective relationship with the speaker.

> In trusting X for the truth as to whether p, Y will resent, even feel betrayed by, any deception or undue carelessness on X's part. This proneness to resentment places a demand on X that X respond in a trustworthy way to Y's need to know whether p. . . . (Faulkner 2014a: 339)

In short, we might be justified in feeling resentful or even betrayed when our interlocutor has not been truthful when that was expected. This can explain the deep, moral opprobrium associated with deception in general and lying in particular (Faulkner 2007).

While we have an ethical commitment to truthfulness, though, this commitment is also contingent. Talk can be "cheap" (Haiman 1998) as well as "expensive" (Pettit 2015: 233–234) and there are many contexts in which trust is not at stake and so lack of truthfulness is not an ethical issue. Truthfulness is often in tension with politeness and social bonding. The more socially adept a person is, the more likely he is to deceive both more often and more successfully. For example, if told to appear "likable and competent," students are more likely to lie than if not primed in this way (Feldman et al. 2002). People showing better social skills tend to be more successful in deceiving others (Riggio et al. 1988). And among both children and adults, socially powerful "leaders" tend to be misleaders (Keating and Heltman 1994). The contingency of our commitment to truthfulness will be explored in particular in Chapter 4.

1.2.3. The Intent to Deceive and Trust

Superficially, it might seem clear that trust is breached only when the speaker deceives, or attempts to deceive, the hearer; in other words, when the speaker (tries to) make the hearer believe something that is false and on which the hearer might subsequently rely. As noted in the Introduction, "intent to deceive" has often been central to formal definitions of lying. Furthermore, it has been linked with breach of faith or trust. For example, in Chisholm and Feehan's view, the liar must be intending to deceive the hearer:

> The object of the liar's intention is, in part, that his victim believe that he is expressing his own acceptance of p and that, in thus expressing his opinion, he is to be trusted. The liar would have his victim believe that, at the moment at least, the liar is someone in whom he may place his faith. (Chisholm and Feehan 1977: 152)

Simpson (1992) developed this link between intent to deceive and lying. He saw lying as a particular form of untruthfulness since "lying involves being untruthful while invoking the trust of the one to whom we lie in what we say" (Simpson 1992: 632). According to Simpson, "we present ourselves as believing something while and through invoking (although not necessarily gaining) the trust of the one we intend to deceive" (1992: 625). He saw this invocation of trust as occurring through an act of "open sincerity" by means of which "we attempt to establish a mutually acknowledged recognition, by the one to whom we lie, both that we believe some proposition and that we intend them to realize that we believe it" (1992: 625). The liar, then, is "doubly insincere in that he or she insincerely presents a belief and insincerely invokes trust in this presentation" (1992: 625).

What Chisholm and Feehan (1977), Simpson (1992), and Faulkner (2014a, 2014b) have in common is that they all believe that the invocation of trust is what marks the lie out from other forms of untruthfulness. Yet other forms of untruthfulness clearly come most often with an intent to deceive. The very names for these non-lying forms of untruthfulness given by philosophers ("*deception* without lying," "*misleading* without lying") suggest we are dealing with deception. When we equivocate, we usually want the hearer to take up the believed-false version rather than the believed-true version. When we take words out of context, we usually want the hearer to interpret them with the new (misleading) framing we have given them, rather than with the original framing. And when we withhold information salient to the hearer, we usually do so to conceal it from them. Other than for the "fetishizing of assertion" (Williams 2002: 100–110), it seems clear that any intent to deceive in whatever linguistic form betrays our trust that the speaker will be truthful.[4]

1.3. Why Not Focus on Deception?

It would appear to be clear, then, that ethically significant acts of untruthfulness seem to be associated with an intent to deceive the other. Nevertheless, I shall argue in this section that an account of insincerity should *not* be rooted in an intent to deceive. I adduce three reasons for this perhaps surprising conclusion: not all cases of insincerity involve deception (1.3.1); deception in any case is not a requisite for breach of trust even in the case of insincerity (1.3.2); and the other face of the broad conception of truthfulness developed here—epistemic irresponsibility—does not involve deliberate deception (1.3.3).

1.3.1. Not All Cases of Insincerity Involve Deception

As noted in the Introduction, a number of "non-deceptionist" philosophers (Carson 2006, 2010; Sorensen 2007, 2010; Fallis 2009, 2010, 2015a; Saul 2012; Stokke 2013, 2018) have adduced types of undisguised lies that apparently do not involve an intent to deceive. Carson (2006) introduced the notion of non-deceptive lying through examples of a mafia-intimidated witness testifying falsely against overwhelming evidence, but hoping that the jury will see through the false testimony in the light of that evidence (2006: 289), and a cheating student, knowing that the Dean will punish him only if he confesses, claiming that

---

[4] Lying, *all things being equal*, probably *does* betray trust *to a greater extent* than other forms of untruthfulness. But context often renders this distinction irrelevant.

he did not cheat despite being caught red-handed (2006: 290). Sorensen subsequently distinguished between such "bald-faced lies" (2007), which he described simply as "undisguised" lies (2007: 252) or "cases where a speaker goes on the record with something even though everybody knows it is false" (Arico and Fallis 2013: 792) and "knowledge lies" (Sorensen 2010), which are "intended to prevent the addressee from knowing that p is untrue but [are] not intended to deceive the addressee into believing p" (2010: 610), as in the succession of slaves declaring "I am Spartacus" in the film *Spartacus*. Rutschmann and Wiegmann (2017) have added "indifferent lies," or ones such as betting that you will only say "yes" on a given day, which "involve no valuation regarding the possible consequences of being believed" (2017: 443). So-called deceptionists, including Meibauer and Dynel, the two most prominent linguistic pragmaticians working on untruthfulness, reject the argument for bald-faced lies on two grounds. First, they claim that bald-faced lies[5] are not lies precisely because they lack the element of "intent to deceive" (Dynel 2011b, 2015; Lackey 2013; Meibauer 2014a). For example, Dynel says of Carson's mafia-intimidated witness example that "it cannot count as a lie, thanks to the speaker's communicative intention not to deceive the jury" (Dynel 2011: 151). This is a somewhat circular argument, though. Second, they claim more plausibly that there might still be some intention to deceive, however remote (Mahon 2008, 2014a; Dynel 2015; Meibauer 2016b).

There is some empirical support for bald-faced lies, though it is far from conclusive. Coleman and Kay (1981) tested informants' understanding of the meaning of the word *lie* through eight carefully constructed scenarios and found that intent to deceive was less salient than falsity of belief. This principal result has been replicated, mostly using the same scenarios, by speakers of Makkan Arabic in Saudi Arabia (Cole 1997) and Spanish in Ecuador (Hardin 2010) and partially replicated for the Mopan Maya of Belize (Danziger 2010).[6] However, Coleman and Kay's clearest example of a putative lie without intention to deceive is a type of "polite" or "prosocial" lie in which a guest thanks his boss's wife for a "terrific party" but with no expectation that she will believe it. Although two-thirds of respondents viewed the guest's compliment as a lie, there was no control for whether they actually perceived an intent to deceive, despite the wording of the scenario (Rutschmann and Wiegmann 2017: 442). Arico and Fallis (2013: 800) found that their informants rated their bald-faced lie (Charlie the Gambler denying to his wife that he has been out gambling

---

[5] "Bald-faced" is American usage. The British equivalent "barefaced" (etymologically, "without beard" and thus undisguised) is arguably more transparent, but I shall follow the now well-established convention in using the term "bald-faced lie."

[6] Danziger's study found that factual falsity was the most salient element, followed by falsity of belief, with intent to deceive least important.

again, despite the wife having found the betting tickets in his coat pocket) as strongly (mean 6.87 on a 7-point Likert scale) as the "straightforward" deceptive lie (6.86). Rutschmann and Wiegmann (2017) found that all three types of undisguised lies they tested ("consistent bald-faced lies" such as Cheating Student, "conflictual bald-faced lies" such as Mafia Witness, and their "indifferent lies") were rated strongly as lies. On the other hand, when Meibauer (2016b) tested a number of the bald-faced scenarios well discussed in the literature, such as Cheating Student and Mafia Witness (Carson 2006, 2010), Charlie the Gambler (Arico and Fallis 2013) and Spartacus (Sorensen 2007), on a group of 128 German students, he found strong evidence that while they were construed as lies, they were also construed (to a lesser extent) as showing an intent to deceive (Meibauer 2016: 259–263). Similarly, Rutschmann and Wiegmann (2017: 451) found that most informants attributed an intention to deceive to Charlie the Gambler of Arico and Fallis's study, though they did not do so for their "indifferent lies" (2017: 450).

How can we account for this attribution of an intent to deceive to bald-faced lies? Meibauer suggests that informants might have thought that "the bald-faced liars conveyed a certain propositional content that is suited (and, in fact, intended) to cause a false belief in the hearer" even if they had little or no chance of deceiving the hearer (2016: 262–263). One could also explain this, though, in terms of cognitive dissonance. We *normally expect* that when people assert a false belief (i.e., lie) they will also have the immediate goal of deceiving the hearer. When confronted with bald-faced lies, informants do not question that they are lies (they involve assertion of false belief), but they have to resolve the dissonance created by the apparent lack of intended deceit. Rather than accept that their normally reliable intuitions linking lying and deception might be wrong in this case, they force the circumstances to fit their expectations by imputing to the liar an implausible intent to deceive. It is also possible, though, that the bald-faced scenarios so far tested are not as watertight as their authors believe, leaving open the remote possibility of intended deception.

Perhaps the clearest examples of bald-faced lies are those where the speaker fears he will be persecuted by the state if he tells the truth. Sorensen (2007: 253) provides the following very clear example of what we might call a "persecution lie" from a journalist's experience of finding a ward full of soldiers in a "civilian" hospital during the Second Iraq War:

Iraqi Doctor
– How many soldiers have you admitted today? I ask a doctor.
– There are no soldiers here, the doctor says.
– But they are wearing uniforms?
– I see no uniforms, he says, and pushes me out. (Seierstad 2003: 262)

I heard many such persecution lies when I expressed curiosity about the State in East Germany and Burma in the 1980s. As an interlocutor in the situated context, as opposed to an informant evaluating an abstract scenario, it was all too obvious that the speaker was making no conscious effort to deceive me. Similarly, while there appears to have been no theoretical or empirical work on the non-deceptiveness of forms of insincerity other than lying, there seems to be a form of *bald-faced evasion* common among politicians when cornered by an aggressive interviewer. As shown in an example discussed in Chapter 5, it can become so obvious that the politician is not admitting to the truth proposed by the interviewer that it seems ingenuous to believe that he is still intending to deceive. What speakers are doing, instead, in the case of both bald-faced lying and bald-faced evasion is, as Sorensen (2007) notes, refusing to *go on record* with the truth.

1.3.2. Deception Is Not a Requisite for Breach of Trust

Even if it is accepted, though, that deception is not an obligatory element of lying, this does not equate with a finding that deception is not necessary for breach of trust. The main reason deceptionists want to hold on to the "intent to deceive" element of lying is because it is considered to underlie the "wrongness" of lying (e.g., Bok 1978; Kant 2012). It might be the case that non-deceptive lies exist but that they do not breach trust. However, there is both intuitive and experimental evidence against this view. Sorensen (2007: 253) argues with at least intuitive appeal that we consider bald-faced lies like Iraqi Doctor not only as wrong, but as more wrong than deceptive lies. He asks, "Why are people outraged by bald-faced lies? Why do they condemn bald-faced lies more stridently than disguised lies?" (2007: 252). Arico and Fallis (2013) found that Charlie the Gambler was rated as even more "wrong" (5.77) than the straightforward lie (5.21). More importantly, Rutschmann and Wiegmann (2017) found that their non-deceptive indifferent lies were rated as more morally wrong than other types of lies (2017: 250).

This finding about the "wrongness" of bald-faced or indifferent lies is very surprising if we associate wrongness with breach of trust, and breach of trust with an intent to deceive. However, it makes more sense if we associate breach of trust not with deception but with broken promises. In outlining the origins of a commitment to truthfulness at the beginning of the chapter, I talked of "reciprocal altruism" and the affront we feel when we are not believed. Just as witnesses swear an oath in court as an *explicit* sincere promise that they will tell the truth, Fried (1978) argues that every time we lie, we make an *implicit* insincere promise that our statement is true: "Every lie necessarily implies—as does every assertion—an assurance, a warranty of its truth" (Fried 1978: 67). Lying, then, is a type of broken promise, but "in lying the promise is made and broken in the same moment" (1978: 67). Carson draws an analogy with invitations. I can issue you an invitation "even if I know that you know that I know that you will not accept the invitation" (2010: 26). The mutual understanding that you will not accept the invitation, though, does not void the invitation itself. In a similar way, "lies can and do invite reliance on what is stated, even if the liar hopes and knows that her audience will not believe or rely on her statements" (2010: 26).

In this sense, there is a surprisingly fine line between a bald-faced lie and a brazen lie. Something that is brazen is "obvious" and "without any attempt to be hidden" (*Cambridge Dictionary Online*) but with the added connotation of shamelessness. Consider an authentic brazen lie.

Leaking Politician
A Defense Secretary is sacked from government after an internal investigation reveals "compelling evidence" that he was behind the leak of sensitive defense information from the Security Council. The list of potential suspects was very small, and everything pointed to him being the culprit. Nevertheless, he swears on his children's lives that it was not him. No one believes him.

This scenario is based on the true story of former UK Defense Secretary Gavin Williamson (Anon. 2019). Virtually no rational observer[7] will have been deceived by Williamson's vigorous denial,[8] and most would see it as a brazen lie, but the only difference between this and a bald-faced lie is that it is more obviously shameless. Indeed, the only reason we might not see Iraqi Doctor as shameless is because there was an understandable goal of self-preservation in a dictatorial state. Meibauer (2016) tested bald-faced lies for "brazenness" and found that both Cheating Student and Charlie the Gambler had very high ratings for brazenness. In both these cases, as with Iraqi Doctor and Leaking Politician, the speaker asserts something when the overwhelming evidence available to both speaker and hearer is that it is false. This, in itself, irrespective of attributions of shamelessness or brazenness, seems to undermine the very workings of truthfulness and trust.

---

[7] I do not consider the epistemically partisan as rational observers.
[8] Columnist Tom Peck satirically described the "tension that has gripped the nation, as it waited for the probability of it having been Gavin Williamson all along to make that final leap from 99.99999999%, all the way up to 100" (Peck 2019). Disturbingly, as this book went to press, Williamson was made Secretary of State for Education by Prime Minister Johnson.

1.3.3. Epistemic Irresponsibility Does Not Involve Deception

Finally, even if insincerity were to necessarily involve deception, the other face of the broad conceptualization of untruthfulness proposed here (epistemic irresponsibility) does not involve a deliberate intent to deceive. If I say to my friend sincerely and confidently, "The train leaves at 5," and then she misses the train because it left at 4, I am in no way intending to deceive her. But I have been irresponsible both in not checking the time and in expressing my belief confidently when I have not checked the time and so have unwittingly distorted the truth. Furthermore, my friend trusted me when I told her that the train left at 5 (otherwise she would have checked herself) and so is entitled to feel to some extent that her trust has been betrayed.

If deception is not central, though, to one of the two proposed faces of untruthfulness, then we need to find the element that is central to them both. I shall argue in the remainder of this chapter and the next that this element is *inquiry*, "the enterprise of forming, testing, and revising beliefs" (Stalnaker 1984: ix) in the context of communicative cooperation. Both discursive insincerity and epistemic irresponsibility close off inquiry, the former by refusing to share a truthful contribution, the latter by failing to take care in the contribution we make. I begin this argument in the next section by turning to the model of communicative cooperation most widely followed in pragmatics, Grice's Cooperative Principle.

1.4. Grice's Cooperative Principle

The standard approach to deception in linguistic pragmatics has been through Grice's Cooperative Principle (CP). I begin by setting out the Principle and its associated maxims in the context of communicative trust (1.4.1). I then introduce the driving force behind the CP, Grice's account of implicature, and its relation to cooperation (1.4.2). Finally, I consider the relative success of his Maxim of Quality in accounting for insincerity (1.4.3).

1.4.1. The Cooperative Principle and Trust

Grice sets his CP and its accompanying maxims within a standard rational account of cooperative communication:

> Our *talk exchanges* do not *normally* consist of a *succession of disconnected remarks* and would not be rational if they did. They are characteristically, to

some degree at least, *cooperative efforts*; and each participant recognizes in them, to some extent, *a common purpose or set of purposes*, or at least a *mutually accepted direction*. (Grice 1975: 45)

He then offers his Principle in a heavily hedged frame:

We might then formulate a *rough* general principle which participants will be expected (*ceteris paribus*) to observe: Make your conversational contribution *such as is required, at the stage at which it occurs, by the accepted purpose or direction of the talk exchange in which you are engaged*. (Grice 1975: 45)

Framed as a rough, all-things-being-equal expectation rather than what necessarily happens, and in light of the previous statement on cooperation, Grice's CP accords well with what linguistic analysis has subsequently revealed about interaction. Conversation Analysis has shown how "talk exchanges" are not simply a "succession of disconnected remarks" but follow strict rules of turn taking and preferential response (e.g., Sacks et al. 1974; Sidnell and Stivers 2014). Genre Analysis has shown how "speech genres" (Bakhtin 1986) follow a "common" or "accepted" purpose or "set of purposes" (e.g., Bazerman 1988; Swales 1990). And Interactional Sociolinguistics has shown how the "direction" of an interaction can be negotiated and thus must surely "normally" result from "cooperative efforts" (e.g., Gumperz 1982; Hanks 1996). So, as an intentionally rational account of cooperative communication, rather than a psychologically or sociologically explanatory one, Grice's CP remains strong.

Although Grice does not talk about his CP in trust terms, he effectively articulates elements of trust in a speaker's contribution through his proposed "maxims" and "specific maxims" of conversation, summarized in Table 1.1.

Despite the maxims being expressed in the language of speaker commitment ("make your contribution," "try to . . . ," "do not say"), they convey default conversational *presumptions* rather than moral *principles* (Bach 2006: 24). The hearer *presumes* and thus *trusts* that, all things being equal, the speaker is observing the CP. This does not mean, though, that we expect speakers to fulfill the individual conversational maxims, as long as the overall CP is being observed. Although Grice draws his terms from Kant's moral philosophy and, in his 1989 Epilogue, he describes the maxims as "[s]omewhat like moral commandments" (Grice 1989: 370), he was certainly *not* setting out a set of conversational prescriptions (Horn 2004: 7). Rather than presupposing "an almost Utopian level of gentlemanly conduct on the part of a speaker" (Campbell 2001: 256), Grice was mainly concerned with how we can blatantly violate, or *flout*, the maxims while still being cooperative.

Table 1.1 Grice's Maxims of Conversation

Maxim	Supermaxim	Specific Maxims
Quantity	[Be appropriately informative][a]	(1) Make your contribution as informative as is required (for the current purposes of the exchange) (2) Do not make your contribution more informative than is required
Quality	Try to make your contribution one that is true[b]	(1) Do not say what you believe to be false (2) Do not say that for which you lack adequate evidence
Relation	Be relevant	
Manner	Be perspicuous	(1) Avoid obscurity of expression (2) Avoid ambiguity (3) Be brief (avoid unnecessary prolixity) (4) Be orderly

[a] Grice strangely provides no supermaxim of Quantity.
[b] I shall argue in Chapter 2 that the maxim should be simply "be truthful."

1.4.2. Implicature and Cooperation

Grice's theory of conversational cooperation was, in the first place, an attempt to account for what he called "implicature," or "the act of meaning or implying one thing by saying something else" (Davis 2014: 1). Through implicature, a speaker so blatantly violates (*flouts*) one of the conversational maxims that the hearer, presuming cooperation, is forced to search both linguistic and contextual evidence for an indirect meaning that makes sense in the context. For example:

Tasha's Teacher
PARENT: How did Tasha do this term?
TEACHER: She attended well.

Tasha's teacher flouts the first maxim of Quantity because her response "attended well" is clearly not "as informative as is required" in the context of a parent-teacher meeting. The parent, trusting that the teacher is observing the CP, infers that the teacher is implicating that Tasha's "good" performance is limited to attendance and does not, for example, extend to academic performance or behavior in class. Similarly:

Fine Intellect
BOB: [*Tells a weak joke poorly*]
JOE (TO OTHERS): Bob has a fine intellect!

Joe flouts the first maxim of Quality because he blatantly says what he believes to be false at that particular point in time. His other mates, trusting that Joe is observing the CP, infer from Bob's evidently weak joke, poorly told, that Joe is implicating that Bob is making a fool of himself. In other words, they understand that Joe is being ironic. Bob, even if not self-aware, is likely to pick up the irony from the ensuing laughter. Accordingly, implicature, when successful, is entirely in keeping with trustful communication. However, the speaker's implicature is often not successful. Speakers can implicate meaning that is not picked up by a hearer, and hearers can infer meaning that was not implicated by the speaker (Saul 2002; Bach 2006).

1.4.3. The Maxim of Sincerity

Theorists have rightly noted the connection between the first maxim of Quality ("Do not say what you believe to be false") and lying. This maxim has been called the "maxim of belief" (e.g., Thijsse 2000) and the "maxim of truthfulness" (e.g., Wilson and Sperber 2002; Dynel 2018) but I shall call it the Maxim of Sincerity for reasons that should become clear. At one level, given the general consensus among theorists that when you lie you say something you believe to be false, lying must be a violation of the Sincerity maxim. Furthermore, most lies are *covert* violations of this maxim because it is indubitably the case that the most *common* immediate goal of lying is to deceive the hearer, and so the speaker will not want the hearer to detect that she is violating the Sincerity maxim (e.g., Wilson and Sperber 2002: 586; Meibauer 2005: 1396; Fallis 2009: 34; Dynel 2011b: 143). Thus, Wilson and Sperber claim:

> Lies are examples of *covert violation*, where the hearer is meant to assume that the maxim of truthfulness[9] is still in force and that the speaker believes what she has said. (Wilson and Sperber 2002: 586)

As we have seen, though, this does not cover non-deceptive lies. Take Carson's much-discussed example of the Cheating Student (Carson 2006: 290; 2010: 21):[10]

---

[9] Like most other theorists, Wilson and Sperber take a narrow view of "truthfulness" as what I shall call "utterance sincerity"—saying what you believe is true. I argue against this view here and in Chapter 3.

[10] This is a simplified version of Carson's more nuanced example, but it is more detailed than some versions (e.g., Stokke 2018: 18) and is sufficient for my argument here.

Cheating Student
A student who failed an exam because she was caught cheating from her crib sheet appeals to the Dean. While the student knows that the Dean knows that she cheated, she also knows that the Dean, fearing litigation, will not punish a student unless they explicitly admit their guilt. Accordingly, the student says: "I didn't cheat. The crib sheet was on my desk, but I didn't look at it."

The student asserts something she believes to be false, but she does not intend to deceive the Dean. Accordingly, her violation of the Sincerity maxim cannot be covert but must be *overt*. Yet she is also not *flouting* the maxim because that would mean she is being ironic, but she means to be taken seriously. Fallis (2009) tried to overcome this problem by suggesting that lying violated the Sincerity maxim, whether covertly *or* overtly, as long as the speaker believed the maxim was "in effect *as a norm of conversation*" (2009: 33); in other words, that the speaker was adhering to the CP. According to Fallis, bald-faced lies are produced when the speaker believes that the Sincerity maxim is *in effect* and so are genuine lies. However, as we have seen, straight irony is a clear overt violation of the Sincerity maxim, yet it is not a lie since it generates the implicature that you mean the opposite of what you are saying (Pruss 2012; Stokke 2013; Dynel 2015). Fallis (2009: 53) claims that the Sincerity maxim is not in effect in such cases but, as seen in the previous section, implicature can only work if the CP *is* in effect, so irony simply could not work if the Sincerity maxim were not being observed.[11] As Stokke puts it, "my purpose is to trade on the fact that the rule is operative, and believed to be operative by everyone involved, so that my overtly violating it will trigger the intended inference" (2019b: 140). Fallis (2012) responds to the criticisms by distinguishing between *saying* (the first maxim of Quality) and *communicating* (the supermaxim of Quality, "try to make your contribution one that is true") and concluding that "you lie if and only if you intend to communicate something false [supermaxim] by saying that thing [first maxim]" (2012: 577). The ironic speaker, on the other hand, intends to communicate something true (supermaxim) by saying something false (first maxim). I shall argue in Chapter 2, though, that we require the supermaxim to do a bigger job than simply distinguishing between lying and irony.

---

[11] Fallis says of the Sincerity maxim that the ironic speaker "turns it off." This sounds like the idea of suspending one's commitment to truthfulness, which I shall develop in Chapter 5. However, irony *performs* a suspension of commitment at utterance level while not actually suspending one's commitment to truthfulness at the communicative level. It does this by *flouting* the CP while it is still in effect.

1.5. Insincerity and Inquiry

The distinction between saying and communicating raised by Fallis is central to the nature of inquiry and its relation to insincerity. Inquiry begins with questions, but it is moved forward through assertion. I thus begin by considering the nature of assertion and its relation to insincerity (1.5.1). I then explore how implicature works with what conversational participants already share (the common ground) (1.5.2). Next I consider how false implicature can be understood in terms of the immediate mutually understood question under discussion (1.5.3). Finally, I consider how misleading disrupts inquiry (1.5.4).

1.5.1. Asserting and Sincerity

While accounts of assertion vary enormously (Pagin 2016), theorists of lying and deception have tended to draw on those in which the speaker is expressing some form of commitment to the truth of the proposition. The most developed of these is Searle's speech-act theoretical account, which built on Austin's (1962) original account of speech acts. According to Searle, "speaking a language is a matter of performing speech acts according to systems of constitutive rules" (1969: 38). Constitutive rules, like the rules of chess, are those that "constitute the activity they regulate" (Searle 2018: 51), whereas regulative rules, like driving laws, merely regulate preexisting activity (Rawls 1955). There are five constitutive rules of assertion:[12]

Searle's Constitutive Rules of Assertion
1. *Propositional Content Rule*: what is to be expressed is any proposition p.
2. *First Preparatory Rule*: S has evidence (reasons, etc.) for the truth of p.
3. *Second Preparatory Rule*: It is not obvious to both S and H that H knows (does not need to be reminded of, etc.) p.
4. *Sincerity Rule*: S believes p.
5. *Essential Rule*: Counts as an undertaking that p represents an actual state of affairs. (Searle 1969: 54–71)

The key rules in terms of insincerity are the Essential Rule and the Sincerity Rule. The Essential Rule effectively establishes the speaker's warranty to the hearer that she is being truthful. The Sincerity Rule establishes the congruence between the

---

[12] I list them all here because I will take up the first two in Chapter 3 and the third later in this chapter.

speech act and the mental state expressed by the act. Given that to assert "that *p* counts as an expression of belief (that *p*)," the speaker (S) must have the requisite mental state of belief in *p* (Searle 1969: 65).[13] If not, she is being insincere. Given that most theorists consider the key element in lying to be falsity of belief, it is unsurprising that many of them understand lying as an insincere assertion (e.g., Chisholm and Feehan 1977; Fried 1978; Simpson 1992; Williams 2002; Stokke 2013, 2018). When a speaker lies, he warrants the truth of his proposition (assertion) while not believing it (insincere).

One problem with Searle's account, though, is that he does not distinguish between stating and asserting. This means we cannot distinguish between contexts of inquiry where information is being exchanged and those where truthfulness is not "in play," such as joking, being ironic, acting, or testing a microphone. Chisholm and Feehan argue that an assertion differs from a statement because, in addition to stating, it is "meant to be taken seriously" (1977: 151). However, they overload their account of assertion because they also require that, in asserting, the speaker believes that the listener is epistemically "justified in assuming" both that the speaker "believes a certain proposition" and that he intends to cause the listener to believe that he believes that proposition (1977: 152). Accordingly, if you are attacked in the street and tell the robber untruthfully that "[a]ll my money is in the bank," you are not actually asserting because you would not believe that the robber was epistemically *justified* in believing that you were being truthful; and if you are not making an assertion, you cannot be lying (1977: 154–155). This would also mean that you could not lie to Kant's murderer at the door (Mahon 2019: 36). Chisholm and Feehan's proposal makes the notion of lying too context-dependent, and I shall argue in Chapter 4 that these are better seen as cases of justified lying rather than the absence of lying. More damningly, Carson points out that Chisholm and Feehan's definition of lying,[14] based on their concept of assertion, "has the very odd and unacceptable result that a notoriously dishonest person cannot lie to people who he knows distrust him" (2010: 23). I shall return to this point that the listener's distrust does not absolve the insincere speaker when discussing moral culpability in Chapters 4 and 7.

While it can clearly be seen as insincere assertion, lying accounts for a comparatively small percentage of cases of deception and insincerity (McCornack 1992; McCornack et al. 2014). My interest, then, is in developing a much broader conception of insincerity that extends to both non-assertoric misleading and

---

[13] Falkenberg (1988: 89) similarly defines insincerity as the "intentional conflict between a state of mind and a synchronic linguistic act" and he sees lying as the opposition of belief and assertion.

[14] My concern in this chapter is not with definitions of lying but in developing a broad conception of insincerity that will serve my analytical purposes, so I do not dwell on the plethora of formal definitions of lying to be found in the philosophical literature.

non-verbal withholding. A first step in this process is to consider how to extend insincerity from lying to cases of misleading without lying or, in other terms, from assertoric to non-assertoric misleading speech. As Williams (2002: 100) puts it:

> The familiar distinction between lying and other forms of misleading speech is that between the speaker's making an assertion the content of which he believes to be false, and his asserting something which he takes to be true, but in such a way that he leads the hearer to believe something false, in particular by exploiting the mutually understood operation of implicatures.

Before turning to false implicature, though, it is essential to understand the cognitive ground shared between speakers and against which implicatures are interpreted by interlocutors.

1.5.2. Implicature and the Common Ground

When discussing invented utterances and brief scenarios, it is easy to forget that we do not enter communicative events with blank slates. In any form of authentic interaction, there is "common ground" shared between speakers right from the start of the interaction (Stalnaker 2002; Allan 2013). Stalnaker describes common ground as "presumed background information shared by participants in a conversation" (2002: 701). We can take it to include *any* presumed shared background information that constitutes "common knowledge" (Lewis 1969) or "mutual knowledge" (Schiffer 1972) among the speakers (Allan 2013). Importantly, this includes what psychologists have identified as the forms of information packaging we store in our brains, variously called "schemata" (Bartlett 1932), "frames" (Minsky 1977), and "scripts" (Schank and Abelson 1977). As interlocutors talk and share information, they contribute to, and incrementally enlarge, the common ground. Therefore, common ground needs to be seen not just as the informational fixed starting point, but also as a dynamic process that is constantly changing according to the sometimes unpredictable directions the talk takes.

The production and uptake of implicature are dependent on the common ground shared between speakers. This is important because if we change the common ground settings, it can entirely change our analysis of implicature and whether or not we are dealing with trustful and/or truthful communication. For example, in the case of Tasha's Teacher, if it is part of the parent and teacher's common ground that Tasha's big problem at school is attendance, then there may be no implicature at all. The parent may be implying (though not implicating)[15] "how did she do *in terms of attendance*" and the teacher's reply (at least as a first response) unproblematically fulfills the maxim of Quantity: "She attended well." In Fine Intellect, I assumed (because I presumed it would be in the reader's common ground with respect to such invented examples) that Bob, Joe, and the others are friends in a symmetrical relationship and that Bob in fact is a fairly intelligent person that his friend is colloquially "taking the piss out of." But imagine that Bob is actually a low-intellect lonely individual whom Joe and his friends cruelly like to taunt. Bob would like to be friends with Joe and thinks he has made a good joke. He does not understand "fine intellect" but he assumes it is positive. He is then devastated when they all seem to be laughing at him. Joe's utterance, "Bob has a fine intellect!" is intended to be perceived as ironic by his friends but not by Bob. One of Grice's conditions of implicature, the "mutual knowledge condition" (Davis 2007: 1658), is that "the speaker thinks [the implicature] is within the competence of the hearer to work out, or intuitively grasp" (Grice 1975: 50). It is patently clear to Joe that Bob is not sufficiently competent to work out the implicature and so he is maliciously exploiting the first maxim of Quality to laugh behind Bob's back. In multiparty talk (Dynel 2010, 2011a), it is not unusual to find situations in which "one hearer (or more) is deceived, whilst others are privy to the truthful meaning and recognize the nonfulfillment [of the maxim] as flouting" (Dynel 2011b: 158). It would seem crucial that any framework of untruthfulness must be able to account for the wrong in such cases. Irony is often given as the paradigm case of overt, non-deceptive untruthfulness (Dynel 2018), but that depends on how it occurs in situated text.

What this account of implicature and common ground tells us is that breach of trust occurs not necessarily when the speaker violates a maxim, but when the speaker's contribution fails to be "such as is required" given the common ground between speakers and the current direction of the exchange.

1.5.3. False Implicature and Questions under Discussion

As Grice pointed out, there is no necessary belief correspondence between what is stated and what is implicated: the speaker may believe both to be true (as in the first reading of Tasha's Teacher); she may believe that the statement is false but the implicature true (as in straight irony); or she may believe that the statement is true but the implicature false. This third case is that of falsely implicating. Take the example of "Mary," one of Coleman and Kay's (1981) scenarios:

---

[15] It cannot be an implicature because implicating is implying by saying something else, yet there is nothing else said. The implication occurs entirely through the common ground between the speakers.

(VI) "Mary"
John and Mary have recently started going together. Valentino is Mary's ex-boyfriend. One evening John asks Mary, "Have you seen Valentino this week?" Mary answers, "Valentino's been sick with mononucleosis for the past two weeks." Valentino has in fact been sick with mononucleosis for the past two weeks, but it is also the case that Mary had a date with Valentino the night before. Did Mary lie? (Coleman and Kay 1981: 31)

Here Mary is stating what she believes to be true (Valentino is sick) and she is warranting the truth of this statement, so it is an assertion on standard accounts. But given their common ground, and perhaps John's jealousy over Valentino, her flouting of the Maxim of Relation will lead to the successful but false implicature that she has not seen Valentino. In making this implicature, she is clearly intending to deceive her boyfriend. She is also clearly exploiting the CP to bring about this deceit. So, there is a *prima facie* breach of interactional trust even if she may well be *justified* in breaching that trust (e.g., because John is overly jealous). But how can we account for such examples in terms of insincerity given that there is no opposition between her actual assertion and her belief?

One option is to argue, along with Meibauer (2005; 2014b: 113–137), that falsely implicating is actually a type of lying because the false implicature is an inextricable part of the assertion. This involves an understanding of assertion in which what is warranted as truthful is not just what is said but what is *pragmatically meant in the context*. One way of accounting for this might be to claim that lying is a covert violation of the supermaxim of Quality ("Try to make your contribution one that is true") rather than the first maxim, "Do not say what you believe to be false" (Stokke 2018: 44). If this view is correct, we might expect informants to judge cases of false implicature as lying.[16] However, in Coleman and Kay's study, just over a quarter of informants (18/67) judged "Mary" as lying, while almost two-thirds (42/67) considered her as "not lying." The reluctance to call out false implicature as lying is also reflected among theorists: most classify falsely implicating as formally and/or morally distinct from lying (e.g., Adler 1997; Strudler 2010; Dynel 2011b; Webber 2013; Stokke 2018).[17] It is also a crucial distinction in the law (Tiersma 1990). In conclusion, then, we cannot safely categorize falsely implicating as lying, so we are left with the problem of how to account for it, and other forms of misleading such as equivocation, in terms of insincerity.

---

[16] This is not a *necessary* conclusion. Academic definitions need not always conform to everyday understanding.

[17] I intuitively used to belong to the one-third minority on this point, so I have some sympathy for Meibauer's argument. However, I now believe there are strong analytical reasons for retaining the distinction between lying and falsely implicating.

One effective solution to the problem of insincerity in misleading is to consider not the linguistic utterance itself, but how what is meant in the context contributes to the common ground. If that contribution to the common ground is incongruent with the speaker's mental state, then she is being insincere. Stokke (2014, 2018) provides a convincing argument of this sort based on Roberts's (2004, 2012) notion of the Question under Discussion (QUD). Roberts builds on Stalnaker's view of discourse (Stalnaker 1984, 2002) as a cooperative activity aimed at the goal of inquiry, or discovering how things are. While this is an impoverished view of communication in the round (communication is as much about affiliation and identity as it is about inquiry), it is useful in terms of an account of sincerity linked to truthfulness. According to Roberts (2004, 2012), inquiry is guided by a set of partially organized QUDs which determine the topic and salience of information and influence the common ground (see also Ginzburg 2012). A QUD can be considered a sub-inquiry, "a strategy for approaching the goal of inquiry" (Stokke 2018: 81). The most salient QUD at any point is called the "immediate QUD," or just "the QUD."

1.5.4. Misleading as Disrupting Inquiry

Following Stalnaker and Roberts, Stokke defines sincerity and insincerity as follows:

> to speak *sincerely* is to consciously intend to truthfully answer QUDs *while avoiding communicating false information in the process*. Conversely, we can see insincerity as lacking a conscious intention to contribute truthful answers to QUDs while not communicating false information in the process. (Stokke 2018: 192; original emphasis)

This definition can account for Mary's insincerity. Mary asserts something she assents to (that Valentino is sick) but the immediate QUD in this case is whether she saw Valentino. With respect to that QUD, she consciously communicates false information she does not assent to by implicating that she did not see him. As Stokke points out:

> It is not enough to simply deliver some truth; if the aim with doing so is to mislead by implicating a falsehood, one's way of addressing the issue with respect to which one carefully confines oneself to speaking the truth is still a form of insincerity. (Stokke 2018: 193–194)

Rather than always being explicitly stated, QUDs are often implicit in the common ground. For example, when Joe, in the straight ironic version of Fine

Intellect, says, "Bob has a fine intellect!" he is responding to an implicit question in the common ground about Bob's ability to tell jokes. Although he says something he does not mentally assent to, he is answering the implicit QUD truthfully by implicating that Bob has not shown himself to have a fine intellect in the way he has recounted his joke. Therefore, he is being sincere.[18] In the deceitful version of Fine Intellect, on the other hand, Joe does not consider Bob sufficiently competent to take up the implicature. Accordingly, he is simply communicating to Bob an assertion he does not assent to. So, he is lying to Bob while being ironic to his friends.

Stokke's proposal enables us to include misleading-without-lying as a form of insincerity since it disrupts the inquiry: "to mislead is to disrupt the pursuit of the goal of inquiry, that is, to prevent the progress of inquiry from approaching the actual world" (2018: 95). Indeed, just as I do here, Stokke considers lying as *one form of* misleading:

> There are ... many ways of contributing misleading information. One may do so by asserting something one believes to be false, by conversationally implicating it, or in some other way. Asserting that one is not going to a party and implicating that one is not going are both ways of contributing this information to the common ground of the discourse, and both effectuate a narrowing of the context set.[19] If one believes that one is not going, both are ways of disrupting the pursuit of the goal of inquiry. (Stokke 2018: 95)

Stokke, like most philosophers of language and linguistic pragmaticians, is explicitly concerned with *linguistic utterances* and so while he accepts that "misleading information" may be contributed "in some other way" than asserting or implicating, it seems unlikely that he is thinking of the deliberate *omission* of information without any form of linguistic signaling (as there is, for example, with implicature and equivocation) as being among those ways. Similarly, while Williams (2002) manifests a very broad understanding of sincerity, noting at one point that "Sincerity at the most basic level is simply openness, a lack of inhibition" (2002: 75), he still defines his Sincerity as "a disposition to make sure that one's assertion expresses what one actually believes" (2002: 96). And while Trilling talks of the general social requirement that the "British" sincere person should "communicate without deceiving or misleading" (1972: 58), he defines sincerity more narrowly as "a congruence of avowal and actual feeling" (1972: 2). Yet the deliberate uncued omission of salient truthful information is the most

---

[18] There is a probable double irony here because one would hope that this would be said only about someone you believe to be intelligent.
[19] The "context set" is the set of possible worlds that are compatible with the information in the common ground (Stalnaker 2002).

common form of deception (Ekman 2009; McCornack et al. 2014) and, I will argue, insincerity. What we need is a notion of *discursive insincerity* that goes beyond the individual utterance but is still narrow enough to be analytically useful when judging cases of insincerity in situated texts.[20]

1.6. Discursive Insincerity

In order to understand how sincerity can be extended not just from the linguistic assertion to the conversational contribution but also to what *might have been said* but was not (Schroeter and Taylor 2018), it is important to gain a basic understanding of how insincere communication actually happens in practice (1.6.1). This will then make it possible to sketch out a notion of discursive insincerity (1.6.2). Finally, I briefly consider withholding as the umbrella category of discursive insincerity (1.6.3).

1.6.1. Discourse, Deception, and the Communication Process

Since all psychological work is on deception rather than insincerity, I shall start with an account of deceptive communication and then adapt it to insincere discourse. Given the context of a speaker in a conversation finding herself in the position of wanting to conceal information from her interlocutor, the overwhelming assumption in deception research in the social sciences has been that the choice is a binary one between telling the truth and lying (Bond and DePaulo 2006). This applies to research on "lie" detection, where informant "detectors," like Coleman and Kay's informants, are almost always given a choice between what are often confusingly called "bald-faced truth" (BFT) and "bald-faced lie" (BFL) (Sporer and Schwandt 2006). It also applies, though, to research on the production of deceptive messages, such as Vrij et al.'s (2010) work on cognitive load and deception. As late as 2014, McCornack et al. (2014) were able to write that "[a]lmost all extant deception research, across disciplines, presumes the BFL versus BFT dichotomy" (2014: 349). Luckily this is starting to change, and so we are beginning to gain a picture of how the process of deception works in situated discourse.

---

[20] There are much broader understandings of sincerity, but they tend to be confused with Rousseau's Romantic notion of "authenticity," which is about "finding" and conveying one's "true" inner self (Trilling 1972). Frankfurt seems to have this conception in mind when he argues that "sincerity" in an individual is in direct opposition to "correctness": "Convinced that reality has no inherent nature, which he might hope to identify as the truth about things, he devotes himself to being true to his own nature" (2005: 65).

Two key points of departure are selectivity and the constraints of working memory. Herrmann (1983) notes that while we construct a propositional base of all the information that would potentially be relevant to disclose, since we cannot reveal everything, "the speaker invariably verbalizes only part of what he has in mind" (1983: 38). For Herrmann, the key factors involved in selection are salience and the speaker's strategic goals. Baddeley (2007) claims that during the highly complex cognitive operation of speech production, a central executive searches and retrieves relevant information from long-term memory and uploads it to a temporary storage system, known as an "episodic buffer," in which such information is combined with perceptual input and other sources to create a coherent episode. The search and retrieval process is guided by the twin factors of salience and ease of access: it gives preference to what seems most relevant to the context and that comes easiest to mind. Accordingly, the selection of material that gets verbalized depends on salience, ease of access, and strategic goals. McCornack et al. (2014) stress that deceptive communication follows exactly the same model as truthful communication:

> When individuals are faced with contexts in which the most salient propositional content is deemed appropriate for disclosure, they will begin utterance construction (and begin speaking) in a truthful fashion. As they construct their utterance incrementally, if information associated with the primary, salient information proves problematic, they will simply delete it from the production process. . . . Importantly, such an "edit-out as you go" process will be largely effortless, as it mirrors what we normally do when we talk with others—that is, select out associated information deemed irrelevant for current disclosure. (McCornack et al. 2014: 361)

Our default is truthful communication, then, and we switch into being insincere only when there is a clash between salience and our strategic goal.

This psychological model can be combined with Stalnaker and Roberts's work on inquiry discussed earlier. First, salience is most likely determined by the QUD: an item that is relevant to the QUD will be more relevant than one that is not. Second, ease of access is likely to be linked to our schemata, frames, and scripts, many of which will be in the common ground: talking about a trip to the dentist, for example, will activate models of "dentist-going" in both speaker and hearer. Finally, while in truthful communication in truth-warranting contexts, the strategic goal will match with the primary goal of inquiry (to find out how things are), it is the insincere speaker's aim precisely to disrupt that goal of inquiry. That will mean at the very least "editing out" problematic propositions that are relevant to the QUD and, failing that, might require verbal intervention that will lead the hearer off the path of inquiry.

In order to show how this can work in practice, I use an example from McCornack et al. (2014) and integrate their description of what goes on in your head with the inquiry account of common ground and QUDs given in this chapter. McCornack et al. ask readers to imagine they are in the following situation:

Flirting
Last night you attended the party of a good friend, Joe. Your romantic partner is OK with you partying and likes Joe. During the course of the party, you consumed two beers, watched part of a football game, and chatted amiably with several acquaintances. You also fiercely flirted for a few minutes with a very attractive person. [Next day your partner] inquires "So, what did you do last night?" (McCornack et al. 2014: 361)[21]

First, then, we have an explicit but general QUD: "What did you do last night?" This will activate the central executive to search our long-term memory for relevant information about both Joe's party and salient party schemata and narrative scripts. This information is uploaded to the episodic buffer in working memory that can easily be accessed. Since "party at Joe's" is highly salient to the QUD and unproblematic for disclosure, this will come first ("Well, I went to a party . . ."). Other unproblematic propositions (drinking beer, watching a game, chatting with friends) will be converted into grammatically and phonologically appropriate speech and added as assertions to the account, incrementally adding to the common ground and apparently pursuing the inquiry about "last night." However, given the traditional monogamous relationship you have with your partner, when the memory unit "flirted" is activated, it will be judged as too problematic for disclosure. Your strategic goal will thus switch from satisfying the inquiry to disrupting it. In the absence of a more specific verbalized QUD, the easiest and safest way of doing this is by editing it out of the account. In other words, you *withhold* the incriminating information from the hearer. The resulting story will be something like this:

Party
Well, I went to a party at Joe's house, and I had a couple of beers, and watched the game on his big-screen. I also chatted for a while with Bill and Jen. It was a lot of fun! (McCornack et al. 2014: 361)

---

[21] Dynel (2011: 157) adduces a similar example of a man responding to his girlfriend's question, "What did you do during the lunch break today?" with "I had coffee," while editing out the fact that he had coffee with his ex-fiancée. One might wonder why theorists of deception seem to be so obsessed with infidelity.

Note that in comparison to the "Mary" scenario, there is nothing *in the text* here that suggests a lack of congruence between speech and mental state. Everything said is true and there is no implicature, presupposition, or equivocation. As in all personal experience narratives (Labov 1972), only a few episodes are selected for narration, and much that happened is left out.

So, in what sense can we say that the speaker is being insincere? The answer is that of all the possible episodes one could have recounted about Joe's party, the flirting is the one that is most salient both in one's own mind and in terms of the common ground one shares with one's partner. We believe it is the *one thing* our partner would want to know. In narrative terms, it is the "Trouble" (Burke 1969). Unlike episodes such as going to the toilet or saying farewell to our host, this one will not be in the background when we are selecting episodes to recount. It will be very salient and, though the editing process is easy, we still have to consciously suppress it to eliminate it from our account. In short, we *believe* that the common ground, now including the QUD itself, calls on us to *disclose* the episode, but we do not actually disclose it in our account and thereby *disrupt* the inquiry.

1.6.2. A Sketch of Discursive Insincerity

Taking into account the view of the deceptive/insincere communication process outlined in the preceding, I define discursive insincerity as follows:

Discursive Insincerity
Discursive insincerity is a lack of congruence between what a speaker believes the common ground calls on them to disclose to the hearer and what they actually disclose to the hearer.

In this definition, I am subsuming QUDs under "common ground" because once a QUD becomes known to the participants, it too becomes part of the common ground. Thus, in "Party," you are being discursively insincere because you believe the common ground (the QUD, your relationship, narrative expectation) calls on you to disclose the flirting to your partner, but instead you edit it out. More gravely, when the defense asks the prosecutor whether she has any evidence to disclose and she offers some small pieces of evidence but not a key piece of evidence that she believes the common ground (the QUD, the law on evidence, a shared sense of justice) calls on her to disclose, she is being discursively insincere. In the latter case in particular, it is clear that the withholding itself disrupts the inquiry. Therefore, I would not restrict the notion of "disrupting inquiry" to misleading (with or without lying) but extend it to withholding.

Indeed, it is withholding rather than misleading that can be considered the umbrella category of insincere discourse strategies.[22] Consider again Carson's example of the Cheating Student (Carson 2006: 290; 2010: 21). The student finds herself, from a communication perspective, in a position with very limited options. She believes that the common ground, including the QUD of whether she cheated, calls on her to disclose the cheating, but she also believes that the personal costs of that disclosure are too high as she cannot afford to fail the exam. The easiest insincere strategy of simply editing out the cheating information (i.e., withholding without misleading) is not available to her as she was caught *in flagrante* and has already been punished. It is difficult to see how verbal misleading without lying could be seen as plausible (e.g., "I wasn't cheating, I was checking"?). That only leaves outright lying, however implausible the excuse. In most cases where one is unlikely to deceive the hearer, it would be rational to switch one's strategic goal to one of damage limitation through confession, mitigation, and apology. However, the student's primary strategic goal is to pass the exam and she knows she can accomplish this by not confessing. She therefore contributes false information to the common ground ("I didn't cheat . . . I didn't look at it") and deliberately disrupts the inquiry in doing so by failing to put her cheating on record. However, note that the student's lie is successful in strategic terms not because it succeeds in deceiving the Dean about her belief but because it *withholds* a truthful statement ("I cheated") which, if revealed, would scupper her chances of a successful appeal. The speaker's estimation of the chances of her lie deceiving the hearer has no impact on this underlying withholding function of lying. If the Dean only suspects, rather than having a justified belief, that the student might have cheated, this will significantly increase the chances of the student deceiving the Dean, but it will make no difference to the fact that she has withheld her truthful contribution to the common ground.

1.6.3. Withholding as Disrupting Inquiry

A truthful contribution, then, can be *withheld* either by not being expressed at all or by being expressed in such a way that it has the potential to lead the hearer epistemically astray. In that case we have *misleading*. And if the method of misleading is to *contradict* one's belief in the truth of the proposition withheld, then we have a case of *lying*. Consequently, from the perspective of discursive insincerity rather than utterance insincerity, lying is a form of misleading, which in turn is a form of withholding. When you lie (assert a false belief), you also

---

[22] I shall explain why I call these *discourse strategies* in Chapter 5.

mislead (lead the hearer epistemically astray) and withhold (conceal a truthful contribution). We can thus see lying and misleading as subtypes of discursive insincerity with "withholding" as the superordinate term:

Withholding exhibits a lack of congruence between what a speaker believes the common ground calls on them to disclose to the hearer and what they actually disclose to the hearer.

Misleading exhibits a lack of congruence between what a speaker believes the common ground calls on them to disclose to the hearer (*i.e., truthful answers to the QUD*) and what they actually disclose to the hearer (*i.e., false or distorted answers to the QUD*).

Lying exhibits a lack of congruence between what a speaker believes the *QUD* calls on them to disclose to the hearer (*i.e., true belief*) and what they actually disclose to the hearer (*i.e., false assertion*).

The proposed hierarchical nature of discursive insincerity has important practical consequences for analysis, for it means that we can start with withholding and then build up to lying only when the evidence permits. I shall use the term "discursive insincerity" to refer to this broad conception of insincerity. Mostly, though, when I use the terms "withholding" or "misleading" I shall mean "withholding without misleading" and "misleading without lying."

In Chapter 5, I shall argue that withholding (without misleading), misleading (without lying), and lying are discursive strategies that come in many guises and I shall explore some of the sub-strategies and pragmatic tactics associated with each of these major categories.

1.7. Conclusion

This chapter has teased out some key theoretical issues relating to the sincerity side of the TRUST framework with regard to the scope, ethical value, and situated analysis of untruthfulness. It began by investigating the main proposition relating to Ethical Value (E), namely that the ethical value of untruthfulness hinges on the notion of trust. I put forward mainly philosophical arguments grounding truthfulness in an indispensable human need for trust and cooperation and noted how untruthfulness can breach trust. I then gave fuller arguments for why the scope (S) of the framework does not focus on deception. The existence of non-deceptive lies is certainly important, as is the fact that deception is not necessary for breach of trust and, as discussed in Chapter 2, epistemic irresponsibility concerns irresponsibility rather than deception. The chapter then focused on the source of much pragmatic work on untruthfulness: Grice's Co-operative Principle. I argued that Grice's implicature is fundamental to understanding insincerity within a framework of communicative cooperation, but his sincerity maxim unnecessarily narrows the scope of insincerity. Instead, I argued that it is best to see sincerity within a context of inquiry and insincerity as disrupting that inquiry. I drew on Stokke's work in particular to extend insincerity from assertion to implied meaning and thus misleading. However, by drawing on a psychological account of how untruthfulness works in situated discursive practice (D), I argued that the concept of insincerity needs to be further extended to cases of insincere "editing out" where there is no textual clue to the insincerity (S1). This broadened conception of insincerity, which subsumes misleading and lying under withholding, I call *discursive insincerity* simply to distinguish it from the traditional narrower *utterance insincerity*.

In Chapter 2, I investigate the other face of untruthfulness: epistemic irresponsibility.

2
Bullshit, Inquiry, and Irresponsibility

We know nothing certainly, for truth lies in the deep.
—Attributed to Democritus

Accuracy is the twin brother of honesty.
—Attributed to Hawthorne

2.1. Introduction

This chapter takes up the other half of the broadened conception of untruthfulness advocated by the TRUST framework: the epistemic responsibility with which one establishes and conveys one's knowledge and beliefs (S2). The traditional understanding of untruthfulness concerns a purely word-to-mind relation rather than the word-to-world one that one might unreflectingly expect. Aquinas noted that even "the word *mendacium* is derived from its being in opposition to the mind" (Aquinas 1989: II–II, Question 110, Article 1). I argue in this chapter, though, that one can be irresponsible, and under certain conditions *ethically* irresponsible, when not taking into account the available evidence. The ethical implications of epistemic irresponsibility had not gone wholly unnoticed before the twenty-first century. Augustine (1961: 18), though he focused mostly on the sin of lying, noted that a man "may sometimes be open to the charge of rashness, if through carelessness he takes up what is false and holds it as true." However, it is only comparatively recently that researchers have taken up the question of epistemic responsibility (Code 1987), particularly through discussion of the concept of bullshit (Frankfurt 2005).

The chapter begins by teasing out the notion of epistemic responsibility and its relation to trust (2.2), first by noting how assertion requires us to take responsibility and to be able to provide justification for what we say, though without requiring us to be objectively true, and then arguing that this responsibility requirement leads to both an intellectual and moral commitment to "getting things right." This groundwork on epistemic responsibility provides a conceptual framework for understanding *bullshitting* (2.3), a "bridge" category which combines discursive insincerity with epistemic irresponsibility, and its relation to Grice's second maxim of Quality. While the strategy of bullshitting disrupts interactional inquiry, the often unintentional discursive product of *bullshit*, or sincere nonsense, disrupts human inquiry (2.4). Consideration of epistemic responsibility as integral to truthfulness leads to a revised maxim of Truthfulness. Finally, the chapter proposes *dogma* (closing off inquiry) rather than *bullshit* as the underlying form of *discourse pathology* resulting from epistemic irresponsibility, and I briefly consider Saul's (2018) concept of negligent falsehood (2.5).

2.2. Epistemic Responsibility and Trust

We take responsibility for what we say by our very act of asserting (2.2.1), and we can be held to account not if we are wrong as such but if we cannot justify our claim to be right (2.2.2). This epistemic responsibility is not just an intellectual virtue but a moral commitment, just like our commitment to be sincere (2.2.3). However, that commitment does not require us to be objectively accurate (2.2.4).

2.2.1. Assertion and Responsibility

Chapter 1 established that in making an assertion we are making a commitment to the truth of what we are saying. But in asserting we are also *taking responsibility* for what we are saying: we are committing ourselves both to *knowing* what we are saying and to being able to *justify* the claim (Kissine 2013: 93). Alston notes that, in asserting, we take "responsibility for (its being the case that) *p*" (2000: 55). The speaker "knowingly took on a liability to (laid herself open to) blame (censure, reproach, being taken to task, being called to account), in case of not-*p*" (2000: 55). In other words, at a very basic communicative level, she has breached the trust of the hearer. Long before Alston, Peirce noted that the assuming of responsibility is not confined to "solemn assertions": "This ingredient, the assuming of responsibility, which is so prominent in solemn assertion, must be present in every genuine assertion" (1960[1935]: V. 546, p. 386.)

Assuming responsibility for one's assertions is not the same as claiming to have secure *knowledge* of what we are talking about. We know that the world is full of uncertainty and that it is often difficult, if not impossible, to arrive at the truth of a matter. Knowledge, after Plato (2004: 201 c–d), is traditionally defined as *justified true belief* (Armstrong 1973).[1] However, it is possible to be epistemically

---

[1] Although Justified True Belief has been seriously challenged as a theory of knowledge by so-called Gettier problems showing justified true belief without knowledge (Gettier 1963), our interest here is not knowledge but "subjectively trying to be true," and all three elements of truth, belief, and justification are relevant to such an analysis.

responsible while holding a justified *false* belief and to be epistemically irresponsible while holding a *true* belief. The question hinges on the notion of *justification*. Justification is quite distinct from either the truth of a claim ("It is true that it is raining") or whether the speaker believes her claim ("I believe it is raining"). Epistemologists make a distinction between "propositional justification," where there are objective reasons for believing p, and "doxastic justification," where the speaker holds the belief appropriately (Montmarquet 1993). Propositional justification indexes objective truth claims: there cannot be objective reasons for believing p that are in fact false. Doxastic justification, on the other hand, indexes subjective qualities of being true in discourse: you can hold a false belief in an appropriate manner, as did academic physicists who believed Newtonian mechanics until special relativity became experimentally indisputable. The justification in "justified true belief" is generally considered to be of the doxastic kind.

2.2.2. Being Responsibly Wrong

We can explore these relations between justification and responsibility through some invented scenarios involving two speakers (Sue and Ben) in a basement office with no access to daylight or the Internet:

Basement Scenario 1: Accidental Justification
It is raining, but neither Sue nor Ben can know that.
    SUE: It's raining.
    BEN: No, it's not.
They both believe they are right, and they believe they are justified in holding their respective beliefs because they are prescient.

In this first scenario, Sue is (and Ben is not) propositionally justified because there are objective reasons (if they bothered to go out) for believing that it is raining. However, neither is doxastically justified in their assertion because prescience is not an appropriate way of forming a belief. In simple terms, we would say that they are accidentally correct or incorrect and are either being playful or are deluded. But consider a second scenario:

Basement Scenario 2: Doxastic Justification
It is still raining and neither Sue nor Ben knows that. Sue leaves the office for a while but remains at basement level and with no view outside of the rain. She then returns to the office:
    SUE: It's raining.
    BEN: Oh, thanks.

Ben wrongly assumes that Sue went outside and so *knows* that it is raining; i.e., she has observed the rain directly through her senses and is thus justified in believing that it is truly raining.

Here Sue, as in Scenario 1, is making an assertion that is propositionally but not doxastically justified. However, because Ben draws an appropriate conversational inference that Sue has witnessed the rain in person, he is doxastically justified in believing that it is indeed raining. As Brandom (1994: 173–175) points out, not only does the speaker, in asserting, undertake a responsibility to justify what she claims, but a hearer is authorized to claim anything that follows from what is asserted. Accordingly, Ben would be *truthful* in passing on this information to a colleague even if it turns out that the proposition that it is raining is false. In that case he would be doxastically justified in believing and conveying the claim even if it lacks propositional justification. Turri (2014) describes such an assertion as a *permissible* one requiring reasonable belief, in contrast to a *good* one requiring knowledge. Adler (2002) similarly distinguishes between *warranted* assertions, requiring full belief, and *proper* assertions, requiring knowledge. Truthfulness requires permissible, warranted, or doxastically justified assertions, rather than good, proper, or propositionally justified ones.

Consider now a more realistic scenario:

Basement Scenario 3: Justified Mistakes
It is now no longer raining and neither Sue nor Ben is being deceptive:
> SUE: I think it's raining. At least it was when I last looked.
> BEN: Actually, it's stopped. I've just checked.

Here, Ben challenges Sue's truth claim but he does not appear to be putting her truthfulness in question. Arguably, this is not just because he blindly trusts that Sue believes what she has said, but also because Sue has taken care both to hedge her claim ("I think," "at least") and to provide empirical justification for that claim ("when I last looked"). Sue is doxastically justified in making her claim even if it turns out to be propositionally unjustified. Ben is simply providing an update on the facts of the matter, which Sue can now use to revise her belief.

Hedging our claims or providing explicit justifications for them opens up a dialogic space (an interactional opportunity) for challenge. However, hedging does not absolve us of responsibility for those claims. If I say, "It is probably raining," and it turns out not to be, "I can properly be called upon to say what made me think it was raining" (Toulmin 2003: 51). If I had no justified reason for saying that it was probably raining, and others were relying on my assertion, then I was being irresponsible. Consider a modified version of Scenario 2:

Basement Scenario 4: Unjustified Hedging
Sue has left the office and then returned without leaving the basement:
  SUE: I think it's raining.
  BEN: Oh, thanks.

Given that Sue, on the basis of prescience, is not doxastically justified in saying that it is raining in the first place, she is still being epistemically irresponsible even if she has slightly attenuated that responsibility by hedging her claim and thus inviting a Toulminian challenge: "Why do you think that?" She would not be able to meet that challenge since prescience is not an appropriate reason for belief. Although the hedge technically opens up the dialogic space, we would normally expect Sue in that situation to have gained firsthand knowledge when she left the room, and so it would not be normal to challenge such an assertion. Consequently, Ben, once again, is doxastically justified and epistemically responsible both in not challenging Sue and in holding the false belief that it is raining.

The determining factor, then, in judging individuals as having a (doxastically) justified false belief seems to be that they have acted in an *epistemically responsible* manner. Furthermore, *epistemic responsibility* (Code 1987; Montmarquet 1993) seems to lie not only in how they have *formed* their belief (in Scenario 3 through empirical observation rather than the prescience of Scenarios 1 and 2), but also in how they have *retained* it (we would expect Sue to drop her belief in the light of Ben's new evidence in Scenario 3) and, crucially for this study, in the way they have *conveyed* their belief in discourse (Scenarios 3 and 4). In telling, they have assumed responsibility for their telling, they stand behind what they say, and they are "ready to justify *or source the justification* for what is told" (Faulkner 2014a: 338). Note that to be justified in believing that *p*, it is not necessary to actively *justify* what we believe, to *argue* for *p* or "to marshal considerations in its support" (Alston 1991: 71). In the vast majority of cases of holding a belief, we do not discursively justify those beliefs. For example, I sincerely believe that special relativity explains the relationship between space and time, but I would be utterly hopeless at trying to justify this belief through an explanation of Einstein's $E = MC^2$. Instead, as Faulkner points out, we need to be able to *source* our justification in an epistemically appropriate manner: in this case I source the beliefs of the twentieth century's most preeminent physicist.

2.2.3. The Commitment to Getting Things Right

In making an assertion, then, we take responsibility for what we assert. Epistemic responsibility, though, goes beyond the felicity of a speech act and one's duties as a speaker. For Lorraine Code (1987), it is an intellectual virtue, a quality of mind that promotes intellectual flourishing (DePaul and Zagzebski 2003), in which the speaking agent takes *active* responsibility for knowing. Epistemically responsible agents are those who "in their knowing, strive to do justice to the object—to the world they want to know as well as possible" and who "value knowing and understanding how things really are" (Code 1987: 59). The virtue lies in "striving to do justice" to the world and in attempting to fulfill an obligation to fellow inquirers, rather than in actually arriving at an elusive truth. Epistemic responsibility seems to be the central intellectual virtue from which others such as open-mindedness, intellectual openness, honesty, and integrity (all incidentally related to truthfulness) "radiate" (Code 1987: 44). It is more central to intellectual flourishing, for example, than epistemic reliability (Goldberg 2012), since one can be passively reliable but "only an active, creative agent can be assessed as responsible or irresponsible, as having fulfilled her obligations to fellow enquirers" (Turri et al. 2009). If moral agents have the intellectual virtue of epistemic responsibility, they will take *care* in arriving at, conveying, and maintaining true belief. Code also later notes the link between epistemic responsibility and advocacy by defining the former as "the responsibility to know well in order to advocate honorably" (2013: 845). When we hear advocates, we trust that they are building their advocacy on evidence that they have acquired responsibly.

While epistemic responsibility is indubitably an intellectual virtue, I would argue, with Williams[2] (2002), that it is also a moral virtue. Aristotle's intellectual virtues—*sophia* (wisdom), *phronesis* (practical wisdom), *episteme* (scientific knowledge), *techne* (technical knowledge), and *nous* (rational intuition)—clearly promote intellectual flourishing but are also clearly not moral virtues. Other intellectual virtues such as clarity, acuity, and critical acumen similarly promote intellectual flourishing without having direct moral implications. Epistemic responsibility, on the other hand, like honesty and integrity, can have ethical weight: we have not just an intellectual obligation but an ethical commitment to get our facts right. Returning to the prehistoric ancestor mentioned in Chapter 1, there is little benefit if our companion reveals that there is an animal behind us but (rather anachronistically) mistakes it for a domestic cat rather than a saber-tooth tiger. Accordingly, there is a mutual advantage in both revealing what we believe is the case (sincerity) and doing so conscientiously (Pettit 2015).

However, there is even more of a need that epistemic responsibility should be raised to a moral virtue because, unlike sincerity, it requires effort. Williams writes of the virtue he calls "Accuracy" (here called "epistemic responsibility" for reasons discussed in the following) that it "encourages people to spend more effort than they might have done in trying to find the truth, and not just to accept any belief-shaped

---

[2] As discussed in the following, Williams somewhat infelicitously calls it "Accuracy" (with a capital A) rather than epistemic responsibility.

thing that comes into their head" (Williams 2002: 87–88). The key value of epistemic responsibility lies not in arriving at the correct answer ("the truth") but in investing sufficiently in the investigation, in making an "investigative investment" (2002: 124) and taking care in representing the results of that investigation. In short, we could say that it is about *caring* for the truth, whereas sincerity is about *sharing* the truth. It is about commitment to the epistemic journey, not necessarily arriving at the destination. And if someone arrives at justified true belief, "[i]t is to say that the person got things right due to his own abilities, efforts and actions, rather than due to dumb luck, or blind chance, or something else" (Greco 2003: 111). In short, we can say of our epistemic commitment that

> [a]n individual who is consciously acting in circumstances of trust to inform other people will take trouble to make sure, to a reasonable degree, that the belief he passes on is true; this is equivalent to saying that an investigative investment can be made on behalf of someone else, or on behalf of the group. (Williams 2002: 124)

However, if epistemic responsibility is more about *striving for* than *arriving at* the truth, then it must be possible to be both responsible and inaccurate.

2.2.4. Accuracy and Epistemic Responsibility

As the "Hawthorne" quote at the beginning of the chapter suggests, we tend to require "accuracy" of speakers, along with "honesty." Williams formalizes this common-sense notion in his conception of truthfulness. Truthfulness, which "implies a respect for the truth" (2002: 11), is a disposition that consists not only in the virtue of saying what you believe to be the case (Sincerity) but also of making an effort to acquire true belief (Accuracy) (2002: 44–45). There is clearly a strong link between *aiming at* accuracy and epistemic responsibility, and Williams makes it clear that his "Accuracy" (with a capital A) concerns the process rather than the product. As in Code's (1987) work, which Williams inexplicably ignores, it is about *striving* to get things right rather than *actually* getting them right. Nevertheless, "Accuracy" is strangely inaccurate as an analytical term since it is difficult to avoid the resultative form "accurate."[3] While there are clear links between the ordinary meaning of "accuracy" (faithful *representation* of the truth) and Williams's "Accuracy" (careful *investigation* of the truth), or being "serious about facts and what's true and what's not," as Barack Obama put it after the election of Trump (Solon 2016), the words are clearly not coterminous, as Williams

---

[3] In a very early version of the TRUST framework, I used Williams's term "Accuracy," but this tended to provoke spontaneous critical reactions at conferences in a way that I have not found using the term "epistemic responsibility."

well recognizes.[4] We are interested in the *process* by which speakers arrive at their claims and how they *represent* that process in discourse, not ultimately in the ontological truth of their claims. Since it is possible to be epistemically responsible while holding a justified false belief, the objective accuracy of an assertion cannot be a determinant of the speaker's subjective truthfulness. In terms of folk psychology, Williams's Accuracy might translate as "trying to be accurate," but in terms of *evaluating* others' putatively untruthful discourse, we are more interested in the "trying" than in the being "accurate." In short, we are interested in whether the claim was *arrived at responsibly* (the speaker has doxastically justified grounds for making the claim) and whether it has been *conveyed responsibly* in discourse. For this reason, virtue epistemologists, who study intellectual virtues and vices (DePaul and Zagzebski 2003), have carefully avoided use of the term "accuracy," with its objective connotations, preferring such terms as "epistemic conscientiousness" (Montmarquet 1987) and "epistemic responsibility" (Code 1987). It seems more reasonable to expect speakers to be *conscientious* or *responsible* in the way they form, convey, and hold onto their beliefs than to expect them to be accurate irrespective of investigative effort. And if we expect that, it seems reasonable to say that speakers are untruthful if they convey a belief that they have formed and retained irresponsibly, even if that belief is actually true.

This distinction between accuracy and epistemic responsibility has been impishly hidden in the attributions to the quotes at the beginning of this chapter. The quotes themselves are examples of what might be called "self-indexical citations," or citations that point to themselves as paradigm cases. With regard to the attribution of the first quote, "We know nothing certainly, for truth lies in the deep," we simply cannot know for certain that Democritus made this remark about certainty because any direct evidence that he said it has been lost in the depths of history. The attribution, then, may or may not be accurate. However, it is epistemically responsible to hedge the citation with "attributed to" (as it generally is). That is the best we can do given the evidence available to us, and it will not deceive the reader into thinking that Democritus definitely said it.

With regard to the second quote, it is *true* that the words "Accuracy is the twin brother of honesty" are generally attributed to Hawthorne. Nevertheless, that attribution is known to be *inaccurate*. The quote (more precisely, "Accuracy is twin brother to honesty") is actually from Charles Simmons's *Laconic Manual and Brief Remarker* (1852). My "Hawthorne" attribution is irresponsible. However, the reason it is irresponsible is not because it is inaccurate: we have seen that

---

[4] Perhaps this is why Williams's distinction has not been taken up by moral philosophers, virtue epistemologists, or linguistic pragmatists. Another explanation is his renowned rejection of theory: his work provides profound and invaluable insights into the nature of truth and truthfulness but no systematic framework, or even clear definitions, that can be drawn on by other researchers.

the Democritus attribution may well be inaccurate, and it is almost certainly the case that Democritus did not say those precise words (even allowing for translation variation). What makes my Hawthorne attribution irresponsible, instead, is a combination of a lack of effort in establishing the facts of the matter, a lack of care in conveying the quote in discourse, and my own professional role as an academic. Having found the "Hawthorne" quote cited multiple times (*without*, incidentally, the hedge "attributed to") on the Internet, it took me just a few minutes to establish that it was a misattribution. No amount of investigation, on the other hand, could take me beyond "attributed to Democritus." Furthermore, unlike Ben taking Sue at her word in Basement Scenario 2, it would have been epistemically irresponsible for me to have genuinely left the "accuracy and honesty" quote as attributed to Hawthorne when we know that quotes on the Internet tend to be unreliable and when I could so easily have cross-checked my original unreliable sources. Crucially, this judgment of irresponsibility holds *even if the misattribution is unintentional*. As an academic, I have a duty to check my sources, so I cannot simply excuse myself on the grounds that "I didn't realize." One of the problems with anonymous posts on social media is that we are unable either to hold an individual responsible for the assertion that is made or to assess the credibility of the writer (Goldberg 2013: 135).

2.3. Bullshitting and Indifference

The previous section established a conceptual frame for viewing the growing pragmatic and philosophical work on bullshitting. In bullshitting, speakers fail to take responsibility for their assertions (2.3.1). However, the lack of responsibility lies not so much at the level of assertion itself as in a failure to contribute responsibly to the ongoing inquiry (2.3.2). Bullshitters are aware of what they are doing. The expression "Money talks, bullshit walks," for example, contrasts two rhetorical strategies for getting one's way. So, bullshitting, unlike other categories of untruthfulness explored in this book, is both insincere and epistemically irresponsible (2.3.3).

2.3.1. Indifference toward Assertions

Frankfurt, in his seminal *On Bullshit* (2005[1986]),[5] upset the standard distinction between sincere and insincere assertion by positing the figure of

---

[5] Building on Max Black's (1983) work on "humbug," "On Bullshit" was first published in *Raritan* (Frankfurt 1986) and reprinted in *The Importance of What We Care About* (Frankfurt 1988), but it became very popular after its publication as a short monograph in 2005.

the "bullshitter" who makes an assertion without caring whether or not she believes it:

> Her statement is grounded neither in a belief that it is true nor, as a lie must be, in a belief that it is not true. It is just this lack of connection to a concern with truth—this *indifference* to how things really are—that I regard as of the essence of bullshit. (Frankfurt 2005 [1986]: 33–34)

He identified this indifference in people like advertisers, salespeople, and politicians, who he thought *bullshitted* audiences, customers, and voters in an attempt to sell them their products. He thus also saw bullshitting[6] as an act of deception. Since Frankfurt took a deceptionist view of lying, he was at pains to distinguish the deception of the bullshitter from the deception of the liar. In his view, both the liar and the bullshitter represent themselves falsely as "endeavoring to communicate the truth" (2005: 54), but whereas the liar takes the truth seriously but contradicts her own belief, the bullshitter is *indifferent* about the truth. She could not care less about the truth value of her assertions as long as they further her rhetorical cause. If the lie works, its victim is deceived on two counts: she will have not only a false belief about the facts, but also a false belief about what is in the liar's mind (Frankfurt 2005: 13). If the bullshit works, on the other hand, the victim will only have a false belief about the facts:

> The fact about himself that the bullshitter hides . . . is that the truth values of his statements are of no central interest to him; what we are not to understand is that his intention is neither to report the truth nor to conceal it. (Frankfurt 2005: 54–55)

Thus, while the liar (or misleader or withholder for that matter) *conceals* the truth, the bullshitter conceals her "enterprise" (2005: 54): in other words, that she is not providing an epistemic warrant for what she is saying. In the terms outlined in the preceding, she is concealing the fact that she is not *taking responsibility* for her assertions, that she is not prepared for the Toulminian challenge "Why do you think that?" In other words, we might say that she is pretending to be asserting, whereas she is only stating.

Frankfurt provides few examples and they are unfortunately mostly infelicitous. One of his main ones is of a politician delivering a 4th of July oration:

---

[6] Frankfurt systematically uses the term "bullshit," but he is clearly talking about the discursive strategy of *bullshitting* rather than the discursive product *bullshit*, which I shall discuss later.

Consider a 4th of July orator who goes on bombastically about "our great and blessed country, whose Founding Fathers under divine guidance created a new beginning for mankind." (Frankfurt 2005: 16)

This is certainly bombastic, but it is not clear either that the politician is indifferent to the truth or even that he is trading in fact. Politicians of the religious right might sincerely believe that the Founding Fathers worked "under divine guidance," while the Declaration of Independence indubitably represented "a new beginning" for *Americans* (which some Americans confuse with "mankind"). As I shall argue in Chapter 3, phrases like "our great and blessed country" are unfalsifiable and so belong to the realm of opinion rather than fact. Furthermore, it seems unlikely that the audience of such an oration, already anticipating flowery rhetoric, would be deceived about the politician's "enterprise" or would use his oration as a source of facts about American Independence.

A perhaps clearer example of bullshitting without exemption can be found in certain cold call scripts. For example, while barratrous "No Win, No Fee" lawyers in the United Kingdom are not allowed to "ambulance chase," or seek clients at the site of traffic accidents and other disasters, they *are* allowed to cold call, or solicit business from potential clients with whom they have had no prior contact. Thus, scenarios like Virtual Ambulance Chaser are quite common:

Virtual Ambulance Chaser
Felicity, a call center employee representing a legal firm, calls a number on a list that has been sold to her company by a vehicle recovery firm. She knows that the great majority of those on the list will only have had a simple breakdown rather than an accident. However, as required by her script, she begins the conversation: "Hello. I believe you have had a car accident in the last few years." The receiver, Reginald, has indeed had a recent car accident and believes that Felicity must be connected with his insurer. He consequently listens to Felicity's sales pitch.

Felicity has no evidence that what she is asserting with regard to Reginald is either true or false. With each call she makes, she cannot know whether or not the respondent has had a car accident recently. She is not taking responsibility for her assertion, and my own experience suggests that she will put the phone down if challenged to substantiate her claim. At the same time, though, she does not necessarily *believe* that the respondent has *not* had a recent accident; indeed, she may well have a cognitive bias to believe that "this next call" will be the one to the accident victim. What is indubitable, though, is both that she lacks doxastic justification, or evidential grounding, for her claim and that she must be aware of this lack of grounding. She is deliberately using a rhetorical strategy scripted by her employers to try to deceive the victim. She is concealing something from her listener but, as Frankfurt noted, the object of concealment is not the truth. The hearer in these cases knows perfectly well whether or not he has had an accident recently, even if some of us with poor memories might be initially perplexed. Instead, she is concealing the fact that *she* does not know the truth of the matter but is just guessing.

A number of theorists have directly challenged whether the cognitive core of bullshitting is epistemic indifference and have adduced cases where people seem to be bullshitting while caring about the truth or falsity of what they say (Kimbrough 2006; Carson 2010; Wreen 2013; Fallis 2015b; Stokke and Fallis 2017; Stokke 2018, 2019a). Stokke (2019a: 267–268) gives the example of friends excitedly discussing a fishing trip and, when one says, "I really hope the fishing is good there," another, "caught up in the excitement," replies, "The fishing there is outstanding!" even if she has no real evidence of this. Stokke argues that while she is bullshitting, she is not indifferent toward the truth because "[s]he wants it to be true that the fishing is good."[7] This may well be the case, but it is also indubitably true that she is not taking responsibility for her assertion: if challenged "Why do you think that?" she will be flummoxed and probably will have to back track.

2.3.2. Indifference toward Contributions

Once again, and after Stokke and Fallis (2017; Stokke 2018, 2019b), we can use the notions of common ground (Stalnaker 2002; Allan 2013) and Questions under Discussion (QUDs; Roberts 2004, 2012) to explain the insincere strategy of bullshitting and why it is also irresponsible. In particular, the indifference in bullshitting is not an indifference toward the truth value of assertions as such, but an "indifference toward contributing true or false answers to QUDs" (Stokke 2018: 139). For Fallis (2015b), the bullshitter is not concerned, in making an assertion, in moving the inquiry nearer to the truth. For example, in the case of filibustering in Parliament or Congress, the setting requires filibusters to make true assertions. But they are not contributing to the common ground or answering QUDs, so they are bullshitting. Similarly, Carson (2010: 62) imagines a scenario in which a student in an exam is asked a question about a legal case

---

[7] There are actually two main planks to Frankfurt's argument: indifference toward the truth value of the bullshitter's assertions and deception about the bullshitter's "enterprise" (Meibauer 2016a: 71–72). Deception is not my central concern in this chapter, but it is worth noting a form of bald-faced bullshitting similar to bald-faced lying. Carson (2010: 60), for example, notes the case of the student who knows that he will receive 60% if he submits an essay of any sort and 0% if he submits nothing, so he submits evident bullshit to get the 60%.

she is ignorant about. She makes sure that what she writes is true because she believes she will get partial credit for this, but since she knows nothing about the case, she is bullshitting with respect to the QUD (the exam question) and the common ground with respect to that question (Stokke 2018: 153). Then there are any number of "Wishful Thinker" cases, such as this one, inspired by an example in Stokke (2018: 142):

> **Reassuring Groom**
> A couple living in Valencia are due to get married in the groom's hometown of Cardiff in a few days' time. The bride is Spanish and is becoming anxious about it raining on her wedding day. The groom reassures her: "It's always dry in Cardiff at this time of year." He has no idea what it is usually like at this time of year and he has not looked at weather forecasts.

The groom cares very much that it should be dry for the wedding but is clearly bullshitting with respect to the underlying QUD: "What are the chances that it will rain at our wedding?"[8] Equally, though, he is not taking responsibility for his assertion and could not provide support for it if challenged. The Virtual Ambulance Chaser can be seen as a more malicious version of the wishful thinker. Like the groom, Felicity is *wishful* that it is true that her call-taker has had an accident because she will receive a commission if she can secure a customer. But whereas the groom is trying to reassure his bride, Felicity is trying to rattle her call-taker into entering vexatious litigation.

2.3.3. Bullshitting, the Maxim of Evidence and Insincerity

There is a clear link between epistemic irresponsibility and Grice's second maxim of Quality: "Do not say that for which you lack adequate evidence." The Evidence maxim clearly signals the case where there has been an insufficient investigative investment. Fallis (2009: 30–31) and Dynel (2011b: 152–153) have both noted the link between this maxim and bullshitting. Thus, for Fallis:

> you bullshit if and only if you intend to violate the norm of conversation against communicating something for which you lack adequate evidence by saying that thing. (Fallis 2012: 575)

---

[8] The in-joke here is that Cardiff is the UK's Seattle: it has the same number of rainy days a year (around 150) and is also the UK's wettest city (115 cm p.a.) (Met Office). Valencia only has 40 rainy days a year.

Dynel (2011) writes that violation of the second maxim "gives rise to *bullshit*" and adds:

> The notion of bullshit pertains to statements which the speaker cannot judge according to their truth ... and which the speaker produces without sufficient knowledge about their validity ..., yet presenting them as if they were truthful and/or the truth. (Dynel 2011: 152)

Both Fallis and Dynel place bullshitting firmly within the camp of insincerity ("*intend* to violate," "*presenting* them as if"). Accordingly, in cases where speakers *believe* they have adequate evidence, they are not bullshitting. We do not think that the five-year-old child Tina is bullshitting when she declares on Christmas Day, "Santa's come!" on the basis of the subjectively "adequate" evidence that Santa has left presents and Rudolf has half-eaten the carrot she left for him. Stokke provides a richer example relating to an older child, Joan:

> **Science Fiction Reader**
> Joan has read a science fiction novel in which one of the characters states that there is life on Saturn. Joan thinks science fiction novels are reliable guides to facts about extraterrestrial life. So, she comes to believe firmly that there is life on Saturn, and she also believes that she has adequate evidence for that claim, that is, the novel's say-so. Indeed, Joan thinks she knows there's life on Saturn. Sometime later, her younger brother asks her whether there's life anywhere else than on Earth. Joan replies: "Yes, there's life on Saturn." (Stokke 2018: 144)

We do not think that Tina or Joan are bullshitting, because they *believe* they are contributing true answers to the local QUDs "Did Santa come?" and "Is there extraterrestrial life?" There is a congruence between what they believe and what they are asserting, and so they are being sincere. However, whether they are violating the second maxim of Quality depends on whether we interpret "adequate evidence" subjectively (they *believe* they have adequate evidence) or objectively (they *actually* have adequate evidence). As seen at the beginning of the chapter, doxastic justification, though subjective, requires epistemically appropriate standards. It could be argued that five-year-old Tina *is* doxastically justified, in the same way that Ben is justified in believing that it is raining, because she trusts that her parents are not lying about Santa coming and she cannot possibly expect that her father would tamper with the evidence. Whether Joan is doxastically justified will depend on her age, since at some point we would expect children to be able to distinguish clearly between fiction and fact. However, I shall argue in the following section for an objective interpretation of "adequate" evidence that makes assertions such as "There's life on Saturn" bullshit if said by a mature adult, whether or not she believes she has adequate evidence.

2.4. Bullshit and Inquiry

The type of inquiry that Grice, Stalnaker, Roberts, and Stokke are concerned with is *interactional inquiry* through conversational cooperation. However, this interactional inquiry takes place against the background of a more general *human inquiry* into the state of the world. While *bullshitting* is concerned with interactional inquiry, *bullshit* is concerned with human inquiry and is epistemically irresponsible with respect to that inquiry. The speaker may be sincere but is producing nonsense (2.4.1). Given the close connection between bullshitting/bullshit and Grice's second maxim of Quality, and given that both maxims are required for truthfulness, I propose taking Grice's supermaxim ("try to make your contribution one that is true") as the maxim of Truthfulness (2.4.2).

2.4.1. Sincere Nonsense

In ordinary language, there are two distinct if interrelated meanings of *bullshit*, which broadly correspond to the meanings of the noun and the verb: *bullshit* is nonsense or complete nonsense either in a linguistic (what is said has no meaning) or empirical (what is said has no grounding) sense; *to bullshit* someone, on the other hand, is to talk nonsense to them in an attempt to deceive them (CED 2003). While most research has effectively focused on *bullshitting* (even when, as in Frankfurt, it has gone under the guise of "bullshit"), Cohen (2002) and a few other philosophers (e.g., Evans 2006; Kimbrough 2006; Maes and Schaubroeck 2006; Wreen 2013) have noted that it is equally important to focus on the *shit* (the discursive product) as well as the *bull* (the rhetorical agent). *Bullshit*, as a discursive product, can be defined informally as *an evidentially worthless claim*.[9] Even more informally, it is "nonsense" or "rubbish." Frankfurt, while focusing on rhetorical bull, appears to unwittingly identify nonsense bullshit in his account of the link between bullshit and hot air:

> Just as hot air is speech that has been emptied of all informative content, so excrement is matter from which everything nutritive has been removed. (Frankfurt 2005: 43)

---

[9] It will be defined more formally in Chapter 6.

We might extend this metaphor to say that if the nutrients are the various forms of evidence that sustain a claim, then *bullshit* is the discursive waste product of poor digestion of the evidence.

A focus on the excrementitious discursive matter itself, rather than a putative strategy of bullshitting, can be found frequently in ordinary usage, as in the following examples from the British National Corpus (BNC 2007):[10]

(1) I did not come out with all the clichéd bullshit. (BNC: Hodkinson 1990, *The Wedding Present*)
(2) Come on guys, get responsible: this is not the first time the strong smell of bullshit has wafted through the air. (BNC: *Guitarist*)
(3) Henry then talks about "the truth" and the Californian Lifestyle Philosophy Bullshit Detectors (BNC: *New Musical Express*)
(4) So, I believe that the people making films have a strong responsibility to foster thought to the general public. Because if we feed them bullshit, they'll think bullshit. You see? (BNC: *Hot Press*)

In (1), we do not generally set out to write clichéd bullshit; it emanates from a lack of epistemic care with our writing. In (2), the "guys" may or may not have been consciously bullshitting, but the focus is on the perfume of emitted ordure. In (3), the focus is not on whether or not the Californian Lifestyle Philosophers are consciously bullshitting but on the detection of the philosophical dung. Finally, in (4), although "feed" is agentive, "bullshit" is the object and seems to correspond to "epistemically worthless matter." Similarly, it is always the content—"Bullshit!"—to which the speaker draws attention in conversation, rather than the person; while it is common to exclaim "Liar!" (attacking the sincerity of the speaker), "Bullshitter!" does not seem to exist. Bullshit is recognized as being of little value ("cut the bullshit") and as being opposed to reason:

> But from somewhere in the fog of received wisdom and what passed for it . . . a persistent and unrepentant voice relayed a subversive message. Bullshit, it said. Preston identified it at once. It was the Voice of Reason. (BNC: Bryers 1993, *The Adultery Department*)

Cohen (2002: 324) rightly notes that "almost any state of mind can emit nonsense or rubbish, with any old mix of sincerity and its lack." In particular, a mental state of earnest belief can produce nonsense. However, Cohen is on less firm ground when he claims that "the character of the process that produces

---

[10] Examples cited from the BNC can be attested at https://www.english-corpora.org/bnc/.

bullshit is immaterial here" and that "[t]he defect of this bullshit does not derive from its provenance" (2002: 324). Bullshit is not bullshit merely because it misrepresents the way things are in the world. The quiz contestant who answers that the capital of Australia is "Sydney" is ignorant about her capitals but is not producing bullshit. What makes "nonsense bullshit" bullshit is not ignorance or epistemic indifference but epistemic *inadequacy* and thus irresponsibility. The speaker has failed to put in any effort to get her facts right. The quiz contestant who has to answer a purely factual question on the spot has no opportunity to get her facts right and it would be very odd to describe her response as "bullshit." On the other hand, a blogger who claims that the MMR vaccine causes autism emits bullshit since we now have overwhelming and readily available scientific evidence that this is not the case.

2.4.2. A Revised Maxim of Truthfulness

Grice's maxim of Quality recognizes that truthfulness requires effort. The Supermaxim solicits us to "*try to* make our contribution one that is true," and we can construe this effortful bending of the will to the good in terms of being *sincere* (the first maxim) and establishing *evidence* (the second maxim):

Maxim of Quality
Supermaxim: Try to make your contribution one that is true.
Specific maxims:
1. Do not say what you believe to be false.
2. Do not say that for which you lack adequate evidence. (Grice 1975: 46)

However, it is the first maxim that has so often been identified as the "maxim of truthfulness" (e.g., Wilson and Sperber 2002; Dynel 2018).[11] This includes Grice himself who, in "Logic and Conversation," described the first maxim rather than the supermaxim as the overriding maxim such that "other maxims come into operation only on the assumption that this maxim of Quality is satisfied" (Grice 1989: 27). There are problems, though, with privileging the Sincerity maxim over the supermaxim. In the first place, as indicated by the imperatives ("Try," "Do not say"), Grice (1975: 45) was concerned, as here, with a speaker's *subjective* discursive relation with the truth: trying to be true, believing what you say, and having evidence for your belief. These subjective relations belong to the realm of truthfulness rather than truth. But if truthfulness

---

[11] Wilson and Sperber (2002), on the other hand, argue that a maxim of truthfulness is unnecessary as it is subsumed by their principle of Relevance.

is being conveyed by the maxim of Sincerity, it is not clear what the function of the supermaxim is meant to be. What subjective quality of truth might have truthfulness *subordinated* to it? What do we call the maxim of Quality, which is apparently so central to effective communication, in everyday terms? We talk of being "relevant" (Relation), "informative" (Quantity), and "clear" (Manner), but it is not apparent how we could have a subjective sense of "being true" that is not "being truthful." Second, if the Sincerity maxim is that of "truthfulness," how do we distinguish between "truthfulness" and "sincerity"? Dynel (2018) makes a brave effort to do so, but her distinctions have to be very subtle indeed to avoid the synonymy.

There seem to be good analytical and practical reasons, then, to raise truthfulness from a subordinate to a superordinate role in terms of the subjective conditions of truth: "saying what you believe" and "having evidence for what you say" (or being able to justify what you claim) are two essential qualities of *being true* in discourse. As some pragmatists (e.g., Wilson and Sperber 2002; Vincent Marrelli 2006) have noted, Grice's retrospective Epilogue does seem to suggest a move to the supermaxim, when he talks of the maxim of Quality "enjoining the provision of contributions which are genuine rather than spurious (truthful rather than mendacious)" and going on to explain that "[f]alse information is not an inferior kind of information; it just is not information" (Grice 1989: 371). Importantly, you can contribute false information to an ongoing conversational inquiry *either* by being insincere (first maxim) *or* by being epistemically irresponsible (second maxim). Furthermore, one of the ways in which Grice describes the supermaxim in this Epilogue is being "truthful," though he also sets "truthful" in opposition to "mendacious," which again suggests insincerity. There is also a direct connection with Searle's (1969: 33–42) constitutive rules for the successful performance of the speech act of assertion outlined in Chapter 1. These included both the "preparatory rule" that the speaker has *evidence* for the truth of *p* (corresponding to Grice's Evidence maxim) and the "sincerity rule" that the speaker *believes p* (corresponding to Grice's Sincerity maxim). Moreover, we saw that the overriding "essential rule" of assertions for Searle is that the speaker is making an undertaking that *p* represents an actual state of affairs (Searle 1969). This seems remarkably similar to Grice's supermaxim "make your contribution one that is true." It is a comparatively small step from here to saying that undertaking that *p* is the case (Searle) and trying to make a true contribution (Grice) are the same as *being truthful* in discourse.

Accordingly, a revised maxim of Truthfulness can be proposed that better captures the broadened conception of truthfulness adopted in the TRUST framework (the wording in italics substitutes Gricean wording while the terms on the right are suggested maxim labels):

Maxim of Truthfulness	
Try to *be truthful*.	*Truthfulness*
(1) Do not *conceal* what you believe *you should reveal*.	*Sincerity*
(2) Do not say *or misrepresent* that for which you lack adequate evidence.	*Responsibility*

Grice's supermaxim "Try to make your contribution one that is true" becomes simply "Try to be truthful." The first "Sincerity" maxim is inverted so that it is about concealing rather than saying: "say" is replaced by "conceal," and "to be false" is replaced by "you should reveal." The second "Responsibility" maxim simply adds "or misrepresent" since adequacy is a scalar phenomenon and careful hedging can compensate for inadequate evidence in many cases. I am not seriously proposing this maxim of Truthfulness as an alternative to Grice's maxim of Quality. Nor does it adequately account for epistemic responsibility, which is as much about what happens *before* and *after* the discursive act (i.e., investigative investment and response to new evidence) as it is about the speech act itself. However, the revised maxim does give an idea of the scope of truthfulness within the TRUST framework.

2.5. Dogma and Discourse Pathologies

Epistemically irresponsible discourse can be seen as reversing the fit between mind and world: we try to make the world fit our beliefs (2.5.1). This is effectively what dogma is, and it inevitably closes off inquiry (2.5.2). Given that dogmatic speakers are frequently not aware of what they are doing, we need to see their discursive output as pathological rather than strategic (2.5.3). Finally, I consider Saul's proposed concept of "negligent falsehood" as a way of introducing the coming chapters (2.5.4).

2.5.1. Direction of Fit

Epistemic responsibility is an intellectual and moral virtue that is manifested as much in the epistemic practices of inquiring, investing, and investigating as in the textual product that is carefully conveyed. As has been seen, one can be epistemically responsible but still get things wrong. Meteorologists carefully investigate a variety of evidence and will tend to hedge their predictions so they are generally epistemically responsible, but their predictions are frequently wrong. Similarly, epistemically responsible claims made in the past can look decidedly irresponsible, if not downright insincere, in the light of more recent knowledge about the facts that the speaker at the time could not have known. When epistemically responsible historical claims are labeled as "lies" in the light of current knowledge, we can call this *hindsight lying*, a type of hindsight bias (Pohl 2007).

Epistemically irresponsible discourse pathologically reverses the "direction of fit" between mind and world (Humberstone 1992). Searle (1979) used direction of fit to help distinguish speech acts: assertions had a words-fit-world[12] direction, while promises had a world-fits-words direction. Later, Searle (1983) noted that direction of fit could be extended to belief. A justified true belief should have a mind-fits-world direction. In other words, rational thinkers should fit their beliefs to the world as they find it through inquiry. If they believe *p* but are presented with clear evidence of *not p*, they should abandon *p*. If I think it is raining because it was raining the last time I looked, but Ben arrives and tells me it is not raining, I should abandon my belief that it is raining. While beliefs should have a mind-fits-world direction, desires have a world-fits-mind direction. We wish that the world *were* as we would like it to be. When the world starts to take the shape we would desire it to be, we talk of our "wishes coming true," but they are not true until that point.

The pathology in epistemically irresponsible discourse, then, is that the normal mind-fits-world direction for belief is switched to a world-fits-mind direction so that the words conveyed no longer fit the world. When presented with clear evidence of *not p*, epistemically irresponsible speakers will not abandon *p* but change their perception of the world so that it fits *p*. For example, the beliefs of many anti-vaxxers in the first decades of the twenty-first century seem to have been completely unaffected by the increasingly overwhelming evidence that there was no link between the MMR vaccine and autism. Each new piece of counter-evidence is either ignored or explained away in anti-vaxxer discourse.

Direction of fit helps to establish the line between what is epistemically responsible and irresponsible in discourse. Take Wreen's example of a non-deceptive bullshitter:

Casino Beater
Imagine that after years of study I come up with a complicated system for beating the casinos that I sincerely believe is flawless. I travel across the United States lecturing about it to various groups, enthusiastically touting its virtues.

---

[12] Searle uses the terms "words-to-world" and "worlds-to-word" and, in his later work, "world-to-mind" and "mind-to-world," but, as Humberstone (1992: 60) points out, it is easy to confuse the directions. Humberstone's "thetic" and "telic," on the other hand, introduce unnecessary technical jargon for the current purpose.

In fact, I couldn't be more wrong: the system is seriously defective and contains multiple errors, silly even egregious errors, errors on a par with those committed by Hobbes in "squaring the circle." In short, my system is humbug or bullshit, and I've been bullshitting, even if I don't believe I've been bullshitting and certainly didn't intend to bullshit. (Wreen 2013: 110)

Wreen is right to note that neither intentionality nor deception are in play here, but he is inadvertently presenting two distinct epistemic situations. When Casino Beater first presents his system, he is probably *not* producing bullshit: he has put in sufficient inquiry ("years of study," "complicated system") and believes he has come up with a good system. He has *tried hard* to fit his system to the world; after all, he will not beat the casinos (the world) if he has not managed the fit. We do not generally consider those who strive to fit their beliefs to the world (i.e., base their beliefs on evidence) as producing bullshit, even if they are wrong. However, once Casino Beater starts touring and promoting his system, his listeners will start trying it out and finding that it does not work. It is also hard to believe he would not try it out himself. He will thus discover himself and come to hear from others that his system does not work. Those who have bought into his system will probably be upset. At that point, if he ignores the constant negative feedback and keeps promoting his system with confidence, his direction of fit has switched; he will be trying to fit the world to his beliefs by believing, for example, that he has had bad luck in his own trials and by claiming that his detractors are not following his system properly or that they are lying. At this point he has become epistemically irresponsible and is now spouting bullshit. He may still genuinely believe at some level that what he says is true but, in a sense, he has become deluded.[13] This example is not purely hypothetical because it is precisely the situation with many lie-detection companies and their technologies that have been scientifically debunked.

While a world-fits-mind/words direction of belief and speech might be pathological, we are all susceptible to this pathology to a greater or lesser extent. There are powerful cognitive biases and emotions leading us to confirm rather than question what we already believe, and it is not at all easy to override them, particularly as these biases and emotions are often necessary for our emotional well-being (Kahneman et al. 1982; Kahneman 2013). Accordingly, we are mostly not aware (or not fully aware) that we are producing epistemically irresponsible discourse, and even when we are aware, almost as passive observers of our own

---

[13] I have a personal attachment to this example since, in my youth, I also came up with an "infallible" casino-beating system. It took one visit to the Genting Highlands casino in Malaysia to recognize that my system was flawed and that any further promotion of it would be bullshit.

verbal behavior,[14] that we are producing such discourse, we are not necessarily being *intentionally* irresponsible, except in many suspended contexts such as hyperbole, joking, and bull sessions.

2.5.2. Dogma as Closing Off Inquiry

Where Casino Beater becomes irresponsible is when he stops listening to others and stops adjusting his beliefs accordingly. Bullshit as a discursive product, then, is part of the much broader phenomenon of *dogma*. Indeed, just as *concealing* rather than *lying* underlies insincere discourse, so *dogma* rather than *bullshit* underlies epistemically irresponsible discourse. Christensen (2011) sums up the dogmatic attitude in the following hypothetical question-begging argument:

> Well, so and so disagrees with me about *p*. But since *p* is true, she's wrong about *p*. So however reliable she may generally be, I needn't take her disagreement about *p* as any reason at all to change my belief. (2011: 2)

This is a clear example of a world-fits-mind direction of belief: even though my usual assessment of the world tells me that she is a reliable source of knowledge, since my belief is not open to question, I must reassess *her* as a source of knowledge. It is this type of dogmatic attitude that can lead to the rejection of the views of experts in a field in favor of "gut instinct" or "just knowing," and it is the fundamental attitude underlying epistemic partisanship. We can see an example of such a dogmatic question-begging argument in Trump's tweet about voter fraud discussed in Chapter 8:

> Of course, there is large scale voter fraud happening on and before election day. Why do Republican leaders deny what is going on? So naive!

What Trump is effectively arguing in that tweet is the following:

> Well, *Republican leaders* disagree with me about *the existence of large scale voter fraud*. But since *large scale voter fraud is happening, they are* wrong about *large scale voter fraud*. So however reliable *these Republican leaders* may generally be, I needn't take *their* disagreement about *voter fraud* as any reason at all to change my belief. In fact, they are the ones who are being naive.

---

[14] Such passive self-reflection has occurred to me a great deal since beginning this project on untruthfulness and raises the question of whether some form of consciousness-raising might help foster rational discourse.

There is a direct link between the notion of investigative investment and skepticism. *Skeptikos* in Greek meant "one who reflects upon" or "investigates," and a skeptical attitude, in this sense, is one that is both open-minded and open to critique. Critical thinking (Kelley 2013) is skeptical in this sense, as are empirical investigations of paranormal phenomena (Irwin 2009). However, the word *skeptic* has often taken on connotations of negativity and mistrust, indicating a nihilistic attitude that closes down the investigation rather than keeping it open (Morison 2014). Sextus Empiricus recognized how skepticism itself could deteriorate into dogma. He contrasted his Pyrrhonian Skeptics "who are still investigating" and perennially searching for the truth with Dogmatic Skeptics who held rigidly to the view that the truth simply "cannot be apprehended" (Sextus Empiricus 2000: I 2). This is the skepticism of the contemporary dogmatic relativist (Norris 1996) or the populist who believes, without need for evidence, that "the EU is out to get us" or that *all* government institutions are so *thoroughly* corrupt that voter fraud can be taken as a *given*.

Concern with the dangers of dogmatism united the two archenemies Popper and Wittgenstein (Edmonds and Eidinow 2001). In *Culture and Value*, Wittgenstein wrote:

> [D]ogma is expressed in the form of an assertion and is unshakable.... It is not a wall setting limits to belief, but like a brake which in practice however serves the same purpose; almost as though someone attached a weight to your foot to limit your freedom of movement. This is how dogma becomes irrefutable and beyond the reach of attack. (Wittgenstein 1998: 32–33)

Popper's primary concern in *The Open Society* (1945) is precisely the closing down of investigation and suppression of alternative voices. Socrates, he believes, taught that "we must have faith in human reason, but beware of dogmatism" and that "the spirit of science is criticism" (1945: 162). Plato in his *Republic*, though, advocated the political elite telling the citizens a "Noble Lie" about the social stratification of society (Plato 1992), one that would lead to what we might today call Gramscian hegemonic consent (Gramsci 1971), in which citizens are complicit in their own subordination, and he maintained that "the state must suppress doubt of any part of this politico-religious dogma" (Popper 1945: 126). In making his case (in a five-page footnote) that the supposed change in Socrates' attitude is a-chronological and thus due to Plato suppressing Socrates' own voice, Popper seems to suggest a cline of critical openness/closure from intellectual humility (Church and Samuelson 2011) to authoritarianism (Stenner 2010):

> The Socrates of the *Apology* and some other dialogues is intellectually modest; in the *Phaedo*, he changes into a man who is assured of the truth of his

metaphysical speculations. In the *Republic*, he is a dogmatist, adopting an attitude not far removed from the petrified authoritarianism of the *Statesman* and of the *Laws*. (Popper 1945: 260 n.56(e3))

The dogmatist, then, falls just short of the authoritarian in terms of critical closure. Critical openness (Fricker 2007), the intellectual virtue opposed to the intellectual vice of dogma, is not a matter of standing on the fence; one must decide at some point where one stands and act on that (Booth 1974). But one's stand slips into dogma when it is seen, in Wittgenstein's words, as "irrefutable and beyond the reach of attack" (1998: 33).

In terms of its discursive manifestation, there is a clear connection between dogma and Bakhtin's *monologic* discourse, which suppresses other voices (Bakhtin 1981). Some of the Socratic dialogues, for example, are arguably monologic (and dogmatic) because Plato is using them to suppress alternative perspectives and others' doubts (Popper 1945; Heffer 2013c). However, it is perfectly possible to put forth a strong argument in a monologic style without being dogmatic, provided the speakers/writers make clear that they are open to critique or, as in academic discourse, openness to critique is a discursive presumption. Russell (2004[1928]) pointed out that open-mindedness should not be mindless: one can retain firm convictions while demonstrating a "critical undogmatic receptiveness" to alternative viewpoints. The "correct" critical outlook combines a strong desire to know with considerable caution in believing one knows.

Dogma, then, underlies both distortion of the truth and evidentially groundless bullshit, and it can be ethically wrong. Yet it is not an intentional discursive strategy.

2.5.3. Discourse Pathologies

We deliberately set out to lie, mislead, or withhold. We do not deliberately set out, though, to be dogmatic, to distort the truth (unless deliberately lying), or to talk bullshit (unless deliberately misleading). Without intentionality, though, we cannot talk of discursive *strategies*. Dogma, distortion, and bullshit, when not motivated by discursively insincere aims, are discursive byproducts that come about when the speaker is focused not on open inquiry but on fitting the world to his beliefs and desires by impressing, convincing, flattering, or defending his faith, face, or faction. When such rhetorical goals are so paramount in the speaker's mind as to override care for the evidence, this can result in forms of epistemically "diseased" discourse.

For this reason, I call irresponsible dogma, distortion, and bullshit *discourse pathologies*. While strategies intentionally aim toward a given goal, pathologies are the "diseased" product of communication that has gone epistemically awry. The notion of "discourse pathology" was suggested by Coady (2006), in referring to gossip, rumor, and urban myth:

> I am going to deal with some of the ways in which various forms of telling things to others come under moral or epistemic suspicion. Since I'm considering this against the background of what is (according to me) our very deep reliance upon testimony and associated trust in others that accompanies it, then I am thinking of these ways as pathologies, in that they present as distortions of or diseases of the normal case of telling and relying on what is told. (Coady 2006: 253)

Coady's use of "pathology," though, is slightly odd since he includes intentional discourse strategies such as lying. Yet disease is something that happens to us, rather than something we instigate. I see epistemically irresponsible discourse pathologies as *happening to* discourse because the speaker has not taken sufficient *care* in investigating and conveying her claims. This does not at all mean that the speaker is not being *strategic* in her discourse. It is just that the discursive strategy does not lie in her being dogmatic or in producing distortions and bullshit, but in other rhetorical goals.

The dogmatic concern is with the avoidance of alternative and potentially critical accounts; in short, with disregarding counter-evidence in all its forms. Just as *concealing* the perceived truth underlies all insincere discourse strategies, so *closing down* inquiry and thus *closing out* the putative truth underlies all forms of epistemically irresponsible discourse pathologies. Chapter 6 will explore the major irresponsible discourse pathologies of dogma, distortion, and bullshit, as well as some sub-pathologies and accompanying discursive propensities.

2.5.4. Negligent Falsehood

During the editing phase of this book (2019), I became aware of Saul's (2018) proposed concept of "negligent falsehood." As with my concept of "epistemic negligence" discussed in Chapter 6, Saul has taken the concept of negligence from the law and used it to distinguish negligent falsehood from lying:

> Negligent falsehood is to traditional lying as negligent killing is to murder. Murder requires intent to kill; and traditional lying requires, if not intent to deceive, then something quite like that. A negligent falsehood, however, does not require this sort of *mens rea*. It is a falsehood negligently propagated *without sufficient attention* to ascertaining the truth of the matter. (Saul 2018: 247)

82   THEORETICAL UNDERPINNINGS

Saul sees negligent falsehood as related to but distinct from Frankfurtian bullshitting because "it does not require a total disregard for the truth value of one's utterance, but only *insufficient* care for ascertaining its truth" (2018: 247). However, this seems much closer to the concept of *bullshit* outlined here, deriving from epistemic inadequacy. Negligent falsehoods are also narrower than my concept of bullshit or epistemic negligence because they must be false: a negligent speaker who does not propagate falsehoods, Saul writes, "may count herself lucky, in much the same way that a negligent driver who manages not to hit any pedestrians is lucky that they have not become a negligent killer" (2018: 247).

Saul defines a "negligent false assertion" as "a false assertion that the speaker negligently believes to be true" (2018: 248). This roughly corresponds to what I call an "epistemically negligent assertion." She gives the example of a famous CNN blunder when their reporters thought they spotted a terrorist flag at an LGBT Pride march in London in 2015. The anchor said:

> An unnerving sight today at a London gay pride celebration: an ISIS flag among a sea of rainbow colors. (Saul 2018: 248)

The flag was a parody composed of drawings of sex toys. This was evident from the footage CNN showed of the man waving the flag, but the network made the story "exclusive" breaking news for several minutes and even interviewed a terrorism expert, who politely pointed out that it was "possible" that this was just a "parody" (Fisherman 2015). There is no question, then, that, as Saul points out, this is a false assertion. Indeed, CNN was thoroughly lampooned in the media for making such a ridiculous mistake (e.g., Fisherman 2015). It is also clear in this "easy" case that the journalist, with a clear duty of epistemic care given her role, was being negligent as she "could easily have investigated properly" before making the assertion (Saul 2018: 248).

While Saul does not "attempt to give a complete account" of "what constitutes insufficient attention" (2018: 252), the TRUST framework aims to provide a more complete account of the entire evaluative process. Indeed, the term "negligent false assertion" effectively combines five different steps in the TRUST framework and we need to be careful with each of these steps:

(1) *Is the assertion verifiably false?*
   Often assertions are simply not falsifiable: "an unnerving sight," for example, adds to the culpability but it cannot be falsified itself. There are few cases like this where it is quite so easy to verify the falsity of the disputed assertion as to look with one's own eyes. Generally, we need to consider the reliability of sources. These issues are explored in Chapter 3.

(2) *Was the speaker justified in suspending her commitment to truthfulness?*
Clearly not in this case, but I could see the utterance as a headline in the English satirical magazine *Private Eye*, above a photo of the "dildo flag." In that case, it would be ironic rather than negligent. Issues regarding the suspension of truthfulness are discussed in Chapter 4. We shall also see, in Chapter 9, that parody always runs the risk of being misconstrued, as the satirical flag evidently was by CNN.

(3) *Is the assertion epistemically irresponsible, and if so how?*
In the TRUST framework, the issue of whether an assertion is epistemically irresponsible is detached from the ethical question of whether it is negligent because most instances of epistemically irresponsible assertions would not be considered unethical. The anchor's utterance is clearly irresponsible as insufficient care was taken in establishing the facts. However, it is more of a *distortion* of the evidence she has received from her reporter (who indicated that it was "an attempt to mimic the ISIS flag") than outright *bullshit*.[15] Epistemic irresponsibility and its categories are explored in Chapter 6.

(4) *Is that epistemic irresponsibility negligent?*
As Saul recognizes, not all unintentional falsehoods are negligent. As I do in Chapter 6, she indicates some "relevant factors," including the crucial one of role responsibility. In Chapter 6 I outline my conditions for epistemic negligence: duty of epistemic care, insufficient investigation, and failure to hedge.

(5) *How morally culpable is the speaker?*
CNN's failed scoop was clearly negligent. This applies in any case where reporters get things wrong when they should not. But we can separately consider moral culpability. Here, for example, the wrong lies partly in CNN's deliberate strategy to find terrorism scoops at all costs. That leads them to lower their guard and risk disseminating false and potentially pernicious information. Chapter 7 will provide a framework for discussing moral culpability in cases of ethical untruthfulness.

The term "negligent falsehood," then, is a useful shorthand for talking about cases of epistemic negligence. However, it does not provide a sufficient account of epistemic negligence, nor allow for the subtleties of its occurrence in situated text.

---

[15] Saul points out that it is not *bullshitting* because "[w]e have no reason to suppose that the anchor failed to care about the truth of her report" (2018: 248–249). This is true but was not in question, as we are clearly dealing with irresponsibility (and thus potential *bullshit*) rather than insincerity (and thus potential *bullshitting*).

2.6. Conclusion

This chapter has principally been concerned with proposition S2, the broadening of the scope of untruthfulness from discursive insincerity to the epistemic (ir)responsibility with which speakers act in forming, retaining, and conveying their beliefs. Subjective responsibility is already embedded within assertion, but it is also an intellectual virtue and a moral commitment. The growing work on *bullshitting* and *bullshit* enriches our understanding of epistemically irresponsible discourse, but it still tends to be tied a little too much to lying and insincerity rather than seeing it as a distinct aspect of untruthfulness. Taking dogma rather than bullshit as a point of departure opens up this aspect of untruthfulness to broader epistemic concerns.

PART II
THE TRUST FRAMEWORK

This central part of the book introduces the steps in the TRUST heuristic (**D3**) in turn. Chapter 3 covers the first two interconnected steps of identifying untruthful claims and establishing the evidence for their untruthfulness. Chapter 4 covers the initial ethical analysis (**E1**) to establish whether the putative act of untruthfulness is ethically significant or "justifiably suspended." Chapter 5 explores the speaker's available insincere discourse strategies (**D1**). Chapter 6 teases out a set of irresponsible discourse pathologies (**D2**). Both chapters 5 and 6 will also explore the conditions under which insincere strategies or irresponsible pathologies might be considered willful or negligent, respectively (**E2**). Finally, Chapter 7 provides tools for analyzing the degree of culpability of the act of untruthfulness (**E3**).

3
Claims of and Evidence for Untruthfulness

> *The truth, unlike a screenful of facts, is a habit of mind, a trust in the teller, a shared hope, a relationship . . . [Trump] said he was hearing them. They believed it. And to hell with the rest.*
> —Collis (2017: 1:30–2:02)

3.1. Introduction

As Collis (2017) nicely illustrates in his journalistic account of Trump's electoral success, "the truth" itself is often a subjective perception, a leap of faith into Democritus's "deep." It is our cognitive capacity to detach "truth" from empirical evidence, if we so desire, that enables populist movements to succeed, but it is also what enables us, more positively, to evince truth through fiction. However, "trust in the teller" and "habits of mind" are highly vulnerable to deception and self-deception, respectively. Where empirical evidence really matters, where lives and livelihoods are at stake (Does the MMR vaccine cause autism? Is voter fraud rife? Is most terrorism on US soil Islamic?), it is dangerous to hide behind the mantle of some "greater truth." The TRUST framework is designed to deal not with greater truths or emotional truths or religious truths, but with empirical truths, or facts, that can be established through evidence. Chapters 1 and 2 established that truthfulness is a subjective quality that does not depend in itself on the objective truth or falsity of a claim. Factual falsity is strictly neither necessary nor sufficient for either discursive insincerity (we can be sincerely mistaken or lie while telling the truth) or epistemic irresponsibility (we can be responsibly wrong or irresponsibly right). However, in this chapter, theory meets the practical problems of situated analysis.

The chapter discusses issues relating to the first two steps in the TRUST heuristic: CLAIMS of untruthfulness and EVIDENCE for falsity. It begins by considering common motives for calling out (or making claims of) lying or bullshit (3.2). Given that some of these motives (e.g., dogma, denial, and distrust) are unwarranted and others (e.g., confession, detection, and self-contradiction) are rare or unreliable, the most common motive for claiming untruthfulness is falsification. However, there is an awkward and unsatisfactory relationship between falsity and untruthfulness (3.3). A focus on falsification has two outcomes. First, it means that the TRUST framework in most cases can only deal with claims that are falsifiable (3.4). Second, it means there is a focus on establishing evidence for falsity and thus the reliability of sources becomes paramount (3.5). The focus on falsification in the framework troubles many colleagues in the humanities and social sciences, so the chapter closes by addressing concerns relating to relativism and social constructionism (3.6).

3.2. Calling Out Lies and Bullshit

The TRUST framework is designed to provide a more sophisticated means of judging untruthfulness in situated text than simple fact checks. One of the main reasons we need such a framework is because while we tend to call out lies all too easily, establishing that an untruth is a lie or bullshit is not at all easy. Indeed, unjustified miscalls of lying and bullshit are all too common and tend to derive from dogma, denial, or distrust (3.2.1). We have four main potentially justifiable motivations for calling out lying and bullshit, but each of them is problematic in its own way: confession (3.2.2); detection (3.2.3); self-contradiction (3.2.4); and falsification (3.2.5).

3.2.1. Miscalls: Dogma, Denial, Distrust

When considering the *in situ* calling out of lying and bullshit,[1] one should start with the observation that, in many contexts, the attribution is clearly unwarranted and the labels are being used primarily for rhetorical effect. Three contexts in particular tend to generate such unwarranted calls: dogma, denial, and distrust.

In *dogmatic* contexts, the speaker will try to close down alternative viewpoints, and the most definitive way of doing so is to describe them as "lies" or "bullshit"; for example:

A: We evolved from apes.
B: That's bullshit!

---

[1] One might add "or any other form of discursive insincerity or epistemic irresponsibility" here. However, in practice, and in cases of unwarranted attribution in particular, it is generally "lies" and "bullshit" that are called out, rather than "misleading," "distortion," or suchlike.

Labeling views as "lies" or "bullshit" seems to preclude in such contexts the need to justify one's own viewpoint. Thus "lie" is removed from its context of personal conviction and becomes simply a false view or mistaken belief. For example, the website of the Church of Jesus Christ of Latter-Day Saints hosts the article "Seven Lies Satan Wants You to Believe." The "lies" are of this sort:

> Lie #7: You've tried and tried, but you're just not good enough. You're never going to make it home to God. (Dickson 2017, n.p.)

In such dogmatic contexts, "lie" effectively means "myth," a widely held but false belief that does not depend for its existence on intentional deception.

A second context where calling out lies is often unwarranted is in the case of *denial*. If we have good reasons for denying an accusation, we can simply *correct* an accuser's mistaken belief: "Actually, it couldn't have been me because I wasn't there at the time. Ask Joe." By calling out lies or bullshit, we deflect the blame and the attention back onto the accuser: "I didn't leak that document. They're lying." This might be rightful indignation at being unfairly accused, but it is also frequently the last defensive resort of the genuine liar who finds himself cornered. Many such denials can be seen by Russian authorities with respect to the Skripal poisoning case (see Chapter 9).

Finally, if we *distrust* an individual or an institution, we are much more likely to believe that they are lying or bullshitting rather than giving them the benefit of the doubt that they might simply be mistaken. If a political party makes a campaign promise in times of economic boom that they will invest more in schools and hospitals, but then the economy unexpectedly collapses and they are unable to fulfill their promise, a large part of the population will accuse them of "lying" in their campaign promise. Similarly, if a leader is distrusted, it is virtually impossible for her, in the eyes of the electorate, to make a genuine mistake: she "*must*" be lying. This distrust can extend to entire groups in society. According to Faulkner, "our testimonial sensibility comes infected with identity prejudice" such that certain kinds of speakers (e.g., women, blacks, the working class) are perceived as having a credibility deficit (2014b: 193). Accordingly, some are more likely to be called out for lying and bullshitting than others.

I should reiterate for linguistic readers that my concern in this book is *not* to explore the *use* of words belonging to the semantic set of "untruthfulness." It is to develop a framework for *analyzing* untruthfulness in a rational and deliberative fashion. I now turn, then, to more rational attempts to call out lies and bullshit.

3.2.2. Confession

Confession can be a very powerful means of calling out one's own insincerity or irresponsibility. Ultimately only we can know definitively whether we have lied since only we can know whether or not we actually believed what we said. It is unsurprising, then, that confession has historically been the main focus of interrogation, whether by Inquisitors or police officers (Leo 2008). On those rare occasions when public figures make full confessions, it can not only be surprising and cathartic, but also demonstrate how easily we can be fooled by protestations of innocence. Such confessions reveal how accomplished some liars can be at insincerely *performing* sincerity. For years, cyclist Lance Armstrong blatantly denied taking performance-enhancing drugs both on camera and in sworn testimony. We see him in one deposition from 2005 answering the lawyer's questions with righteous indignation. When asked about one potential drug-taking incident, he replies, "How could it have taken place when I've never taken performance-enhancing drugs? How could that have happened?" And then, "If it can't be any clearer than 'I've never taken drugs,' then incidents like that can never have happened" (https://www.youtube.com/watch?v=klz86uQMrVg). While he is evidently nervous, as most witnesses are when testifying, there are no obvious signs that Armstrong is lying in such clips. Then, eight years later, and only after he had been found guilty and been stripped of his cycling awards, he made a full and frank confession to Oprah Winfrey (https://www.youtube.com/watch?v=N_0PSZ59Aws). While such a confession makes the previous lying absolutely certain, it should be noted that Armstrong's guilt had already been proved beyond reasonable doubt. In the vast majority of cases, though, we can only expect to arrive at standards of proof equivalent to the civil "on the balance of probabilities" or the criminal "beyond reasonable doubt," as mostly people do not make Perry Mason–style confessions.

Furthermore, there are serious problems with relying on others' confessions as a means of analyzing untruthfulness in situated text. First, in most contexts it is extremely rare for a speaker to confess to lying. In none of the cases analyzed in this book is a confession available. It is more common for a speaker to confess to having been irresponsible ("I'm sorry, I should have checked my facts better"; "that was an oversight"; "I misread that"). Second, though, where there is a genuine confession of insincerity or epistemic irresponsibility, this will tend to preclude the need for an analysis of untruthfulness in the first place. Finally, for a confession to confirm a judgment of insincerity or irresponsibility, it needs to be made freely, voluntarily, and in a rational state of mind (as in Armstrong's confession to Oprah). Unfortunately, where confessions are most common (i.e., in police interrogation), we now know that many are coerced and turn out to be false (Kassin et al. 2005; Kassin 2008; Perillo and Kassin 2011).

3.2.3. Detection

In the absence of voluntary confession, the holy grail of veracity assessment is detection of insincerity through verbal or non-verbal means (Vrij 2008). Given its utility, one might expect us both evolutionarily and in terms of child development to develop highly sophisticated natural abilities in lie detection. Indeed, many of us believe we are good at detecting lies (Hartwig and Bond 2011). These supposed natural abilities can be supplemented with techniques and technologies of lie detection that go back thousands of years and range from chewing on rice to the polygraph and "brain fingerprinting" (Littlefield 2008). Police forces have used innumerable techniques from "statement analysis" (SCAN) to analysis of bodily behaviors to detect lying in suspects (Inbau et al. 2001).

The reality, though, is that not only are we very poor natural lie detectors—our ability to detect lies is more or less at the level of chance (Bond and DePaulo 2006)—but lie-detection techniques and technologies are mostly highly unreliable (Vrij 2008; Granhag et al. 2015). There are both phylogenetic and ontogenetic reasons why lying is so difficult to detect. In terms of evolution, Trivers (2011) has argued convincingly that there are good reasons why we should have developed better skills at lying than in detecting lying. Essentially, these skills in deception develop because we learn to deceive ourselves. Despite our sense organs having evolved "to give us a marvelously detailed and accurate view of the outside world . . . once this information arrives in our brain, it is often distorted and biased to our conscious minds":

> We deny the truth to ourselves. We project onto others traits that are in fact true of ourselves—and then attack them! We repress painful memories, create completely false ones, rationalize immoral behavior, act repeatedly to boost positive self-opinion, and show a suite of ego-defense mechanisms. (2011: 2)

In developing such means of self-deception, we become proficient in deception: "we deceive ourselves the better to deceive others" (2011: 3).

Evolutionary arguments are somewhat speculative, but we have clear evidence from child development studies that we develop strong lying strategies from quite an early age. We can see the ontogenetic emergence of insincere strategic interaction through the "temptation resistance paradigm" (Sears et al. 1965). According to this common experimental method in child psychology, a young child is told by the researcher not to peek at or play with a hidden toy when he is left alone. Most young children succumb to temptation and disobey the instruction. When the researcher returns and asks the child whether he peeked at or played with the toy, the child who has transgressed effectively has a strategic choice to make: to tell the truth or lie. By the age of three or four, many children will lie, presumably with the strategic goal of avoiding perceived admonishment for not obeying instructions. However, most children of this age will subsequently trip up and reveal themselves as liars by showing awareness of the identity of the toy. By the age of six to seven, though, half of the children manage to successfully feign ignorance of the identity of the toy, thus withholding guilty knowledge, and have learned to evade incriminating answers, thus maintaining "semantic leakage control" (Talwar and Lee 2002), or consistency between their initial lie and subsequent statements. In this way, they render themselves both indistinguishable from the children who did not peek and undetectable by adults. A successful insincere discourse strategy in this case, then, involves not just an initial strategic choice to lie, but maintenance of that covert strategy through subsequent interactional turns. This is a complex and effortful task but one that many children develop quite early and that most adults have mastered to some degree. The crucial achievement in an insincere discourse strategy is that, in terms of performance, there should be nothing to distinguish a lie or act of misleading from a sincere assertion and deliberate withholding from mere omission.

Formal techniques and technologies of "lie detection" not only tend to ignore the most common forms of linguistic insincerity (misleading and withholding), but they also assume that lying is cognitively distinct from truth-telling. Yet adult liars maintain plausibility by building their lies from truths (McCornack et al. 2014: 367) or from "a related episodic memory of an event, personally or vicariously experienced" (Walczyk et al. 2014: 30). By recounting irrelevant but known truths rather than fabricating new material, they are able to give the impression of truth-telling. Accordingly, as seen in Chapter 1, the discourse processing of a liar is not substantially different from that of a truth-teller because most of what a liar says will be true. Indeed, Ganis concludes an overview of neuroimaging research on lying that "it is not clear that any of the observed patterns of neural activation are specific for deception production processes" (2019: 467).

Furthermore, even if reliable means of lie detection were eventually developed, it is unlikely these would be available to the discourse analyst judging putative cases of untruthfulness in discourse. There are two general exceptions to this rule, which are not normally considered under "lie detection": self-contradiction and falsification.

3.2.4. Self-Contradiction

Although it is perhaps our most effective means of catching out insincerity or irresponsibility, identifying contradictory statements is generally not considered to be a lie-detection technique. However, just as the interrogator's preferred goal is confession, so the cross-examiner's preferred goal is formal impeachment, i.e., "The discrediting of a witness's testimony by confronting the witness with his or her specific untruthful acts, prior convictions, prior inconsistent statements, or the like" (Garner 2009: 821).

Self-contradiction, though, is not always indicative of insincerity. There can be many sincere reasons why our account might change on different tellings. Chief among these is the fallibility of memory (Loftus 1979). There is also the necessary selectivity of any narration: taking a certain narrative line might lead us to ignore details that would have been relevant in another narrative direction. Furthermore, while it is extremely difficult to be accurate in perceptions, this can be turned into a claim of self-contradiction by cross-examiners: "You said in your interview that the car was going at 180 km per hour. Now you are saying it was going at 170 km per hour. Which is it?" Finally, it is virtually impossible to remember verbatim what someone has said, so different reportings of the same speech event are almost inevitably going to differ linguistically.

3.2.5. Falsification

Since voluntary confession and genuinely incriminating self-contradiction are comparatively rare and since lie detection is mostly unreliable, our main motivation for rationally calling out lying or bullshit is a perceived lack of correspondence between what is claimed and what we know to be the case from the available evidence. This is the realm of fact checking: speaker makes claim x; we doubt x; we investigate x and we discover (ideally) that x is either true or false. Alternatively, we already *know* from prior knowledge and experience that x is false. According to cognitive linguist Eve Sweetser, in our folk theory of information and evidence, "the speaker's saying something entails the truth of the thing said" (Sweetser 1987: 47). This is a presumption of *truth* rather than *truthfulness*. It follows, according to Sweetser, that if speakers say something *false*, they *know* it is false and thus it is a lie. Such a correlation between falsity and insincerity, if it exists, is reinforced through the fundamental attribution error, the belief that others' behaviors are always consciously motivated whereas our own are often dictated by circumstances (Ross 1977). If people are always consciously aware of what they are doing, it follows that a speaker is more likely to be lying rather than being ill-informed when it is revealed that she has said something false.

However, this unreflective correlation between factual falsity and insincerity is challenged by three phenomena:

(1) Believed-true assertions that are innocently false, i.e., sincere mistakes;
(2) Believed-false or unjustified assertions that are true, i.e., true lies or true bullshit;
(3) Believed-true assertions that are irresponsibly true, i.e., irresponsible truths.

First, people are able to overcome the folk correlation between falsity and insincerity when faced with obvious mistakes or with distortions attributable to human fallibility. No one consciously denies, on reflection, the existence of sincere mistakes, even if it is often difficult to distinguish a sincere mistake from an insincere lie or an irresponsible falsehood. The other two phenomena are more controversial.

The notion of the "true lie" has a long pedigree: Augustine condemned as a liar he "who with his mouth speaks the truth without knowing it, but in his heart wills to tell a lie" (Augustine 1961: 18). Coleman and Kay's true lie scenario scored second highest for lying (1981: 31). More recently, the true lie has been challenged. Carson (2006, 2010) has argued that "[s]howing that a statement is true is always sufficient to counter the accusation that one has told a lie" (2010: 15). This intuition was tested by Turri and Turri (2015), who came to the surprising conclusion that "[i]f someone makes a dishonest assertion that turns out to be true, then he does not lie. Instead, he *tried* to lie but failed to do so—he *only thinks* that he lied" (2015: 166). Unfortunately, though, the authors built this conclusion into their multiple-choice options, which were constructed according to their anticipated conclusion that "lie," like "deceive," is a two-part success verb involving trying and then succeeding or failing, for example:

(1) He tried to tell a lie but failed to tell a lie;
(2) He tried to tell a lie and succeeded in telling a lie. (2015: 164)

When Wiegmann et al. (2016) replicated Turri and Turri's experiments using their original loaded questions, only 26% of informants considered the true lie to be a lie, but when they included endings that explained the relation with truth (e.g., "He tried to lie and actually did lie [although what he said turned out to be true]"), 81% of respondents saw the true lie as a genuine lie (Wiegmann et al. 2016: 40). While these results provide a form of evidence that at least *some* people might see lying as a success verb, they are not nearly strong enough to question the view of lying as fundamentally a form of insincerity rather than falsehood. The same also holds for true bullshit. As seen in Chapter 2, we can have both a doxastically justified false belief (i.e., be responsibly wrong) and a doxastically unjustified true belief (i.e., be irresponsibly or accidentally right).

Third, we have the case of true assertions that are irresponsibly true. This is the "prescient" basement worker who guesses correctly that it is raining or the horoscope that "predicts" correctly that you will meet someone new today. While their assertions cannot be falsified, these speakers are untruthful because they are being epistemically irresponsible.

3.3. Factually Falsifiable Claims

While we can be both insincere and irresponsible while telling the truth or sincere while saying something false, the constraints of discourse analysis mean that we have to begin with justified evidence of falsehood (3.3.1). If evidence of falsity is analytically necessary for judgments of untruthfulness in situated discourse, then it follows that we must work with claims that are both factually significant (3.3.2) and falsifiable (3.3.3).

3.3.1. Justified Evidence of Falsehood

Discussion in the previous section has led to a conundrum. Factual falsity is not strictly necessary for insincerity: you can make a mistake without lying, and you can lie while inadvertently telling the truth. Factual falsity is also not strictly necessary for epistemic irresponsibility: you can get things right by luck, or get things wrong despite your best efforts. It is possible to explore such types of insincerity and irresponsibility under social scientific experimental conditions or in philosophical thought experiments. In situated discourse, though, it is rare to be able to establish evidence of untruthfulness without first ascertaining either that the speaker has said something false or that he has no justification for the claim he has made. A true lie can only be picked up through an unlikely confession. On the other hand, Mary's misleading implicature could be falsified through an eyewitness seeing her entering Valentino's house, or her boyfriend finding a selfie of her in bed with Valentino, or through any number of other occurrences. A lie that you didn't eat the cake could be falsified through a crumby mouth. In general, then, we need to begin a TRUST analysis with evidence of falsity. Such types of prima facie evidence of untruthfulness are the mainstay of criminal jury trials and they are made possible (to some extent) by extensive questioning of witnesses by assiduous trial lawyers. Outside legal contexts, though, we seldom have the luxury of being able to test claims in the way a cross-examiner can. We generally have to rely on publicly available evidence.

At the same time, with respect to public discourse, at least, we often do have available evidence of factual falsity, without the need for cross-examination, particularly when the speaker/writer is referring to public knowledge that can be accessed through the media or through academic research. And then we have "settled" cases such as those involving Bush's and Blair's claims of Iraq possessing weapons of mass destruction (see Chapter 8), in which long investigations have already been carried out. So, it is often quite possible to establish evidence for falsity, but it needs to be remembered that such evidence is analytically necessary but certainly not sufficient for judgments of lying, bullshit, and so on.

3.3.2. Factually Significant Claims

In order to be able to falsify a claim, it needs to be "factually significant" (Ayer 1946: 35). In other words, it needs to be able to establish a fit between word and world. It involves a claim of correspondence with the facts of the world as far as those can be ascertained. A false claim, then, is simply one that does not correspond with the facts, where fact is "that of which we may have empirical or *a posteriori* knowledge" (Mulligan and Correia 2013, n.p.). This underlies Hume's distinction between "Matters of Fact" and "Relations of Ideas" (Hume 2007: S.4), the basic legal opposition between "fact" and "opinion" in law (Keane and McKeown 2016), and the distinction between "knowledge" (or "justified true belief") and "opinion" in epistemology (Armstrong 1973). It is useful to make a further distinction between "brute" facts and "institutional" facts (Searle 1964; 1969: 50–53; 2018). It is a brute fact that the Earth is 93 million miles from the sun (imprecision makes it no less of a brute fact). Stating that fact requires the institution of measurement, but changing the measurement (e.g., the Earth is 150 million kilometers from the sun) will not change the brute fact that is being measured: the brute fact itself does not depend on our understanding of the conventions of measurement. It is an institutional fact, on the other hand, that Boris Johnson is, at the time of writing, the prime minister of the United Kingdom. For that fact to exist requires political institutions with quite elaborate constitutive rules; e.g., despite the United Kingdom being a political democracy, Johnson is, at the time of writing, a legitimately unelected leader. While institutional structures such as money, property, and government require complex constitutive rules that do not depend on brute facts, we can know these rules as we know brute facts, and claims about institutional facts can thus be falsified (e.g., "Theresa May is PM" is now false, whereas it was true when I last revised this chapter; Sydney is still not the capital of Australia, though it could be made the capital if the institutional rules changed).

While each of these dichotomies can be troubled and the boundary between facts/knowledge and ideas/opinions is fuzzy rather than clearly delineated, from a practical perspective we can strive to "get our facts right" as far as that is appropriate; and that effectively is what is required to be epistemically responsible. However, while there is something in Aristotle's claim that in dialectic and rhetoric "the underlying facts do not lend themselves equally well to the contrary views" (Aristotle 2007: Bk1, Ch1), sincere and responsible speakers will always legitimately hold differing views based on a careful assessment of the facts.

3.3.3. Falsifiability

It is not sufficient for a claim to be factually significant; it also needs to be falsifiable. The claim "God created the world" is factually significant to the extent that it establishes a fit between word and world, but it is not falsifiable since no evidence could be adduced that could assess the claim one way or the other. Falsifiability, when applied to truth claims, is the capacity for the statement or proposition to be proved wrong (Popper 1959). When considering the falsifiability of an utterance, what is of concern is the underlying propositional claim being made, rather than the particular linguistic form in which that claim is made. Accordingly, the untruthfulness may be in the form of a claim that is stated, implied, or presupposed over one or more utterances. For example, (b) and (c) in the following imply and presuppose (a), respectively.

(a) "The Chinese invented global warming." (statement)
(b) "Where does global warming come from? Ask the Chinese." (implication)
(c) "Why did the Chinese invent global warming?" (presupposition)

The untruthfulness, though, may also be in the form of a materially relevant fact that is deliberately or irresponsibly omitted. In (d) the speaker deliberately withholds the fact that she has not actually looked for such studies, and in (e) she fails to mention that most studies indicate global warming:

(d) "I am not aware of studies showing global warming." (withheld fact)
(e) "This study shows that global warming isn't happening." (failed mention)

Many utterances claimed in the media or in debate to be cases of lying or bullshit cannot be subject to an assessment of truthfulness because they cannot potentially be falsified. The issue here is not the nature of the speech act. The hortative "Let's reduce the skyrocketing crime rate!" is open to analysis because it falsely presupposes a rapidly rising crime rate. But the hortative "Let's make America great again!" is not accessible, despite the implied disputable assertion that "America was once great and is now no longer so," because the adjective "great" is an entirely subjective measure that cannot be falsified. Similarly, the prediction "Britain will be able to halt EU immigration and remain part of the single market" is open to analysis because it depends (at least in part) on current EU policy that absolutely prohibits this, whereas "Brexit will be the best thing since sliced bread" is not open to analysis since there is no falsifiable quality of sliced bread that we can measure Brexit against, nor a way of establishing what is "best." In theory, any overtly unfalsifiable statement such as "America is no longer great" or "Brexit is the best thing since sliced bread" is actually potentially open to an analysis of sincerity because what counts with sincerity is not coherence between word and world but between word and mind (does the speaker really *believe* that America is no longer great or Brexit is best?). One can certainly lie through unverifiable assertions. However, in practice, it is extremely difficult to find clear evidence of insincerity in such cases, and in regulatory contexts such statements would be regarded as "puffery."

The relationship between falsifiability and epistemic irresponsibility can be seen in MacFarlane's (2014) account of "assessment sensitivity." McFarlane is making what he clearly sees as a straightforward distinction between forms of assessment that he assumes everyone would make (the emphases are mine):

> It is useful to compare "tasty" to color words like "red" and non-evaluative flavor words like "salty." We do not universally agree in our judgments about what is red or salty. But when there is disagreement, we do not blithely continue to maintain our own views without hesitation. The fact that others report seeing red where you saw green, or tasting saltiness where you tasted none, makes you less confident in your own color or flavor judgments. It makes you suspect that the lighting is funny, or that you are ill or under the influence of a drug, or that your perceptual equipment is defective (as it is in color-blind people). To insist without further investigation that your own judgment is right, and that the other's is wrong, would be rash and unwarranted. But when it comes to disagreement about whether something is "tasty," we find no comparable hesitation. (MacFarlane 2014: 5).[2]

McFarlane is suggesting that with factually significant terms like "red" and "salty," alternative assessments should lead to a search for evidence. This might lead to a realization that we are mistaken in our claim.

Claims are not either falsifiable or unfalsifiable but fall on a continuum. We can borrow MacFarlane's example to establish a simple cline of falsifiability (Figure 3.1).

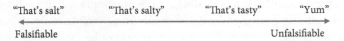

Figure 3.1. A cline of falsifiability.

---

[2] MacFarlane's choice of "salty" as a paradigm "non-evaluative" term is not entirely felicitous because "salty" is very often used evaluatively in discourse to mean "*too* salty."

At one end of the cline, we can judge statements like "That's salt" as clearly falsifiable assertions of fact. Table salt, for example, is a mineral primarily based on the scientifically confirmed chemical compound sodium chloride (NaCl). At a more practical level, we instantly falsify the factual status of sugar when we accidentally add salt to our coffee, exclaiming "Yuk! That's salt! (not sugar)." Factual accuracy is context-sensitive. There are many different types of salts, and a chemist is unlikely to be satisfied with the assertion "That's salt," but this is a perfectly appropriate degree of accuracy for the dinner table. Other "*salt*-like" assertions that are clearly open to judgments of both epistemic sincerity and responsibility include:

Canberra is the capital of Australia. (political institutional fact)
The knee bone is connected to the thigh bone. (anatomical brute fact)
Hitler invaded Poland. (historical institutional fact)
About 71% of the world's surface is covered in water. (statistical brute fact)

At the other end of the cline of falsifiability are purely expressive utterances such as "yum" and "yuk" that convey subjective affective reactions. Cuttlefish in squid ink makes my wife go "yum" and my eleven-year-old daughter go "yuk," but while my wife might claim better "taste," these are not claims that can be falsified and so are not open to an analysis of epistemic responsibility. They *are* open theoretically to an analysis of sincerity: if my daughter says "yuk," she is claiming that she finds the cuttlefish disgusting; if she actually loves it, she is contradicting what she believes and so is lying. However, as indicated earlier, this could only be falsified through confession or self-contradiction.

While *salt*-like assertions simply need to be fact-checked (not to diminish the difficulty of doing this in many cases) and *yum*-like expressions are clearly beyond falsification, *salty*-like assertions, as MacFarlane indicates, invite further investigation. With regard to *salty* itself, for example, the sensation of saltiness as a basic taste is scientifically established as occurring when alkali metals or hydrogen ions enter the taste buds. An inability to distinguish salty from sweet would certainly suggest a defect in the taste buds. And even marked differences in assessment of the degree of saltiness might result (after further investigation) from the level of physical habituation to very salty food (as anyone who has drastically reduced their salt intake will know). On the other hand, while the protagonist of the Norwegian comedy *Dag* (Karlsen 2015) finds bacon with lashings of salt "tasty," many of us would equally genuinely find it revolting. There is no ultimately falsifiable fact of the matter in this case. Claims of global warming require more than a simple fact check—it is still theory rather than empirical fact—but further investigation will reveal that the overwhelming weight of scientific evidence is in favor of the theory of global warming. So, although *salty*-like claims require further investigation, they can be empirically grounded to such an extent that it would be irresponsible to disagree without providing strong grounds for doing so. On the other hand, *tasty*-like claims are the sorts of opinions that are unlikely to lead to agreement through further investigation: "America is no longer great" suggests political nostalgia, but it would be impossible to agree on clear measurable criteria for "greatness"; "we have lost control to the EU" might hide xenophobic feelings about the free movement of EU citizens, but it would be impossible to agree on what constitutes "control" in this case; "*Citizen Kane* is the best film ever" is clearly a matter of aesthetic taste which will inevitably vary from person to person; and "abortion is wrong" is a moral stance and morality may be right or wrong but cannot be true or false.

3.4. The Reliability of Sources

Having identified a factually significant and falsifiable claim, evidence needs to be adduced for its falsity. Evidence needs to be sourced, and some sources of evidence are more reliable than others (3.4.1). Furthermore, if we rely on global media sources, we depend to some extent on third-party organizations that assess the reliability of media sources (3.4.2).

3.4.1. Cues to Source Reliability

The reliability of a source of information is an evaluation of its trustworthiness. Ultimately, no oral or written source is 100% reliable, just as no source is 100% accurate, and there is no direct correlation between perceptions of source reliability and actual source reliability. For example, while eyewitness testimony tends to be trusted by jurors, it is known to be fairly unreliable in many crime contexts due to the fallibility of memory (Loftus 1979). We are concerned, then, with *degrees* of reliability, but sources can vary from the highly trustworthy (e.g., an impartial expert report) to the thoroughly untrustworthy (e.g., conspiracy websites). Some of the key cues to source reliability are direct experience, expertise, impartiality, and track record.

Despite the problems with eyewitness testimony, direct *experience* is more likely to be trustworthy than hearsay, and indeed hearsay is generally not admissible as evidence in court. In media terms, direct filming of events as they happen appears more reliable than indirect reporting, though video evidence can be highly misleading as it can be manipulated through shot selection, editing, and verbal interpretation (Goodwin 1994). The "ISIS dildo flag" mentioned at the end of the previous chapter is an example of how video evidence can be distorted through interpretation, though it is notable that the video itself was what enabled the debunking of CNN's claims. Had there not been the video evidence, the claim might have held sway for much longer than it did.

A genuine *expert* in an area is more likely to be reliable than a non-expert. This should be obvious, but it needs to be reiterated at a time when expertise is often denigrated and the opinion of the random passenger interviewed on the Clapham omnibus[3] sometimes seems to be given equal weight to the expert. Four factors tend to diminish the perceived reliability of experts. First, experts, particularly in adversarial contexts, often arrive at contrasting opinions about the same evidence. There are certainly issues with bias, particularly where experts are paid by an adversarial party, but also a misperception that if experts cannot agree, then anyone's opinion is as good as anyone else's. Second, experts often get things spectacularly wrong. However, this often occurs when they go beyond their actual expertise or when the evidence is simply not strong enough to warrant a definitive opinion. Third, experts tend to be misreported. For example, experts are trained to hedge their opinions but people like trading in certainties, so the nuances are often lost in lay translation in the media and in courts. Finally, there are far too many pseudo-experts, people who either unduly claim expertise in an area (e.g., quacks in relation to medicine) or who unduly claim that the area they are expert in is valid and reliable (e.g., many lie-detection companies).

From this final factor there follows the problem of discrimination, first identified by Socrates, of how we can reliably distinguish the expert from the non-expert (Gentzler 1995). People often rely on demeanor, how a speaker looks and sounds, but this is a very unreliable form of meta-expertise (Collins and Evans 2007). More reliable, but by no means infallible, are credentials (degrees, awards, professional memberships), status in a field (one tends to trust a consultant cardiologist more than the family doctor), peer review (where available), and a good track record (where success is measurable) (Collins and Evans 2007). Despite the many issues in assessing experts and expertise, the rule that an expert is more likely to be reliable than a non-expert is generally a good one. It follows from this rule that trained journalists on balance will be more reliable than untrained ones. So, the mainstream media, which usually employ trained journalists, are more

---

[3] The "man on the Clapham omnibus" is an English legal fiction representing the ideal view of the reasonable person. Lord Reed memorably said: "The Clapham omnibus has many passengers. The most venerable is the reasonable man, who was born during the reign of Victoria but remains in vigorous health. Amongst the other passengers are the right-thinking member of society, familiar from the law of defamation, the officious bystander, the reasonable parent, the reasonable landlord, and the fair-minded and informed observer, all of whom have had season tickets for many years." Reed stressed that the views of actual passengers on the real Clapham bus would be irrelevant to what is an ideal legal standard (*Healthcare at Home Limited v. The Common Services Agency* [2014] UKSC 49 at [1]–[4]).

likely to be reliable than social media outlets and fringe websites employing "citizen" (i.e., non-expert) journalists.[4]

Nevertheless, experts are only more reliable if they are impartial. "Hired guns" are not particularly reliable in court, nor are "experts" in totalitarian regimes who are not permitted an impartial opinion. There is a strong folk sense that a partisan speaker or writer is likely to be a less reliable one. This explains the very low trust scores in the United Kingdom and the United States for politicians and journalists, despite these groups having more training in dealing with information than the average person, and the very high trust scores for doctors and scientists (perhaps under the misperception that the latter do not have a vested interest in their results) (Ipsos 2017). The BBC are generally considered to be more trustworthy than Fox News because they are funded by UK citizens as a whole, and so have a strong ethos of impartiality, rather than representing the ideological interests of their owners.

Finally, there is the issue of *track record*. How often does the source tend to get things right? Some speakers (e.g., Trump, Johnson) are notoriously poor in terms of their track record of reliability, and so it is rational not to trust what they say. Some media sources (e.g., BBC, *New York Times*) have a strong record of accurate reporting while others (e.g., Fox News, the British tabloids) have a very poor record, which should inspire mistrust. Social media and the Internet in general should be treated with particular distrust, particularly where the sources of information are not clear.

3.4.2. Source Evaluators

Since it is not possible to have direct experience of the majority of information sources across the world, we need to rely to some extent on media watchdog sites that rate publications for epistemic quality. Media Bias/Fact Check (MBFC) rates publications for both bias and factual reporting and offers extensions on Chrome and Firefox (MBFC 2019). With respect to the TRUST framework, the factual reporting rating is more important than the bias rating since it is possible to be factually reliable while conveying strong ideological opinions. Thus, *Huffington Post* (left bias) and *National Review* (right bias) are both rated "High" for the quality of factual reporting but are very different in the ideological opinions they convey. However, publications or websites rated "Low" for factual reporting tend to correlate with MBFCs separate ratings of "Conspiracy-Pseudoscience" (e.g.,

---

[4] There are exceptions to this rule where sites such as Bellingcat are primarily investigative and where technical expertise is more important than journalistic assessment and balance.

InfoWars) and "Questionable Sources," i.e., those propagating hate and propaganda (e.g., *Britain First*, whose content Trump has retweeted) or extreme bias and fake news (e.g., *The Gateway Pundit*). The owner of MBFC, Dave Van Zandt, is clear that he is not an expert and that his methods are not rigorously objective (Solender 2018),[5] but this is a growth area that both Facebook and Google are currently investing in and, despite current issues, we can expect to see more robust measures being developed in the coming years.

Such measures are crucial in the fight-back against epistemic partisanship because extremely partisan sources simply describe fact-checking sites as "fake." The alt-right site *WND*, rated by MBFC as "Mixed" for factual reporting, published an article "Phoney Baloney: 9 Fakest Fake-News Checkers" (WND 2017), which listed not only MBFC but PolitiFact, Snopes, and FactCheck all as "fake." Such calling out as "fake" of genuine sites dedicated to helping readers in their necessary assessment reliability task might be seen as a form of gaslighting, designed to destabilize readers to the point that they take genuinely unreliable sources of information as more trustworthy than the objectively more reliable ones. It is common in such circles simply to dismiss the entire mainstream media ("MSM") as "fake." Similarly, proponents of alternative medicine often dismiss the entire traditional medical establishment as "evil," while New Age believers tend to have a blanket rejection of rationalism and the scientific method and thus of reliable methods of establishing the truth (Drury 2004).

3.5. Falsity, Pragmatism, and Relativism

This chapter has argued that, for operational reasons, the analysis of untruthfulness in situated text needs to begin with an assessment of the factual falsity of the putatively untruthful claim. However, many in the humanities and social sciences reject the possibility of establishing factual falsity in the first place. This section briefly addresses such claims. First, I argue that the view of falsity required by the TRUST framework is compatible with a pragmatic conception of truth and knowledge as warranted assertibility (3.5.1). It is not compatible, though, with epistemological relativism or truth by popular consensus (3.5.2). Next I address the challenge of social constructionism (3.5.3). Finally, I consider non-rational epistemologies (3.5.4).

---

[5] MBFC does occasionally get things wrong: classification of the sensational UK tabloid *The Daily Express* as "Right" bias but "High" in factual reporting will amuse many British readers.

3.5.1. Falsity as Unwarranted Assertibility

Central to the notion of untruthfulness as explored in Chapters 1 and 2 is a disruption of inquiry: insincerity disrupts inquiry by concealing relevant information from the hearer; epistemic irresponsibility disrupts inquiry by feeding the hearer information that cannot be trusted. McFarlane (2014), in the passage cited earlier, captures the essence of a norm of inquiry in human communication when he assumes that "when there is disagreement, we do not blithely continue to maintain our own views without hesitation." He seems to take for granted the need for "further investigation" in the face of disagreement in assessment about *salty*-like claims. However, he is assuming norms of rational discursive practice that are not necessarily "normal," in the sense that people do not necessarily follow them in their everyday lives. What he is actually maintaining in the case of *salty*-like claims is something normative rather than descriptive: that "when there is disagreement, we [should] not blithely continue to maintain our own views without hesitation." While it may be "rash and unwarranted" to blithely ignore the overwhelming scientific evidence on global warming, it is certainly not uncommon. Blithely or blindly continuing to maintain our own views is the distinct characteristic of the dogmatic frame of mind that tends to lead to epistemic partisanship. It is closing out alternative views because we do not want to accept them.

Always keeping one's views open to "further investigation" is precisely what underlies the pragmatist Dewey's notion of "warranted assertibility":

> The attainment of settled beliefs is a progressive matter; there is no belief so settled as not to be exposed to further inquiry. It is the convergent and cumulative effect of continued inquiry that defines knowledge in its general meaning. In scientific inquiry, the criterion of what is taken to be settled, or to be knowledge, is being *so* settled that it is available as a resource in further inquiry; not being settled in such a way as not to be subject to revision in further inquiry.... When knowledge is taken as a general abstract term related to inquiry in the abstract, it means "warranted assertibility." (Hickman and Alexander 1998: 161)

Pragmatists like James, Peirce, and Dewey were reacting to what Putnam subsequently described as "metaphysical realism": "the thesis that the objects, properties and relations the world contains exist independently of our thoughts about them or our perceptions of them" (Khlentzos 2016, n.p.). The realism/anti-realism debate, though, is an abstract metaphysical one which does not affect everyday assessments of falsity. Indeed, the pragmatists were realist to the extent that they still believed that there was an external reality we need to address through empirical inquiry. The early pragmatists imagined they belonged to a community of highly rational and intelligent peers for whom "continued inquiry" and knowledge that is never so "settled" that it cannot be "subject to revision" was the norm. What Dewey seems to be describing is similar to Schlick's (1936) "verifiability principle" and even Popper's (1959) "falsifiability" and, in general, demonstrates a highly responsible epistemic attitude. It is effectively the scientific community in its ideally functioning form. Dummett (1978) and Putnam (1981) both later argued that truth is nothing more than what can be supported by the best possible evidence. For example, Putnam (1981) associated truth with "idealized rational acceptability": a true belief is one that would be accepted by anyone under ideal epistemic conditions. In terms of inquiries into untruthfulness, all that is *necessary* for a claim to be regarded as false is that it is falsifiable and that it is clearly *not* supported by the evidence.

3.5.2. Falsity and Epistemological Relativity

Inquiries into untruthfulness, though, are not compatible with radical epistemological relativity, the belief that truth is relative to a particular person, group, or community perceiving the world and is unaffected by independent epistemic warrants. It cannot be both the case that Neil Armstrong stepped onto the moon's surface in July 1969 (according to NASA) and that he stepped onto a studio floor (according to the conspiracists). Given even far from ideal epistemic conditions, the latter claim cannot possibly be warranted. According to consensus-based theories of truth (e.g., Rorty 1991), truth is relative to the discourse/interpretative community in which the truth is being claimed. If all people in the interpretative community of British Brexiteers believed that "bent bananas are banned by Brussels" (as the tabloids claimed) then it is "true" that this is the case. This relativist vein of thought began with Protagoras, who famously declared in the opening sentence of his *Truth* that "Man is the measure of all things..." (Plato 2004: 152a). Socrates retorted that, since most people would not accept his claim of relativity, if his claim is true, it must be false.[6] Similarly, Putnam pointed out that there are no Western norms that could justify a putative pragmatic claim that "[a] statement is true (rightly assertible) only if it is assertible according to the norms of modern European and American culture" (1983: 239).

Relativity is more complex than such "recoil" arguments seem to suggest (Blackburn 2005; MacFarlane 2014), but from an analytical perspective there is a real problem in locating truth effectively in consensus. At its extreme, a consensus-based approach can lead to a situation where the truth corresponds to

---

[6] As is often the case in Plato (Popper 1945; Heffer 2013c), the one-sided Socratic dialogue leads to Protagoras's argument being misrepresented (Billig 1996; Blackburn 2005).

the most popular view—we might call it "truth-by-likes"—as in Yahoo Answers (https://uk.answers.yahoo.com/info/about). For example, to a query as to the origin of the phrase "Liar, liar, pants on fire," Yahoo Answers awards its trophy for the "Best Answer" (with almost 700 "likes") to the following:

> 🏆 **Best Answer**: "Liar, liar, pants on fire. Hangin' on a telephone wire!" is a paraphrased version of the 1810 poem "The Liar" by William Blake. (https://answers.yahoo.com/question/index?qid=20100424202531AAk6ilr)

The answer then includes the full "Blake" poem. While the poem, which is widely available on the Internet, does not look at all Blakean, a comment providing clear evidence that it is indeed a fake (it is not in the Blake Archive) was evidently the "worst" answer with only five likes and one dislike. The judgment of truth-warranting assertions as subjective *tasty*-like opinions can therefore lead to absurdities.

"Truth-by-likes" is actually a gross distortion of the consensus theory of truth as proposed by philosophical pragmatists. Richard Rorty once apparently said that truth is "what your contemporaries let you get away with" (Blackburn 2005: 31; Dapía 2016: 28). In true Socratic style, though, his contemporaries not only failed to let him get away with his consensus version of truth, but also distorted what he said. Rorty was asking whether there is a need for ontological explanations for the relation between nature and its "mirror" (language):

> The aim of all such explanations is to make truth something more than what Dewey called "warranted assertibility": more than what our peers will, *ceteris paribus*, let us get away with saying. (Rorty 1979: 176)

Given its rooting in rationally achieved warranted assertibility, Rorty's claim is considerably less flippant than the Rorty "quote" that has been reproduced innumerable times. However, the reading of Rorty as anti-rational is not confined to his opponents. The literary critic Sam Slote has also picked up on this miscitation of Rorty, but his interpretation of it, from a rational perspective, is somewhat mystifying:

> [T]he miscitation is in effect a self-fulfilling prophecy precisely in being recited by others; apparently citing (or misciting) Rorty is what your contemporaries (or our peers) let you get away with saying. (Slote 2013: 75)

This is an extraordinary interpretation, privileging *de dicto* (what Rorty's peers say he said) over *de re* (what Rorty actually said). Yet then Slote effectively glosses what Rorty is *actually* saying (wrongly, in my opinion) as: "Can there be a truth that withstands and survives the perpetuation of misreadings and misapprehensions?" (2013: 75). While the question is rhetorical and the "correct" answer within Slote's rhetoric is clearly "no," in revealing the "*mis*citation," Slote is precisely demonstrating that what Rorty *wrote* (as opposed to what he meant) "withstands and survives the perpetuation" of miscitation. Rather than the miscitation being a "self-fulfilling prophecy," Slote has decidedly *not* let Blackburn, Dapia, and others "get away with" misciting Rorty because he has flagged up the *truth* of what Rorty said. Furthermore, Slote is not just pointing out a minor inaccuracy in copying. Pointing is not simply deictic here ("oh, look, they've made a mistake in copying what Rorty said") but ethically evaluative ("hey, they've misrepresented what Rorty said"). There is an implication of irresponsibility in academic miscitation because there is an expectation in academia that writers will invest some effort into ensuring that they are accurate: "accuracy is a duty," as Housman said (Gow 1936: 32).

3.5.3. The Challenge of Social Construction

It is indubitably the case that many phenomena that people take to be "real" (nation, gender, identity, culture) are partially or wholly socially constructed, and these tend to be the phenomena that are particularly salient in our social and political lives (Hacking 1999). Nation, for example, as Benedict Anderson (2016[1983]) ably demonstrated, is a socially constructed community "imagined" by people who believe they share the same language, history, culture, or beliefs. The idea of nation generally begins with the emergence of print in the vernacular and then is sustained and reinforced through constantly repeated nationalist discourse (Anderson 2016[1983]). This does not make the notion of nation *false* or *wrong*: repurposing Goffman's (1974) terms, it might be a "benign fabrication," or social construction, encouraging a sense of belonging among people living together, as well as an "exploitative" social construction encouraging hatred toward immigrant Others. Feminist writers have equally shown how our notions of gender have been constructed over centuries of patriarchal discourse (Spender 1980).

Evidence of social construction, though, is sometimes taken as evidence of relativity. If certain discourses about the abstract notions of nation and gender are repeated over time, they can become normalized to the point that they are reified and become perceived as concrete "things" that are "true." Up to this point, the argument is watertight. The problem is when this subjective perception is taken as objective reality: because people perceive it as true, it *is* true. Furthermore, if this notion is extended from specific cases like nation and gender to *all* information, one can see how one can arrive at a notion that there is no objective truth to any matter.

There are two problems with radical social constructionism. First, not all phenomena can be socially constructed. Prominent, focal, socially constructed concepts such as identity and culture are set against a background of dull and inconspicuous facts. For example, while *nations* are imagined, *states* are political institutional facts. States have territorial borders defined in law and political leaders and institutions with sovereignty over the people within that state. One can challenge those borders or political leaders or institutions, but one cannot generally dispute that (rightly or wrongly) they exist at an institutional level. One can say truthfully (if provocatively) that there is no English nation. But it is a factual mistake to assert that there is no UK state (unless intended figuratively or said after Brexit has led to the breakup of the United Kingdom). Similarly, while gender is clearly a performance of identity (Butler 1990), biological sex is a brute fact (though not a binary one).

The second problem with socially constructed relativity is that even where notions have been socially constructed, one can often distinguish between the social construct and empirical facts. For example, while most nations claim to have ancient histories, they are actually mostly modern constructs (Anderson 2016[1983]), and while nationalists in Croatia, Serbia, Bosnia, and Montenegro imagine they speak four very different languages corresponding to their four different imagined communities, they actually speak very slight dialectal variations of the same linguistic variety known as late as the 1990s as "Serbo-Croatian."[7] Whether a linguistic variety is labeled as a separate language has always been a political rather than linguistic question, but linguists can empirically observe the similarities and differences between language varieties. Similarly, the tabloid press in the United Kingdom have been propagating myths about the European Union for the past thirty years or so, and the discourse of tabloid-reading "leave" voters would suggest that they consequently have a socially constructed, and highly distorted, view of the European Union. However, this does not prevent the EU Commission from being able to dismantle each of these myths with hard evidence (EU Commission 2018). The British tabloid view of the EU does not become the "truth" because large sectors of the UK population believe these myths are true. Indeed, the analysis of social constructions themselves would not be possible without being able to abstract from those constructions: we need to be able to see them objectively (i.e., from without) to see that they are socially constructed.

---

[7] This is a source of much humor among anti-nationalists in the Balkans. For example, a widely circulated Internet meme shows cigarette packet warnings in Bosnia with "Pušenje ubija" (Smoking kills) written three times, twice in Roman script and once in Cyrillic script, all with the same spelling.

3.5.4. The Challenge of Other Epistemologies

As a final point, it should be noted that while there are a number of different epistemological paradigms operating in the world today (Fernandez-Armesto 1997; Lynch 2004), rational inquiry open to challenge is the most reliable means of arriving at knowledge. Where societies operate within an epistemological paradigm based on authority or religious dogma, for example, knowledge tends not to advance. Rational inquiry depends on a conception of truth that allows for some form of objective assessment of truth value. This was demonstrated in a debate between Sam Harris and Jordan Peterson, which failed to get off the ground because Peterson's "Darwinian" conception of truth allowed for no objective assessment of the truth value of anything (Harris 2017).

There are many occasions in everyday life when we are not warranting the truth, and these will be discussed in the following chapter. It is quite possible, then, to follow other epistemological paradigms in contexts where we are not warranting the truth: the religious scientist is not necessarily an oxymoron provided she leaves her faith at the laboratory door (though see Coyne 2015). However, where questions of factual falsity are at stake, rational inquiry is a methodological necessity.[8]

3.6. Conclusion

This chapter addressed the first two elements of the TRUST framework: CLAIMS and EVIDENCE. I noted the apparent paradox that while truthfulness is a subjective phenomenon, its analysis in situated discourse requires empirical evidence of falsity as a point of departure. True lies and true bullshit are insincere and irresponsible, respectively, but they mostly escape analysis. The requirement of falsification to call out insincerity and irresponsibility in most cases in turn means that claims subjected to analysis through TRUST need to be falsifiable. Nevertheless, establishing that a falsifiable claim is indeed false is only the start of an analysis of untruthfulness. It does not tell us whether the untruthful claim was justified in the context, whether it was discursively insincere or

---

[8] This claim is unaffected by the current debate about indigenous knowledge. Indigenous knowledge of local environments has generally come about through hundreds of years of informal experimentation leading to expert knowledge. The issue is generally about voice (Heffer 2017), about the established scientific and medical establishment's unwillingness to listen to these local experts, rather than the scientific status of these beliefs. However, if some of those local beliefs (e.g., regarding the medical efficacy of a specific plant) turn out to be empirically false, it would be dogmatic and potentially harmful to retain those beliefs on the basis of religion or authority.

epistemically irresponsible, whether it was willful or negligent, or how culpable is the speaker in producing such a claim in that particular context. These forms of analysis will be teased out in the following chapters. I start, in Chapter 4, with the question of whether an untruthful claim might be justified in the particular discursive context.

4
Justified Untruthfulness

Falsehood and delusion are allowed in no case whatever: but, as in the exercise of all the virtues, there is an oeconomy of truth.
(Burke 1999[1795]: 99)

4.1. Introduction

Lying and deception are part of what makes us human in terms of both evolution and child development. I noted in Chapter 3 that the development of self-deception in humans gave us an evolutionary advantage because it became easier to deceive others (Trivers 2011). The emergence of lying and deception is considered to be an important milestone in a child's socio-cognitive development because it shows a developing understanding of others' minds (Baron-Cohen et al. 2013). Autistic children are noted to have difficulties with this milestone (Baron-Cohen 1992) and particularly with the stage of developing from producing a lie to being able to cover up for it afterward (Talwar and Lee 2002). Even as adults, "everyone has to lie" to maintain social cohesion, as Harvey Sacks, the godfather of Conversation Analysis, observed (Sacks 1975). Social psychologists have claimed that some form of deception occurs in at least a quarter of all conversations (DePaulo et al. 1996), presumably mostly without harmful consequences. So, while many forms of untruthfulness in many discursive contexts might be considered unethical, being impelled to tell the truth on all occasions, as Jim Carrey's character in the film *Liar, Liar!* demonstrates, would lead to social disintegration.

Every discursive context, then, makes slightly different demands on truthfulness. As Burke said, there is an economy of truth, and it is important to understand the local economy before making judgments of culpable untruthfulness in a given situation. The alethic economy, like the financial economy, is subject to so many variables that it is difficult to predict in advance what ethical conditions will hold in a given context. Wittgenstein (2009) was right to point out the link between truth and the rules of a discursive game, but it is not so much the nature of truth that varies but our *ethical evaluation* of its presence or absence. It is an empirical brute fact that elephants cannot fly, but we are delighted rather than dismayed when Dumbo manages to do so because we "suspend our disbelief," or our presumption of truthfulness, at the beginning of a Disney film.

This chapter tackles the first level of ethical engagement in the TRUST framework by asking the following question: Is the act of untruthfulness *justified* in the context and therefore not *wrong*?

The chapter begins by considering three different communicative premises to this question: speech acts, speech contexts, and suspension of the speaker's commitment to truthfulness (4.2). Then, following the age-old Golden Rule that we should treat others as we would wish to be treated ourselves, it argues that the cases in which speakers' suspension of their commitment to truthfulness might be justifiable are those in which we would want others to be untruthful to us (4.3). The cases fall into three main types: conventional contexts in which we consider that truthfulness is not in play because we are not pursuing an inquiry (4.4); consequential contexts where other moral considerations override the pursuit of inquiry and thus overturn the presumption of truthfulness (4.5); and condonable contexts in which we would want to be excused for disrupting inquiry (4.6). In all these cases the speaker considers that the pursuit of inquiry is not paramount. The chapter concludes with a summary of types of justifiable suspensions and an example of a suspension analysis in context (4.7).

4.2. Analyzing the Economy of Truthfulness

Most of the work on the justifiability of untruthfulness has been confined almost exclusively to the question "When is it not wrong to lie?" Furthermore, this has mostly been in the form of case-based philosophical discussion of murderers at the door, innocent fugitives, dying parents, polite guests, and so on. Such work is difficult to bring together into a systematic framework that can be used in judging specific cases of untruthfulness in situated context. Here I consider instead three potential communicative premises for a systematic analysis of cases where untruthfulness is not also unethical: the overtness of the speech act (4.2.1); the relevance of truth to the discourse context (4.2.2); and justifiable suspension of the speaker's commitment to truthfulness (4.2.3).

4.2.1. Overtly Untruthful Acts of Speech

Since truthfulness is, at its core, about openness and untruthfulness about concealment, an obvious place to look for ethical distinctions is in the overtness or covertness of the untruthfulness (e.g., Vincent Marrelli 2006; Dynel 2011b, 2018). Lying and other forms of willful insincerity are generally covert, hiding a "noncommunicative and intentionally not communicated super-goal" (Vincent Marrelli 2006: 21). With overt untruthfulness, on the other hand, the speaker wishes to make his insincerity manifest, generally by flouting Grice's first maxim of Quality:

> The speaker wishes the hearer to recognize the intended meaning of the overtly untruthful utterance, which they both know not to be what the speaker believes or wants the hearer to believe at the level of what is said, but which carries *implied meaning* emerging from *implicature* materialized by *flouting* the Quality maxims. (Dynel 2011b: 141)

This accounts for rhetorical figures such as metaphor ("You are the cream in my coffee") and irony ("What a lovely mess"). Vincent Marrelli argues that overt untruthfulness can "plausibly" be taken further to cover "*ritualized social*, and, perhaps some ego- and alter- face-saving or protective 'lies' where an underlying assumed social contract of 'collusion' for pretending or mutual deception, is doing the cueing, rendering the strategy 'overt'" (2006: 21). However, while social contracts of collusion undoubtedly exist, it is not clear how the cueing of overt untruthfulness can take place in discursive practice in the case of pretending. If I say to my host, "I loved the turnip and custard crumble—so original!" it can only be face-saving to the extent that it is covert; as soon as it is taken as overt, it will be ironic (and far from face-saving). Even in the case of ritualized British greetings (A: "How are you?" B: "I'm fine"), we cannot assume that B is being overtly untruthful; she may well indeed be fine. The main issue with this approach, though, is that not all overt untruthfulness is justifiable (e.g., irony, as we have seen, can be harmful under certain conditions) and many cases of clearly covert untruthfulness (such as polite compliments to a distinctly average child musician) are considered ethical.

4.2.2. Truth-Irrelevant Contexts

The example of ritualized greetings suggests an alternative way of analyzing the economy of truthfulness: start with the assumption that each discourse context comes with a given epistemic value or epistemic grounding of which interlocutors are aware. Sweetser (1987: 49), in seeking theoretical explanation for the results of Coleman and Kay's study of the meaning of *lie*, offers a "taxonomy of speech settings" in which the primary variable for statements is whether their truth value is relevant or not in the setting. Her "+Truth Value Relevant" settings are ones in which "knowledge is beneficial and informing helpful" (1987: 49–50). If, in such a setting, the speaker is "fully informed" (+Know) but says something false, he "lies." According to Sweetser's folk model, the word *lie* can only be defined within this "idealized informational-discourse world": "Only within this world can the hearer properly link utterance with informativeness, sincerity and factual truth" (1987: 49). If the speaker is not fully informed (–Know), for example, she makes a mistake, which might be "honest" or "careless," depending on whether she has "adequate evidence or justification" for the mistake. In the case of "–Truth Value Relevant" settings, on the other hand, the question of truth simply does not come into play. Sweetser gives the examples of fiction (e.g., a story), politeness (e.g., a compliment), and entertainment (e.g., a joke).

Sweetser provides a fascinating and systematic theory of how people conceive of lying. However, there are a number of problems if we try to extend this model to our current purpose of providing a framework for judging cases of untruthfulness. First, the relative truth-relevance of a setting can be quite complex. So while fiction is notionally –Truth Value Relevant, the relevance of truthfulness actually varies widely across subgenres: biopics are fiction (they are not documentaries) but both sincerity and epistemic responsibility are relevant (if perhaps attenuated with respect to a documentary), while costume dramas commit to epistemic responsibility (often investing heavily in getting period details such as dress and furnishings "right" at the risk of incurring the wrath of some viewers if they do not do so) while making no commitment to sincerity in terms of the veracity of the storylines (though verisimilitude, or life*like*ness, is generally still important). Second, there is significant sociolinguistic and sociocultural variation regarding perceived epistemic value. Seventeenth-century Quakers famously refused to use titles, greetings, or politeness formulae because they saw them as "lies" (Bauman 1984). Plato saw the poets as deceptive, and the Athenians had to argue for the justification of comedy. Finally, it is not clear whether we can find consensus on truth value relevance even within a given speech community. We perhaps all know of people who cannot watch a fiction film (supposedly "–Truth Value Relevant") without constantly complaining about its factual inaccuracy. And not all of us are happy to lie or be lied to as a way of boosting positive face (Goffman 1981).

4.2.3. Warranting the Truth and Suspending One's Commitment to Truthfulness

A third type of approach to the economy of truthfulness is to see the speaking agent not as passively detecting the truth relevance of the context but as actively warranting the truth or actively suspending her commitment to truthfulness. Truth warranting, as indicated in Chapter 1, is often associated with the act of assertion. However, Carson (2006, 2010) argues that the warranting function is not part of the inherent meaning of assertion but is linked to aspects of the context.

One actively warrants the truth of a statement when "one promises or guarantees, either explicitly or implicitly, that what one says is true" (2010: 26). Conversely, "[i]n the context of a work of fiction or when saying something in jest, one is not guaranteeing the truth of what one says" (2010: 26). This warranty is not to be found within the speech act of assertion itself but "depends largely on the context and the relevant local conventions embedded in that context" (2010: 27). Placing the focus on actively warranting the truth, though, seems to suggest that the default presumption in discourse is that we are not normally warranting the truth of what we say. Yet, as argued in Chapter 1, the default presumption in discourse is one of truthfulness: the speaker commits to being truthful, and the hearer presumes that the speaker is being so.

If one starts with the speaker's default commitment to truthfulness, one can then consider when the speaker *suspends* that commitment and under what conditions that suspension might be morally justifiable. One of the main types of context in which that commitment is likely to be suspended is precisely in those conventional speech settings such as joking and fiction where both speaker and hearer are likely to share a belief that either sincerity or epistemic responsibility are irrelevant. However, the notion of *suspension* allows for a more dynamic and nuanced analysis. Fallis claims that the norms represented by Grice's maxims, including his first maxim of Quality, "can be turned off or suspended" by the speaker through discursive signaling such as winking or stress:

> Basically, you can signal to your audience—in a manner that is collectively accepted by the relevant linguistic community for this purpose—that you will not be obeying the norm of conversation in question. (2009: 53)

Fallis still seems to be thinking in terms of what I shall call "conventional" suspensions based on mutually agreed discourse conventions in a given speech community. Furthermore, what Fallis calls "suspension" seems more like overt flouting and thus more relevant to the overt/covert approach to the economy of untruthfulness.

Shiffrin (2014) provides a more subtle context-based account. Seen from the hearer's perspective, Shiffrin talks of "epistemic suspended contexts" to cover those specific contexts in which "ascertainable facts about the situation itself, or the actions or utterances of one or more participants, deprive the listener of the epistemic warrant to presume, in a predictive sense, that the speaker will tell the truth" (2014: 16). Sitting in a comedy club, reading a novel, watching a curtain rise on stage are all ascertainable facts that should deprive the listener of an epistemic warrant of sincerity. But also, a speaker prefacing what he says with "This is only speculation but . . . " should, *ceteris paribus*, deprive the listener of an epistemic warrant. In making ethical judgments of untruthfulness in situated discourse, though, we are more interested in the actions of the speaker than those of the listener. Certainly, the predictability of the suspension by the listener will play a major part in assessing the speaker's verbal act. But although my previous experience of listening to Donald Trump or Boris Johnson might deprive me of an epistemic warrant to presume that they will tell the truth, this does not justify Trump or Johnson's own suspension of truthfulness. Shiffrin uses the term *justified suspended context* to refer to "contexts in which the speaker's (potential) insincerity is reasonable and justifiable" (2014: 16). This rightly puts the ethical focus back on the speaker, but the terminology is still one of setting rather than agency.

For the purpose of situated analysis, the notion of suspension needs to be extended in three ways. First, it needs to cover contexts not only of cooperative overt untruthfulness but also of non-cooperative covert untruthfulness. Second, it needs to cover *suspensions of epistemic responsibility* as well as *suspensions of sincerity*. Third, it needs to cover not only types of speech setting but also the complex nuances of locally situated discourse. Furthermore, once we make a distinction between speech setting and situated commitment, it becomes necessary to distinguish between suspensions that are *justifiable in principle* given the *type* of discursive context and suspensions that are *justified in practice* given the specific circumstances of the situated discourse.

The problem at this point is to establish how to identify the types of cases where we might consider a suspension of truthfulness morally justifiable at least in principle. Furthermore, suspensions that are *justifiable in principle* also need to be *justified* in the *practice* of situated discourse. To solve the case selection problem, and in some debt to Carson (2010), I turn to what is arguably the single best candidate for a universal moral principle: the Golden Rule that we should treat others as we would wish to be treated ourselves.

4.3. The Golden Rule and Justified Untruthfulness

The Golden Rule offers a universal moral precept for grounding judgments of untruthfulness (4.3.1). Furthermore, by considering the types of cases where we would want others to be untruthful to us, we can identify three general types of justifiable suspensions of truthfulness (4.3.2).

4.3.1. The Golden Rule and Moral Reasoning

In Chapter 1, I argued that a presumption of truthfulness was necessary for the trust required in human communicative cooperation and that such a presumption was part of the much broader phenomenon of reciprocal altruism. But I also suggested that there would be good evolutionary reasons for raising this presumption from the instrumental stratagem of reciprocal altruism to a character virtue to be encouraged. In terms of recorded history, there is one very strong candidate for a folk formalization of the stratagem of reciprocal altruism into an ethical virtue: the Golden Rule (Wattles 1996). The Golden Rule is the age-old principle that we should treat others as we would wish to be treated ourselves. The rule seems to be the closest we have to a universal moral principle both diachronically and synchronically. It seems to go back to the beginnings of recorded history. It can be found in the ninth-century BCE Sanskrit masterpiece, the *Mahābhārata* ("treat others as you treat yourself"; *Shānti-Parva* 167:9), in the Attic orations of the fourth-century ancient Greek rhetorician Isocrates ("Do not do to others that which angers you when they do it to you"; *Nicocles* 3.60), and in the Roman stoic Seneca ("Treat your inferiors as you would be treated by your betters"; Seneca 2014: 93). Expressions of the Golden Rule are found across all the world's major religions. For example:

Islam: "As you would have people do to you, do to them; and what you dislike to be done to you, don't do to them" (Kitab al-Kafi, vol. 2, p. 146 *Hadith*).

Judaism: "What is hateful to you, do not do to your fellow: this is the whole Torah" (Hillel the Elder, Shabbath folio:31a, *Babylonian Talmud*).

Christianity: "Do unto others as you would have them do unto you" (Matthew 7:12).

Buddhism: "Hurt not others in ways that you yourself would find hurtful" (*Udanavarga* 5:18).

Confucianism: "What you do not wish for yourself, do not do to others" (*Analects* XV.24).

But it is also, arguably, the fundamental principle underlying secular ethical accounts such as John Rawls's influential theory of justice (1972). The rule is expressed both positively (e.g., "Do unto others as you would have them do unto you") and, more commonly, negatively (e.g., "What is hateful to you, do not do to your fellow"). The negative version is sometimes called the Silver Rule as it is less demanding.

The Golden Rule has tended to be rejected by Western philosophers in the past, even if it directly influenced both Utilitarianism and Kant's Categorical Imperative. According to Kant, the Rule enables a criminal to argue that he should not be punished because the judge would not want to be punished in his place (Kant 2012). Similarly, critics have argued that the masochist would be able to justify inflicting pain on others because he would have others do this to him. However, Carson (2010), who forcefully defends a version of the Golden Rule as a basis for moral reasoning, points out that these criticisms misconstrue the nature of the Rule as it functions in moral practice. According to Carson, in order to make a moral judgment, we need to be (1) "consistent"; (2) "adequately informed"; and (3) not cognitively impaired (2010: 129). Criminals who claim they should not be punished are being inconsistent because they do not believe that "those who commit crimes against *them* should go unpunished" (2010: 139). Masochists who believe they are justified in inflicting pain on non-masochists are not adequately informed because part of being informed is having "a vivid understanding of the experiences of other people" (2010: 130) and this would mean understanding that the non-masochist would object to "others inflicting pain on him" (2010: 137). Finally, a heroin addict who is so afflicted that he no longer cares what happens to himself is not entitled to do what he likes to others because he is cognitively impaired and so incapable of making a rational moral judgment.

Carson states the Golden Rule in more formal terms as follows:

> [I]f I claim that it is permissible for someone to do something to another person, then, on pain of inconsistency, I cannot object if someone else does the same thing to me (or someone I love) in relevantly similar circumstances. (2010: 135)

This version of the Golden Rule both explains the rationale behind the principle and provides two important extensions and a crucial qualification. The rationale of inconsistency is based on the universalizability principle that if one holds a certain moral judgment in one case, one must be able to extend that to all similar cases (Gensler 1998: 205; Carson 2010: 132). Consistency of application is fundamental to the law, to education, and to most other institutions. Otherwise, others would not be able to trust our judgments and social cooperation would soon break down. Carson rightly extends the Golden Rule from the purely injunctive "Do unto others ... " to the moral judgment of others' actions. We want to be able to judge not only the actions of a president taking a country to war, but also our own actions. Carson also rightly extends the receiving end of the principle "do unto you" to our loved ones too: partner, children, close friends. The crucial qualification is "in relevantly similar circumstances." These circumstances need to be judged in terms of our current rational understanding. For example, the judge in sentencing a murderer needs to imagine not what the criminal is thinking now (i.e., "I don't want to be punished") but what action would be right if she herself were standing in the dock as a criminal convicted of the same offense. She might imagine *now* that if she murdered another person, it would be right that she should be deprived of liberty but not, for example, that she should be deprived of life through the death penalty. This example shows that the Golden Rule does not lead to an absolute moral judgment, but it can rule out obviously inconsistent judgments.

4.3.2. The Golden Rule and Judgments of Untruthfulness

The Golden Rule necessarily involves role reversal. We need to imagine what it would be like to be in another's shoes. The Rule therefore hinges on empathy. When we lie to a five-year-old about the existence of Santa Claus, we empathize with the five-year-old wanting to believe in Santa. On the other hand, when we lie to the murderer at the door, we cannot empathize with the dangerous criminal, but we would want him to be stopped. When applied to untruthfulness, the Golden Rule might be stated as follows:

> **Golden Rule for Untruthfulness**: Be untruthful only in those cases where you would have others be untruthful to you or your loved ones in relevantly similar circumstances.

We need to consider, then, what *types* of cases are those where we would consider it justifiable for another to be untruthful to us. I suggest that these cases fall into three main types.

First, we would want others to be *exempted* from being truthful when *conventionally* truthfulness is deemed not to be in play because we are not pursuing an inquiry. This covers many speech genres, such as comedy, fiction, joking, banter, and so on. In these cases, inquiry is *expressly* not paramount. We would not want a stand-up comedian joking about her trials and tribulations to feel obliged to provide an accurate report, as that would be far less entertaining for us. But conventional suspensions also cover figurative language such as irony, hyperbole, and metaphor, in which inquiry *may be* paramount but the inquiry is not *disrupted* by the figurative language. For example, since irony means the opposite to what is stated, what is meant can still pursue the inquiry. We generally want to maintain the possibility of using figurative language ourselves and so we usually accept the overt untruthfulness.

Second, we might want others to be untruthful to us in cases where truthfulness is *in play* and inquiry at one level is *disrupted* by the untruthfulness, but other moral considerations *override* the pursuit of inquiry and thus overturn the presumption of truthfulness. In these cases, the *consequences* of the speaker being untruthful are considered to be *better* than the consequences of telling the truth. These might involve politeness ("that custard and gravy pie was *delightful*") or the protection of privacy ("I'm afraid I don't have my credit card details on me"), of emotional well-being ("this won't hurt much"), or of security ("he's not at home," said to the murderer). There is generally much less agreement than with conventional suspensions about when such consequential suspensions are desirable. Some of us would have others be more truthful than others in such contexts.

Finally, we would generally want others to be *excused* when truthfulness is in play and the untruthfulness disrupts the inquiry but finding ourselves in similar circumstances we would also want to be excused. These *condonable* suspensions cover playful pranks but also cases of pathological lying or bullshit where the speaker has effectively lost control of the suspension process.

It should be noted, though, that while the Golden Rule itself is a candidate for universality and while these categories of suspension might have wide intercultural acceptance, the specifics of their application to untruthfulness are socially, culturally, and individually bound. In the following sections I shall discuss these types of suspension in more detail.

4.4. Conventional Suspensions: Genre and Performativity

Conventional suspensions of a speaker's commitment to truthfulness are those in which there is a sociocultural discourse convention, recognized by both speaker and hearer in a given discourse community, that renders discursive sincerity and/or epistemic responsibility non-salient in the current discourse. After justifying an account of such cases in suspensional rather than definitional terms (4.4.1), I further divide conventional suspensions into those that are *prescribed* ("written in") by the speech genre (e.g., fiction, comedy) (4.4.2) and those that are *performed* by the speaker in their utterance (e.g., irony, hyperbole, metaphor) (4.4.3).

4.4.1. Definition versus Suspension

If conventional suspensions are justifiable to the extent that those discourse conventions are recognized by both speaker and hearer in their given discourse community, it could be objected that there is no need to account for them in suspensional terms at all. Indeed, researchers generally build these suspensions into their definitions of lying. Saul, for example, effectively covers *prescribed* conventional suspensions by requiring that liars take themselves to be "in a warranting context" (2012: 65): fiction and comedy are not contexts in which the truth is generally warranted. These are Sweetser's "-Truth Value Relevant" contexts. However, there are at least two problems with this definitional approach. First, *performed* suspensions do often occur in a warranting context (cross-examiners are often ironic, and politicians can produce a joking aside). So, Saul feels the need to add to her definition that "the speaker is not the victim of linguistic error/malapropism or using metaphor, hyperbole or irony" (2012: 65). Second, like all suspensions of commitment to truthfulness, conventional suspensions are not automatically *justified* since communication always involves *risk*: the hearer may not actually share the same discourse conventions or may be vulnerable and unable to pick up the discursive cues. Irony, as already indicated, can be particularly insidious. And even in the case of conventional genres, it is by no means a given that speaker and hearer will interpret the epistemic status of the genre in the same way. Truthfulness in autobiography, for example, is by no means always warranted, but is often expected by the reader. Suspensions start with the discourse context rather than the speech act or speech genre and so are more amenable to the evaluation of untruthfulness in situated discourse.

4.4.2. Prescribed Suspensions and Cultural Relativity

Prescribed conventional suspensions are "written in" to the genre. Often the metadiscursive labels for the speech genres themselves ("comedy," "fiction," "satire") cue community expectations about truthfulness. When we enter a "comedy" club or watch a "comedy" program, see a "fiction" film or read a "novel," we feel deprived of an epistemic warrant to presume that the comedian or narrator is telling the truth. When a comedian says on a comedy program that he has invented an office "de-laminator" (something that returns laminated paper to just paper), we do not ask to see his patent.[1] Prescribed suspensions, though, are almost never universally recognized. There is a long tradition, for example, of linking fiction with lies, and the distinction between the two is not self-evident (Maier 2019). It is often said that "fiction is the lie through which we tell the truth."[2] And some fundamentalist Muslims consider the "profane" knowledge of fiction unethical (Kareem 2017). Furthermore, as noted earlier, prescribed suspensions of sincerity do not always come with prescribed suspensions of epistemic responsibility. Even stand-up comedians like Michael McIntyre bank on verisimilitude (life*like*ness) for effect, drawing our attention to (and humorously exaggerating) the absurd minutiae of everyday life that so many of us recognize

---

[1] Sean Lock, *8 Out of 10 Cats*. Channel E4, UK. Personal viewing.
[2] This is usually attributed to Camus, but I can find no evidence that he actually said this. Contrary to many claims, it is *not* in *The Outsider*. But if the quote is fictive, there is a truth to it.

as being "true."[3] Similarly, most adult non-comedic and non-fantasy fiction tends to avoid defying the laws of physics. On the other hand, Oakley Hall, in his advice to those writing novels based on real events, says: "Truth is more important than facts, and fiction deals with what should have happened rather than what did happen" (1994: 72). Yet the award-winning historical novelist Hilary Mantel (*Wolf Hall, Bring up the Bodies*) is fastidious about getting her facts right and sees the task of historical fiction as "filling the gaps" in the historical record (Mantel 2017), while the Netflix series *The Crown* has caused controversy by changing or inventing details in the Queen's life (Vickers 2017).

Plato's exiling of the poets from his Republic is an interesting case with regard to prescribed suspensions. Plato, infamously, did not accept that poets could suspend their commitment to truthfulness. It is often said that he considered poets to be "liars," but in the *Republic*, it is more that Socrates accuses them of being epistemically irresponsible:

> "Then," said I, "have we not next to scrutinize tragedy and its leader Homer, since some people tell us that these poets know all the arts and all things human pertaining to virtue and vice, and all things divine? For the good poet, if he is to poetize things rightly, must, they argue, create with knowledge or else be unable to create. So, we must consider whether these critics have not fallen in with such imitators and been deceived by them, so that looking upon their works they cannot perceive that these are three removes from reality, and easy to produce without knowledge of the truth. For it is phantoms, not realities, that they produce. (Plato 1992: 598d–599a)

In TRUST terms, Plato is effectively accusing the poets not of lying but of bullshit because they have no evidential grounding for the claims they make. They cannot have invested sufficiently in their investigation because it is not possible for any mortal to "know all the arts and all things human pertaining to virtue and vice, and all things divine." And like bullshit, poetry is "easy to produce" because it does not require grounding in the truth. What makes poetry particularly negligent for Plato, though, is that he sees the poets as educators who have an epistemic duty of care toward their pupil readers. In presenting "phantoms, not realities" to those they are educating, they are breaching their readers' trust and having a pernicious effect on society. The warranting of truth, then, and what types of genres can be justifiably suspended are not always as straightforward as it might first seem.

---

[3] Stand-up comedian Louise Reay was recently sued for defamation by her ex-husband for using sensitive material about their marriage in a show at the Edinburgh Fringe festival. Juries in the United Kingdom have never accepted material used in comedy routines as defamatory and the husband dropped the case before it went to court.

Not only is the truth value relevance of a genre not always clear cut, but it can change over time, as occurred first with fiction and then autobiography. More recently, when Jack Dorsey created a new platform for social media, he adopted the name "Twitter" as he identified the new genre of the tweet with "a short burst of inconsequential information" (Sarno 2009). However, since its creation in 2006, Twitter has entered the mainstream social media and is now an integral part of media strategy in most large organizations. When even a US president relies on Twitter for much of his communication with the public, it is no longer possible to argue that truthfulness is conventionally suspended, or even attenuated, in the case of tweets from someone with a duty of epistemic care.

4.4.3. Performed Suspensions and Contextual Sensitivity

While prescribed suspension is "written in" to the genre itself, *performed* conventional suspensions are dynamically cued to the hearer by the speaker during the course of the interaction. Performed suspensions are cases of "overt untruthfulness" (Vincent Marrelli 2006; Dynel 2011) in which the speaker "does not subscribe to the meaning of his/her utterance taken literally and wants the hearer to appreciate its untruthfulness" (Dynel 2011: 141). Precisely how such suspensions are pragmatically conveyed is a matter of considerable dispute and is beyond the scope of this book (see, for example, Wilson and Sperber 1992). It is of note, though, that while performed conventional suspensions may be constrained by the genre, the genre itself does not permit or prohibit them: performed suspensions occur in many truth-warranting contexts.

The case of irony can demonstrate that while performed suspensions are justifiable in principle, they are by no means always justified in practice. With irony, as indicated in previous chapters, Grice's maxim of Sincerity ("Do not say what you believe to be false") is flouted, while the supermaxim of Truthfulness is observed by providing the contextual cues to the irony and making the falsehood overt. When Mark Anthony says in his funeral oration in *Julius Caesar*, "For Brutus is an honorable man," Shakespeare is performing irony on two levels, neither of which relies on a suspension of sincerity prescribed in the genre of the funeral oration itself. On the one hand, through virtual oxymora like "the honorable men whose daggers have stabbed Caesar," Anthony intends the funeralgoers to pick up his flout of Quality, along with the super-level "truth" that Brutus is anything but honorable. On the other hand, Shakespeare also arguably intends the theater audience to understand that Anthony's irony is false, and thus to pick up the super-level truth that Brutus is indeed an honorable man, while Anthony is being treacherous. By duping the citizens of Rome into believing that he has justifiably suspended his commitment to sincerity, he covertly lies while overtly performing insincerity.

Irony cannot be justified, then, when it is deliberately concealing the truth; some, for this reason, have even considered irony to be a form of lying (Barbe 1995). It also cannot be justified where the addressee cannot reasonably be expected to register the suspension, as in the insincere version of Fine Intellect in Chapter 1. For example, autistic children and adults are well known to have difficulty distinguishing literal and non-literal language (Happe 1995). This is particularly relevant when irony is used in such contexts as police interrogation or cross-examination where the suspect or witness is a child, autistic, or of subnormal intelligence. But even in the case of non-vulnerable adults, irony can be a risky game: when Randy Newman wrote the lyric "Short people / Got no reason to live" (1978) in the voice of an unreliable narrator, many people took the song as a prejudiced attack on short people (Fish 1989: 180).

One curiosity of the philosophical research on bullshit is how often the argumentation appears to depend on examples that appear to be justifiable suspensions of epistemic responsibility. Frankfurt, for example, discusses only two examples. One, the 4th of July orator, was discussed in Chapter 2. The other is an anecdote about Wittgenstein related by Fania Pascal:

> I had my tonsils out and was in the Evelyn Nursing Home feeling sorry for myself. Wittgenstein called. I croaked: "I feel just like a dog that has been run over." He was disgusted: "You don't know what a dog that has been run over feels like." (Frankfurt 2005: 24)

While Frankfurt recognizes that this is a simile (and thus a performed conventional suspension in TRUST terms), he considers it from Wittgenstein's subjective perspective as someone who is misrepresenting reality because she cannot possibly know how a run-over dog feels: "He construes her as engaged in an activity to which the distinction between what is true and what is false is crucial, and yet as taking no interest in whether what she says is true or false" (2005: 33). However, this example seems to tell us more about Wittgenstein's character than the ethical value of bullshit.

Conventional suspensions, then, whether prescribed or performed, are best not dealt with in purely formal or definitional terms when judging untruthfulness in situated discourse. They rarely provide a blanket exemption and the analyst always needs to consider whether the putative suspension is justified or not in the particular context.

4.5. Consequential Suspensions: Privacy, Politeness, and Protection

Consequential suspensions of a speaker's commitment to truthfulness are those in which the speaker believes that there is a greater good to be obtained by concealing rather than revealing the truth. After justifying a suspensional approach rather than one based on distinguishing different types of non-ethical lies (4.5.1), I further divide consequential suspensions into those considered to be *private* (saving the face of the speaker) (4.5.2), *polite* (saving the face of the hearer) (4.5.3), or *protective* (avoiding harm to self or others) (4.5.4).

4.5.1. Lying/Misleading versus Suspension of Sincerity

There is a very long history of philosophers discussing contexts in which insincerity might be considered consequentially justifiable (e.g., Aquinas 1989; Plato 1992; Kant 2012). However, the major focus of this work has been on the ethical difference between lying and the other major forms of insincerity (misleading and withholding). The distinction between lying and misleading is often rooted in a faith-based linguistic ideology that the "natural" purpose of communication is to communicate one's thoughts and thus not doing so is an offense against nature and God (Kant 2012: s.9). But, with Saul (2012: 73), I would argue that once we have decided that a speaker is consequentially justified in suspending her commitment to sincerity in responding, for example, to a would-be murderer, it matters little whether that insincerity is in the form of misleading or lying (except that lying is likely to be the more efficacious discourse strategy). On the other hand, in the less serious cases of polite suspension, there does seem to be an ethical difference between lying, misleading, and withholding in at least some contexts (Webber 2013). Nevertheless, where the scales tip from sincerity to consequentiality is highly dependent on both cultural norms and individual sensibilities, so while cases can be justifiable in principle, it is more difficult to justify them in practice.

Accordingly, many cases of consequential suspension are described in terms of types of socially acceptable lies (Dietz 2019). Thus "white lies" ("love your hat"), "butler lies" ("have to go, waiter's here"), and general "conversational lies" ("How are you?" "I'm fine") (Sacks 1975) are examples of polite consequential suspensions; "defensive lies" and similar are examples of protective consequential suspensions; "kidding" is a condonable playful suspension. Others characterize mitigating factors that I shall discuss in Chapter 7.

4.5.2. Private Suspensions

With *private suspensions* of sincerity, commitment to truthfulness is considered to be overridden by the greater good of saving "face," your sense of self-esteem and self-respect (Goffman 1955). Such suspensions are justifiable when the hearer has no countervailing right to know. We all have the right to private thoughts, feelings, and opinions. In everyday life, more often than not, the right to privacy trumps the right to know. Privacy is essentially "control over knowledge about oneself" (Fried 1968: 483). It is a fundamental part of human dignity that we are able to maintain this control as far as possible. Privacy is a valuable coin of social capital that we trade for intimacy and security. We give over private knowledge to increase trust in love and friendship, or to increase security in society (think passports and medical details). Complex social rituals develop in society to avoid infringing privacy, including "civil inattention" rites such as avoiding eye contact in crowded trains (Goffman 1963). Institutional representatives have the power to usurp those rights but, in a democratic state, those powers are circumscribed: the traffic officer can "ask" (i.e., demand) to see your license but not your credit card; the doctor can view your medical details but not your financial records; the trial lawyer can ask quite intimate details but only to the extent that they relate directly to the case. Since one withholds only if the hearer has a right to know what the speaker is holding back, withholding needs to be counterbalanced against the right to privacy and security.

Where an interlocutor has no right to know about your personal knowledge, a private suspension can be justifiable. Sjaak van der Geest (2018) revisits one of his early anthropological field trips to Ghana in 1973, in which he lived with a village family for a year and gradually gleaned from them and forty-two of their extended family members information about their sexual relationships and practices of birth control. With the benefit of forty-five years of hindsight, he is able to recognize the potential abuse of power inherent in this situation: being an outsider, and therefore not a threat to one's respect within the family, van der Geest was able to find out a great deal of intimate knowledge which the members of the family trusted him not to make known to other members:

> They were reluctant to speak on the issue of birth control, in particular abortion, but knowing that I already knew a lot (through gossip with others, for example) they usually "admitted" things that they had initially tried to conceal. Some—half jokingly—called me a "dangerous person" because I "knew too much." (2018: 544)

He effectively notes a conflict between the perceived right to know of the young anthropological field researcher inquiring for the sake of academic knowledge and the very intimate, and thus privacy-infringing, nature of the questions he was asking. In effect, he unwittingly abused his status as a trusted outsider to find out things he did not really have a right to know. What is particularly interesting about van der Geest's reflection, though, is that he also administered a questionnaire to 279 of the town's residents. The women's questionnaire was administered by nurses at a local hospital and, in those pre-consent days, the women assumed the questions served a medical purpose rather than being part of his anthropological research. It turned out that six of the women surveyed were part of "his" family, and by comparing their answers with what he knew about them, he found that, in the non-anonymous and orally delivered questionnaire, "[t]hey had lied profusely, presenting themselves in terms that they expected would make the nurses respect them" (2018: 545). In this intimidating formal context bereft of mutual trust, they had engaged in "impression management" (Goffman 1969) and lied to defend their privacy, and this might therefore be seen as a justified private suspension of sincerity. While it has been argued that privacy is a culturally relative concept (El Guindi 1998), most anthropological research suggests that all cultures respect some form of privacy even where physical and social conditions make privacy virtually impossible, as in an Indonesian "longhouse" shared by many different families (Loeb 1947).

The right to privacy, though, needs to be balanced against professional duties and other obligations that give the hearer the right to know. We would now accept that van der Geest's questionnaire informants had a right to know that they were taking part in a piece of anthropological research and that the information they provided (e.g., on illegal abortions) would not be passed to the police. Given that they were denied that right to know, it was understandable that they should take measures to defend their privacy. In contrast, in an ethically sensitive contemporary research setting where participants are not only informed of the general context of the research but also must give their written consent to participate, and are allowed to withdraw that consent at any time, it is arguable that in agreeing to participate, informants are entering a contract in which truthfulness is warranted. In such a context, a privacy suspension would seem less justified.

4.5.3. Polite Suspensions

With *polite suspensions* of sincerity, commitment to truthfulness is considered to be overridden by the greater good of saving your interlocutor's face (self-esteem) or showing warmth and friendliness. Polite suspensions lead to "social" or "prosocial" insincerities that could be said to effectively protect social life (Sweetser 1987: 54; Meibauer 2014b: 152) and to maintain kindness and reduce the possibility of hurt in relationships (DePaulo et al. 2009). Generally, it is assumed that rights are protected and trust is not breached in these contexts, but there is extreme cultural and individual variation regarding when and what forms of polite insincerity are ethically appropriate. Lying for politeness can be common in some Mexican communities (Agar 1996) while being utterly prohibited in seventeenth-century Quaker communities (Bauman 1984).

Polite consequential suspensions need to be distinguished from prescribed or performed conventional ritualistic utterances. For example, the Tzeltal Maya have a special tone of voice that they can use in polite contexts which releases "the speaker from the responsibility of believing the truth of what he utters" (Brown and Levinson 1987: 173). This is arguably a conventionally performed suspension, cued precisely through the special tone, rather than a consequential polite suspension (see also Saul 2012: 128). The question "How are you?" might receive the ritualistic response "I'm fine, thanks" or a genuine response about the interlocutor's wellbeing. The ritualistic response might suggest something about the respondents' reading of the question. They might consider themselves in a context of formal greeting and thus may be simply producing a prescribed conventional response. Or they might pick up performance cues that the question is merely formal rather than a sincere request for information. The respondents might also read the question as having the illocutionary force of a request but may wish to exercise their right not to disclose private feelings. Finally, though, they may not wish to impose their troubles and woes on the interlocutor, in which case they are making a consequential polite suspension by withholding relevant information.

Even insincere compliments are not straightforward within a given discourse community. After a disgusting dessert of turnip crumble and lumpy custard, we might leave our dinner hosts with any of the following forms of insincerity:

(1) "I had a lovely time" (withholding the truth about the dinner);
(2) "That was an exquisitely original dessert" (misleading the host into thinking that you enjoyed it);
(3) "I loved the dessert" (a straight lie).

While US and UK writers tend to presuppose the acceptability of tactful lying to hosts, I have found very considerable variation in attitudes even within a very narrow socioeconomic band of middle-class, middle-aged educated British people. I am by no means alone in assiduously avoiding (3) in the preceding list, and always preferring (1) (at best), and would feel aggrieved if I discovered that my guests had not been straight about my dessert.[4] There are certainly British

---

[4] I admit to a slight sense of *schadenfreude* when more socially adept friends complain about receiving the same undesirable present again and again because they once politely and enthusiastically told the gifter that they "loved" it.

people who will lie in such circumstances, just as there are Italians who prefer to be insincere when asked for directions rather than be "unhelpful" by saying they do not know. Hardin (2010) found that Ecuadorians rated a vignette about a store owner giving false directions through ignorance as less of a lie than did Americans. For Italians and Ecuadorians, *calore umano* ("human warmth") often seems to trump truthfulness in the same way that "saying the right thing" does in the United Kingdom. Knowing this means that "in-the-know" listeners will lower their trust in the information provided to them (best not rely on just one person giving directions in Ecuador; best not take "you must come round for dinner" as an actual invitation in the United Kingdom), but many others (both foreign and local) will be deceived and may feel betrayed. Polite insincerity, then, while being justifiable in principle, should certainly not always be taken as a *justified* suspension of the speaker's commitment to sincerity in situated practice.

4.5.4. Protective (and Self-Protective) Suspensions

With *protective* suspensions of sincerity, truth is considered to be overridden by the greater good of protecting oneself or others from harm. They go beyond the social to such situations as avoiding breaches of confidentiality or protecting from physical harm. There is an enormous literature on Kant's "murderer at the door" scenario (e.g., Bok 1978; Carson 2010; Saul 2012: 73–81). Kant famously claimed that if a murderer came to our door and asked for the whereabouts of someone he wanted to kill, we still would not be able to lie because communicating "the contrary of what the speaker thinks on the subject is an end that is directly opposed to the natural purposiveness of the speaker's capacity to communicate his thoughts, and is thus a renunciation of his personality" (Kant 2012: 6:429). We would have to try to mislead him instead. For most of us, though, this is getting our ethical priorities horribly wrong (Saul 2012: 73): in such a context, the priority must surely be to save the victim by misdirecting the murderer, to whom we owe no respect and who does not "deserve the truth" (Williams 2002: 114), and lying is a more effective insincere strategy than misleading since it closes down the inquiry. In short, the threat to life morally overrides the interactional breach of trust: threat trumps trust. Kant notwithstanding, most philosophers and religious thinkers accept protective suspensions. In religion, there is the *taqiyya* in Islam and the *pikuach nefesh* in Judaism. In her replication of Coleman and Kay in a Saudi Arabian context, Cole (1997) added two "lying" stories supposedly to bring out cross-cultural differences: claiming to be Iraqi to avoid capture by Iraqi soldiers, and a brother sugar-coating to his brother-in-law what his sister said in order to save his sister's marriage. These were chosen because they reflected

Islamic *haditha* on exceptions to the moral condemnation of lying. However, if we consider these in terms of protective suspensions rather than elements in a definition of lying, it seems unlikely that Western informants would judge these cases any differently.

A more difficult case is the subset of protective suspensions that we might call *paternalistic suspensions*, where we try to protect others from emotional rather than physical harm. Do we tell a woman on her deathbed who asks how her son is that he died in a car accident that morning, or do we lie to avoid making her last days ones of extreme sorrow? And does it make a difference whether we lie ("He's fine") or mislead her by saying, "I saw him yesterday and he was fine" (Saul 2012: 87–88)? The first question is a purely ethical one, but the second inextricably links discourse and ethics and thus merits further discourse analytical inquiry. Even more difficult are *self-protective suspensions*. There is the famous case of St. Athanasius (Geach 1977), pursued by killers, who uses dodgy deictics ("He is very close to here"—pointing to the ground next to him) to mislead his pursuers. Again, this is a rather silly lying versus misleading case that is easy to solve for anyone not embroiled in Kantian ethics. But there is a continuum from protecting oneself or others *from* a murderer (a clear *protective* suspension with the greater good of saving life) to protecting oneself *as* a murderer (a clear *willful* insincerity with purely selfish ends). Toward the ethical end, du Boulay (1976) found on the Greek island of Euboea that lying was considered a legitimate strategy to protect one's personal secrets, and there is probably some cross-cultural consensus on that. Somewhere in the middle of the continuum is the case of defendants avoiding self-incrimination in court, but it is best to deal with that as an attenuated case of willful insincerity (Chapter 7) rather than as a justifiable suspension.

4.5.5. Consequentialism and Culture

While private, polite, and protective suspensions are all predicated on the ends justifying the means, the consequentialist argument can be a dangerous one. Certainly, if the Enigma machine really did shorten World War II (and thus potentially save millions of lives), it is difficult to dismiss out of hand the decision to conceal its existence by deliberately not passing on intercepted German messages to warships that were sunk. However, consequentialism has been used to justify torture during the interrogation of terrorist suspects, with no evidence that such torture actually "works"; it is used to justify lying and other forms of deception during police interrogation in the United States, resulting in high levels of false confessions (Leo 2008); and it has been used to justify closed societies with governments and multinationals withholding information to "protect" state and company "secrets." There is nothing universal about these practices, though, and cultural relativism should not be used to justify dishonest practices: there is a close correlation globally between institutional corruption and individual dishonesty (Gächter and Schulz 2016). There has been a historical trend toward considering citizens in democratic countries to have greater rights to know (see the growing prevalence of Freedom of Information requests). As these rights grow, institutions find themselves having to justify suspensions of discursive sincerity in contexts such as information about CEOs' salaries and politicians' tax declarations where this value of sincerity formerly did not come into play.

4.6. Condonable Suspensions

Condonable suspensions of a speaker's commitment to truthfulness are neither conventional (manifestly cued by the context or discourse as suspensions) nor consequential (carried out for a perceived greater good) but are nevertheless not *willful* (in the sense of malicious). Condonable suspensions may be *playful* (where the intent to deceive has humorous rather than harmful ends) (4.6.1), or *pathological* (where the *will* of the speaker itself is in doubt) (4.6.2). They are justifiable in principle to the extent that they are either not *willful* or not *harmful*.

4.6.1. Playful Suspensions

Playful suspensions (usually of sincerity but also of epistemic responsibility) are those in which the speaker appears genuinely insincere or irresponsible (unlike with conventional suspensions such as comedy or irony) and the hearer will be deceived if the suspension is successful, but the speaker ultimately *reveals* the insincerity with the intent that this should result in humor or greater understanding. At its simplest, this is *kidding*, when finally revealed by a metadiscursive cue such as "just kidding," "I'm only joking," or "I'm pulling your leg." Gilsenan describes the playfully insincere Lebanese practice of *kirzb*, which can go on for some time before the perpetrator, victorious, reveals that "I was lying to you, you ate it" (1976: 192). Playful suspensions also account for untruthful discourse performed within the frame of "prank days" such as April Fool's Day (April 1) or Innocents' Day (December 28). The convention of prank days can render the prank justifiable in principle, though even gentle hoaxes such as the BBC's famous "Spaghetti Harvest" (BBC 1957) have been controversial. Outside such culturally demarcated prank days, it is more difficult to justify hoaxes in principle, and they can be very dangerous in practice. The Royal Hoax Call scandal, in which two Australian DJs impersonated the Queen and the Prince of Wales in a call to the hospital where the Duchess of Cambridge was recovering from severe morning sickness, led to the nurse who put through the call committing suicide (Davies 2014).

4.6.2. Pathological Suspensions

With *pathological* suspensions of truthfulness, the speaker is in a context where sociocultural discourse conventions would require them to tell the truth and they are not consciously claiming a consequential suspension, and yet they are unaware of not telling the truth and so there can be no willfulness involved. An interesting case is the traumatized asylum seeker suffering from post-traumatic stress disorder (PTSD). There is now considerable empirical evidence that PTSD can seriously affect memory and recall, leading genuine asylum seekers to unwittingly change details in their accounts from one reporting to the next, which is then erroneously taken by authorities as evidence of deceit through self-contradiction (Herlihy et al. 2012; Memon 2012). There is currently no clear consensus, on the other hand, on whether the so-called pathological liar lacks conscious awareness of telling lies (Dike et al. 2005), but if this does turn out to be the case, then what we have here is not a suspension of sincerity (a match between belief and speech) but of epistemic responsibility (a match between world and speech) and the so-called pathological lie is properly pathological bullshit resulting from a pathological recklessness with regard to the truth. To the extent that traumatized asylum seekers or pathological bullshitters are not fully aware of what they are doing, their (unconscious) suspension of epistemic responsibility is, to a greater or lesser extent, condonable.

4.7. Summary of Suspensions and a Sample Analysis

In this final substantive section of the chapter, I shall summarize the suspensions in terms of their ethical import (4.7.1) and then provide a sample analysis of suspensions with respect to a putative case of politeness (4.7.2).

4.7.1. Summary of Suspensions and Trust

Suspensions of the speaker's commitment to sincerity and/or epistemic responsibility that are justifiable in principle are summarized in Table 4.1.

Epistemic suspensions should all follow the Golden Rule and should not harmfully breach the trust of the hearer. However, they also have more specific

Table 4.1 Justifiable Suspensions of Truthfulness in Discourse

Epistemic Suspension	Ethical Justification	Examples
Conventional	Known to hearer	
Prescribed	Mutually understood	Fiction, comedy
Performed	Made manifest by speaker	Irony, hyperbole
Consequential	For the greater good	
Private	Save face of speaker	Reticence
Polite	Save face of hearer	Compliments
Protective	Avoid harm to self or others	Self-defense, *taqiyya*
Condonable	Not willful or harmful	
Playful	Insincerity soon revealed	Pranks, kidding, *kirzb*
Pathological	Lacks intentionality	Trauma talk

justifications. Conventional suspensions are justifiable to the extent that they are known to the hearer and so cannot lead to a breach of trust between speaker and hearer. In the case of prescribed suspensions, the suspension forms part of mutually understood expectations about the given genre in play, but we have seen that expectations about genres are not always mutually understood. Performed suspensions, on the other hand, are not pre-given by the discursive context but are made manifest by the speaker during the course of the interaction. Performed suspensions always come with a degree of risk because they depend on hearer uptake, and this cannot be guaranteed in certain contexts such as when speaking to a vulnerable audience. Consequently, performed suspensions may require interactional work to justify the suspension. *Consequential* suspensions are intended to deceive the hearer and so breach conventional interactional trust. The ethical justification for such an interactional breach of trust is that it is being performed for the greater good. Private suspensions such as reticence save the face of the speaker when the hearer does not have an overriding right to know. Polite suspensions such as insincere compliments are intended to save face and/or boost the positive face of the hearer. Protective suspensions such as *taqiyya* are intended to avoid a greater harm to self or others than a mere interactional breach of trust. Finally, *condonable* suspensions superficially breach trust but they are either not willful or not harmful. With playful suspensions such as kidding, pranks, and *kirzb*, the breach of trust is short-lived and the insincerity is soon revealed without harmful consequences (if it goes well). With pathological suspensions such as trauma talk, there is also a breach of trust, but there is a lack of intentionality and thus willfulness.

4.7.2. A Sample Suspensions Analysis

My sample Suspensions Analysis is based on a "Politeness and Untruthfulness" questionnaire. This is the only analysis in the book based on survey data. All of the other analyses are of naturally occurring discourse data. However, a survey approach is particularly useful for exploring inter- and intracultural variation in perceptions of putative polite suspensions, and I hope to demonstrate in my analyses in Chapters 8 and 9 that there is more than one way of applying the TRUST framework.

The questionnaire was administered to three groups of students: an undergraduate class of mostly British students; an MA class of British and international students; and a TESOL class of international students.[5] The total sample was 52, with 37 home students and 15 international students. The questionnaire presented a vignette adapted from a website called "Skills You Need" (https://www.skillsyouneed.com/):

> Two people meet in the street. They have known each other for years but neither particularly likes the other. They greet, say hello and ask about each other's families—engaging in some small-talk. One glances at their watch and makes excuses to leave the conversation. As they leave, they say: "It was nice to see you, we should do this more often. Call me and we'll have coffee." In reality the feelings were more like "It was not nice to see you and I hope I don't bump into you again anytime soon. Don't call me!"

Superficially, there seem to be two types of putative suspension here: a quasi-conventional ritualistic farewell, "It was nice to see you," and an explicitly false invitation that would suggest a putatively polite consequential suspension.

Students were first asked whether they ever made false invitations like "Call me and we'll have coffee": 33 (63%) said they did, but 19 (37%) said they did not. There was a difference in proportions: 70% of home students agreed, while only 50% of international students did (the numbers are too low for statistical significance). Of those who replied to the frequency question, 16 indicated that they made false invitations "rarely" (5) or "sometimes" (11), while only 6 said they did so "fairly often" (5) or "frequently" (1). In terms of whether they found the false invitation "dishonest" (Q2), 20 (38%) did, while 32 (62%) did not. Those who found the false invitation dishonest noted that it was unnecessary for politeness and that there was a lack of intention to carry through with the invitation. Of those who did not find it dishonest, 6 noted that the other person would know

---

[5] I thank my MA Research Experience group of 2017 for helping me with this survey.

that it was not going to happen, while 5 said they would go through with the invitation if the hearer misconstrued the false invitation as true. The results of these first two questions seem to suggest that there is a *tendency* for British people to accept false invitations either as prescribed conventional suspensions (if there is mutual understanding of no uptake) or as polite consequential suspensions (if there might be deception). However, crucially, this is merely a probability. Roughly a third of the British students did not make false invitations themselves and found the false invitation dishonest. Thus, contrary to received wisdom, when you make a false invitation, even in a British context, you are taking a considerable risk: in a third of cases you might be breaching trust, and not in a way that the "victim" will perceive as for their greater good. With a non-British interlocutor this chance of deception grows. Thus, while making false invitations might theoretically be a *justifiable* suspension in British contexts, in practice it will very often not be *justified* in the context.

The third question in the survey asked about the status and acceptability of "It was nice to see you" as a putative lie here. The majority of students (56%) did not see it as a lie, and many saw it as a conventional greeting, suggesting that it is a prescribed conventional suspension, but a considerable number (44%) saw it as an "acceptable lie," which strongly suggests they were seeing it as a consequential suspension.[6] Those seeing "It was nice to see you" as an acceptable lie noted that it was "polite," a "white lie," boosted face, and was harmless, thus suggesting a polite consequential suspension. The survey then asked whether participants felt there was a difference in simply saying, "It was nice to see you," or adding the false invitation in terms of, first, "dishonesty" (Q4) and then "politeness" (Q5). When asked to see things in this way, an overwhelming 85% of participants saw the addition of the false invitation as more dishonest. Respondents noted that the false invitation is unnecessary and goes beyond what is socially required in this context. They noted that it could lead someone on and give them false hopes and that it suggests a desire to rekindle a relationship that had fallen cold. Or, as one participant put it, "you are digging yourself a hole and getting deeper into the lie."

All of this questions whether the false invitation is a *justified* consequential suspension in this context. When asked specifically about "politeness," 54% said it did make a difference, and some said it was just "trying to be pleasant" or "make people feel better." However, for 39% of that group, the addition of the false invitation made the interaction *less* rather than more polite. It was seen to "negate" the initial politeness or was construed as "sarcastic" or creating "awkwardness" or "false hope." At the same time, of those who did not see a difference in politeness, a few saw the false invitation itself as a "formal greeting" or "a socially acceptable

---

[6] Two even saw it as an unacceptable lie ("it makes the situation awkward").

way of ending the conversation," thus suggesting a prescribed conventional suspension. One possibility that could not be explored through a written questionnaire is that both "It was nice to see you" and the false invitation are *performed* conventional suspensions in such a scenario. One can imagine both being said with prosodies that clearly cue overt insincerity. But then it is difficult to conceive them as being polite at all.

What this short, informal survey shows is that there might be considerable intercultural but also *intra*cultural variation in the way people judge acts of insincere politeness. As the literature on intercultural pragmatics shows (e.g., Kecskes 2013), we cannot make generalizations about the way different people or peoples perceive politeness. Therefore, as with irony, speakers should be aware of potential risks involved in forms of potentially polite insincerity such as false invitations.

4.8. Conclusion

This chapter addressed proposition E regarding the ethical value of untruthfulness and how this can be neutralized through the suspension of one's commitment to truthfulness (E1). I considered but ultimately rejected other approaches to ethical justifiability based on the overtness of the communication and the epistemic categorization of conventional speech settings. The framework of suspensions set out here provides for a more flexible and nuanced analysis that does not prejudge the epistemic status of a given discursive context. Suspensions are putatively *justifiable*, and justifiability is linked to sociocultural and sociolinguistic variation and to the discourse systems (Scollon et al. 2012) in which we are participating. But suspensions also need to be *justified* in a particular discourse context, which renders them sensitive to more specific situational factors, such as shared and negotiated knowledge between speakers, that can be brought out through discourse analysis. Analysis of suspensions inter- and intraculturally can help bring out the dangers of cultural essentialism. While a folk norm to "say the polite thing" in the United Kingdom might lead to a greater tendency to see the making of a false invitation as a justifiable polite suspension of sincerity, and the folk norm to convey *calore umano* in Italy might lead to a greater tendency to see the giving of false directions to a stranger as a justifiable suspension of epistemic responsibility, many British and Italian people do not see false invitations or directions as justifiable suspensions.

I now turn to the next element of the TRUST framework: the analysis of discursive insincerity. For the sake of setting out categories of insincerity, I shall put the question of putative suspensions to one side, but, when I come to carry out full TRUST analyses, I shall start with suspensions and only proceed to an analysis of sincerity if the speaker's commitment to truthfulness is not clearly and justifiably suspended. Similarly, though, it is worth considering putative suspensions even if, at first blush, there seems to be a clear case of willful insincerity or irresponsibility. For example, although I conclude in Chapter 8 that putative suspensions are not justified in the cases I present, the analysis of suspension can anticipate possible defenses for unethical untruthfulness and generally enrichens the analysis.

5
Insincere Discourse Strategies

Sincerity. Use no hurtful deceit; think innocently and justly, and, if you speak, speak accordingly.
—Benjamin Franklin (Franklin 1996: 65)

5.1. Introduction

Speakers are discursively insincere if they fail to disclose to the hearer what they believe the common ground calls on them to disclose. There are three points to note from the start that have been argued for in previous chapters. First, insincerity is a subjective intentional state of the mind rather than an objective state of the world: speakers are not being insincere if they accidentally omit mentioning something, and they are not being insincere if they mention something false that they believe to be true. Second, discursive insincerity concerns communicative behavior, not the general character of the speaker. A partner may be unfaithful but he is only discursively insincere if the topic of infidelity is made conversationally relevant in some way and he deliberately withholds revealing the truth. Third, as seen in the previous chapter, in many contexts we can be insincere without being unethically, or *willfully* insincere. Van der Geert's lying informants were indubitably insincere, but they were arguably not *willfully* insincere because they were justified in defending their privacy. Guests who say they had a lovely time, when they were bored stiff, are indubitably being insincere but generally not willfully so, as they believe they are being polite. And if a scammer is trying to access your password, any form of discursive insincerity would be ethically justified. Given this starting point, we need to consider the nature of insincerity in discourse and some major strategies of not-sharing in discourse (D1), along with the conditions under which those strategies become unethical (E2).

The chapter begins by considering previous typologies of insincerity and deception, including those based on violations of Grice's maxims or on speaker intentions and goals, and then grounds the TRUST distinction between the strategies of withholding, misleading and lying based on four communicative tests (5.2). I then explore each of the major insincere discourse strategies in turn. First, I consider sub-strategies and tactics relating to withholding (without misleading) and provide grounds for distinguishing between omitting, evading, and blocking

(5.3). Second, I explore different sub-strategies of misleading (through semantics, degree, pragmatics, and reframing) and their accompanying pragmatic tactics (5.4). Third, I define lying and note some subcategories of lying (5.5). Next, I turn to the question of when the insincere discourse strategies become unethical and note that there are two discursive conditions that make them *willful* (5.6). Finally, I summarize the strategies and provide a sample TRUST analysis of Sincerity based on Trump's claim that he had "great respect for women" (5.7).

5.2. Categories and Typologies of Insincerity

Although theorists have proposed typologies of deception rather than insincerity, these are the closest we have to what we need. First, I consider a common pragmatic approach to deception based on violation of Grice's maxims (5.2.1). Then I consider typologies based on intentions and goals (5.2.2). Next, I ground the TRUST distinction between lying, misleading, and withholding in communicative tests (5.2.3). Finally, I show the link between the TRUST categories and other taxonomies (5.2.4).

5.2.1. Deception as Violation of Grice's Maxims

Given that insincerity is often uncooperative, one evident way of approaching the categorization of its discursive forms is through Grice's maxims. Chapter 1 noted attempts to account for irony and lying in terms of overt and covert violations of the first maxim of Quality (the Sincerity maxim). Chapter 2 noted attempts to account for bullshitting in terms of the second maxim of Quality (the Responsibility maxim). However, Grice's maxims have also provided the analytical framework for a number of attempts to map out the entire domain of "deception" (Turner et al. 1975; Metts 1989; McCornack 1992; Buller and Burgoon 1996; Dynel 2011b; Gupta et al. 2013; Ortony and Gupta 2019). For example, according to McCornack's (1992) Information Manipulation Theory (IMT), "[g]iven that conversational interactants possess expectations regarding information quantity, quality, manner and relevance, it is possible for speakers to violate any or all of these expectations in attempting to deceive listeners" (1992: 13). Buller and Burgoon (1996) developed their Interpersonal Deception Theory (IDT) on the back of McCornack's IMT, but they changed the names of the maxims to Veridicality (Quality), Completeness (Quantity), Directness/Relevance (Relation), and Clarity (Manner). They also added a new norm of Personalization, which "captures the extent to which the information presented conveys the speaker's own thoughts, opinions and feelings" (Burgoon et al. 1996: 55). We can hide ownership, for example, by using constructions like "People say" rather than "I think," or "You are required to" rather than "I want you to." Despite following maxim-based approaches, neither McCornack (1992) nor Buller and Burgoon (1996) tried to construct taxonomies of deception. According to McCornack:

> [B]y placing messages into global categories (rather than construing them as existing at the intersection of multiple dimensions) we necessarily lose information relevant to the subtle message features that potentially influence deceptiveness. (1992: 11)

While I agree that "subtle message features" are inevitably lost in categorization, if we are to judge cases of untruthfulness in situated text rather than just being interested in the social psychological process of deception, we need to be able to categorize different forms of untruthfulness.

Several theorists have, though, developed taxonomies based on or relatable to Grice's maxims. McCornack (1992) related Turner et al.'s (1975) major forms of information control—Concealment, Distortion, and Diversionary Responses—to Quantity, Quality, and Relation, and he linked Bavelas et al.'s (1990) *equivocation* to Manner. Turner et al. (1975) identified *half-truths* and *secrets* as subtypes of Concealment and *lies* and *exaggeration* as subtypes of Distortion. Metts (1989) did not use Gricean maxims, but Gupta et al. (2013) note that her categories of "Omission" (Quantity), "Falsification" (Quality), and "Distortion" (Manner) fit with a Gricean perspective. Dynel (2011) does not propose a taxonomy as such, but she does show in more detail than other theorists how Grice's maxims relate to certain types of deception. The most complete neo-Gricean taxonomy is provided by Gupta et al. (2013) and Ortony and Gupta (2019). They identify seventeen "verbal deception strategies" deriving from the violation or flouting of one of the four maxims. Table 5.1 includes their major deception strategies, along with the strategies proposed by Turner et al. (1975), Metts (1989), Bavelas et al. (1990), and Dynel (2011). Column 2 indicates the meaning of the violation, while column 4 lists corresponding terms in the TRUST framework that will be introduced in the remainder of the chapter.

Attempts to link deception to Grice's categories are descriptively interesting partly because they link a known framework (the Cooperative Principle) to a relatively uncharted domain (deception). There are clear links between Quantity violations and types of withholding. The link between Quality violations and lying/bullshitting is attractive if, as seen in previous chapters, not entirely unproblematic. There is also a clear link between Manner violations and the misleading strategies of *obfuscation* and *equivocation*. However, ultimately such maxim-based categorizations do not really help us in terms of a trust perspective

Table 5.1 Grice's Maxims and Deception Categories

Maxim	Violation means...	Deception Category	TRUST Category
Quantity	Not informative enough (first maxim)	*Concealment* (Turner et al. 1975) *Secret* (Turner et al. 1975) *Omission* (Metts 1989) *Half-truth* (Turner et al. 1975; Dynel 2011; Gupta et al. 2013) *Silence* (Dynel 2011) *False Implicature* (Gupta et al. 2013)	*Withholding: Omitting* *Misleading: Falsely Implicating*
	Too informative (second maxim)	*Augmentation* (Gupta et al. 2013)	*Withholding: Evading*
Quality	Believed false (first maxim) [Overt *flouts* include: *Irony* and *Metaphor* (Grice 1975; Dynel 2018); *Hyperbole* and *Meiosis* (Dynel 2018); *Banter* (Leech 1983; Terkourafi 2019)]	*Lying/lies* (Turner et al. 1975; Dynel 2011) *Falsification* (Metts 1989) *False irony/hyperbole/meiosis* (Dynel 2011, 2018) *Denial* (Gupta et al. 2013) *Fabrication* (Gupta et al. 2013) *Over/understatement* (Gupta et al. 2013)[a] *False Implicature* (Gupta et al. 2013)	*Lying: Deceptive* *Lying: Fabricating* *Lying: Exaggerating/ minimizing* *Misleading: Falsely Implicating*
	Lacks evidence (second maxim)	*Bullshit* (Dynel 2011; Fallis 2015)	*Bullshitting*
Relation	Is irrelevant	*Contrived distraction* (Gupta et al. 2013) *False Implicature* (Gupta et al. 2013)	*Withholding: Evading* *Misleading: Falsely Implicating*
Manner	(1, 3, 4) Is obscure, prolix, disorderly (2) Is ambiguous	*Obfuscation* (Gupta et al. 2013) *Equivocation* (Gupta et al. 2013) *False Implicature* (Gupta et al. 2013)	*Misleading: Obfuscating* *Misleading: Equivocating* *Misleading: Falsely Implicating*

[a] I use these terms to describe types of pathological distortion (see Chapter 7). According to Gupta et al's definitions, understatement and overstatement are clearly degree lying in TRUST terms.

on untruthfulness. There are three issues in particular: missing categories; the primacy of Quality; and correspondence with the speech process.

In terms of missing categories, McCornack recognized that there was "a realm of deceptive messages beyond the immediate scope of IMT: messages that mislead not through the manipulation of information, but through the generation of deceptive implicatures" (1992: 14). *Falsely implicating* is difficult to accommodate, first because the insincerity occurs while *overtly* observing the Cooperative Principle rather than covertly violating it, and second because one can falsely implicate in relation to *any* of the maxims or submaxims. Gupta et al. (2013: 27) include *false implicature* in their taxonomy, but only by incorporating it into each of the four maxims and showing the distinct relation of flouting rather than covert violation. Covert violations of Relation are virtually impossible because it is generally obvious to the hearer when the speaker is not being relevant. Gupta et al. contrive the Relation category of *contrived distraction*, in which the speaker is "evasive by finding some pretext to urgently change the subject" (2013: 22), as when a young child comes home from school and says, "My friends say that Santa Claus isn't real," and the mother replies, "Never mind that now. Show me what homework you have today" (2013: 22–23). This is their *only* category of evasion, and yet evasion is a fundamental category in withholding information. Other categories that are not accommodated well are bald-faced lying (a category of insincerity but not deception), exaggerating and minimizing (as degree lying), faking, and taking words out of context. There is a particular problem with the way misleading is handled because it only partially correlates with Manner. Finally, maxims notoriously combine and clash in myriad ways, and this is not accounted for well in the Gricean frameworks.

A second issue is the primacy of the maxim of Quality in Grice's account. If an utterance is insincere, it must be violating the supermaxim of Quality ("try to make your contribution one that is true," or, simply "be truthful") whatever other maxim it might also be violating. Grice claimed that the other maxims did not hold unless the first maxim of Quality was observed. This can be seen from the list of meanings of the maxim violations in column 2 of Table 5.1: not informative enough; too informative; believed false; lacks evidence; is irrelevant; is obscure, prolix, disorderly; is ambiguous. Of these meanings, only "believed false" seems relevant to insincerity or deception. Particularly in light of the revised maxim of Truthfulness presented in Chapter 2, one could say that the insincere speaker covertly violates or maliciously flouts the maxim of Quality while often *also* violating Quantity or Manner.

Finally, this way of looking at deception (or insincerity) does not conform to our understanding of how the communicative process of deception actually works. The short account of this given in Chapter 1 suggests that deception takes place in real-time discourse processing, and the main impetus is to hold back discursively relevant truths. When we find ourselves having to conceal information, we do not think, "I'm going to deceive the hearer; now let me choose the maxim of conversation to covertly violate." We choose the best available strategy rather than the best available category.

5.2.2. Speaker Intentions and Strategic Goals

Speakers are insincere when they intentionally try to disrupt the pursuit of the goal of inquiry. But if the strategic function of discursive insincerity is to attempt to disrupt inquiry by concealing (or not putting on record) what we know, then such concealing requires intention. While, if we are open, we will naturally say what we believe, "[i]nsincerity requires me to adjust the content of what I say" (Williams 2002: 75). That adjustment of the content requires intentional effort,[1] which is why lying and other forms of insincerity tend (with the exception of fabrication) to take place in small doses (Vrij 2008). If you "go wrong in your utterance" (Austin 1970) and unintentionally say something you do not believe, as in the malapropism "Samuel Johnson was a famous entomologist," you cannot be *intentionally* lying. If, because you are very nervous, you accidentally come across as misleadingly ambiguous, you are not *intentionally* misleading. If, because you are traumatized, you accidentally omit a material fact in your eyewitness account of a crime, you have not *intentionally* withheld that fact. We would say in these cases that you have not been insincere at all. On the other hand, as seen in Chapter 6, intentionality is not a determinant of epistemic irresponsibility.

Several typologies of deception have been concerned with the speaker's intentions and goals (Chisholm and Feehan 1977; Vincent and Castelfranchi 1981; Bradac 1983; Gupta et al. 2013; Ortony and Gupta 2019). However, the intent has always been that of deceiving, and the goal to bring about some effect on the hearer's beliefs. In their seminal account, Chisholm and Feehan (1977) identify eight types of deceptive intent. A speaker may either *cause* ("deception by commission") or *allow* ("deception by omission") another person to (a) *acquire* a false belief ("positive deception *simpliciter*"), (b) *continue* to hold a false belief ("positive deception *secundum quid*"), (c) *cease* to hold a true belief ("negative deception *simpliciter*"), or (d) be *prevented* from acquiring a true belief ("negative deception *secundum quid*"). Gupta et al. (2013) and Orton and Gupta (2019) take up Chisholm and Feehan's deception types but see them as

---

[1] The notion that lying requires effort has been challenged by the concept of "easy lies" (Harwood 2014), but these "easy lies" occur in contexts where the presumption of sincerity has arguably been suspended. There is considerable consensus that deceptive lies do require more effort (Granhag et al. 2013), but the effort comes not so much in producing them in the first place, as we saw in Chapter 2, but in remembering that we have told them.

the speaker's communicative goals. So, *Acquire, Continue, Cease,* and *Prevent* become the speaker's four "belief manipulation goals" (Gupta et al. 2013: 29; Orton and Gupta 2019: 152):

> We think that the most informative and psychologically descriptive way in which to systematically organize the different types of deception is to view them as strategies that speakers use to attain goals of this kind with respect to their hearers. (Gupta et al. 2013: 29)

The idea of seeing deception or insincerity in terms of communicative goals is not new. Vincent and Castelfranchi (1981) wrote that "[o]ne can talk of sincerity or insincerity only in the case of communicative goals where the hearer is meant to understand that the speaker is committing himself" (1981: 757) and they were particularly interested in indirect deception and pretending, where the play of intentions and goals is particularly important. Bradac (1983) was concerned with the connection between belief and both deceptive and non-deceptive communicative goals when he proposed the verbal deception strategies of *secrecy, evasion,* and *lying.*

The TRUST framework is not designed to analyze the psychological process or goals of deception, but to evaluate cases of *linguistic* untruthfulness in situated text. However, these deception models can be related to the understanding of insincerity developed in Chapter 1 as concerning a speaker's disruption of the pursuit of the goal of inquiry. Essentially, if you are causing or allowing your hearer to acquire or hold on to a false belief or to cease holding or to be prevented from acquiring a true belief, you are contaminating the common ground and disrupting the pursuit of the goal of inquiry. But you are doing this also if you are stubbornly, cynically, or brazenly refusing to put a true belief on record (bald-faced lying). You are doing it if you could not care less whether or not what you say is true (bullshitting). And you are doing it if you have not taken care to ground what you say in evidence (see Chapter 6).

While the TRUST framework is not concerned with psychological categories of belief manipulation, the Sincerity framework is rooted in discourse strategies. A discourse strategy (Gumperz 1982), like a speech act, is a way of doing things with words, but it operates beyond a single utterance and is always goal-directed. It might involve designing discourse for a specific audience (Bell 1984), code-switching to perform identity (Rampton 1995), providing cues to how one's discourse should be contextualized by the hearer (Gumperz 1982), or navigating the "super strategies" of positive, negative, and off-record politeness (Brown and Levinson 1987). In each case, there is an overall strategy and a number of pragmatic tactics that contribute to fulfilling that strategy. Just as the military strategist has many deceptive strategies and tactics on which to draw, so the discursive

Persuasion (ultimate communicative goal)

Deception (immediate epistemic goal)

Misleading (discourse strategy)

Falsely implicating (pragmatic tactic)

Figure 5.1. The communicative nesting of insincerity.

strategist can draw on several insincere discursive strategies (withholding, misleading, lying) and a variety of sub-strategies and pragmatic tactics for realizing those strategies.

Insincere discourse strategies generally serve broader communicative goals. Deception is often, though not always, the immediate epistemic goal of insincerity. Deception, in turn, is often a super-strategy for achieving persuasive goals. These may be self-defensive, such as the child's efforts to persuade her mother not to punish her or Mary's efforts to persuade her boyfriend that all is well in their relationship, or proactive, as in lying in one's CV to persuade the interview panel to shortlist you. Thus, Mary's false implicature that she has not seen Valentino might be analyzed in terms of the communicative hierarchy in Figure 5.1.

Mary uses the pragmatic tactic of falsely implicating ("Valentino is in bed with mononucleosis") in pursuing the discourse strategy of verbally misleading John into acquiring the false belief that she has not seen Valentino this week. Her immediate epistemic goal is to deceive John, but her ultimate communicative goal might be to assure/persuade him that everything is fine in their relationship.

5.2.3. Grounding the Distinction between Lying, Misleading, and Withholding

In TRUST, *withholding* is the umbrella category for discursive insincerity. Withholding constitutes a speaker's relationship with the truth in which she keeps her perceived truth concealed because she considers it *worth* keeping secret. So, insincere speakers, as Williams (2002) and Frankfurt (2005) both note, *value* the truth and will often go to considerable effort to conceal it. If, like the bullshitter, they did not *care* for the truth, they would not go to such effort. Misleading and lying are subsets of withholding. *Misleading* is a type of concealment in which the speaker does not merely keep back the truth by not proffering it, but deliberately tries to *lead* the listener to believe what is not the case. *Lying* is a type of misleading (and thus also withholding) in which the speaker deliberately tries to lead the listener to believe what is not the case by *unequivocally asserting* what the speaker knows is not true.

Lying, then, is a specific category of misleading, which in turn is a specific category of withholding. This nesting (Figure 5.2) enables a richer account of insincerity in context than would be possible with discrete category systems, since it permits discussion of the ways a claim withholds and misleads as well as lies (if it does all three).

Such hierarchical categorization is not unknown in the literature, but the categorizations have tended to be binary rather than threefold: lying versus misleading, or lying versus deception, or lying versus bullshit (Mahon 2016). Ekman, though he simply talks about "two primary ways to lie" (2009: 28), comes closest to the nesting organization proposed here in seeing "falsifying" ("lying" here) as taking "an additional step" beyond "concealing" ("withholding" here):

> In concealing, the liar withholds some information without actually saying anything untrue. In falsifying, an additional step is taken. Not only does the liar withhold true information, but he presents false information as if it were true. (2009: 28)

Strictly speaking, we should talk of "misleading without lying" (as some philosophers do) and "withholding without misleading," but in discussing the categories of withholding and misleading in this chapter and in the analyses in

Figure 5.2. Nesting of insincere discourse strategies.

Chapters 8 and 9, I shall mostly take the "without" element as given. One could also talk of "merely misleading" or "merely withholding," but that suggests attenuated moral gravity, which is by no means the case.

This basic framework can be made more robust through an analysis of the discursive conditions that hold in the case of each of the major insincere discourse strategies. We can consider: (1) whether and how the speaker makes a false contribution to the QUD; (2) how the believed-false proposition (p) is expressed; (3) the speaker's subsequent option to change her epistemic stance; and (4) the extent to which the speaker can subsequently deny that she was concealing a believed-false p (Table 5.2).

We can apply these tests to a famous exchange in the seminal Supreme Court case *Bronston v. United States* (409 U.S. 352). The film producer Samuel Bronston was being cross-examined during a bankruptcy hearing (I have fabricated the exchange after the dotted line for illustrative purposes):

Q1: Do you have any bank accounts in Swiss banks, Mr. Bronston?
A1: No, sir.
Q2: Have you ever?
A2: The company had an account there for about six months, in Zurich.

Q3: Yes, but have *you* ever had one?
A3: No, I haven't.

It transpired that Bronston had held a large personal bank account in Switzerland for five years.

Table 5.2 Tests for Insincere Discourse Strategies

	False Contribution wto QUD	Expression of Believed-False P	Options to Change Epistemic Stance	Deniability
Withholding (−misleading)	Not offered	Not conveyed	Open	Strong: didn't say, forgot to mention
Misleading (−lying)	Offered indirectly	Implied/ implicated/ presupposed	Limited	Moderate: didn't intend to suggest
Lying	Offered directly	Asserted	Removed	Weak: believed it was the case

(1) *False Contribution to the Question under Discussion (QUD)*
A first distinguishing element is whether and how the speaker makes a false contribution to the QUD. Here the general QUD, understood by both the lawyer and Bronston, is whether Bronston had money in a Swiss account (a key question in high-level bankruptcy hearings) (Q1). The false contribution is that he has never held a Swiss bank account (A3). In his first answer (A1: No, sir), he *does not offer* that false contribution, but he *withholds* a truthful contribution (that he formerly held a Swiss account) which he almost certainly believes the common ground calls on him to disclose. In doing so, he is *evading* the QUD, which is thus a sub-strategy of withholding. In his second answer (A2: The company had an account...), he *indirectly offers* the false contribution via the false implicature ("but I didn't"), so he is verbally *misleading*. In the final (invented) response (A3: No, I haven't), he *directly offers* the false contribution and so is lying.

(2) *Expression of Believed-False P*
Related to false contribution is whether and how the believed-false proposition is expressed through language. In the withholding contribution (A1), Bronston does not *convey* anything false. In the misleading contribution (A2), he *implicates* the believed-false proposition. In the lying contribution (A3), he *asserts* the believed-false proposition.

(3) *Options to Change Epistemic Stance*
A third distinguishing element is the availability of options to change one's epistemic stance, or the way one conveys one's beliefs. After his first less-than-truthful withholding response (A1), Bronston is still completely *open* to change his mind and could have provided a truthful contribution in response to the lawyer's second question (e.g., A2b: Yes, I did have one for a while but it's now closed). Indeed, in the context of cross-examination, his response to A1 would not necessarily be seen as insincere if he gave this putative second response at A2. Instead, he provides a false implicature. In doing so, he severely *limits* his options, but he could still answer Q3 without self-incrimination (e.g., A3b: Well, yes, I did for a while but it's now closed). Instead, by asserting what he knows to be false (A3), he *removes* any option to change his stance and will be guilty of perjury. He also limits the options for the questioner who suspects he is lying: the lawyer can only try to coerce feelings of guilt by seeking confirmation (Q4a: Are you sure?), or directly challenge the veracity of the assertion (Q4b: That's not true, is it?).

(4) *Deniability*
The final element distinguishing the three insincere discourse strategies is the extent to which it is possible to *deny* that you were being untruthful when you are caught. We wish for our denials to be plausible if we want

to save face (or worse). If the exchange ends at A1 and the lawyer subsequently asks him why he did not mention that he used to have a Swiss account, Bronston can rightly argue that he was not asked whether he used to have one or he might claim (less plausibly) that he forgot or that he did not think it was relevant to mention. Withholding generally comes with strong deniability. If the exchange ends at A2 (as it did in court), Bronston can argue that what he said was true and (less plausibly) that he did not mean to implicate that he did not have one himself. In other contexts, one might even use a counter-strategy of claiming that the accuser is being devious (Vincent and Castelfranchi 1981: 770). However, once an outright lie has been made, it is very difficult indeed to deny. The fictional Bronston of A3 could only claim (extremely implausibly) that he forgot that he held the account.

5.2.4. The Link between TRUST Categories and Other Taxonomies

The principal categories of withholding, misleading, and lying have been qualitatively generated from consideration of both the virtues of sincerity and the dynamics of strategic interaction. They are not, however, data-driven categories and they have not been empirically tested. Nevertheless, they do conform to a great extent with the major categories of other taxonomies that have been proposed in philosophy, communication theory, and pragmatics. Table 5.3 lists deception categories proposed by other scholars that are similar to the main categories or subcategories of withholding, misleading, and lying. Clearly there are many distinctions among the different uses, but the table should give some idea of the general domain. Very similar terms to those used in the TRUST framework are indicated in bold.[2]

Furthermore, most of the subcategories proposed here are well-established in the literature even if they might have slightly different meanings within the TRUST framework. The following sections will discuss the three insincere discourse strategies of withholding, misleading, and lying, as well as some substrategies and pragmatic tactics.

---

[2] I have used active participles rather than abstract nouns for the TRUST terms (omitting, evading, obfuscating, equivocating, etc.) to stress the active nature of insincere discourse strategies. I have ignored this choice of ending in choosing similar terms. This list is intended to be indicative rather than comprehensive.

Table 5.3 Deception Categories Similar to Withholding, Misleading, and Lying

Withholding (Failing to mention)	Misleading (Verbally leading hearer astray)	Lying (Contradicting one's belief)
Withholding (Barnes 1994; Ekman 2009; Carson 2010; Dynel 2011b)[a]	*Misleading* (Adler 1997; Green 2001; Saul 2012; Stokke 2018)	*Lying* (most researchers)
Omission (C & F* 1977; V & C* 1981; Metts 1989)	*Falsely implicating* (Adler 1997)	*Fabrication* (Gupta et al. 2013)
Evasion (Bull 2003)	*Obfuscation* (Gupta et al. 2013; V & C 1981)	*Bald-faced lies* (Sorensen 2007; Carson 2010)
Blocking (Shuy 2017)	*Equivocation* (Bavelas et al. 1990; Bull 2003; Gupta et al. 2013)	*Falsifying/ Falsification* (Metts 1989; Buller and Burgoon 1996; Ekman 2009)
Concealment/concealing (Turner et al. 1975; Ekman 2009)	*Taking words out of context* (Galasinski 2000)	*Straight/Straightforward lies* (Arico and Fallis 2013)
Secrecy (Bradac 1983)	*Deception without lying* (Dynel 2018; Carson 2010)	*Deception by commission* (C & F 1977)
Half-truth (Vincent Marelli 2006; Gupta et al. 2013)	*Indirect lying* (V & C 1981; Meibauer 2014)	*Lies of commission* (Douglas 1976)
Reticence (V & C 1981)	*Lying while telling/saying the truth* (V & C 1981; Meibauer 2014)	*Denial* (Gupta et al. 2013)
Contrived distraction (Gupta et al. 2013)	*Distortion* (Metts 1989)	*Knowledge lies* (Sorensen 2010)
Keeping someone in the dark (Carson 2010)	*Deliberate/pernicious/deceptive ambiguity* (V & C 1981; Solan 2004; Shuy 2017)	*Indifferent lies* (Rutschmann and Wiegmann 2017)
Abstraction (Gupta et al. 2013)	*Insinuation* (V & C 1981)	*Group lies* (Lackey 2019)
Dissimulation (Snyder 2009)	*Evasion* (Bradac 1983)	*Fake News* (Levinson 2017)
	Pretending to lie/act/joke (V & C 1981)	

[a] As indicated in the following, Carson's conception of withholding is much narrower than here, so is not really coterminous.

* C & F = Chisholm and Feehan; V & C = Vincent and Castelfranchi.

5.3. Withholding as Concealing Relevant Information

Withholding without verbal misleading ("withholding" for short) covers those cases of discursive insincerity that do not involve *linguistically misleading* the hearer either through implicit suggestion (misleading) or explicit assertion (lying). After defining withholding and distinguishing it from other uses (5.3.1), I discuss three discourse sub-strategies for achieving withholding: insincere *omitting* (5.3.2), *evading* (5.3.3), and *blocking* (5.3.4).

5.3.1. Withholding and Its Sub-Strategies

Withholding without linguistic misleading involves a vitally important set of insincere discourse sub-strategies and pragmatic tactics, but it has been comparatively neglected in work on untruthfulness (Fallis 2019). In the TRUST framework, withholding is a deliberate failure to voice salient truths or a deliberate attempt to block others from discovering or voicing them: it is a failure to state, or allow to be stated, what it would be "right" to state in a given context. In that sense, it is a violation of a revised Gricean first maxim of Quantity: make your contribution as informative as is required *to maintain discursive sincerity*. Withholding can be defined more formally as follows:

Withholding (without misleading)
Withholding is a discursive strategy of failing to mention or blocking others from conveying salient information that you believe the common ground calls on you to disclose.

In terms of the insincere discourse strategy tests (Table 5.2), in withholding, (1) a false contribution to the QUD is not offered; (2) a believed-false proposition is not conveyed; (3) the option to change one's epistemic stance is open; and (4) there is strong deniability.

Withholding has traditionally been called "omission." In Catholic theology, "sins of omission" are committed by those who know what is the right thing to do but fail to do it (James 4:17): the two men in the parable of the Good Samaritan who pass by the injured man lying by the side of the road without helping him are committing a sin of omission. When the failure to act is verbal rather than physical, for example not speaking up when you know that someone has been unjustly accused, it has traditionally been called "lying by omission" (Vincent and Castelfranchi 1981; Smith 2004; Vrij 2008; Ekman 2009; Scott 2010). However, most contemporary definitions of lying require speech acts of saying, stating, or asserting (Mahon 2016), and without such a verbalization requirement for lying, it becomes difficult to distinguish between the various forms of insincerity. The term "withholding" makes clear both that the speaker is consciously keeping back what he believes to be true, rather than simply neglecting to mention it, but that he also is not actively engaged in responding to the QUD in a verbally misleading manner. As Dynel puts it, "a piece of information vital from the hearer's perspective remains unavailable to him/her as a result of the speaker's purposeful communicative action" (2011: 157).

Withholding is often distinguished from *concealing* (e.g., Carson 2010; Lackey 2013). According to Carson, *withholding* is simply failing to offer information (which may or may not be deceptive), whereas "[t]o conceal information is to do things to hide information from someone—to prevent someone from discovering it" and so is always deceptive (2010: 57). However, for withholding to "keep back" or "refrain from giving" (CED 2003), rather than simply neglecting to mention, the speaker must be aware that the common ground is calling on them to disclose that information. So, withholding must be discursively insincere whether or not it is deceptive. There are two features, though, that the withholding/concealing distinction brings to light. First, although withholding is an insincere discourse strategy, it is very often a *justified* one, particularly in terms of private, polite, and protective suspensions of truthfulness. So, as will be discussed in the following, withholding is very often not *willfully* insincere. Second, withholding can involve more or less discursive effort. As used by Carson, Lackey, and others, "withholding" corresponds to what I call "omitting" in the following discussion. This is a key sub-strategy of withholding, but it requires the modifier "insincere" to distinguish it from the sincere sense of "neglecting to mention." The other two sub-strategies of withholding (evading and blocking) more actively conceal. However, all three strategies serve the function of keeping back information that the common ground calls on the speaker to disclose while avoiding responding to the QUD.

The TRUST framework, then, proposes three discourse sub-strategies of insincere withholding: (*insincere*) *omitting, evading,* and *blocking. Insincere omitting* is what is generally understood by "omission" or "withholding," while *evading* and *blocking* are not generally included in such accounts. Figure 5.3 represents the relationship between the three proposed discourse sub-strategies of withholding (W = Withholder).

With (*insincere*) *omitting,* the Withholder (W) simply does not reveal the concealed information. *Evading* occurs where a Questioner tries to extract that concealed information from the Withholder (as in the Q1–A1 pair in the Bronston case described earlier). *Blocking,* on the other hand, occurs where the Withholder tries to prevent a Respondent from discovering concealed information or from revealing it to others.

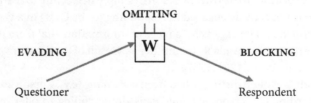

Figure 5.3. Sub-strategies of withholding.

5.3.2. Omitting and Plagiarizing

In insincere *omitting*, the speaker tries to keep truthful information interactionally "offstage" (Goffman 1959). The insincerity lies in not bringing this truth "onstage" when she believes the common ground calls on her to disclose it. *Omitting*, as a deliberate sub-strategy of withholding, can be defined as follows:

(Insincere) Omitting
Insincere *omitting* occurs when the speaker *intentionally omits information when answering an explicit or implicit Question under Discussion* as a way of withholding salient information that she believes the common ground calls on her to disclose.

As noted in Chapter 1, speakers normally *omit* information simply by editing it out of their account as they are speaking. The textual product of such *omitting* is often called a *half-truth* (e.g., Vincent Marrelli 2006; Carson 2010; Dynel 2011b). Dynel (2011b: 155) defines *half-truth* as "not giving the hearer all the information that would be the goal of the hearer if he/she knew the speaker had it, because it is relevant or important to the hearer." Insincere omitting has also been called *dissimulation* (Snyder 2009) in contrast with the active falsification involved in *simulation*.

Plagiarism (Pecorari 2008), a type of academic dishonesty (Jordan 2003), is a form of insincere *omitting* in which a writer deliberately *omits* disclosing the source of her ideas and/or words while believing that the common academic ground calls on her to do so. In other words, it is information the hearer/reader has a right to know and that it would be right and honest to reveal. In a general sense, the plagiarist is clearly deceiving the reader into thinking that she is the source and/or the author of the words. Furthermore, she is effectively "pretending to communicate" (Parret 1993) in those roles. However, it is not what is linguistically *present* that deceives the reader, but what has been linguistically/graphically *omitted*. Using Goffman's participation framework (Goffman 1981), we can tease out three distinct types of plagiarism with different forms of omission (Table 5.4).

In *ideational plagiarism*, the plagiarizer pretends to be the *principal* (responsible for the ideas) and so does not acknowledge that the ideas are not his own even if the words are. What is omitted textually is explicit acknowledgment of the source of the ideas in the form of a short citation or bibliographic footnote. In *linguistic plagiarism*, the plagiarizer acknowledges the source of her ideas but pretends to be the *author* (responsible for the words). This is manifested textually in the presence of a formal citation but the absence of quotation

Table 5.4 Types of Plagiarism

Type of Plagiarism	Faked Role	Type of Omission	Textual Omission
Ideational	Principal	Source of ideas not attributed	Omitted reference
Linguistic	Author	Author is cited but his or her words are not attributed	Omitted quotation marks
Full	Principal + Author	Neither the ideas nor the words of the author are attributed	Omitted reference and quotation marks

marks. In *full plagiarism*, the plagiarizer pretends to be both the principal and the author of the words, so both reference to the source and quotation marks are omitted.[3]

5.3.3. Evading and the Political Interview

Whereas, in insincere *omitting*, the truthful information simply remains interactionally "offstage" (Goffman 1959), in *evading*, the insincerity lies in circumventing that truthful contribution once it has been brought interactionally onstage through direct questioning. Insincere *evading*, as a deliberate substrategy of withholding, can be defined as follows:

> **Evading**
> *Evading* occurs when the speaker intentionally *avoids answering an explicit Question under Discussion* as a way of withholding salient information that she believes the common ground calls on her to disclose.

There are many *evading tactics*. As Bull (2003) notes, many of these can be seen in hardball political interviews: ignoring the question, or acknowledging it without answering it ("That's a fair question but the real issue is . . . "); questioning the question, e.g., by asking for clarification or reflecting the question back to the

---

[3] I have simplified a rather complex situation here. It could be argued, for example, that linguistic plagiarism is actually a case of misleading since the presence of the author citation combined with the lack of quotation marks *implies* that the words are a paraphrase rather than a direct quotation of what the author said. And it could be said that full plagiarism has something in common with lying since, in academic discourse, in asserting p you are also asserting that you are the author of p; by not signaling what you believe to be the original author, you are effectively insincerely asserting that you are the author of p.

questioner ("What do you think?"); attacking the question, e.g., by claiming that it is based on a false premise, that it is merely hypothetical or speculative, that it is inaccurate, that it takes the interviewee's words out of context (Galasiński 2000), or that it is simply objectionable; attacking the questioner, e.g., that she is unscrupulous or "out to get" the interviewee; or, finally, simply declining to answer on various grounds (Bull 2003). In everyday contexts, Gupta et al. (2013: 22) add "contrived distraction." There is some empirical psychological evidence that "artful dodging" can be a particularly successful insincere discourse strategy. Rogers and Norton (2011), for example, discovered that test informants not only found it difficult to detect a political candidate's dodges but even rated fluent dodgers more positively than those who answered the moderator's questions accurately but disfluently.

Evading is sometimes seen as being in an intermediate position between lying and withholding and thereby corresponding to misleading here (e.g., Bradac 1983). In some cases, this might be because "evasion" is being used as a synonym for "misleading." However, *evading* as defined here and in some key texts (e.g., Bull 2003) passes the tests for *withholding* rather than *misleading*. First, it does not offer, even indirectly, a false contribution to the explicit QUD: the whole purpose is to *avoid* addressing the QUD. Second, since it does not address the content of the QUD at all, the believed-false p is not conveyed. What is conversationally implicated by an evasive answer is not the believed-false p but simply that the speaker does not want to answer the question. Third, the evader's option to change her epistemic stance is left open: she can decide at any point to stop evading and actually answer the question. Finally, if she is subsequently confronted with her believed-false p, she can simply deny that she ever asserted or implied that p. Speakers are often *justified* in being evasive: the question may truly be unfair or invasive and the questioner unscrupulous irrespective of whether the interviewee/interlocutor has anything to conceal.

Politicians are often expert evaders, while political interviewers are often expert in tackling these evasions. Former BBC journalist Jeremy Paxman's infamous *Newsnight* interview with then Home Secretary (minister of internal affairs) Michael Howard in 1997 is a master class both in *evading* (Howard) and doggedly pursuing an answer to a QUD (Paxman) (Smith and Randerson 2014). Paxman asked Howard no less than thirteen times whether he had threatened to overrule the Director General of prisons Derek Lewis if he failed to suspend the governor of a prison (John Marriott) from which three dangerous criminals had escaped. Lewis claimed that Howard *had* threatened to overrule him, while Howard was determined to keep his hands clean of the scandal. The following excerpt covers six explicit iterations of this QUD (P = Paxman; H = Howard; [= overlap with following turn; <u>threat</u>en = emphasis):

Evading Politician
1 P: Did you threaten [to overrule
2 H: I- I was not entitled to instruct Derek Lewis and I did not instruct him hh [an the
3 P: Did you threaten to overrule [him
4 H: The truth of the matter is that Mister Marriott was not suspended [I did not-
5 P: Did you threaten to overrule him?
6 H: I did not overrule [Derek
7 P: Did you threaten to overrule him?
8 H: I took advice on what I could or could not do.
9 P: Did you threaten [to overrule him?
10 H: And I acted
11 P: [Mr Howard
12 H: scrupulously in accordance with that advice. I did not overrule D[erek
13 P: Did you threaten to overrule him?

(Transcript based on Clayman and Heritage 2002: 256)

Howard demonstrates a variety of evasive tactics, including reinterpreting the question ("I was not entitled to instruct Derek Lewis"; turn 2), shifting from the threat to the outcome of the process ("the truth of the matter is that Mister Marriott was not suspended"; turn 4), denying the act rather than the verbal threat ("I did not overrule Derek Lewis"; turn 6), providing relevant but not requested information ("I took advice on what I could or could not do"; turn 8) and simply ignoring the question ("and I acted scrupulously"; turn 10). Note that Howard's response in turn 6 ("I did not overrule Derek") is not a false implicature because it is *already* in the common ground that Howard did *not* overrule the prisons boss. The explicit QUD is precisely whether he *threatened* to overrule him, as emphasized by Paxman in the following turn. When specifically drawn back to the question later by Paxman, Howard simply switches to a more "relevant" question:

P: But, with respect, you haven't answered the question of whether you *threatened* to *overrule* him.
H: Well, you see, the question is what *was* I entitled to do and what was I *not* entitled to do? I was *not* entitled to instruct him and I *did not do that*.

By the end of this sequence of questioning, only the naïvest of viewers could think that Howard had not threatened to overrule Lewis. Indeed, we might see this almost as a case of *bald-faced evading*, in which the speaker does not seriously intend to deceive the listeners but also is quite determined not to go "on record" as lying. If Howard denies unequivocally that he threatened to overrule

Lewis, he not only may be lying, but he will be indirectly calling the prisons chief a liar. But without a confession, no-one can claim either that Howard has lied or that he has accused Lewis of lying: the papers lose their front-page headline and the opposition lose their taunt of "liar."

As the last exchange cited in the preceding Howard-Paxman interview demonstrates, *evading* is very much about trying to change the topic or introduce a new QUD (Stokke 2018: 157). In trying to evade or change the topic, an evader like Howard might be very concerned with the truth value of what he is saying while evading. However, as Carson (2010: 60) points out, many evaders also bullshit in their evasive answers. He gives as an example of *evasive bullshitting* an anti-abortion presidential candidate who, when specifically asked in a presidential debate whether he will make opposition to abortion a requirement for nomination to the Supreme Court, replies:

> Look, there are lots of things to be taken into account when nominating someone for the Supreme Court. This isn't the only relevant consideration. I want someone with a good legal mind and judicial experience who supports my judicial philosophy of following the constitution as it is written. (2010: 60)

As with Howard, the candidate is clearly intent on avoiding a politically damaging answer and so is insincerely *evading* the question to *conceal* the truth. However, while Howard tries hard to keep his answers as relevant as they can be to the QUD without actually answering it, the presidential candidate uses the question as a way of providing campaign material that is quite unrelated to the QUD.[4]

5.3.4. Blocking and the Meeting of Political Targets

The third sub-strategy of withholding without misleading is *blocking*, in which a speaker deliberately prevents a *hearer* from providing or being provided with interactionally relevant material. *Blocking* can be defined as follows:

Blocking
Blocking occurs where the speaker intentionally either prevents the hearer from finding, or prevents a third party from disclosing, the answer to an explicit or implicit Question under Discussion as a way of withholding salient information that she believes the common ground calls on her to disclose.

---

[4] Carson (2010: 60) appears to suggest that this is bullshit mainly on the grounds that it does not answer the question (Meibauer 2016a: 79). But that would make all cases of evading ones of bullshitting and that does not seem to be the case. The key insincerity category here is withholding through evading, while bullshitting is embedded within the evasive answer.

Both *evading* and *blocking* try to circumvent a truthful contribution once it has been brought interactionally onstage, but whereas speakers do this directly in *evading*, they need to do this indirectly in blocking. Blocking is similar in some ways to Carson's "keeping someone in the dark" (2010: 53–55). However, Carson uses this term in the general sense of "preventing others from learning the truth" (2010: 54) and this might be achieved through lying and other forms of deception as well as withholding (so the term has the same status as "spin" and "bluffing," discussed in the following). Certainly, one of the two types of blocking is to prevent hearers from finding out the truth themselves, as when a seller tries to distract you from reading the contract. However, blocking also refers to preventing a third party from disclosing salient information.

Shuy (2017) uses the term *blocking* to describe the way police officers and undercover agents prevent suspects and witnesses from revealing exculpatory evidence during interrogations and undercover conversations (e.g., by abruptly changing topic or by lowering the volume of recording equipment so that the exculpatory material becomes inaudible). Similarly, the UK government *blocked* local councils from revealing the true proportion of families that had been helped by their Troubled Families Programme, launched by David Cameron in the wake of the 2011 riots in London. They did this by permitting councils to record not how many families they had *tried* to help, but only the number they had *succeeded* in helping (according to the government's strict and short-term criteria). The result was that the government could misleadingly claim a 99% success rate (Press-Association 2016). Furthermore, when the National Institute of Economic and Social Research (NIESR), which they had commissioned to carry out an official national study, found that the scheme had not had "any significant or systematic impact" (Day et al. 2016), the government *blocked* the release of the report for over a year. In criticizing ministers' suppression of these critical findings, the Public Affairs Committee stressed the importance of "transparency," or revelatory honesty, in institutional settings (Press-Association 2016).

5.4. Misleading as Discursively Leading Astray

While withholding attempts to avoid addressing the salient QUD, misleading attempts to lead the hearer astray linguistically with respect to the QUD. After some clarification of the concept of misleading (5.4.1), the section discusses discursive means of misleading through semantics (5.4.2), inference (5.4.3), and reframing (5.4.4). Finally, I consider the case of *spin* (5.4.5).

5.4.1. (Mis)Conceptions of "Misleading"

There are two key strategic ways of misleading:

(1) *Explicitly asserting* what you do not believe (i.e., lying);
(2) *Implicitly suggesting* what you do not believe while not committing that false belief to explicit assertion (i.e., misleading without lying).

Misleading (without lying) can be defined formally as follows:

Misleading (without lying)
Misleading is an insincere discourse strategy that exhibits a lack of congruence between what a speaker believes the common ground calls on her to disclose to the hearer—truthful answers to the QUD—and what she actually discloses to the hearer by implicitly suggesting false or distorted answers to the QUD.

The "mere" misleader, unlike the liar, is not willing to go "as far as" to openly contradict what he believes is the case. This might either be because of an internalized categorical moral imperative not to lie (Kant 2012) or, particularly in the case of politicians, lawyers, and witnesses, because the potential costs of being caught lying (losing trust, being forced to resign, being debarred, being indicted for perjury) outweigh the immediate benefits of closing down the interrogation.

The term "misleading" is, perhaps aptly, misleading. First, as indicated by the previous sentence, misleading, unlike lying, can be accidental rather than deliberate. For this reason, Carson (2010: 47) uses "deceiving" for intentionally rather than inadvertently misleading. However, "deceive" can also be used in an accidental sense: "the light/perspective deceived me." Furthermore, as I have noted, deception is best seen as the most common strategic *goal* of insincerity as a whole, rather than as an insincere discourse strategy for arriving at that goal. Meibauer goes further than Carson and suggests that misleading is merely "a by-product of misunderstanding" and so can only be accidental (2014: 136). But this leads him to stretch the category of lying into many areas covered by "misleading" here, thus losing a potentially very important category of insincerity. Furthermore, this approach tends to lead to talk of "indirect lying" (Vincent and Castelfranchi 1981), which seems to be a proxy for misleading, or the oxymoronic "lying while saying the truth" (Meibauer 2014: 123–127), which is quite different from but can be confused with the true lies discussed in Chapter 3. It is certainly true that the hearer can be misled inadvertently, just as he can be deceived inadvertently, but we are concerned in this chapter with a speaker's *intentional insincere discourse strategies*, so that automatically excludes accidental misleading. I can see no way of avoiding ambiguity with respect to any of these labels without stipulating a specific analytical meaning.

Second, "misleading," like "deceiving," is often considered to be a success verb: "A has not misled B unless B believes A" (Saul 2012: 71). However, as with "deceive" ("A has deceived B"), this is partly a semantic effect of the perfect aspect in English ("has misled") rather than being inherent in the meaning of "mislead." The *Collins English Dictionary* defines "mislead" as "to give false or misleading information to" (CED 2003). There is no suggestion in this definition of accomplished perlocutionary effect. Furthermore, I take my term of art *mis-lead-ing* from the more literal meaning of "to lead or guide in the wrong direction." If the destination of that wrong discursive direction is false belief, then lying takes the hearer straight there, whereas misleading without lying merely leads in that direction. The misleader guides the hearer to take up a false implicature or the wrong meaning of an ambiguous term, or to falsely believe that the speaker knows what he is talking about. The liar, on the other hand, will simply give the hearer false assertions without any room to doubt the direction.

One can mislead in a variety of ways: through semantics, inference, or reframing. Each of these is connected with a number of pragmatic tactics.

5.4.2. Misleading through Semantics: Obfuscating and Equivocating

One can insincerely mislead by drawing on the semantic obscurity or indeterminacy of words or grammar. This form of misleading thus covertly violates the maxim of Manner "Be perspicuous."

Obfuscating is deliberately using technical jargon or unclear grammar or vocabulary, "assuming and intending that the hearer will not be able to understand the full import" of the utterance (Vincent and Castelfranchi 1981: 764). Etymologically, obfuscate comes from Latin *obfuscare*, "to darken," and obfuscating casts a dark shadow over a text so that its meaning is less transparent. Terms and Conditions often insincerely obfuscate to discourage buyers from reading them. Obfuscating can occur in conventionally suspended humorous cases, as in Fenimore Cooper's writing rule "eschew surplusage" (Twain 2013[1895]: 6). Insincere obfuscating needs to be distinguished from the pathological bullshit category of "gobbledygook" common to bureaucratic language and certain types of academic discourse (see Chapter 6).

Equivocating is deliberately using ambiguous vocabulary or grammar with the intent that the hearer should construe the false version (Bavelas et al. 1990; Bull 2003). The classic example is Athanasius's dodgy deictic "He is very close to *here*" (Geach 1977), which, as noted in Chapter 4, is a self-protective suspension. Insincere equivocating has been described as "deceptive ambiguity" (Shuy

2017), "deliberate ambiguity" (Vincent and Castelfranchi 1981), and "pernicious ambiguity" (Solan 2004). The contemporary paradigm example is President Bill Clinton's "I did not have sexual relations with that woman," which equivocates between the ordinary meaning of "sexual relations" and the stipulated meaning agreed by lawyers in the case, which excluded fellatio (but not cunnilingus) (Solan and Tiersma 2005). Similarly, when Clinton said in a PBS interview that "[t]here is no improper relationship" with Monica Lewinsky, he relied on the inherent temporal ambiguity of the present tense (current state "now" or timeless existential) to mislead his audience (Saul 2012: 47–48). Given the inherent ambiguity of *is*, he is able to suggest in the context what he knows is not the case, i.e., that there is no question of an improper relationship that he needs to account for. The linguistic ambiguity, though, enables him to subsequently plausibly deny that he intended the more plausible interpretation. The same applies in the case of false implicature.

Another example of equivocating can be seen in the use of "turned around" in reporting the success of the Troubled Families Programme mentioned in the previous section. In a speech in June 2015, Prime Minister David Cameron said:

> I can announce today that almost all of the 117,000 families which the programme started working with have now been *turned around*—in terms of either school attendance or getting a job or both. (Cameron 2015)

That was then recontextualized in a government press release as:

> In a speech in the north west on Monday he announced that the programme had succeeded in turning around 99% of the actual number of families targeted. (Gov.UK 2015)

Collins English Dictionary defines "turnround" as "a complete reversal of a situation or set of circumstances" (CED 2003) but, as Cameron himself suggested in his speech, "turn around" here is measured by specific and potentially temporary indicators (temporarily returning to school, gaining a temporary job), a point that was not lost to the Public Affairs Committee in their review of the program:

> The implication of "turned around" was misleading, as the term was only indicative of achieving short-term outcomes under the programme rather than representing long-term, sustainable change in families' lives. (Day et al. 2016; PAC 2016)

Equivocating is an extremely common tactic of semantic misleading in public discourse.

5.4.3. Misleading through Inference: Falsely Implicating and Falsely Presupposing

In addition to misleading through semantics, we can also mislead pragmatically by triggering false inferences in the hearer through falsely implicating and falsely presupposing.

Falsely implicating is a pragmatic tactic of using Grice's Cooperative Principle to suggest a believed-false *p* while asserting a believed-true *p*. Falsely implicating, the strategic manifestation of "false implicature," has also been called "deceptive implicature" (McCornack 1992) and "covertly untruthful implicature" (Dynel 2018). This pragmatic tactic was discussed extensively in Chapter 1 and was part of the Bronston illustration at the beginning of this chapter, so little more will be said here. However, the tests for misleading can now be applied: (1) clearly, the false contribution to the QUD is offered indirectly, provided one accepts that implicature is indirect; (2) it is specifically implicated rather than asserted; (3) there are limited options to change one's epistemic stance, as we saw at the beginning of this chapter; and (4) there is some degree of deniability. Meibauer, on the other hand, claims that the false implicature is inseparable from the assertion because, drawing on Burton-Roberts (2013: 26), it is "an integral part of the total signification of the utterance" (Meibauer 2014b: 123–124). If, as Meibauer and Burton-Roberts claim, the implicature is not "cancellable," then the option for the speaker to change his epistemic stance is removed and deniability becomes very weak, thus making the false implicature a lie. It is certainly the case that in most everyday contexts, we would take the implicatures as an inevitable part of the meaning of what is said. However, as discussed in Chapter 1, the majority of people appear able to distinguish what is explicitly asserted from what is implicated or presupposed, and an alert hearer can take up and challenge what is implicated. Furthermore, while the speaker can make a false implicature, there is no guarantee that the audience will work it out. I would not go so far as Green's *caveat auditor* principle regarding misleading that "a listener is responsible for ascertaining that a statement is true before believing it" (2006: 165), or even Adler's claim that "each individual is a rational, autonomous being and so fully responsible for the inferences he draws, just as he is for his acts" (1997: 444). Principles of truthfulness and trust require the speaker to be putting in the work rather than relying on the hearer. The hearer cannot be held responsible simply for following the Cooperative Principle in unpacking the speaker's implicature. But the question of hearer responsibility is very different from the question of plausible deniability. The hearer may be charitable in allowing the speaker to plausibly deny in a way she could not be with deceptive lying.

Falsely presupposing is a pragmatic tactic of using presupposition to suggest that a believed-false *p* is true. The classic example is "When did you stop beating your wife?" where it is falsely presupposed that you used to beat your wife. Presupposition differs from implicature because it is unaffected by negation ("Did you/didn't you see the broken glass?") or antonymy ("When did you *start* beating your wife?"). Presupposition is "triggered" through certain lexical items (e.g., change of state verbs like "stop" and "start") and grammatical constructions (e.g., definite descriptions like "the King of France"). These are a little problematic for our tests because it is difficult to see how one could change one's epistemic stance or deny that one presupposed what is automatically triggered through the definite article or a verb like "stop." For this reason, Meibauer claims that falsely presupposing, like falsely implicating, is in fact lying (2014: 55–56). However, many cases of falsely presupposing are much less definitive. For example, in "It's a pity the Queen can't make it to our daughter's wedding," the speaker is presupposing that the Queen was invited to their daughter's wedding, but it is easier to deny here that the presupposition was intended.

5.4.4. Misleading through Reframing: Faking and Taking Words Out of Context

The final pair of misleading tactics covered here involves misleading through interpretatively reframing the speech context.

Faking counterfeits what the hearer is meant to assume about the speech context. Vincent and Castelfranchi (1981) note that we can pretend to act, joke, or even lie. In a game of poker, if a player says, "I've got a royal flush," the others are likely to assume that she is lying, so she could mislead them by telling the truth. In that case, we have a conventional suspension. But a speaker may also fake the discourse frame, by pretending, for example, to be joking ("I hate you . . . only kidding") or by misleading with rhetorical questions, saying, for example, "Am I responsible for that disaster?" when he knows he is (Meibauer 2014: 92). Meibauer argues that such a faked rhetorical question is, in fact, a lie since it is simply an indirect form of the assertion "I am not responsible for that disaster." However, most researchers agree that it is precisely the indirectness that makes it a case of misleading rather than lying. Applying the four tests: (1) the believed-false proposition is indirectly offered in response to an implied QUD; (2) it is conveyed in the form of a rhetorical question rather than being explicitly asserted; (3) there is still space for a change of epistemic stance ("Well, actually, I'm afraid I am"); and (4) the speaker can somewhat plausibly deny that she was making the suggested assertion ("I was just asking").

Taking words out of context involves reformulating what someone has said to give a misleading impression of what they meant (Galasiński 2000). This is particularly common in adversarial political and trial discourse. Every time we report others' words, we first extract them from their original context (decontextualization) and then place them in a new context (recontextualization) (Bauman and Briggs 1990). These processes will inevitably alter the meaning of the words to some extent, however careful we are in reporting them. Undergraduate students often distort by choosing quotes without understanding the contexts in which they are used. This is not intentional misleading, though, but pathological *distortion* (see Chapter 6). There is also a fine line between using quotes in persuasive argumentation and being willfully misleading about the original contexts. However, many contexts are clearly intentionally misleading, as when concessive clauses are taken as main clauses or a phrase with negative scope is converted into an affirmative. A student once reported to one of my colleagues that "Heffer swears in class": she did not give the context of discussing swear words academically in a lecture on taboo language.

5.4.5. Spin and the TRUST Categories

Several terms relating to insincerity and deception refer to what might be called "super-strategies." These super-strategies make use of several of the insincere discourse strategies outlined earlier. One such super-strategy is the notion of *spin* (as in "to spin a yarn," used in political contexts) (Gaber 2000). A "spin doctor" might use all of the strategies and tactics of withholding and misleading mentioned in the preceding. Indeed, many of the sub-strategies talked about with regard to "spin" can be talked of in TRUST terms: "cherry picking" is a type of deliberate *omission* of information salient to the QUD; "burying bad news" is a type of *blocking* since the idea is that media outlets will be so focused on the "big" news of the day that they will not be able to spend time on the "buried" news; the "limited hangout," or volunteering some scandalous information to hide more incriminating information, is a form of *evading*; the "non-denial denial" and the "non-apology apology" are types of *equivocating* since they use ambiguous language to make it seem as if they are making a denial or an apology but while leaving space for plausible denial; "cherry-picking" is also used to describe misleading selection of quotes, which is a case of *taking words out of context*; and "misdirection" is often used to mean *falsely implicating*. What spin doctors will tend to avoid, though, is *lying* as it prevents plausible deniability, which is particularly important in political contexts.

5.5. Lying as Self-Contradiction

Lying attempts to lead the hearer astray not by implicitly suggesting but by *explicitly asserting* what the speaker does not believe. The liar's insincerity lies in a lack of epistemic conviction in the claims she is sharing. Lying pretends to give information (Castelfranchi and Poggi 1994) while withholding what the speaker actually believes. I begin with a more formal definition of lying (5.5.1). I then distinguish between deceptive lying and bald-faced lying (5.5.2). I next discuss the subcategories of fabricating (5.5.3) and degree lying (5.5.4). Finally, I discuss the super-strategy of bluffing (5.5.5).

5.5.1. A Definition of Lying

The definition of lying is a substantial research area in the philosophy of language and has spawned a wealth of often highly complex formal definitions (Mahon 2016). My concern here, though, is merely to provide a workable definition that will fit the TRUST framework and serve in the context of judging discursive untruthfulness. My rather simple formal definition of lying, then, is as follows:

Lying
A speaker S lies if and only if:
(1) S asserts P;
(2) S believes P is false;
(3) S's commitment to truthfulness is not conventionally suspended.

The first two conditions are fairly standard in the literature. The third is particular to the TRUST framework and it is required because we do not say of an ironic speaker, for example, that he is "lying" but that his commitment to truthfulness is suspended. "Lying," unlike "misleading" and "withholding," inherently exempts conventional suspension.

We can compare this definition with a similar one by Saul (2012: 19):

If the speaker is not the victim of linguistic error/malapropism or using metaphor, hyperbole, or irony, then they lie iff (1) they say that P; (2) they believe P to be false; (3) they take themself to be in a warranting context.

My first element ("S asserts P") covers both Saul's first element ("they say that P") and the first half of Saul's initial condition ("If the speaker is not the victim of linguistic error/malapropism"). Saul is thinking of cases like "Samuel Johnson was an entomologist" (instead of etymologist) and "you inferred I was lying" (instead of implied), where linguistic errors lead the speaker to say what she does not mean. However, my first element requires the speech act of assertion, and linguistic well-formedness is a preparatory condition of assertion.[5] Such mistakes are common in online user comments but tend to be picked up immediately as performance mistakes rather than assertions with a different meaning. Were it not part of my definition of lying, it would also fail the general requirement of insincerity that it be intentional. Regarding the requirement for verbal expression in (1), some (e.g., Eco 1994) claim that lying can occur in any semiotic mode. However, we have many other words to describe such non-verbal deceptions (e.g., "pretending," "faking," "camouflaging," "trompe l'oeil") and such deceptions tend to distort rather than directly contradict what the deceiver believes to be the case. It seems odd to describe the doctored image of a crowd or a cardboard tank as "lies" even if they deceive the viewer into believing something false. The use of "assert" rather than "say" or "state" in (1) is also controversial because "assert" comes with speech act baggage such as preparatory conditions. However, opting for "say" or "state" does not avoid the difficult line between what is said and what is suggested, discussed in the previous section.

My second element ("S believes P is false") is identical to Saul's second element ("They believe P to be false") and it is the one element that tends to remain stable across most definitions (Mahon 2016). As noted in Chapter 3, a few researchers such as Carson (2010) and Turri and Turri (2015) believe that P itself should be false because it is far from uncommon for people in practice to equate factual falsity with lying when not asked to deliberate on specific scenarios that challenge that folk equation. However, my pragmatic definition of lying attempts to provide a "best fit" between expert opinion and popular usage. The fact that many people use "lie" loosely in speech to include mere factual falsity or non-verbal instances of deception is not good grounds to include these in an analytical definition.

My third element ("S's commitment to truthfulness is not conventionally suspended") covers both Saul's third element ("They take themself to be in a warranting context") and the second half of her initial condition ("or using metaphor, hyperbole, or irony"). In Chapter 4, I classed metaphor, hyperbole, and irony as performed conventional suspensions and, by "warranting context," Saul effectively means those contexts not covered by prescribed conventional suspensions.

Lying is sometimes called "falsification" or "falsifying" (Buller and Burgoon 1996; Ekman 2009). However, while this term captures the intentionality of

---

[5] Saul does not have this option because she takes a non-assertoric approach to lying.

making false that is inherent in lying, it does not convey the cognitive state of disbelief that is central to most accounts of lying. "Falsification" also comes with semantic baggage that tends to link it with the falsification (i.e., altering) of documents. The words "lie" and "lying" are far from transparent, but they are firmly entrenched in both popular and professional use.

5.5.2. Deceptive Lying and Bald-Faced Lying

Deceptive lying adds to the basic definition of lying the traditional Augustinian element of intent to deceive (4). We can thus define deceptive lying as follows:

Deceptive Lying
A speaker S deceptively lies to a hearer H if and only if:
(1) S asserts P;
(2) S believes P is false;
(3) S's commitment to truthfulness is not conventionally suspended;
(4) S intends to deceive H.

Given that, in TRUST, discursive categories are analytically separable from ethical import, what I call *deceptive lying* is not the same as what has been called "straight lies," "proper lies," or "straightforward lies" (Arico and Fallis 2013: 791), which add the element of willfulness that I keep as a separate ethical condition (see 5.6). Deceptive lying is not necessarily willful because lies intended to deceive can be used in consequentially or condonably suspended contexts. Several subcategories of deceptive lying might be posited. For example, a *group lie* (Lackey 2019) is one in which a group of people such as a government, organization, or company are collectively responsible for a deceptive lie. Often group lies will be conveyed through a spokesperson, who tells the lie *on behalf of* the group. Group lies are at the heart of disinformation (see Chapter 9).

Bald-faced lying (e.g., Sorensen 2007; Carson 2010), discussed in Chapter 1, adds to the basic definition of lying a specific lack of intent to deceive. It is thus the direct opposite of deceptive lying:

Bald-faced Lying
A speaker S bald-faced lies to a hearer H if and only if:
(1) S asserts P;
(2) S believes P is false;
(3) S's commitment to truthfulness is not conventionally suspended;
(4) S does not intend to deceive H.

168　THE TRUST FRAMEWORK

As with deceptive lying, there seem to be several possible subcategories of bald-faced lying, including *knowledge lies* (Sorensen 2010)[6] and *indifferent* lies (Rutschmann and Wiegmann 2017), discussed in Chapter 1.

5.5.3. Fabricating and False News

Finally, whereas deceptive lying and bald-faced lying tend to conceal incriminating facts (from the speaker or from the record) in an otherwise truthful account, **fabricating** constructs an alternative fictional world. Fabrications are fictions without a justifiable conventional suspension of sincerity. However, the fabricator does not have the careless attitude to the truth that characterizes the bullshitter. The self-confessed fabricator Stephen Glass began his career in journalism as a fact-checker and was, at least at first, quite meticulous in establishing the "truthfulness" of his fabricated articles in the *New Republic* (Rabaté 2005: 94–101). He published twenty-seven articles that were either partial or complete fabrications, but the fact checkers at *New Republic* failed to pick up his fictions. Spies will similarly concoct meticulously planned fabrications designed to fool their dupes.

False news is a subcategory of fabrication. The term has recently replaced *fake news* (Levinson 2017), after Donald Trump's appropriation of that term to describe the mainstream media. False news has a very long tradition. For example, the European Commission has a blog with an alphabetical list of hundreds of "Euromyths" from hygiene rules causing UK "Abattoirs" to close down to "Zoos" being forced to use a universal elephant symbol (EU Commission 2018). Many, if not most, of these myths have been invented by the British tabloid press over the past fifty years (Cross 2008).

5.5.4. Degree Lying: Exaggerating and Minimizing

The final category of lying, which we might call *degree lying*, includes the very common pragmatic tactics of *exaggerating* and *minimizing*. With degree lying, one lies not about an underlying proposition, which may be true, but by deliberately distorting the perceived proportions or degree of something. For example, consider this exchange between parents after putting the children to bed:

---

[6] Sorensen himself sees knowledge lies as distinct from bald-faced lies.

FATHER: I've spent simply ages tidying up after the kids.
MOTHER: What do you mean? You've hardly started.

The father believes he has spent some time tidying up but he hopes to give his partner the false impression that he spent much longer than he did. The mother knows her partner has spent some time tidying up but she hopes to give him the false impression that she thinks that he has spent much less time than he did. They are thus insincerely *exaggerating* and *minimizing* to score rhetorical points. Similarly, a student believing that an exam was moderately difficult might say, "it was incredibly tough" or "it was relatively easy," depending on the impression she wants to make on the hearer.

Degree lying can be defined as follows:

Degree Lying
A speaker S degree lies if and only if:
(1) S asserts *P*;
(2) S believes *P* is false *with respect to the degree to which it holds*;
(3) S's commitment to truthfulness is not conventionally suspended.

Exaggerating degree lies by claiming that *P* holds to a *greater* degree than S actually believes. *Minimizing* degree lies by claiming that *P* holds to a *lesser* degree than S actually believes. Thus, the parents both believe the core proposition that the tidying up has taken some time, but they dispute and intentionally distort the length of that time. Similarly, the student believes the proposition that the exam was difficult but she intentionally exaggerates or minimizes the degree to which that proposition holds. Condition 2 rules out epistemically irresponsible *overstatement* and *understatement*, where the speaker may not be consciously aware of the distortion of degree (see Chapter 6). Condition 3 rules out performatively suspended *hyperbole* (Grice 1975; Claridge 2011; Dynel 2018) and *meiosis* (Grice 1975; Dynel 2018), where the distortion of degree is overt and thus sincere (see Chapter 4).

Given that degree lying is both very common and often fairly harmless, it is tempting to see it as something "less than" lying. However, this would be to confuse again insincere discourse categories with their ethical value in context. Polite compliments are often lies, though usually beneficial ones. Similarly, degree lying is often found in suspended contexts. But it can also be malicious. For example, if I want you to miss your plane and I know it takes two hours to drive to the airport, I am being thoroughly malicious if I deliberately minimize with "it takes no time at all to get there." Furthermore, degree lying clearly meets the tests for lying: (1) it offers a false contribution to an explicit or implicit QUD about degree (e.g., how much tidying up did you do? How difficult was the exam?); (2) it explicitly asserts the false contribution about degree; (3) it leaves no option to change epistemic stance without admitting to exaggerating or minimizing; and (4) it leaves little scope for plausible deniability.

5.5.5. Bluffing and the TRUST Categories

Like *spin*, **bluffing** is a super-strategy of deception but one used primarily in negotiation and games. Whereas *spin* focuses on the strategies of withholding and misleading, *bluffing* can make use of all three discourse strategies, particularly including lying. In bluffing, "one attempts to misrepresent one's intentions or overstate the strength of one's position" (Carson et al. 1982: 14). We can see this in US police interrogations (Leo 2008).[7] In attempting to negotiate a confession from suspects, officers may *lie* about having found the murder weapon or about the suspect having failed a polygraph test; they often *minimize* the nature of the crime and *exaggerate* (if not completely faking) empathy for the suspect; and they *omit* telling the suspect details that might be exculpatory and *block* other suspects from communicating with the suspect. As with *spin*, then, one can be aware of the super-strategy of bluffing without needing it to analyze specific cases of untruthfulness in situated text.

5.6. *Willful* Insincerity

Previous sections have detailed a taxonomy of insincere discourse strategies, involving withholding the truth and disrupting inquiry in one way or another. So far in this chapter, though, the ethical value of such strategies in context has been put to one side. Chapter 4 demonstrated that a speaker can be morally justified in *suspending* his commitment to truthfulness in many types of cases. Here, then, I argue that for a speaker to be unethically insincere, he must not only withhold the truth but also do so *willfully*. In this section I define and establish conditions for willfulness (5.6.1) and then explore the application of these conditions to the major insincere discourse strategies of withholding, misleading, and lying (5.6.2).

5.6.1. Willfulness and Its Conditions

The concept of willfulness I am proposing here combines intention with a degree of impropriety. The legal understanding of willfulness can help, despite the

---

[7] Lying by police officers is not permissible in Europe.

vagueness of the term in legal discourse (Craswell 2009). *Black's Law Dictionary* defines "willful" as "voluntary and intentional, but not necessarily malicious" (Garner 2009), yet the concessive clause is indicative of the way "willful" is construed in the legal community. Some jurists claim that willful "does not require any actual impropriety," while others claim that "the requirement added by such a word is not satisfied unless there is a bad purpose or evil intent" (Perkins and Boyce in Garner 2009: 1737). In short, the threshold for willfulness seems to be something ethically stronger than merely intentional but something less than outright malicious. It is perhaps best summed up in a Delaware Superior Court ruling with respect to the meaning of the word "willful" as used in the Workmen's Compensation Statute:

> In the present statute we believe it was used to define an act done intentionally, knowingly, and purposely, without justifiable excuse, as distinguished from an act done carelessly, thoughtlessly, heedlessly or inadvertently. (*Lobdell Car Wheel Co. v. Subielski*, 2 W.W. Harr. 462, 125 A. 462, 464)

Here the two elements of legal willfulness the TRUST framework borrows are set out clearly: that the insincerity is done "intentionally, knowingly, and purposely" and that it is done "without justifiable excuse." The first element indicates that it is not sufficient for the insincerity to be intentional, which is a constitutive condition for all insincerity, but it must be done "purposely." Generally, the immediate purpose will be to deceive or otherwise breach the trust of the hearer. The second element indicates that even when an act of insincerity is intentional and deliberate, it can still be justifiable.

I thus propose the following two formal conditions for willful insincerity:

Willful Insincerity
   A speaker S is willfully insincere if and only if:
   (1) S *breaches trust* in deliberately attempting to disrupt the inquiry;
   (2) S is not *justified in suspending* his or her commitment to truthfulness.

The *Breach of Trust* condition (1) requires that the interactional trust that the speaker will be truthful in contributing to the inquiry is breached. Interactional trust is not breached when a speaker overtly states something he believes to be false (e.g., in irony or hyperbole) if he is still contributing truthfully to the inquiry. Trust *is* breached, on the other hand, if a speaker says something she believes to be true while suggesting something she believes to be false, as it is the suggested falsity that contributes to the inquiry. In most cases, interactional breach of trust corresponds to an intent to deceive. In the case of bald-faced lying or withholding, the breach of trust usually resides in the selfish refusal to put the truth on record.

The *Suspension* condition (2) requires that the speaker's commitment to truthfulness is *not* justifiably suspended in the context. The daughter telling her dying mother that her son (who died that morning) is fine (Saul 2012: 86–88) is clearly intending to deceive and so is superficially breaching interactional trust, but she is arguably performing a protective consequential suspension and so is not being *willfully* insincere. On the other hand, if she stands to gain a selfish benefit from that insincerity, such as avoiding the will from being rewritten, then a consequential suspension is no longer justified and we would say that her insincerity is willful. Similarly, when we lie to the murderer at the door, we breach interactional trust, but we are clearly justified in suspending our commitment to truthfulness. As seen in Chapter 4, there will often be disagreement: an American tourist might feel that his trust has been breached in a truth-warranting context when the Ecuadorian shopkeeper intentionally misdirects him, but this may be construed as a justified polite suspension rather than a willful insincerity in the Ecuadorian context.[8]

5.6.2. Willfulness in Withholding and Lying

There is an ample gray area between willful and non-willful insincere discourse. First, with regard to withholding, plagiarism is generally understood to be *willfully* insincere and thus sanctionable: it is intentional, attempts to deceive, and is unlikely to be the result of a justified suspension. "Innocent plagiarism" or "accidental plagiarism" seem to be oxymora. However, we can understand contexts where ideational and linguistic "plagiarism" on their own might not be considered willful. For example, ideational plagiarism can only come about when the writer is *aware* that he is copying someone else's ideas. Yet it is perfectly possible for two researchers to independently develop very similar ideas at around the same time. Accidental linguistic "plagiarism" is common among students who take verbatim notes when studying and then forget that they need to paraphrase them when writing essays. There is also relatively low awareness among students that linguistic plagiarism is wrong (Dawson and Overfield 2006). For this reason, many universities (including my own) now talk of "unfair academic practice" to avoid having to prove willfulness in case of appeals. In this sense, "plagiarism" is rather like the term "perjury" in that it has willfulness built into it.

Lying is similarly not always willful, as can be seen from the number of terms we have for non-willful lying: white lies, prosocial lies, benevolent lies,

---

[8] This sentence should be read in the light of my empirical findings at the end of Chapter 4: there is no suggestion here that Americans would *normally* find misdirection a breach of trust or Ecuadorians find it a polite suspension.

etc. On the other hand, the Platonic "noble lie," "a contrivance for one of those falsehoods that come into being in case of need" (Plato 1992: 414b–c), is an enormous breach of trust that coercively manipulates the citizenry and so is a willful deceptive lie. Bald-faced lying is not always willful. If a group of people see a man harassing a woman in the street, they might go up to the man and say, "she's with us." It might be obvious that they have never met the woman before, but the group are protecting the woman by sending a face-saving message to the man that he should back away rather than risk being attacked by the group. When bald-faced lying is *willful*, on the other hand, the liar generally pursues a selfish gain that does not require deceit. Often the impropriety consists in the selfish refusal to put the truth on record. When the student tells the Dean that she has not cheated, she thereby unfairly avoids punishment (Carson 2010); when the suspect tells the officer, "You've got me Guv, now prove it!" he potentially avoids conviction. Finally, with regard to degree lying, *exaggerating* in the form of *puffery* ("washes whiter than white") is generally considered not to be willful as it occurs in the partially suspended context of advertising: advertisers are not permitted to lie directly, but they are allowed to "gild the lily." On the other hand, exaggerating in the form of *spin* in government press conferences is generally considered to be willfully insincere since the government cannot similarly suspend its commitment to truthfulness.

5.7. Summary of Insincere Discourse Strategies and a Sample Sincerity Analysis

In this final substantive section, I summarize the insincere discourse strategies (5.7.1) and apply the Sincerity framework to a Trump claim about respecting women (5.7.2).

5.7.1. Summary of Insincere Discourse Strategies

The main insincere discourse strategies and sub-strategies are summarized in Table 5.5. Withholding (without misleading) tries to keep incriminating information off the interactional stage: omitting by leaving it out of one's account, evading by trying to divert away from the interlocutor's pressing, and blocking by trying to prevent the interlocutor from revealing the incriminating information to others. Misleading tries to conceal the information once it is on the interactional stage: by obfuscating or equivocating on the meaning of words; by suggesting an alternative reality through falsely implicating or presupposing; or by reframing what is said through faking or taking words out of context. Finally,

174 THE TRUST FRAMEWORK

Table 5.5 Insincere Discourse Strategies

Strategies	Sub-Strategies	Pragmatic Tactics/ Further Sub-Strategies
Withholding (– misleading)	Omitting	Plagiarizing
	Evading	Ignoring the question Attacking the question or questioner Contriving a distraction Declining to answer
	Blocking	Preventing finding Preventing disclosing
Misleading (– lying)	Misleading through Semantics	Obfuscating Equivocating
	Misleading through Inference	Falsely implicating Falsely presupposing
	Misleading through Reframing	Faking Taking words out of context
Lying	Deceptive lying	Group lying
	Bald-faced lying	Knowledge lying Indifferent lying
	Fabricating	False news
	Degree lying	Exaggerating Minimizing

lying misleads by contradicting what one actually believes: deceptive lying tries to manipulate the hearer's beliefs; barefaced lying avoids putting the truth on record; fabricating creates an alternative reality; while exaggerating and minimizing deliberately convey a distorted picture of the world.

5.7.2. A Sample Sincerity Analysis: "Nobody has more respect for women"

Given the central element of speaker belief and the difficulty in making a cognitive appraisal, the Sincerity analysis in TRUST will often, on its own, be inconclusive. However, the *process* of undertaking the analysis is often thought provoking. The example I would like to discuss is an assertion made by Donald Trump during a presidential election debate in Nevada on October 19, 2016. The utterance came early in the debate:

Nobody has more respect for women than me. Nobody. Nobody has more respect.

We can safely assume that "nobody" is performed hyperbole that would be picked up by most of the audience and that the "normal" figurative interpretation of the utterance would be:

>I have a huge respect for women<

There are two key pieces of evidence that warrant a claim of untruthfulness in this case:

(1) The text-internal evidence of him subsequently talking over Hillary Clinton during the presidential debate and snarling, "Such a nasty woman";
(2) The historical evidence of him apparently disrespecting women, including the "pussy grabbing" bus episode, accusations of sexual molestation, and calling women with derogatory names (Daily Telegraph DT Sexism Tracker).

Despite being manifestly untruthful, this is a complex case in terms of sincerity. On the one hand, text-internal contradiction ("Huge respect . . . Such a nasty woman") is evidence for insincerity but, on the other, in Trump's deluded world, it is not clear whether he is aware of the contradiction, and so it is not clear to what extent he is being *willfully* insincere.

In terms of *withholding*, one could argue that he is willfully omitting all those cases where he seems to have been disrespectful to women. But it is not at all clear whether he accepts that he was being disrespectful to them (sadly, there are still men who believe that women are flattered by being groped by powerful men). One can also argue that he is *willfully equivocating*. First, the stative meaning of the present simple ("Nobody *has* more respect . . .") allows him to equivocate between what is his normal character ("I normally respect women") or his current character ("I now respect women") and all those historical "exceptions" to his normal or current character. Second, the word "respect" can be interpreted in a more "salty" or a more "tasty" way. As a "salty" assertion, we could list a number of concrete behaviors that we might associate with "respect for women," including allowing them to speak, judging them on relevant qualities rather than looks, and not abusing one's position of power to molest or demean them. But "respect" can also be used in a more subjective "tasty" way. So, Trump may well have "respected" in his own way women like his wife Melania, his daughter Ivanka, and his counselor Kelly-Anne Conway, but he may not have "realized" in his own mind that respect needs to be extended to all women. It could also be argued that Trump is *willfully lying* on the grounds that he appears to contradict himself when he is abusive to Clinton. However, it is possible that he fails to recognize the contradiction because, in his mind, Clinton is not *worthy* of respect. He is certainly *exaggerating* to a very great extent: he must know his reputation and cannot possibly believe that he is *extremely* respectful to women.

Nevertheless, as in many cases where the speaker is somewhat deluded, it is ultimately difficult to make a judgment of willful insincerity. On the other hand, it is much easier to demonstrate epistemic irresponsibility. Trump had an epistemic duty given not only his institutional role as presidential candidate, but also the universal responsibility to respect the rights of others. The word "respect" comes from Latin *respicere* (to look back, to pay attention) and one of the (lesser) meanings of respect is to treat courteously or kindly. Trump has not paid attention to his lack of basic courtesy during the debate, and he has not looked back and reflected respectfully on his behavior with women in the past. In other words, he has failed to sufficiently investigate his own behavior, and so he is at the very least epistemically irresponsible in claiming that he has a great respect for women.

5.8. Conclusion

This chapter has teased out a framework for analyzing discursive insincerity in terms of a speaker's intentional insincere discourse strategies, sub-strategies, and pragmatic tactics (D1). I have suggested that these many strategies and tactics can be grouped together into three main strategies deriving from the notion of intentionally withholding what one believes to be the case. The three key insincere discourse strategies can be distinguished according to their relation to the QUD, their linguistic manifestation, the extent to which they leave space for epistemic change of mind, and the extent to which they can plausibly be denied. However, while it is possible to distinguish the strategies discursively, it is far more difficult to establish willfulness on the part of the speaker because of the inherent difficulty in making a cognitive appraisal (E2). We might "know" instinctively that someone has lied, misled, or withheld, but it is quite another thing to get inside the insincere speaker's head to prove it. But, as will be seen in Chapter 6, where there is insufficient evidence to make a judgment of willful insincerity, there is often sufficient evidence to make a judgment of epistemic negligence.

6
Epistemically Irresponsible Discourse Pathologies

> By collecting contrasting divergent opinions, I hope to provoke young readers to push themselves to the limit in the search for truth, so that their wits may be sharpened by their investigation.... It is by doubting that we come to investigate, and by investigating that we recognize the truth.
> —Abelard (1976[1121–1132], Prologue)

6.1. Introduction

In order to make a judgment of insincerity, we must infer the mental state of the speaker through evidence. Such evidence might come through confession, self-contradiction, lie detection, or prior record. However, as indicated in Chapter 3, it is surprisingly difficult to make reliable judgments of insincerity on the basis of such evidence: too many confessions are false, conflicting remarks are not uncommon in honest speakers, some people sincerely (if sadly) believe that they have been abducted by aliens, and our natural ability to detect deceptive insincerity in others is roughly at the level of chance. Judgments of epistemic irresponsibility, on the other hand, though not always easy to make, are more accessible to the extent that they depend, at least to a degree, on the relation between two phenomena—word and world—that are empirically observable or institutionally defined. Since being epistemically responsible involves making some investigative effort, the complete lack of empirical evidence that you were abducted by aliens, even if you sincerely believe that, or that thousands of Muslims were out celebrating in New York on 9/11, even if President Trump disturbingly believed that (Reuters 2015), is actually clear evidence that investigative effort cannot have been made. There is an ethical gulf, though, between the innocent delusions of a would-be alien abductee and the culpable hate-mongering of a deluded but democratically elected US president. It needs to be considered, then, what makes a proposition not merely irresponsible but also ethically *negligent* because it breaches trust in a morally blameworthy way.

I begin this chapter by considering the hybrid category of *bullshitting* introduced in Chapter 2 (6.2). Bullshitting is insincere since the speaker knows what he is doing and knows that he is disrupting inquiry. Nevertheless, it is rooted in an epistemically irresponsible attitude that distinguishes it from the other forms of insincerity explored in Chapter 5 and makes it similar in this respect to the discourse pathologies explored here. Then I address in turn the discourse pathologies of *dogma* (6.3), *distortion* (6.4), and *bullshit* (6.5), each manifested in subpathologies or "discursive symptoms" that can be identified in the text itself in relation to the world, rather than requiring a cognitive appraisal. Next, I discuss the conditions under which epistemically irresponsible discourse becomes *epistemically negligent* and thus morally blameworthy (6.6). Finally, I summarize the analytical categories and use them and the negligence conditions to carry out a brief analysis of epistemic responsibility with regard to a news tweet (6.7).

6.2. Epistemic Irresponsibility, Bullshitting, and Pathological Discourse

A link between discursive insincerity and epistemic irresponsibility can be found in the hybrid category of *bullshitting*, which I further discuss and define (6.2.1). I then identify three different types of *bullshitting* (6.2.2) before outlining the key discourse pathologies of dogma, distortion, and bullshit (6.2.3).

6.2.1. Bullshitting as a Hybrid Category: Insincere and Irresponsible

To the extent that bullshitters are withholding information about their lack of commitment to truthfulness and are deceptive about their rhetorical goals, bullshitting seems to be an insincere discourse strategy. The expression "Money talks, bullshit walks," for example, contrasts two rhetorical strategies for getting one's way. As seen in Chapter 2, the intentionally deceptive strategic nature of bullshitting was the primary concern of Frankfurt (2005) and of most of those who have followed in his footsteps. Although bullshitting is a deliberate insincere strategy, it is also epistemically irresponsible since it is rooted in a lack of investigative investment. If the speaker knows what is the case but says otherwise, she must be lying; she can only be bullshitting if she has not invested in discovering the facts of a case. Whereas the insincere discourse strategies discussed in Chapter 5 are aimed at concealing what you *know* to be the case, *bullshitting* aims to conceal that *you do not know* what *is* the case. Indeed, many supposed cases of insincere *bullshitting* in the philosophical literature can be explained in terms of the other categories of insincerity. Carson's example of *evasive bullshit* (2010: 59–60), as seen in Chapter 5, is best understood as a specific *tactic* of evasion while pursuing the insincere discourse strategy of withholding. Carson goes on to say that "[o]ne can tell a lie as a part of an evasive bullshit answer to a question" (2010: 61). His example is being asked by an administrator at a religious university intolerant of atheists whether one's colleague is an atheist, and instead of lying "no" (which is likely to be found out and get me into trouble), replying with a claim that is unlikely to be investigated: "as a boy he always went to church and loved singing Christmas Carols" (2010: 62). However, this response cannot be *evading* in TRUST terms because it indirectly addresses the QUD "Is your colleague an atheist?" Given Grice's maxim of Relation, you will be taken (falsely) as implicating "so he's probably still Christian." Furthermore, this false implicature holds irrespective of the truth status of your assertion about your colleague as a boy. If the assertion is true, this is a standard false implicature. If you do not know whether it is true or not, this is bullshitting at the level of what is said, but it still conveys the false implicature and so is misleading at the level of what is meant. In Carson's version, "I know this to be false" (2010: 62), so what is said is a lie but, in terms of responding to the QUD, the false implicature still holds, so we still have a case of misleading in terms of the QUD. Bullshitting at the level of the QUD simply does not come into the picture. Furthermore, in terms of the overall TRUST framework, the insincerity takes place in a context of justifiable (and probably justified) suspension of epistemic commitment for the consequential greater good of protecting one's colleague from discriminatory practice.

I define bullshitting as follows:

Bullshitting
Speaker (S) is bullshitting Hearer (H) if and only if:
(1) S asserts p.
(2) S does not commit to the truth of p.
(3) S does not disclose or suggest to H that she is not warranting p.

Condition 1 excludes conventional suspensions. In Carson's terms, the speaker must be in a warranting context. Some polite suspensions are also arguably excluded. *Benign bull*, or "benign bullshit" (Nagel 2002) deliberately emitted to boost positive face ("how nice to see you"; "anybody can do anything"; "you'll be fine"), is so emphatically phatic rather than referential that it is unlikely to be construed as assertoric. Condition 2 is very different from the "believe false" condition of lying because not committing to the truth of a proposition is very different from committing to its falsity. This condition is about lack of responsibility rather than lack of sincerity. It violates Searle's first preparatory rule—"S has evidence (reasons, etc.) for the truth of p"—rather than the sincerity rule—"S believes *p*." Indeed, it is Condition 3 that is the sincerity one in terms of the understanding of sincerity outlined in Chapters 1 and 5: S does not disclose what she believes the context calls on her to disclose, i.e., that she is not warranting *p*. This condition incorporates a lack of linguistic signaling that you have a low degree of confidence in what you are asserting. Indeed, some see the hedging of one's degree of confidence as indicating a lack of assertion altogether (Marsili 2019).

We can apply these conditions to the Virtual Ambulance Chaser introduced in Chapter 2. First, she opens the call with a clear assertion (1): "Hello. I believe you have had a car accident in the last few years." "I believe" would normally be construed as a hedge, but in service encounters it is generally a polite way of saying "I know" or "I am reasonably confident that." Second, she cannot commit to the truth of this claim (2) because she knows that many of the people she calls have *not* had a car accident. At the same time, she equally does not believe the claim is false because *some* of the receivers *have* had accidents. Finally, though, she does not disclose to the receiver that she cannot warrant the truth of her assertion (3) and does not hedge the assertion in a way that would suggest this (e.g., "I believe you might have had … ").

6.2.2. Types of Insincere Bullshitting: Rhetorical, Knowledge, and Wishful

Several types of insincere *bullshitting* have been identified in the literature and might be formalized as categories of bullshitting here.

Rhetorical bullshitting is focused on achieving a given rhetorical goal (selling a product, convincing voters, impressing a business partner, etc.) at the expense of everything else, including the truth value of the assertions one makes. This is classic Frankfurtian bullshit in which there is both indifference to the truth values of the assertions one makes and a clear intent to deceive the hearer about the nature of one's enterprise. This does not mean one can say anything, though, since in order to maintain the pretense of epistemic commitment, what one says needs to be *believable*.

Knowledge bullshitting occurs when a speaker lacks knowledge of a subject but is put in a position where he is meant to speak knowledgeably about that subject. Carson's exam sitter trying to gain partial credit by saying true things (2010: 62) is a knowledge bullshitter. The type is also common among teachers and lecturers suddenly finding themselves in the position of having to teach a subject they know little about. Knowledge bullshitters are not *indifferent* to the truth. Indeed, they very much care that they should be telling the truth as much as they possibly can. It is just that they do not have the knowledge to be able to do that reliably, but feel that the costs of admitting that ignorance are too great in the context.

Wishful bullshitting clearly derives from what Stokke (2018: 142) calls "wishful thinking." We saw several examples of this in Chapter 2, including Reassuring Groom and Virtual Ambulance Chaser. In these cases, the speakers are not indifferent to what they are saying, indeed they *hope* that what they say is true, but they are indifferent to the truth value of their assertion with respect to the QUD: the Reassuring Groom has no idea what the weather is like in Cardiff at this time of year; the Ambulance Chaser does not know that you have had a car accident that would warrant the attention of a claims lawyer.

6.2.3. Categories of Pathological Discourse

Having covered the hybrid category of *bullshitting*, in the remainder of the chapter I shall focus on epistemically irresponsible discourse that may well be sincere. Unlike with the insincere discourse strategies illustrated on the left of Figure 6.1, there are no existing typologies of epistemically irresponsible discourse pathologies, illustrated on the right of Figure 6.1. Bullshit is now a well-established category (though the focus is still on bullshitting). Dogma is a

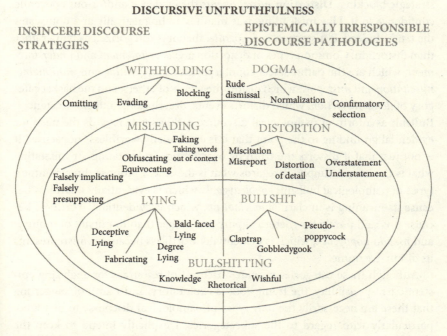

Figure 6.1. Discursive categories of untruthfulness.

well-discussed phenomenon, but it has not generally been discussed in the context of untruthfulness, insincerity, or deception. Distortion tends to be discussed as an intentional strategy similar to lying, rather than as a pathology (Turner et al. 1975; Metts 1989). For example, Turner et al. (1975) identified "lies" and "exaggeration" as subtypes of distortion, so this sense of distortion corresponds to *lying* here. As with the main insincere discourse strategies discussed in Chapter 5, I suggest that the major differences between epistemically irresponsible discourse pathologies are hierarchical rather than binary (see right half of Figure 6.1). I shall talk of specific categories of the three main pathologies as being either sub-pathologies or *discursive symptoms* of those pathologies.

The umbrella category is **dogma**, or closed-minded discourse that *disregards* counter-evidence. It is quite possible for such dogma to be true, but it is true by accident rather than through the epistemic responsibility of the speaker. Dogma, like withholding, concerns a lack of openness (but in this case lack of open-mindedness) and, again like withholding, is more about absence than presence in discourse. Common discursive symptoms of the discourse pathology of dogma are: *confirmatory selection*, which is the pathological counterpart to strategic omission; *rude dismissal* of counter arguments, which, like strategic evading, is a way of avoiding the issue once it is brought on stage; and *normalization*, which naturalizes a claim beyond question and so has some affinity with strategic blocking. **Distortion** *misrepresents* the evidence and/or our epistemic confidence in it. Like misleading, it is manifested linguistically and obfuscates the truth. Indeed, if distortion is *deliberate*, then it is categorized as lying rather than distortion. Common types of distortion are: *overstatement* and *understatement*, which are the pathological counterparts of *exaggerating* and *minimizing*; *miscitation* and *misreport*, which distort the words of others; and the basket category of *detail distortion*, which distorts events, descriptions, and circumstances. **Bullshit** as a form of pathological discourse recklessly disregards the need for evidential grounding to the point that it is evidentially worthless "nonsense." It is not just that it distorts the truth by overstating, understating, or misstating what is the case; it simply disregards what is the case. I propose three common types of pathological bullshit: *gobbledygook*, which is evidentially worthless because its meaning is unclarifiable; *claptrap*, which is evidentially worthless because it is said purely for rhetorical purposes rather than in pursuit of inquiry; and *pseudo-poppycock*, which is evidentially worthless because it misrepresents its discursive frame.

Although these categories provide a rich set of resources for analyzing epistemic irresponsibility, the framework is exploratory, and I am not suggesting that these are necessarily the *only* types of pathological discourse to be found, particularly with regard to the subcategories. I explicitly intend to keep the inquiry open.

6.3. Dogma as the Disregarding of Counter-Evidence

Ideally, we would want to be able to take it for granted that in the case of "salty" assertions people would not "blithely continue to maintain" their own views in the face of disagreement (MacFarlane 2014: 5). Sadly, though, it is all too often the case that people fail to question their views in the case of "salty-type" disagreement. This leads to the discourse pathology of *dogma*, or unwarranted discursive closure. I first define the conditions of pathological dogma (6.3.1). I then explore three discursive symptoms of this pathology: confirmatory selection (6.3.2), rude dismissal (6.3.3), and normalization (6.3.4).

6.3.1. Dogma and Closure

The quote from Peter Abelard at the opening of this chapter nicely illustrates the distinction between dogma understood as an authoritatively laid down set of principles and dogma understood as the pathological discursive manifestation of a dogmatic attitude. In his medieval scholastic text *Sic et Non* (Abelard 1976[1121–1132]), Abelard presented his students with 158 contradictory theological assertions that they were to grapple with. Within the confines of the then hegemonic Christian theological dogma, he was encouraging critical openness and critical thinking in his dialectic approach and so was anything but dogmatic. Indeed, it was too much for the theological establishment of the time, who removed him from his teaching post (Luscombe 1969).

We can define pathological dogma more formally as follows:

Dogma
Discourse is pathologically dogmatic under the following conditions:
(C1) a sound alternative account was available to the speaker;
(C2) the speaker has disregarded that alternative account;
(C3) the speaker conveys her beliefs confidently;
(C4) the speaker is not intentionally withholding the alternative account.

Dogma is defined in relation to discourse rather than a specific claim because it concerns as much what is not said as what is said. C1 requires both that the speaker could reasonably have been expected to be aware of an alternative account and that the alternative account is a sound one. How reasonable it is to expect someone to be aware of an alternative account is very much dependent on context. A climate change denier cannot plead ignorance of the theory of global warming, but there are many contexts where alternative accounts are less readily available. Furthermore, if we are presenting, as in climate change, a very strong argument with a very strong consensus behind it, we cannot be expected to take account of deniers' views (unless this is part of a debate). C2 requires the dogmatic speaker to *disregard* the alternative account. If sound reasons are given for rejecting the alternative account, the speaker has not disregarded that account but has addressed it directly. C3 requires the speaker to be confident. We can explicitly suggest, speculate, wonder, guess, venture, and so on without being dogmatic. In ordinary usage, "dogmatic," when applied to statements and opinions, means "forcibly asserted as if authoritative and unchallengeable" (CED 2003). This forceful expression condition will be more evident when we come to the "stronger" forms of dogma: distortion and bullshit. Dogma without linguistic distortion or bullshit is similar to withholding in that it is not so much identifiable from what is manifested linguistically as from what is not there but should be (though I shall indicate linguistic cues to such absence in the following). Finally, if the speaker is intentionally withholding the alternative account (C4), then we have a case of strategically insincere withholding rather than pathological dogma.

Three discursive symptoms indicative of a discourse pathology of *dogma* (without explicit distortion or bullshit) are *confirmatory selection, rude dismissal,* and *normalization.*

6.3.2. Confirmatory Selection and the Filter Bubble

Confirmatory selection is a discursive symptom of dogma in which the information presented and positively evaluated exclusively confirms one's preexisting beliefs while ignoring or dismissing disconfirming information. Confirmatory selection is the discursive manifestation of the cognitive confirmation bias, or the tendency to select and evaluate evidence in such a way that it will confirm our preconceptions (Oswald and Grosjean 2004). The effect of confirmation bias was demonstrated in a seminal experiment in which groups for and against capital punishment were asked to read two studies, one on each side of the argument. As expected, the informants rated the study confirming their own view more highly but, unexpectedly, they became *more* convinced of that view, rather than less so, after reading the study supporting the opposing view, thus increasing polarization (Lord et al. 1979). What the researchers did not consider in this case is whether the informants were reacting emotively not only to a "hot button" subject, but also to being subjected to a view they would not normally allow themselves to encounter. Indeed, this is the real danger with confirmation bias: not so much that we preferentially select and favorably evaluate confirmatory information but that we *avoid* conflicting views. So, with confirmatory selection, sound alternative views are clearly available to select (C1), but they are cognitively disregarded during the selection phase of the speech process (C2), and the ensuing polarization is likely to lead to more strident claims (C3). However, the speaker is not intentionally withholding the ignored information (C4).

Many other well-established cognitive biases (Kahneman et al. 1982; Gilovich et al. 2002; Kahneman 2013) can contribute to the discursive symptom of confirmatory selection, such as fundamental attribution error (overemphasizing the role of dispositional factors in others' behavior but situational factors in our own), and focusing and framing effects (focusing too much on one aspect of the information at the expense of others, and interpreting the same information differently according to how it is framed). Bias, or a tendency to lean toward a particular perspective, is often understood agentively, particularly in media studies, as a blind refusal to consider the possible merits of alternative views or, worse, as a deliberate distortion of the facts. But the cognitive biases are "forms of interpretation processing that take place more or less unintentionally" (Oswald and Grosjean 2004: 79), even if they act as a hurdle in working toward an epistemically responsible attitude. Indeed, rather than being deliberately deceptive strategies, we need to go to a considerable effort to *overcome* these natural biases.

The danger of confirmatory selection has grown with the rise of Internet search engines that predict what we want to read and view. Pariser (2011: 9) argues that predictive search engines, which learn what we like and give us more of the same, end up creating for us our own little personalized world of information. This results in an insidious form of bias called the "filter bubble," which radically affects the way we encounter information:

> Because you haven't chosen the criteria by which sites filter information in and out, it's easy to imagine that the information that comes through a filter bubble is unbiased, objective, true. But it's not. In fact, from within the bubble, it's nearly impossible to see how biased it is. (Pariser 2011: 10)

Filter bubbles effectively guarantee confirmatory selection. In so doing, they also potentially create an issue for our first two conditions for dogma, since if "it's nearly impossible to see how biased" information is in a bubble, one could argue that alternative accounts are *not* available to the speaker (C1) and so cannot be disregarded (C2). However, alternative accounts are always potentially available on the Internet if the user is willing to look for them and, as with the law, we might say that ignorance is no excuse for epistemic irresponsibility. Nevertheless, we have a situation where both subconscious cognitive biases and hidden software algorithms can lead to speakers being unaware of how biased their discourse world is and, consequently, how biased their discursive production is too. This is why we are dealing with pathological rather than insincere dogma.

6.3.3. Rude Dismissal and the Echo Chamber Effect

Rude dismissal is a discursive symptom of dogma in which others' beliefs, or correction and critique of one's own beliefs, are dismissed arbitrarily rather than through reasoned argumentation. Uncomfortable with our beliefs being challenged, we emotionally switch the direction of fit of mind and world so that they are no longer open to challenge. "Rude" is intended here in the "coarse, unconsidered" sense ("a rude awakening") rather than the "uncivil" sense ("rude behavior"), though rude dismissal is also often uncivil. Rude dismissal can occur in the form of *ad hominem* (or *ad feminam*) attacks on the capacity ("what would you know?"), disingenuity ("so naïve!"), or identity ("racist!" "snowflake!") of the critical other. The beliefs or critique can also be *dismissed out of hand* ("nonsense," "bullshit," "lies") or through *pejorative* (in context) *idea-packaging labels*: "fascist," "Marxist," "sexist," "transphobic," "anti-American," "essentialist," "relativist," "Islamophobic," "alt-right," etc. Another type of rude dismissal of critique is the *simple reversal*. When the mainstream media in the United States fact-check Trump's tweets and find clear evidence of false information, Trump responds by calling the mainstream media "fake news."[1] Rude dismissals, though, can be more subtle. On the website of the controversial lie-detection company Nemesysco, there is a section on research where the company promises:

> For the purpose of proper disclosure, we will provide below research that supports the technology as well those with negative findings (*those we believe were conducted in good faith*). (http://nemesysco.com/research-2)

Given their absence from the list, the two major peer-reviewed critical studies of "Layered Voice Analysis" (Damphousse et al. 2007; Eriksson and Lacerda 2007) were evidently considered not to have been conducted "in good faith."

Rude dismissal is facilitated by echo chambers. A media echo chamber is "a bounded enclosed media space that has the potential to both magnify the messages delivered within it and insulate them from rebuttal" (Jamieson and Cappella 2008: 76). In an acoustic echo chamber, sounds reverberate off the walls of an enclosed room. In a media echo chamber, ideas reverberate within an enclosed media space that effectively allows no access to alternative perspectives. Jamieson and Cappella use "echo" both literally to refer to direct citation between

---

[1] In Chapter 9 we shall see how the Russian government responded to accusations that they had poisoned Sergei Skripal with claims that the accusation was a "provocation" or even a false flag operation. However, this is part of a deliberate insincere campaign of disinformation.

the conservative media sources they are studying and figuratively to refer to the processes of mutual legitimization between the sources. With the rise of social media, particularly as a source of "alternative" news, and the effects of filter bubbles, the echo chamber effect has become even greater. Within these echo chambers, *rude dismissal* of alternative viewpoints goes completely unchecked. *Ad hominem* attacks, out-of-hand dismissals, and pejorative idea-packaging labels abound and are continually reinforced. When, as in the case of reader comments on articles, a stray alternative perspective is expressed, it is generally met with immediate rude dismissal.

As with filter bubbles, though, echo chambers create a potential problem for our definition of dogma. If echo chambers insulate ideas from rebuttal, it could be argued that alternative accounts are not available to the speaker (C1) and so cannot be disregarded (C2). However, echo chambers are never airtight. Nor are we forced to enter or remain within them. Sound alternative accounts are always available if we are willing to exit from our echo chambers, and so the choice to remain within them is effectively a choice to disregard those accounts. We may not be fully aware of what we are doing, and we are not deliberately blocking those accounts, but the net effect is to shut down open inquiry.

6.3.4. Normalization and Trump Talk

Normalization is a discursive symptom of dogma in which disputed information or debatable views are presented as if they were part of a societal common ground and thus beyond challenge. Normalization manifests linguistically particularly in forms like "normal," "obviously," "of course," and "common sense"; e.g., "*Of course* immigrants shouldn't be allowed in," or "*Obviously* we should have a referendum on capital punishment." The term *normalization* has been used in sociology to refer to the way society imposes strict norms that lead to some members of society, such as homosexuals and those suffering from mental illness, being considered deviant (e.g., Foucault 1977). In psychology it has been used to refer to the processes by means of which those suffering physical, mental, or emotional disability can become "normalized" and thus integrated into society (Wolfensberger and Tullman 1982). In the latter case, we are talking about deliberate processes designed to counteract societal prejudice, whereas in cases of *dogmatic normalization*, the normalizing language often stokes societal prejudices.

Trump's speech, for example, is permeated with normalizing language that stokes prejudice and effectively closes out alternative views. In "Trump Talk," it is "common sense" that immigrants should be persecuted, even if that "common sense" is in opposition to the law:

[*On radical Islam*] ... These warning signs were ignored because political correctness has replaced common sense in our society. (Campaign website, Aug 15, 2016)

[*On deporting illegal immigrants*] Sort of simple. It's amazing what common sense can do, isn't it? (Rally, Concord, NC, November 3, 2016)

[*On Muslim travel ban*] It's common sense. You know some things are law, and I'm all in favor of that. And some things are common sense. This is common sense. (Press Conference, Washington, DC, February 7, 2017)

And, in Trump Talk, "of course" Hillary Clinton was corrupt:

... of course she took the calls from her slimy friends. (Rally, Sacramento, CA, June 1, 2016)

Of course, the moderators didn't call her out and they didn't call out this lie she told. (Rally, Ambridge, PA, October 10, 2016)

She's got bad judgment of course (Rally, Roanoke, VA, September 24, 2016)

Normalization cues are effectively assumption markers: what they modify is treated as a foundational assumption that cannot be challenged. Accordingly, while a sound alternative to a Muslim travel ban (i.e., no ban) is available to the speaker (C1), there is no point in taking it into account because it challenges a foundational assumption ("it's common sense") (C2). Since the debatable belief is foundational, it can be conveyed quite stridently (C3). At the same time, the speaker probably believes that it *is* common sense and so the alternative belief is not being deliberately withheld (C4).

The net effect of normalization within an echo chamber is that already radical views with respect to a societal norm can seem "normal" so that, as with drug taking, one can cease to get the "effect" and so one becomes *more* radical and states even more strident views (Aiken 2016). When combined with confirmatory selection and rude dismissal, with filter bubbles and echo chambers, normalization can help promote and maintain a dogmatic attitude.

6.4. Distortion as the Misrepresentation of Evidence

A dogmatic attitude is likely to lead not only to the *suppression* of voice (in the form of the alternative account), but also to the *distortion* of voice in the account presented. In the case of *pathological distortion*, the speaker has unintentionally misrepresented a state of affairs because he has not made a sufficient investigative investment in establishing and/or conveying the facts. Where that investment is more or less absent, we have a case of *bullshit*. In the case of distortion falling short of bullshit, the speaker has made some effort to arrive at the truth but it is simply not sufficient for the contextual demands. After discussing and defining distortion in general (6.4.1), I consider a number of the discursive symptoms of this pathology: *overstatement* and *understatement* (6.4.2), *miscitation* and *misreport* (6.4.3), and general *distortion* of *detail* (6.4.4).

6.4.1. Irresponsible Distortion

Distortion, as a form of epistemically irresponsible discourse pathology, symbolically "twists against" (*dis+torquere*) what is known to be the case without contradicting it. Whereas lying gives us a clear picture of a false world, distortion gives us a disfigured picture of a true world. At one level, distortion, like omission, is an inevitable aspect of communication: everything is seen from an angle that will distort the view from another angle. For example, distortion in one's perception of the past occurs naturally as a consequence of the passage of time and the influence of the present: "Hindsight throws a retrospective shadow over people and events which distorts light and shade as they were actually perceived at the time" (BNC: Hennessy 1990, *Cabinet*). Distortion in one's perception of the present comes about through insufficient availability of evidence and, as seen with dogma, through natural reasoning biases (Kahneman et al. 1982). Predictions of the future will almost inevitably turn out to be distorted with hindsight bias (Taleb 2007). Moreover, in many contexts, a fuzzy picture is good enough; we cannot possibly be expected to have accurate knowledge of everything we talk about.

Distortion, as a discourse pathology, follows from a dogmatic attitude rather than a deliberate attempt to deceive. Since our cognitive biases lead us toward distortion, we are often not aware of our distorting the truth. In our psychologically biased perception, our opponents distort our ideas, our words, our meanings: we do not do the same with theirs. While Fowler defines "bias" as a "deliberate distortion for some ulterior motive" (1979: 12), if a distortion [+ false] is deliberate [+ belief] and made for an ulterior motive that surely must involve an attempt to manipulate hearer belief [+ intent], then it is a *deceptive lie* and concerns insincerity rather than epistemic irresponsibility. Similarly, if I know it takes three hours to drive to London from Cardiff and I say, "it won't take you more than an hour" because I want you to miss your plane, I am *willfully minimizing* rather than pathologically distorting. The fact that time and distance are gradable in this case is irrelevant. Again, if I have seen pictures comparing the crowds at the presidential inaugurations of Obama and Trump and have evidently realized that the former had a much larger attendance than the latter, it is not distortion but a deceptive lie to claim that Trump had the largest crowd ever at a presidential inauguration. To avoid such a lie, Trump's counselor Kellyanne Conway had to invent the term "alternative fact" (D'Ancona 2017: 13).

There are many shades of gray between an "accidental" distortion in the form of an innocent mistake and the "deliberate" distortion that we call a lie. However, given the psychological cline between the accidental and the deliberate, it is very difficult to judge willful insincerity in these cases of distortion. In the Internet age, for example, it can be challenging to judge the authenticity of a text since "acts and information are not located in a particular space or time and, because of the nature of bits, it is easy to alter content, making it more challenging to assess its origins and legitimacy" (boyd 2010: 53). In a sense, then, the judgment of pathological distortion often depends on a reverse Principle of Charity (Wilson 1959): instead of presuming that the speaker is being rational and therefore pursuing a deliberately insincere discourse strategy, we charitably presume that the speaker is being irrational, epistemically irresponsible, and thereby inadvertently producing pathological discourse in the form of distortion.

Given this context, I define *distortion* as follows:

Distortion
Discourse is pathologically distorted if:
(C1) it linguistically misrepresents the known evidence;
(C2) the degree of misrepresentation is not acceptable in the context;
(C3) the speaker is not intentionally lying or misleading or using hyperbole or meiosis.

C1 distinguishes distortion from dogma or withholding, both of which lack *linguistic* misrepresentation or misleading. C2 recognizes that there is *always* a degree of distortion when representing the world and that different contexts accept different degrees of distortion without them being considered in any way irresponsible. Austin (1962) gives the example of describing France as hexagonal. Clearly this is a gross geographical simplification, but it would not be considered a distortion in the context of teaching children. Similarly, a basic weather app might legitimately describe today as "sunny" because it predicts that there will be a 70% chance of sun at any one point in the day. We should not describe that prediction as distorted if the weather is overcast for part of the day. C3 excludes intentional insincerity and performed suspensions overtly flouting Grice's first maxim of Quality, which again must be intentional rather than pathological.

6.4.2. Distortion of Numbers: Overstatement and Understatement

Overstatement and *understatement* are discursive symptoms of pathological distortion in which either proportions or the interpretation of those proportions is greater than (*overstatement*) or lesser than (*understatement*) what is warranted from the known evidence. The terms "overstatement" and "understatement" are used by many theorists to indicate the *degree lying* tactics of *exaggerating* and *minimizing*, which were discussed in Chapter 5, but in the TRUST framework it is vital to distinguish insincere discursive tactics from irresponsible discursive symptoms. *Overstatement* and *understatement*, then, are reserved for the pathological discursive symptoms of an irresponsible approach to inquiry.

One of the principal ways in which dogma progresses to distortion is in interpreting the significance of numbers. Most non-scientists are relatively innumerate. This leaves us open to statistical manipulation by others and even to "statistical panic" (Woodward 2009). Woodward notes how a statistic can become a prospective future narrative, so that even when statistics are meant to be reassuring, they can have the opposite effect: "we feel that a certain statistic, which is in fact based on an aggregate and is only a measure of probability, actually represents our very future" (1999: 185). If we are told reassuringly by the airline industry that only two people have died from air turbulence in the last fifteen years, many will dwell on the conditions that might lead to such a fatality, rather than the extreme infrequency of the event (1999: 180). Furthermore, confirmation bias will lead us to select and convey statistics in a way that will support our existing beliefs.

The more strongly we hold to a belief, the more difficult it is to see epistemically irresponsible distortion in discourse. Clearly, for example, we would all agree that any level of sexual harassment between academics and students should not be tolerated and we might expect that, in this asymmetrical power relationship, many victims will feel too intimidated to report it. Nevertheless, right advocacy needs to be built on epistemically responsible foundations (Code 2013). In March 2017, *The Guardian* ran the following front-page headline and byline:

Sexual harassment "at epidemic levels" in UK universities
Exclusive: Almost 300 claims against staff have been made in six years, but victims and lawyers say those are just tip of iceberg. (Batty et al. 2017)

The reporters were epistemically responsible in establishing the empirical evidence, as they indicate in the news item:

Freedom of information (FoI) requests sent to 120 universities found that students made at least 169 such allegations against academic and non-academic staff from 2011–12 to 2016–17.

However, the way the newspaper conveyed that evidence in general ("300 claims," "169 allegations," "at epidemic levels") was grossly distorting. What the FoI statistics actually showed is that there were, on average per university, 1.4 allegations by students against academic and non-academic staff over a six-year period, or approximately 0.2 allegations per university per year. That is against a base annual university population in the United Kingdom of about 2.3 million students, 200,000 academic staff, and 200,000 non-academic staff (UUK 2018). It is evidently an *overstatement*, then, to describe such figures as an "epidemic."

Some on the political right might claim that the reporters were *willfully exaggerating*, but this does not sit well with the fact that the *Guardian* was very open in providing the full data set.[2] It is more likely that the reporters fell victim to a combination of a dogmatic approach and a classic cognitive bias. The reporters evidently invested a considerable amount of time and effort (by today's journalistic standards) into their investigation and they used the investigative reporter's favored tool of the Freedom of Information request to provide empirical data to support their points. All of this is epistemically responsible. Where the investigation most likely became irresponsible is that the journalists approached the issue with a dogmatic attitude: they set out, on the basis of the anecdotal evidence of lawyers and victims, not to *establish whether* but to *prove* that staff-student sexual harassment was a serious problem. Already predisposed to confirmatory selection of the FoI results, they then fell victim to the base rate fallacy, or the tendency to ignore base rates of the phenomenon and focus on specific cases (Baron 2007). Accordingly, they failed to see that the figures they were openly publishing showed very low levels of recorded harassment when compared to the base populations of students and staff. It would have been possible to retain justifiable advocacy while maintaining an epistemically responsible approach by declaring the results as surprisingly low, but then challenging their validity on the grounds of under-reporting due, for example, to intimidation or fear; in other words, to focus on the putative hidden iceberg rather than its confirmed meager tip. By grossly *overstating* the currently established level of the problem as an "epidemic," on the other hand, the reporters irresponsibly risked causing both statistical and moral panic among parents and students.

---

[2] *The Guardian* helpfully provided an interactive facility to search each university's figures and these confirmed that most universities had between 0 and 2 allegations over the six-year period.

6.4.3. Distortion of Words: Miscitation and Misreport

Miscitation and *misreport* are discursive symptoms of pathological distortion in which either a direct quote from a source is inaccurate (*miscitation*), or the indirect reporting of the source misrepresents what was actually said or written (*misreport*).

Miscitation generally occurs in writing and usually requires speech marks or some other graphic cue (e.g., indenting or speaker name followed by colon) to cue that the speech is being presented as direct rather than indirect. Some conventionally suspended oral genres, such as the performance of plays, the recital of poems, or the singing of songs, *prescribe* direct speech and so can also miscite. Innocent mondegreens such as the mishearing of "Scuse me while I kiss the sky," in Jimi Hendrix's *Purple Haze*, as "Scuse me while I kiss this guy," are technically miscitations even if they generally occur in suspended contexts. The misquoting of Rorty as saying that truth is "what your contemporaries let you get away with" (Blackburn 2005: 31; Dapía 2016: 28), discussed in Chapter 3, is a clearer example of irresponsible distortion through miscitation. It is always possible in these cases that the speaker is *insincerely* misciting to deliberately mislead the hearer about what was said. We might see such cases as a subtype of *taking words out of context*: the words actually cited are taken out of the context of what was literally said. If the words "miscited" are completely different from the original, then we have a case of *fabricating* rather than miscitation. Since direct citation involves not only repeating words but attributing them to a source, then *misattribution* can be seen as a subtype of *miscitation*. Thus, the "Hawthorne" epigraph at the beginning of Chapter 2 manifests both standard *miscitation* (the words are quoted inaccurately) and *misattribution* (Hawthorne is not the source).[3]

Misreport is a very broad category including all those cases where what someone said or wrote is misrepresented but there is no claim that the words are being quoted directly. Once again, we need to distinguish this discursive symptom of irresponsible distortion from insincere misleading. Many of the examples Galasiński (2000) presents of insincerely taking words out of context might more charitably be seen as, at worst, misreports. When a politician on a talk show reformulates an audience member's opinion "We have no right to *interfere* in Russian internal politics" as "We cannot *intervene*. It's not our direct responsibility" (Galasiński 2000: 49), he is not necessarily intentionally distorting what the audience member said. *Interfere* is a negatively evaluative term suggesting unfairly getting in someone's way, while a country may

---

[3] To complicate matters, I was being thoroughly insincere in this case because I was perfectly aware that both the quote and the attribution were false. This was (hopefully) a justified condonable suspension of the delayed sincerity "prank" kind.

intervene diplomatically to solve conflict between two parties. The reformulation might misreport the audience member's intentions, but it is not clear the politician is being insincere, at least with respect to this particular reformulation. In the "staff-on-student sexual harassment" case discussed earlier, the *Guardian* clearly misreported the FoI documentation. Furthermore, while "at epidemic levels" began as a citation (hopefully not a miscitation) attributed to a sexual harassment lawyer, over the following days it became first presupposed ("Calls for action by universities on 'epidemic' of harassment on campus"; Weale and Batty 2017, n.p.) and then fully reified as an established fact ("When will universities wake up to this epidemic of sexual harassment?"; Livingston 2017, n.p.). The original *Guardian* misreport of the FoI responses indicating "epidemic" levels of harassment was then unquestioningly reproduced across the global media as fact established through evidence, rather than as opinion. While the progressive readers of the original article, as indicated by below-the-line comments, were horrified at the level of statistical irresponsibility shown, I have only found one media article pointing out the serious statistical anomaly (Zushi 2017).

6.4.4. Distortion of Detail

Finally, *detail distortion* is a discursive symptom of pathological distortion in which a narrative, descriptive, or circumstantial detail misrepresents what is known to be the case without being a distortion of numbers or words. This is evidently a "basket" category to cover cases not covered by the preceding categories. It covers all those cases where the precise action (e.g., "she went to the Post Office and then the bank" rather than the opposite), the description (e.g., "she was carrying a Smith and Wesson" rather than a Beretta), or the circumstantial details (e.g., "it was raining" [it was sunny], "she wore a blue jacket" [it was green], "it was half past ten" [it was midday]) linguistically misrepresent the known evidence (C1) while the other two conditions of distortion are in place: the degree of misrepresentation is not acceptable in the context (C2), and the speaker is not intentionally lying or misleading or using hyperbole or meiosis (C3). Very often the care required to make the misrepresentation responsible rather than irresponsible is simply to convey the proposition with a much lesser degree of confidence (i.e., *hedge* it): "I'm not sure but . . . "; "it might have been . . . "; "this is just a guess . . . "; "the details are not clear yet but . . . "; "some reports are suggesting that . . . but these are currently unsubstantiated." Sometimes *detail distortion* can be insignificant in context, but it can be highly significant when, for example, the race or religion of a suspect is misidentified.

In all cases of distortion discussed in this section, the speaker recognizes the need to match what she says to the available evidence but she irresponsibly (if unwittingly) *distorts* that evidence. In the case of *bullshit*, on the other hand, the speaker disregards the need for evidential grounding altogether.

6.5. Bullshit as Disregarding Evidential Grounding

The chapter began with discussion of the hybrid insincere-irresponsible category of *bullshitting*. Here, on the other hand, I explore the pathological category of *bullshit*. First, I define *bullshit* formally (6.5.1) and then I consider three particular consistencies of pathological bullshit: gobbledygook (6.5.2), claptrap (6.5.3), and pseudo-poppycock (6.5.4).

6.5.1. Bullshit as Pathological Discourse

Bullshit was explained informally in Chapter 2 as *an evidentially worthless claim*. Its structural properties (De Waal 2006) can now be defined more formally as follows:

Bullshit
A proposition p is bullshit if and only if:
(C1) p has no grounding in the known evidence;
(C2) either evidence disproving p, or no evidence supporting p, is available to the speaker;
(C3) the speaker conveys the claim with undue epistemic confidence.

Consider the following calling of bullshit from a fictional character Ace from the fictional component of the British National Corpus:

"I'd say these carvings were at least fifteen million years old." His voice was uncharacteristically hushed. "Bullshit," Ace scoffed. "Even I know man hasn't been around that long." (BNC: McIntee 1993, *White Darkness*)

The proposition p is that the carvings are at least fifteen million years old. This has no grounding in known evidence (C1) because it is a scientific fact that *Homo sapiens* has "been around" for approximately 200,000 years. This correct aging is common knowledge and can easily be checked, and there is no evidence that the human race has existed for millions of years (C2). Finally, the speaker conveys the claim with undue epistemic confidence (C3): "I'd say" sounds more considered than "I think," and "at least" suggests that some form of calculation is taking place rather than a completely wild guess. Ace is therefore right to call out the bullshit.[4]

While *dogma* disregards alternative accounts, preventing us from seeing the full picture, and *distortion* warps the picture as in a carnival house of mirrors, with *bullshit* we get an alternative picture that does not belong to the world as we know it but, like "alternative facts" or Ace's carvings, belongs to some alternative parallel universe. Within our current world, though, bullshit is evidentially worthless. Distorted discourse can arise from irresponsible speculation rather than responsible inferencing. To speculate is to "conjecture without knowing the complete facts" (Collins 2013) and so arises from insufficient investigative investment. Bullshit, though, arises from something epistemically worse than speculation: an abandonment of any attempt to connect with reliable facts. Accordingly, just as lying is usually considered (though not always correctly) the most grievous form of insincerity, *bullshit* may be considered in many truth-warranting occasions as the most grievous form of epistemically irresponsible discourse. At the same time, bullshit, like bullshitting, can occur in epistemically suspended contexts. With *bullshit-from-a-bottle*, for example, comes a drug-induced suspension of disbelief generally occurring during playful suspensions:

> Any conference she'd been to, everyone wound up in her room long after midnight, playing poker and spouting Bacardi bullshit, wine-bottle wisdom. (BNC: Cooper 1991, *Jay Loves Lucy*)

Several different types of pathological bullshit can be identified depending on the way in which a speaker's claim is evidentially worthless. These may result either from intentional bullshitting or earnest belief, but the focus of pathological *bullshit* is on the discursive excrement itself, which has come about as a result of the speaker being epistemically irresponsible, whether or not he is aware of being so. The three proposed special consistencies of bullshit are:

Gobbledygook: worthless because semantically unintelligible;
Claptrap: worthless because rhetorically reckless;
Pseudo-Poppycock: worthless because framed as something it is not.

Gobbledygook and *claptrap* are rustic words already found in ordinary usage referring to similar phenomena to those intended here. *Pseudo-poppycock* is a neologism consisting in a similarly rustic term for "nonsense" combined with

---

[4] However, as this is fiction, it turns out that the carvings are evidence of an alien presence on Earth millions of years ago. Fiction frequently plays with our epistemic vigilance.

a prefix suggesting "faking." There is no suggestion that the specific meanings applied to these terms here match directly with ordinary usage. Indeed, many would see the words as synonyms to refer to "nonsense." I could have used or coined more obviously technical terms, but it seems appropriate to use coarse terms in everyday usage to refer to the very earthy concept of bullshit. I shall now briefly explore each of these proposed bullshit types.

6.5.2. Gobbledygook

Gobbledygook is a type of pathological bullshit that is evidentially worthless because it is semantically unintelligible. This most likely results from the speaker being recklessly careless in her use of words, with the result that the connection between word and world is lost. The term "gobbledygook" appears to have been coined by the congressman Maury Maverick, who speculated that, in coining the term, he might have been thinking of a turkey "gobbledygobbling and strutting with ridiculous pomposity" (1944: 11). Maverick defined gobbledygook as "talk or writing which is long, pompous, vague, involved, usually with Latinized words" (1944: 11). Accordingly, it was more similar to "jargon," "verbiage," "doubletalk" and "humbug" than "gibberish," which can refer to meaningless sounds produced through chronic medical disorders or temporary incapacities (Robertson and Shamsie 1959). Gobbledygook as understood here is produced by cognitively competent speakers who are being recklessly careless in their use of words. It is more than jargon-filled discourse; it is effectively meaningless. Just as turkey gobbling is no more than annoying noise for most human listeners, so gobbledygook presents a world of words signifying nothing or very little.

Gobbledygook can be defined more formally as follows:

Gobbledygook
An utterance is *gobbledygook* if and only if:
(C1) it is semantically incoherent;
(C2) its meaning cannot be clarified.

Regarding the semantic incoherence condition (C1), gobbledygook is generally syntactically correct while meaningless, as illustrated by the most famous piece of gobbledygook in linguistics: "Colorless green ideas sleep furiously." Chomsky's novel utterance is a performed suspension with respect to semantic responsibility, but as Steiner points out, "No safety-wire in the publicly available grammar stops us from talking nonsense correctly" (1998: 226). A test for semantic incoherence was proposed by Cohen (2002), who pointed out that if an utterance is incoherent, the meaning will not change if the polarity of the sentence is switched. For example, "Colorless green ideas *don't* sleep furiously" is equally as incoherent as the version with positive polarity, as are both polarity versions of the following: "Wholeness *quiets/does not quiet* infinite phenomena" (Pennycook et al. 2015: 549). Semantic incoherence is necessary but not sufficient for gobbledygook. A nervous speaker might garble what he is trying to say but subsequently clarify what he meant. Some academic writing may be conceptually complex (e.g., Einstein's account of relativity) or stylistically dense (e.g., Kant) and accordingly might appear incoherent to students, but it can be explained or clarified in simpler terms in introductory textbooks and lectures.

The second condition for gobbledygook, then, is that the meaning cannot be clarified (2). Cohen exquisitely describes this as "unclarifiable unclarity," or discourse "that is not only obscure but which cannot be rendered unobscure" (2002: 332–333). Any attempt to clarify unclarifiable discourse will not be recognizable as a version of the original. In his response to Cohen, Frankfurt noted that unclarifiability can be tested through translation (Frankfurt 2002). Lewis Carroll's *Jabberwocky*, for example, though conventionally defined as a "nonsense" poem, is arguably not entirely gobbledygook because it can be translated very carefully to convey its somewhat clarifiable meaning. On the other hand, when I once requested clarification from a distinguished Italian art critic whose article I was finding impossible to translate, he wrote back that I should just "translate the words and not worry about the meaning."

Gobbledygook corresponds to George Campbell's academic categories of *learned nonsense* ("to talk plausibly without any meaning") and profound nonsense ("the merest nothing, set off with an air of solemnity, as the result of very deep thought and sage reflection") (Duff 2009: 49).[5] It also corresponds to the *humbug* of Orwell, who lamented in the 1940s that "modern writing" "consists in gumming together long strips of words which have already been set in order by someone else, and making the results presentable by sheer humbug" (Orwell 1946: 259). Pathological gobbledygook is distinct from the deliberately insincere strategy of *obscurantism*, in which "the speaker [sets] up a game of verbal smoke and mirrors to suggest depth and insight where none exists" (Buekens and Boudry 2015: 126). The gobbledygook equivalent to obscurantism is perhaps what Pennycook et al. call "pseudo-profound bullshit," or "buzzwords randomly organized into statements with syntactic structure but no discernible meaning" such as "Wholeness quiets infinite phenomena" (mentioned earlier) or "Hidden meaning transforms unparalleled abstract beauty" (2015: 549). When asked to rate the profundity of statements randomly generated from two "new age bullshit" generators (http://wisdomofchopra.com/ and http://sebpearce.com/bullshit/), certain types of informants proved to be particularly susceptible to believing such *pseudo-profound gobbledygook*.

[5] I thank my colleague Mercedes Durham for pointing out this link.

Gobbledygook often occurs in epistemically suspended contexts. MathGen (http://thatsmathematics.com/mathgen/), for example, generates gobbledygook math papers by randomly stringing together prefabricated formulae. Hoax papers such as Sokal's "Transgressing the Boundaries," a piece of deliberate critical theoretical gobbledygook published in *Social Text* (Sokal 1996), or the famous Dr. Fox lecture in which an actor delivered a gobbledygook academic paper supposedly on game theory (Naftulin et al. 1973), are arguably condonable (if controversial) pranks. It is indubitably the case that some genres have greater demands for clarity than others and that this varies considerably across cultures, but a truthful writer will not produce gobbledygook except in a suspended context. Finally, gobbledygook can also be the discursive product of misleading through obfuscation (see Chapter 5), though it is often not easy to establish insincerity in such cases.

6.5.3. Claptrap

Claptrap is a type of bullshit that is evidentially worthless because it results from the speaker focusing purely on trying to please the audience rather than grounding her claims in evidence. The word *claptrap* is an eighteenth-century compound *clap+trap* and so etymologically means a type of discourse that traps the audience (perhaps inadvertently) into clapping. This is an ideal description of this type of bullshit (Frankfurt's main focus, but from an intentionalist perspective), which is distinguished by a reckless focus on the rhetorical goal of persuading an audience at the expense of veracity. The term "claptrap" has been used in the study of political speeches to mean the use of any rhetorical device likely to result in audience applause (Atkinson 1984), such as contrasts, three-part lists, naming, puzzle-solution, and so on (Bull 2016). However, while claptraps may help to persuade an audience (assuming there is a link between applause and attitude change), only cases where this is done while disregarding the evidence can be considered forms of bullshit.

Claptrap can be defined as follows:

Claptrap
An utterance is *claptrap* if and only if:
(C1) what is proposed is not grounded in evidence;
(C2) it is said primarily to persuade an audience.

When Michelle Obama delivered the following lines at the Democratic National Convention in 2008, she was certainly producing claptraps that aroused applause, but the speech also appeared genuine and heartfelt:

> Barack and I were raised with so many of the same values, that you work hard for what you want in life, that your word is your bond and you do what you say you're going to do. And Barack and I set out to build lives guided by these values, and pass them on to the next generation. Because we want our children—and all children in this nation—to know that the only limit to the height of your achievements is the reach of your dreams and your willingness to work for them. (NPR 2012)

When Melania Trump delivered virtually the same lines at the Republican National Convention in 2016 (Drabold 2016), it was claptrap bullshit because the lines had been plagiarized from Obama's speech by an unscrupulous speechwriter who evidently noted that the words themselves would arouse applause irrespective of the grounding in reality. In this case the speechwriter was actively and rhetorically bullshitting (as well as withholding through plagiarism). However, if Melania was not aware of the speechwriter's plagiarism, then she was not necessarily bullshitting herself, even if she was clearly producing claptrap bullshit.[6] As always with bullshit, it is irrelevant whether Melania Trump's parents really did happen to inspire her in exactly the same way as the Obamas' parents. What makes this bullshit is that the speechwriter lacks any evidential grounding for making this claim, and what makes it specifically claptrap is that she chose the words solely for their likely effect in arousing applause and gaining approval from the audience.

Frankfurt compares the product of rhetorical bullshitting (claptrap here) to counterfeit:

> What is wrong with a counterfeit is not what it is like, but how it was made. This points to a similar and fundamental aspect of the essential nature of bullshit: although it is produced without concern with the truth, it need not be false. The bullshitter is faking things. But this does not mean that he necessarily gets them wrong. (Frankfurt 2005: 48)

This reminds us again that epistemic responsibility involves the speaker's subjective relations with the world rather than the objective accuracy or reliability of her claims.

---

[6] There have been suggestions that Melania herself plagiarized the lines and the speechwriter "took the hit" for the sake of the campaign, in which case Melania would be guilty of insincere withholding (for the plagiarism) but not necessarily claptrap if she was simply finding more effective words for what she really believed.

6.5.4. Pseudo-Poppycock

Finally, the distinguishing feature of *pseudo-poppycock* is that the bullshitter places his work in an ill-fitting epistemic frame. Myth passed off as history is pseudo-poppycock, but so would be history passed off as myth. Fiction passed off as non-fiction is pseudo-poppycock, but so would be non-fiction passed off as fiction. The link between the substance of this bullshit and the term I am using to refer to it is not as straightforward as for the terms "gobbledygook" and "claptrap" (for which I am merely stipulating more precisely their analytical scope). "Poppycock" in ordinary usage simply means "nonsense." However, the word "poppycock" comes from Dutch dialect *pappekak*, "soft excrement" (CED 2003), and this captures both the excremental nature of this type of bull and the lack of a firm basis for epistemic grounding.

Pseudo-poppycock can be defined as follows:

Pseudo-Poppycock
A text is *pseudo-poppycock* if and only if:
(C1) it is in the style of an established discourse type;
(C2) the information conveyed is not appropriate for that discourse type.

Pseudo-poppycock manifests discursively, then, in a mismatch between expression (which superficially matches the discourse type) and content (which is wholly inappropriate). Specific subtypes of *pseudo-poppycock* can be named according to the field of discourse that is parasitically copied, e.g., "pseudo-historical poppycock," "pseudo-legal poppycock," and "pseudo-scientific poppycock."

One example of *pseudo-legal poppycock* is a Sovereign Citizen "legal" document. Sovereign citizens believe that the state and its institutions are fraudulent and that, as free citizens, they have the sovereign right not only to reject their institutional status in the form of birth certificates, social security numbers, and so on, but also that they have the free choice to decide not to pay taxes (Loeser 2015). However, they also believe, somewhat paradoxically, that they can achieve what they want through the existing legal system by drawing up their own "legal" documents. Sovereign Citizen documents, then, are presented in the form of existing legal documents, often mirroring formatting and attempting to imitate legal style (C1). However, the information conveyed through such documents bears no relation to established legal systems or principles, having more connection with ritual magic than legal discourse, and the documents have no legal legitimacy (C2) (Griffin forthcoming).

The most common type of pseudo-poppycock is *pseudoscientific poppycock*, in which the speaker adopts scientific language (C1) and claims scientific status for work that is not grounded in scientific method, reasoning, or understanding (C2). Astrology framed as entertainment in popular magazines is not pseudoscientific poppycock, but it is if astrologers claim to be scientific. Biblical myth is not pseudoscientific poppycock, but Intelligent Design, which purports to be scientific, is (Coyne 2009). If the speaker *knows* that her scientific claims are false, then she is being willfully insincere and we probably have a case of fabrication. However, those who inadvertently produce pseudoscientific poppycock *believe* their bullshit, and there is probably a strong element of self-deception involved both on the part of the speaker and of the listener who is taken in by the poppycock. Pseudoscientific poppycock is very common in the world of lie-detection technologies.

I have now outlined a number of discourse pathologies and their associated sub-pathologies or discursive symptoms, but I have not yet tackled the question of their ethical value in situated discourse.

6.6. Epistemic Negligence

Epistemic irresponsibility becomes ethically salient when the speaker's discursive behavior can be described as "negligent" (6.6.1). I propose three conditions for describing a proposition or text as epistemically negligent: the speaker has a duty of epistemic care (6.6.2); he fails to investigate sufficiently in accordance with that duty (6.6.3); and the speaker fails to hedge his commitment to his claim (6.6.4).

6.6.1. Suspension, Intellectual Vice, and Negligence

We are frequently epistemically irresponsible in contexts where we have not suspended our commitment to truthfulness but where we would not tend to see the irresponsibility as having an ethical value. Intellectual vices (Cassam 2019) such as epistemic irresponsibility do not lead to good reasoning or good decision-making but, in and of themselves, they are not unethical: we all make irresponsible mistakes when describing the world and it would hold us to too high account not to expect us to make them. For example, the aria *Pietá Signore* is traditionally attributed to the Baroque composer Alessandro Stradella (1639–1682) even though musicologists have long known that the piece was actually most likely composed in the 1830s by the Belgian composer Francois-Joseph Fétis, who falsely claimed that he held Stradella's original score (Glenn Paton

1991). However, it would seem churlish to hold to account (or even correct) a cello teacher waxing lyrical to her child pupil about the genius of Stradella, who was "composing music 200 years ahead of his time." Similarly, it seems harsh to blame the would-be alien abductee or the Californian I once met who thought that New Zealand was a US state.

The speaker's epistemic irresponsibility goes beyond mere intellectual vice and becomes **epistemically negligent**, and thus morally blameworthy, under the following conditions:

Epistemic Negligence
(1) The speaker has a **duty of epistemic care**, either in her current professional or institutional **role** or with respect to another's **reputation**;
(2) The speaker **fails to investigate sufficiently** in accordance with her specific duty of epistemic care in the context; and
(3) The speaker **fails to hedge her commitment** to her claims in accordance with the available evidence.

Note that these conditions, as must be the case with ethics, relate to speaker behavior rather than characteristics of the pathological text, though in analysis they will be derived from the context (1 and 2) and the text (3). These conditions can now be teased out in a little more depth.

6.6.2. Duty of Epistemic Care

In considering a duty of epistemic care, we can begin with Hart's notion of "role responsibility" (Hart 1949). Hart argues that:

> [w]henever a person occupies a distinctive place or office in a social organization, to which specific duties are attached to provide for the welfare of others or to advance in some specific way the aims or purposes of the organization, he is properly said to be responsible for the performance of these duties, or for doing what is necessary to fulfil them. Such duties are a person's responsibilities. (Hart 2008: 212)

Hart gives the examples of a sea captain being responsible for the safety of his ship, parents being responsible for the upbringing of their children, and a sentry being responsible for alerting the guard at the enemy's approach, but role responsibilities can include any "'sphere of responsibility' requiring care and attention over a protracted period of time" (Hart 2008: 212–213). We can apply this notion of role responsibility to epistemic responsibility because many professional roles come with "prospective responsibilities" (Cane 2002: 31) regarding truthfully accurate discourse: doctors, politicians, journalists, scientists, academics, teachers, and even lawyers all have a **duty of epistemic care** that goes with their professional role. Furthermore, if they fail in that duty they can be said to have *retrospective responsibility* (i.e., they can be blamed) for that failure (Moore 1998; Pettit 2001) and we can thus say that they have been **epistemically negligent**. For example, if I tell my Linguistics 101 class that "phonetics and phonology are more or less the same thing," I am not just making a careless mistake or even just being epistemically irresponsible, but I am being epistemically negligent because my students trust that I know what I am talking about and will depend on that knowledge (to some extent) in their studies. If, on the other hand, I drop a casual remark during the lecture that "*La La Land* won the Oscar for Best Picture last night" (it was actually *Moonlight* in 2017), I am simply making a careless mistake that is likely to be picked up almost instantly by students tapping away at their iPhones. But when Warren Beatty and Faye Dunaway performatively declared at the 2017 Academy Awards that *La La Land* had won the Best Picture award, the organizers who gave them the wrong card were being epistemically negligent: there was a clear breach of trust with respect to the huge audience and damaging emotional consequences for those who thought they had won (Smith 2017).

The duty of epistemic care is not restricted to professional or institutional roles. As individuals, we all have a duty of epistemic care to respect others' reputations. By this I mean that we all have a responsibility not to publicly disseminate inaccurate information that can potentially damage the reputation of others. I am thinking here, for example, of Internet trolling: the posting of psychologically harmful messages about vulnerable subjects (Aiken 2016). Trolls do not have a *role* duty of epistemic care (unless they are also journalists) but, like all individuals, they do have a duty of epistemic care toward the *reputation* of others. Reputation might be seen as the public aspect of Goffman's concept of *face* (Goffman 1955). While *face* is a positive self-image, a social mask that the individual privately tries to keep in place in public performances and that others support through politeness, *reputation* is the esteem in which a person is actually held by others. As recognized by defamation law (Price et al. 2009), reputation can be seriously damaged by the dissemination of deliberate falsehoods. Importantly for the argument in this chapter, legal defamation does not require intent. According to US law (Sack 2017), libel requires that a statement was false, that it was made without adequate research into its truth (effectively the second condition of epistemic negligence), and that it caused harm. Intention affects the perceived gravity of the offense and the expected remedy. For example, in English law, "unintentional defamation" can often be remedied with a sincere apology (Price et al. 2009).

EPISTEMICALLY IRRESPONSIBLE DISCOURSE PATHOLOGIES   205

While it is important to note the link between reputation and legal defamation, the duty of epistemic care toward another's reputation, in the TRUST framework, is a *moral* rather than a legal one. This is important because the regulation of defamation is in tension with freedom of speech. Article 10 of the European Convention on Human Rights, for example, opens with the general principle that "[e]veryone has the right to freedom of expression" but then notes "duties and responsibilities" connected with that freedom, including "the protection of the reputation or the rights of others" (http://www.hri.org/docs/ECHR50.html#C.Art10) (Rainey et al. 2017). Unfortunately, strict defamation laws, as existed for example in the United Kingdom before 2014, can have a "chilling effect" on free speech (Schauer 1978). In other words, they seriously discourage publishers from exercising their legitimate right to free speech for fear of being sued at great expense. This made it difficult, for example, for the academic community in pre-2014 UK to criticize pseudoscientific methods such as alternative medical treatments (Singh and Ernst 2008) and voice analysis for lie detection (Eriksson and Lacerda 2007). Although authors were speaking scientific truth to commercial power, publishers self-censored for fear of going bankrupt.[7] Analysts need to be cautious, then, when applying the "reputation" sub-condition of duty of epistemic care.

From an analytical perspective, the duty of epistemic care is established by the general discursive context. It may lie in the established institutional role of the speaker (journalist, politician, academic, parent) but may also be claimed by the speaker in interaction ("trust me on this, I know what I'm talking about") or invoked by making an attack on the hearer or a third party.

6.6.3. Failure to Investigate Sufficiently

Given a duty of epistemic care, the speaker is obliged to make a sufficient investment in establishing the facts. One cannot seriously distort the facts and then claim the epistemic negligence was unintentional, for even if one really did not intend to distort the facts, the fact that one actually did so demonstrates that one did not invest sufficiently in pursuing the truth in the first place. The lack of intentionality, as in unintentional defamation, might mitigate the wrong but it does not absolve it. When British columnist Katie Hopkins insinuated in a tweet that anti-austerity campaigner Jack Monroe (who is from a military family) approved the defacement of a war

---

[7] For example, the Eriksson and Lacerda article was retracted by Equinox while the author and broadcaster Simon Singh was forced to crowdfund to the tune of £200,000 to defend a libel claim by the British Chiropractic Association.

memorial—"Scrawled on any memorials recently? Vandalised the memory of those who fought for your freedom? Grandma got any more medals?"—the fact that she indisputably confused Monroe with another female journalist did not absolve her of responsibility for the attack on Monroe's reputation, as was recognized in Monroe's successful libel action (Kennedy 2017). Hopkins was being epistemically negligent in not establishing that she had the right target of attack in the first place.

The issue of how we can ascribe culpability to those who unintentionally produce discourse pathologies will be taken up in Chapter 7. For the moment it is sufficient to recognize that we do not ascribe ethical value to the discourse pathologies themselves but to the processes that lead to them. The ethical value of epistemic negligence lies in the *insufficient investment* that is made in *investigating* and *conveying* the facts while maintaining a *duty of epistemic care*. If I know my visitor will miss her plane if I give her a grossly inaccurate estimate of the time it will take to get to the airport, it is negligent of me as a host and local "expert" to base that estimate on a very vague idea I have gleaned from talking to others. If I know that my country will go to war if I give Parliament a grossly inaccurate estimate of the likelihood of Iraq having weapons of mass destruction, it is negligent of me as prime minister to base that estimate on unreliable evidence.

Analytically, this condition will be established by the co-text (the previous and subsequent discourse) and the intertexts (other discourse related to the case). What constitutes "sufficient" investment will depend on the context, the availability of evidence, and the gravity of the potential consequences.

6.6.4. Failure to Hedge One's Commitment

While having a duty of epistemic care increases responsibility, it is very often not possible to invest sufficiently to arrive at a confident assertion, either because the evidence is simply not available or it is not possible to access the evidence in the time available. In this case, the speaker may *hedge*, i.e., conversationally mitigate (Fraser 1980), her epistemic commitment to her claim in accordance with the available evidence (Kalenböck et al. 2010). Warren Beatty, for example, tried to non-verbally hedge his false Best Film announcement, first by hesitating at length and then by passing the award card to Dunaway. Notably, while Beatty was merely the animator (the sound box) of the award announcement, he still felt a strong need subsequently to justify his mistake to the audience.

Failure to hedge one's commitment is a very important condition from a discourse analytical perspective as it is the only one that depends entirely on an analysis of the discourse itself. The speaker's assessment of the evidence for her statement is conveyed through various forms of evidentiality (Jakobson 1957; Aikhenvald 2004): epistemic modals (*may, might*) and adverbs (*possibly, probably*), performative prefixes (*I guess, I suppose*), tone of voice (Kissine 2013: 93), and clausal evidentiality hedges such as "I don't know" (Weatherall 2011), "as far as I know/can tell," "as I understand it," "if I'm not mistaken," "I may be wrong but," "speaking conservatively," "my best guess is," and so on (Fox 2001; Bednarek 2006). Epistemic modals and adverbs decrease the degree of certainty of the claim (Marsili 2019), while clausal evidentiality hedges "avoid potential charges of carelessness or irresponsibility by not allowing the hearer to under- or overevaluate the evidence supporting the hedged assertion" (Sweetser 1987: 56).

In conditions of epistemic uncertainty, it is clearly irresponsible for a speaker with a duty of epistemic care not to hedge her assertion to show a lack of confidence in her claim. For example, in the case of the staff-on-student sexual harassment "epidemic," the reporters had a role duty of epistemic care but they failed to hedge their claims sufficiently in accordance with the available evidence, which showed anything but epidemic levels of harassment. Trump's use of evidentials such as "of course" or "it's common sense" similarly give a completely wrong assessment of the evidence.

6.7. Summary of Irresponsible Discourse Pathologies and a Sample Analysis

In this final substantive section, I summarize the epistemically irresponsible discourse pathologies (6.7.1) and apply the Irresponsibility framework to a Fox News tweet about a terrorist attack (6.7.2).

6.7.1. Summary of Irresponsible Discourse Pathologies

The main epistemically irresponsible discourse pathologies (dogma, distortion, bullshit) are set out in Table 6.1. The second column indicates some discursive types or symptoms of these pathologies, as discussed earlier. The third column suggests some cues the discourse analyst should look out for when considering these types. These are not intended to be exhaustive and I would hope they can be added to.

208 THE TRUST FRAMEWORK

Table 6.1 Epistemically Irresponsible Discourse Pathologies

Pathologies	Discursive Types/ Symptoms	Analytical Cues
Dogma (– distortion)	Confirmatory selection	One-sided discourse
	Rude dismissal	*Ad hominem* attacks Out-of-hand dismissal Pejorative idea-packaging labels Simple reversal
	Normalization	Normalizing lexis (e.g., "normal," "obviously," "of course," "common sense")
Distortion (– bullshit)	Overstatement Understatement	Statistical anomalies Epistemic boosters/minimizers (e.g., "incredibly," "epidemic," "not a bit," etc.)
	Miscitation Misreport	Comparison with original source
	Detail distortion	Comparison with original source
Bullshit	Gobbledygook	Semantic incoherence (Polarity Test) Unclarifiability (Translation Test)
	Claptrap	Empty rhetoric
	Pseudo-poppycock	Content-expression mismatch

6.7.2. A Sample Analysis

The categories outlined earlier, along with the negligence conditions discussed in the previous section, can be put to work in a brief sample analysis of epistemic irresponsibility in the media. In January 2017, Fox News tweeted the following identification of a suspect in the Quebec mosque terrorist attack (BBC 2017).

Suspect in Quebec mosque terror attack was of Moroccan origin, reports show fxn.ws/2k9is8W

The putative untruthful proposition here is:

>Reports show that the suspect in the Quebec mosque terror attack was of Moroccan origin<

There are some truthful presuppositions in the headline assertion: there was indeed an attack in Quebec; it was of a terrorist nature; it was an attack on a mosque; and there was a single suspect. However, the terrorist, far from being of "Moroccan origin," was a French-Canadian university student, and Canada asked Fox News to remove the tweet long before they actually did (BBC 2017).

The tweet is not a mere mistake but is epistemically irresponsible. Fox was clearly being *dogmatic* because, in succumbing to its prejudices, it produced a *confirmatory selection* of clearly unreliable reports. Furthermore, Fox's failure to remove or correct the tweet when it received authoritative information from the Canadian prime minister and the police that it was wrong is evidence of a *rude dismissal* of counter-evidence. The tweet is a clear example of *distortion*. We do not know if the distortion results from a *misreport* of the mentioned "reports" or whether the reports themselves were wrong. There is, however, very significant *detail distortion* in the identification of the suspect as an African Muslim rather than a white Canadian. Finally, this is arguably a case of *bullshit* since the tweet claims that "reports show" but Fox has produced no evidence for any reliable source for its claim. It is probably claptrap bullshit arising from a desire to appeal to Fox's audience.

The tweet also amply fulfills the conditions for epistemic negligence. First, as a mainstream news organization, Fox News has an extremely strong *duty of epistemic care* and it has the universal duty of care to respect the *reputation* of minority groups. Second, its *investigation of the evidence* falls well short of the expectations one might have of a mainstream news organization: there is no evidence that the news item was sourced carefully, and no evidence has been adduced of the putative "reports" showing Moroccan origins. Third, the claim is not hedged in accordance with the available evidence: "reports *show*" is categorical; "suggest" might have been more responsible, though still misleading, *if* there had been at least unreliable reports. Also, the position of "reports show" at the end of the sentence puts the focus on the straight assertion that the suspect was of Moroccan origin. Finally, there can be no justification for Fox to suspend its epistemic commitment in this case.

Demonstrating epistemic negligence does not preclude willful insincerity. *If* Fox knows the claim is not true, then it is a *deceptive lie*. If the putative "reports" are from unreliable sources (e.g., Facebook or Internet rumor) and the author of the tweet knows this, then this could be construed as *misleading* through *equivocation* since the reader is likely to presume that "reports" mentioned in mainstream media are to be understood in the sense of "reliable reports" rather than hearsay. If the original reports (if there are any) hedge the assertion (e.g., "it is possible that") and the author is aware of this, then this is also *misleading* since the author has *exaggerated* the likelihood. If the sources are known to be unreliable, then Fox is also guilty of *withholding* for failing to report the unreliable sources (e.g., "According to Facebook . . . "). However, while one can easily imagine plausible scenarios in which Fox is being willfully insincere, it is difficult to *prove* willful insincerity in this case. Calling out lying in such cases often says more about one's own epistemic partisanship than it does about the actual state of affairs. However, it *is* quite possible to prove epistemic negligence, and this should be considered a major ethical wrong for a media organization. *How* wrong will be explored in Chapter 7.

6.8. Conclusion

This chapter has necessarily been exploratory in nature since there is no tradition of systematically analyzing epistemic irresponsibility in an analogous fashion to an analysis of discursive insincerity (at least to the extent that insincerity overlaps with deception). I radically proposed analyzing dogma, distortion, and bullshit as discourse pathologies resulting from the intellectual vice of closed-mindedness (D2) and I explored a number of novel discursive types or "symptoms" of these main discourse pathologies. With these pathologies the ethics hinge not on willfulness but on the notion of epistemic negligence and its link with institutional and interpersonal trust (E2). Those who are epistemically negligent are most often not held *legally* responsible for their negligence, but I would argue that people are at least *morally* responsible for being dogmatic, distorting the truth, and talking bullshit while communicating under a duty of epistemic care.

7
Culpability and Breach of Trust

> *[C]ertain ways of acting or failing to act will open up the person who is an object of trust to a charge of betrayal. Where nothing will count as betrayal, nothing will count as trust.*
>
> —Hertzberg (2010: 200)

7.1. Introduction

This chapter completes the exposition of the TRUST framework by developing a sub-framework for analyzing moral culpability. Culpability has already entered the framework in terms of the concepts of *willfulness* and *negligence* (E2). Chapter 5 argued that insincere speakers are morally culpable if their act of insincerity is *willful*; i.e., it purposely and knowingly breaches trust without justification. Chapter 6 argued that epistemically irresponsible speakers are morally culpable if their irresponsible act is *negligent*; i.e., they were in a duty of epistemic care, they did not investigate sufficiently in proportion to their role, and they did not hedge their claims. What is still missing, though, is a way of assessing the *degree* of culpability once an untruthful act has been judged willful or negligent; in other words, a way of determining the extent to which the hearer, in Hertzberg's words quoted at the opening of this chapter, has been betrayed (E3). The chapter argues that this assessment of degree of culpability can be achieved in two ways: first, and mainly, through an assessment of the *gravity of the breach of trust* involved; and, second, through an assessment of the further *aggravating and mitigating factors* involved in the specific case.

I begin with the question, postponed from Chapter 6, of whether we can attribute blame to an epistemically irresponsible speaker who is not aware of being wrong (7.2). I then discuss, through an authentic example, why we need to take account of the degree of culpability and I suggest that we should do so through an analysis of communicative rather than strategic trust (7.3). Next, I outline my nine proposed dimensions for assessing the gravity of the breach of trust and thus degree of culpability (7.4). I then turn to the second means of assessing degree of culpability: an assessment of the further aggravating and mitigating factors involved in the case (7.5). Finally, I use the breach of trust dimensions and the aggravating/mitigating factors to reanalyze my initial example (7.6).

7.2. Culpability and Irresponsibility

Before proceeding to an analysis of the degree of culpability, it is necessary to return to the question of whether speakers who are being epistemically irresponsible can be considered morally accountable for their untruthful discourse. This is an important question in terms of the literature on moral responsibility. Just as the relativist and the radical social constructionist may doubt whether it is possible to ground an analysis of untruthfulness in empirical evidence, so traditional accounts of moral responsibility would preclude the possibility of blaming a speaker for a negligent remark (7.2.1). However, in discussing "culpable ignorance" (7.2.2), I argue that awareness is not a necessary condition of blame, and thus epistemic negligence can be construed as morally blameworthy.

7.2.1. Wrongness and Blameworthiness

Moral philosophers tend to make a distinction between the "objective" *wrongness* of an action and the agent's *blameworthiness* in performing it (Herman 1993; Khoury 2011). Thus, a doctor who performs a medical procedure that is considered standard at the time but is subsequently found to be extremely damaging to patients is said to be objectively wrong in carrying out the procedure but is not morally blameworthy in doing so because he could not have known better at the time. He is said to be *excused* from blame. However, as Chapters 1 and 2 demonstrated, there is no *objective* standard of truthfulness: truthfulness is always a subjective relation between mind, word, and world. If it is not known in medical circles that a certain procedure is dangerous, a doctor cannot be held morally responsible for saying that it is safe. It might be said that he is *justifiably ignorant*. He is factually wrong but not untruthful. If, on the other hand, it had become established in the medical literature that the procedure was unsafe, then if the doctor says that the procedure is safe, he is being epistemically negligent because he *should have known better*. This, however, is a controversial perspective within moral philosophy.

Philosophers have posited two necessary conditions for moral responsibility: a *control* condition and an *epistemic* condition (Rudy-Hiller 2018). When applied to speech behavior, the control condition requires that the utterance has been made *freely*: if a police interrogator coerces an innocent suspect into confessing to a crime he did not commit, one cannot hold the suspect morally responsible for being untruthful, since he lacked control over what he said due to the coercion. The epistemic condition, on the other hand, requires that the speaker is *aware* of what she is doing, that "the agent's epistemic or cognitive state was such that she can properly be held accountable for the action and its consequences" (Rudy-Hiller 2018: 1): if a politician is not aware that what he is saying is false, we cannot hold him morally culpable for lying. While the literature on moral responsibility has focused mostly on the control condition, it is the epistemic condition that is problematic for the assignment of culpability to the speaker who has been epistemically negligent. According to the account in Chapter 6, epistemically negligent speakers may be wholly unaware that what they have said is highly dogmatic, grossly distorted, or complete bullshit. Yet can we then hold a speaker morally culpable for saying something she is not aware is wrong?

7.2.2. Culpable Ignorance

Blaming an agent for an action or omission resulting from ignorance is called "culpable ignorance" (Smith 1983). The idea of culpable ignorance is not new. For example, while Aristotle mostly considered ignorance to be exculpatory, he also realized that careless ignorance, for example with respect to the law, could be blameworthy "on the grounds that it was up to them not to be ignorant, since they are in control of taking the appropriate care" (Bartlett and Collins 2011: III.5.30). Similarly, Descartes noted that in cases where

> I don't clearly and distinctly grasp what is true ... if I stumble onto the truth, I'm still blameworthy since the light of nature reveals that a perception of the understanding should always precede a decision of the will. (Descartes 1996: Meditation IV: 59–60)

However, given the centrality of the epistemic condition in contemporary accounts of moral responsibility, moral philosophers have gone to great lengths to establish some form of agent awareness while allowing for culpable ignorance.

Smith (1983) noted that culpable ignorance involves two separate acts: "an initial act, in which the agent fails to improve (or positively impairs) his cognitive position, and a subsequent act in which he does wrong because of his resulting ignorance" (1983: 547). She called the initial act a "benighting act," since it leads to the state of moral ignorance, and she noted that it could also be an omission. The subsequent act is the "unwitting wrongful act" that derives from the state of moral ignorance (1983: 547). In the case of epistemically irresponsible utterances, the benighting acts might involve omission of investigation or the reading of unreliable sources. The solution, then, is to defer moral responsibility to "an action or omission the consequence of which is lack of true belief about the impermissibility of one's conduct" (Rudy-Hiller 2018: 12). Thus, a politician's bullshit tweet might be morally accountable because it depended on the benighting act of reading and relying on unreliable sources such as conspiracy websites or social media, both of which will lead to a lack of true belief about the permissibility of emitting the bullshit tweet. The problem with this solution is that it leads to moral regress (Rosen 2004: 307). For the politician to be morally accountable for reading and relying on unreliable sources, she needs to be *aware* that doing so is wrong. If she is not aware of this, and this is the suspicion in postfactual populism, then we have to look upstream for a further benighting act in which the speaker knows that what she intends to do is wrong, that it is wrong in the current circumstances, and that she goes ahead and acts despite this knowledge. Philosophers have pointed out that there is the risk of interminable regress (Rosen 2004), but even finite regress places an enormous, and generally intractable, burden on the ethical discourse analyst. What is needed is some way of assigning "responsibility without awareness" (Sher 2009).

Fortunately, philosophers have recently begun to question the necessity of the link between awareness and accountability. In particular, it has been argued that culpable ignorance can be morally blameworthy if it is based on epistemic vices of which the speaker *should have been* aware (Montmarquet 1995, 1999; FitzPatrick 2008). For example, in responding to Zimmerman's (1997) claim that there can in fact be no culpable ignorance, Montmarquet notes that "a certain quality of *openness* to truth- and value-related considerations is expected of persons and that this expectation is *fundamental*" (1999: 845). FitzPatrick notes the corresponding effect of closed-mindedness on an individual, Potter:

> Perhaps Potter's complacency, self-indulgence, and arrogance have led him to dismiss competing views and arguments as naive and foolish, without adequate critical reflection on his own views, and he remains quite confident that he is in the right, just retaining and compounding his moral ignorance as time goes by. (2008: 605)

FitzPatrick argues that certain vices that lead one to act against one's better judgment (called *akrasia*) can in turn lead to culpability:

> It is enough for culpability if Potter made his epistemically debilitating choices—cavalierly dismissing opposing arguments, insulating himself from open, critical discussion or relevant sources of information, and so on—out of indulgence of vices, in a context where he could reasonably have been expected to know better and to do a better job of informing himself morally, given his capabilities and culturally available opportunities. (FitzPatrick 2008: 606)

FitzPatrick's consequent definition of culpable ignorance (CI) is one that fits well with the TRUST framework:

CI: Ignorance, whether circumstantial or normative, is culpable if the agent could reasonably have been expected to take measures that would have corrected or avoided it, given his or her capabilities and the opportunities provided by the social context, but failed to do so either due to akrasia or due to the culpable, nonakratic exercise of such vices as overconfidence, arrogance, dismissiveness, laziness, dogmatism, incuriosity, self-indulgence, contempt, and so on. (FitzPatrick 2008: 609)

The work of the moral philosophers Smith, Montmarquet, and FitzPatrick, then, provides a warrant for claiming that epistemic negligence can indeed be morally culpable.

7.3. Degree of Culpability: Gravity of Breach of Trust

Having established that both willful insincerity and epistemic negligence are morally culpable, it is now necessary to consider how one can roughly measure the *degree* of culpability involved. I begin with an authentic example showing why we need an analysis of degree (7.3.1). I then argue that we need to consider culpability in terms of communicative rather than strategic trust (7.3.2). Finally, I propose analyzing degree of culpability in terms of the gravity of the breach of trust (7.3.3).

7.3.1. The Need for an Analysis of Degree of Culpability

With respect to most of the examples of willfully insincere and epistemically negligent claims discussed so far, the speaker has been fairly evidently culpable. However, some examples are much less evident in terms of culpability. Consider the case of Intimidated Employee:

Intimidated Employee
A tough female boss strides up angrily to a young flustered female office trainee and demands: "Did you send that email I expressly told you not to forget? Because I've had an angry client on the phone saying that she hasn't received it." Feeling intimidated by the boss and afraid of not passing probation and thus losing her job, the trainee replies: "I thought I had already sent it. I'm sure I did."[1]

---

[1] I am grateful to my MA Research Experience student Anfal Almarshd for providing this personal example.

There is a clear "salty" assertion here (>I thought I had sent it<) and a clear statement of conviction (>I'm sure<). The trainee knows perfectly well that she has not sent it, so the assertion is clearly untruthful. In terms of suspensions, there is no conventional suspension since we are in a truth-warranting professional context and the trainee is not being ironic. It might be claimed that this is a self-protective consequential suspension on the grounds that she is potentially saving her job. However, for self-protection to be a justifiable suspension rather than a mitigating excuse for wrongdoing, the interlocutor must be behaving unethically; otherwise a murderer could use this excuse when lying to avoid capture. Yet an employer has a right to request, even order, an employee to do something that is within her expected professional role (sending an email certainly was, in this case). Nor is there a formally condonable suspension here.

Moving to the analysis of sincerity, the trainee has clearly withheld the truth that she did not send the email; she has done so through a misleading proposition ("I thought I had actually sent it"); and she has explicitly asserted ("I'm sure I did") what she does not actually believe, so is lying. Furthermore, given that she is aware of what she is doing, that she is breaching her employer's trust and that she is not justified in suspending her commitment to truthfulness, her insincerity is *willful* and thus morally culpable. At this point we do not need an analysis of epistemic responsibility, though clearly the assertion is false, the trainee has a certain duty of epistemic care, and she has expressed discursive overconfidence. Following the TRUST framework, we must conclude that this is a morally culpable deceptive lie.

At the same time, though, most of us would feel that the trainee is not worthy of particular moral condemnation: there is a breach of trust, but the gravity of that breach and the degree of culpability of the trainee are both quite low. A final component is needed then in our analysis of untruthfulness in situated discourse: an analysis of the *degree of culpability* of the willful or negligent untruthfulness. I propose (E3) that this should occur first through an analysis of the gravity of the breach of trust, by considering the conditions of interpersonal and/or institutional trust that hold in a given discursive context and, second, through assessment of other factors pertaining to the particular setting that might mitigate or aggravate the speaker's culpability in that particular speech situation.

7.3.2. Strategic and Communicative Trust

To accuse someone of breaching or betraying one's trust is to assign moral blame to them; it is to consider them morally culpable. However, we need to make a distinction between communicative and strategic trust in others. *Communicative trust* follows naturally from our mutual dependence, from the Cooperative

Principle, from the presumption of truthfulness. It precedes considerations of the trustworthiness of specific individuals and is "a continuation of the normal run of life" (Lagerspetz 2015: 70) in which "people are standardly trusted to do their part" (Williams 2002: 89). It is the type of trust that was discussed in Chapter 1 and is the background trust noted by Luhmann (1979). *Strategic trust*, on the other hand, involves conscious or semi-conscious decisions to trust others. Often called "cognitive trust" (Becker 1996), this has been the main focus of philosophical and psychological work on trust. Cognitive (i.e., strategic) trust "is a way of managing uncertainty in our dealings with others by representing those situations as risks" (Becker 1996: 45). It is often focused on the sorts of conditions that warrant investing trust in a speaker (McLeod 2015) and it is a highly rational, strategic, and sometimes game-theoretical approach to trust:

> Once we have beliefs and expectations about the trustworthiness of others, we can convert uncertainties about their behavior into an estimate of the risks of dealing with them. Then the theory of strategic choice can be wheeled securely into place—to discuss not only when it is rational to trust particular people in particular situations but also whether it is rational to be trusting in general. (Becker 1996: 45)

Linguists have also tended to focus on the warrants for investing trust and how those are negotiated in discourse (Candlin and Crichton 2013). However, while both communicative and strategic trust occur in everyday life, the focus in contemporary literature on strategic trust to the exclusion of communicative trust leads to a misfocus from our perspective here. First, it leads to a focus on the person who trusts (the trustor) rather than the person who is trusted (the trustee), but we are interested in evaluating the behavior of the person who is being dishonest (the object of trust) rather than the perception of the trustor. Second, strategic trust tends to lead to negative ethical evaluations of the trustor rather than the trustee. As Hertzberg (1988) points out, failures of trust tend to be put down to the misperception, even naïveté, of the trustor rather than to unethical behavior by the trustee. Thus, a history of untrustworthy behavior should lead us not to trust an individual. Yet the acts of trust we tend to consider most highly are those in which the trustor bestows trust against the odds, as when a foster parent trusts a child despite a history of delinquency or an employer takes on a worker with a criminal record. On the other hand, the fact that certain politicians continually spout bullshit might make them less trustworthy in our eyes, but it does not make their epistemic negligence, each time it occurs, any less unethical a breach of trust.[2]

---

[2] Indeed, I shall argue in the following that it is a further aggravating factor.

An example of the danger of focusing on strategic trust at the expense of communicative trust can be seen in Wakeham's (2017) explanation of his category of "Contextualized Bullshit" mentioned in the Introduction. Wakeham notes that certain professionals such as lawyers, politicians, and CEOs "have a reputation for being flexible with the truth" (2017: 31). He then goes on to say the following:

> While criticism often has a moralizing tone, people generally understand that these professions have powerful financial incentives and even professional obligations to lie, obfuscate, or otherwise avoid the truth. Because this caveat is widely understood, what a lawyer, politician, or CEO says typically gets bracketed off from the usual epistemic standards of honesty. In other words, culture provides people with a particular kind of epistemic framing as a way to deal with the typically questionable claims of such professions. Believing what a lawyer, politician, or CEO says not only represents a kind of epistemic naïveté but also amounts to a kind of cultural incompetence. (Wakeham 2017: 31)

While Wakeham begins by somewhat disparagingly noting the "moralizing tone" with which people criticize these professionals' dishonest speech, he goes on to suggest that "culture provides" us with an "epistemic framing" of these speech events that leads to their being "bracketed off from the usual epistemic standards of honesty." Accordingly, if you believe a lie uttered by one of these professionals, the fault lies not with the dishonest professional but with your own lack of epistemic vigilance, your own "epistemic naïveté," or even your "cultural incompetence."

There are two serious problems with accounts of this sort.[3] First, they seem to imply that our "culture" tolerates professional dishonesty. Yet this is not at all the case. Professional and institutional dishonesty are considered a major cause of concern in contemporary society (O'Neill 2002) and populist parties all over the world are gaining power partly on the back of claims that they will "clean things up" or "drain the swamp." Furthermore, far from having a professional obligation to lie, efforts are made to deal with the problem: all these professions have internal codes of conduct prohibiting dishonesty and many are regulated externally against dishonesty. We feel that we *should* be able to trust them at least not to lie or overtly bullshit, even if they are constantly betraying our trust. We do not "bracket off" what these professionals say "from the usual epistemic standards of honesty" in the way that we do with banter, bull sessions, or other harmless contexts of bullshit. We know that these professionals are speaking in truth-warranting contexts and we feel perfectly justified in holding them to account

---

[3] My intent here is not to critique Wakeham's work as such, but the type of approach to untruthfulness that this article on bullshit represents.

when they are called out for dishonesty. And some *are* held to account and lose their jobs and/or their reputations accordingly.

Second, this type of approach to untruthfulness assumes a form of cultural essentialism in which everyone in a culture *should* think and react in the same way. Yet there is extreme variation in any culture. There are the "savvy" citizens who do not fall for politicians' weasel words, but also large parts of the population that are still vulnerable to them. Effectively blaming the voter for believing the politician, or the juror for believing the trial lawyer, or the shareholder for believing the CEO is like blaming the phishing victim for not detecting the linguistic cues to deception in the email that duped him. Similarly, in countries where levels of political corruption are particularly high, citizens might *expect* a politician to be corrupt, but this does not mean they *accept* that politician being corrupt.[4] Dishonest politicians, lawyers, and CEOs are suffered, not sanctioned, in society; they are not simply accepted as "part of the culture."

The focus on strategic trust leads to a sense that we enter situations of trust with a "cautious reliance" (Baier 1986) and an awareness of risk. However, as Lagerspetz (2015: 56) notes, caution and a sense of risk would tend to suggest an attitude of suspicion rather than trust, and "given the kinds of relations in which trust has a place, suspicion in the absence of positive grounds would strike us as pathological" (Hertzberg 1988: 13). Rather than trust being a marked situation we "enter into," it is the *breach* of trust that stands out as significant. This was demonstrated at a routine level by Garfinkel, who investigated the social effects of breaching the "constitutive expectancies" of "normal" communication by getting his students to clarify, for example, the sense of commonsense remarks ("I had a flat tire." "What do you mean you had a flat tire?") or to address a customer as if he were a salesperson or waiter (1963: 380–384). The effects of breaching trust in normal conversational cooperation often led to social anomie or plain annoyance in the victim. And these were very minor breaches. Rather than trust being a communicational tool we can wield at will, then, we find ourselves *in* relations of trust. In such relations, as indicated in the epigraph, failing to act in ways we are trusted to act will open us up to a "charge of betrayal" (Hertzberg 2010: 200). On the other hand, whether or not the trusting party actually trusts is immaterial since it is "the fact of dependence that generates the demand to be trustworthy" (Faulkner 2014a: 341). Or, as Løgstrup notes, "in trust or in mistrust the other person's life has to a greater or lesser degree been delivered into our hands" (1997: 110).

---

[4] I have personal experience of this, having lived in Italy before and during the Mani Pulite ("Clean Hands") corruption investigations in the 1990s.

7.3.3. Gravity of Breach of Trust

How can we measure the gravity of a breach of trust? In law, gravity is the seriousness of an offense or harm "as judged from an objective, legal standpoint" (Garner 2009). Murder is objectively graver than manslaughter, and grievous bodily harm is objectively graver than actual bodily harm. This legally objective difference leads to mandatory differences in length of sentence depending on the gravity of the offense. Gravity is generally determined by the set of aggravating and mitigating circumstances pertinent to the case:

> The premise underlying gravity is that the existence of a factor which makes the offence a graver example of its genus is aggravating, while any fact that diminishes gravity ought to mitigate from the proportionate response. (Manson 2011: 43)

There has been relatively little theoretical discussion of the concepts of aggravation and mitigation (Ashworth 2010: 156), though sentencing guidelines always indicate the types of factors that might be considered aggravating or mitigating in a criminal case.

We have no equivalent guidelines, though, for judging the gravity of a case of unethical untruthfulness. However, having located the moral wrong in an unjustified breach of trust, what needs to be found is a way of assessing the extent of the betrayal in cases where trust is unjustifiably breached. In criminal law, gravity is generally measured by both the actual harm caused and "the level of harm that was intended or ought to have been reasonably foreseen" (Manson 2011: 43). Perceived harm is certainly relevant to breach of trust, but it is by no means the only or even the most important measure. Two other key elements are asymmetrical power relations and the vulnerability of the trustor. These two elements could combine to create "high trust" (strong asymmetry of institutional or epistemic power and high vulnerability of the trustor) or "low trust" (symmetrical power relations and low vulnerability) discursive contexts. However, this is a little too abstract to operationalize in the analysis of situated discourse and leaves out the important elements of perceived harm and reprehensibility of motive.

It is tempting to use the substantial research into the judgment of message deceitfulness as a proxy for degree of culpability. For example, a number of researchers have shown that violations of Grice's Quality and Relation maxims are perceived as more deceitful than violations of Quantity and Manner (e.g., McCornack et al. 1992; Yeung et al. 1999; Levine 2001; Levine et al. 2003). These findings might be seen to link with the perennial observation that lying (a Quality violation) is worse than misleading (often a Manner violation) or withholding (usually a Quantity violation). Perceptions of Quantity violations vary among individuals but tend to be judged as highly deceptive when the consequences are severe (Levine et al. 2013: 216). And, not surprisingly, untruthfulness with regard to important information is regarded as more deceitful than untruthfulness with regard to trivial information (McCornack and Levine 1990). However, deceitfulness is not necessarily linked to breach of trust, let alone moral culpability. As Levine et al. point out, a dishonesty rating by an informant could indicate the informant's perception of message features, degree of confidence, or degree of lie importance:

> For example, if a message was rated as moderately deceptive, that moderate rating could reasonably mean that the rater thought the message contained a mixture of true and false information, that the rater was not sure if the message was deceptive or not, or that the rater thought that the message, although clearly deceptive, was, to some extent, either morally justified or innocuous. (Levine et al. 2003: 210)

In terms of culpability with respect to untruthfulness, we are only interested in the last of these factors: the extent to which the insincerity or irresponsibility was morally justified or not. Levine et al. (2003: 211) conclude that "it is reasonable to think in terms of gradations of information along multiple dimensions when describing deceptive messages." Degree of culpability with respect to breach of trust is also best seen along a series of dimensions. I now turn to these proposed dimensions.

7.4. Nine Dimensions for Analyzing Gravity of Breach of Trust

I set out in Table 7.1 nine dimensions that should be taken into consideration when making an ethical evaluation of the gravity of the breach of trust once willful insincerity or epistemic negligence has been established. It is proposed that high values on these dimensions represent more serious breaches of trust, and low values represent more minor breaches of trust.[5]

---

[5] These dimensions have been explored in a wide variety of different contexts with my Research Experience students at Cardiff University. It is indubitably the case, though, that the dimensions can be further refined.

222 THE TRUST FRAMEWORK

Table 7.1 Ethical Dimensions of Breaches of Trust

	Dimension	High → Serious Breach	Low → Minor Breach
1	Vulnerability of Trustor	E.g., irony addressed to low-intelligence hearer	E.g., pranks to other pranksters
2	Mutual Attachment	E.g., lying about infidelity to intimate	E.g., lying about infidelity in casual relationship
3	Infringement of Rights (of trustor or third party)	E.g., spreading lies about vulnerable social groups	E.g., misleading about powerful social groups
4	Epistemic Power of Speaker	E.g., expert witness being epistemically negligent at trial	E.g., irresponsible claim from declared non-expert
5	Institutional Power of Speaker	E.g., political leader being epistemically negligent	E.g., misleading by low-level institutional representative
6	Institutional Warranting of Truth	E.g., false claims made in Government publication	E.g., defendant misleading the court under cross-examination
7	Potential Harm of Breach	E.g., lying about safety where there is a known risk	E.g., bullshitting about safety where there is no known risk
8	Reprehensibility of Motive for Breach	E.g., privileging commercial gain over safety	E.g., privileging overcoming fear
9	Information Importance	E.g., withholding major source of income from tax return	E.g., withholding small gift from tax return

7.4.1. The Vulnerability and Rights of the Trustor/Third Party

A vulnerable trustor is both more likely to trust and is less able to defend themselves from betrayal and cope with the consequences of betrayal. I propose three dimensions relating to the vulnerability and rights of the trustor or third party:

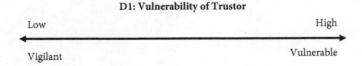

Trustors may be vulnerable because they are immature (e.g., a young child), cognitively impaired (e.g., low intelligence or autistic), emotionally traumatized (e.g., rape victim), or under the physical or psychological control of the trustee (e.g., captives or abused spouses). Under such conditions of vulnerability, the trustor is less likely than average to be able to process implicatures and frames, misleading words, and performed suspensions. Accordingly, when a cross-examiner in court uses irony with a young child witness, the jury are likely to take it up as a performed suspension that discredits the witness, but the child witness may simply take it as a lie and respond in a way that worsens her image before a jury. A vigilant interlocutor, on the other hand, can normally be expected to pick up such indirectness and ambiguity. Similarly, performing a prank on a confirmed prankster is an attenuated breach of trust because one would expect, also following the Golden Rule, that the prankster would be vigilant for people attempting to return his pranks, while performing a prank on someone who is very insecure about his identity would be an aggravated breach of trust.

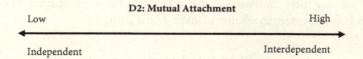

Two people in a strong emotional bond will lower their guard, become very trusting, and thus be mutually vulnerable. As Boon and Holmes put it:

> An appreciation of interdependence is critical to an understanding of interpersonal trust because the degree of interdependence between individuals determines the relevance of trust for the interaction between them: the greater the interdependence, the more crucial is the state of trust. (Boon and Holmes 2008: 191)

Accordingly, breaches of trust in interdependent relationships are likely to be heavier betrayals than in cases where the two parties are more independent. What is important here is the degree of mutual attachment or dependency rather than the institutional status of the relationship. Some married couples, for example, are highly interdependent, while others lead more independent lives with greater degrees of guardedness.

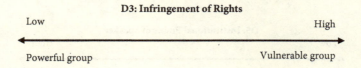

One generally thinks of relations of trust obtaining between individuals (interpersonal trust) or between institutions and the people those institutions serve (institutional trust). However, we should also be able to trust that our universal human rights will be respected. Members of some vulnerable social groupings (e.g., ethnic, sexual, and linguistic minorities), though, are more at risk of their rights being breached than others. In these cases, trust can be breached also by spreading untruthful assertions about these groups. Claiming that all Muslims are terrorists or all Mexican immigrants are criminals may lead to those groups' human rights not being respected and thus the general societal trust that one's human rights *will* be respected will be breached. Although one can infringe the rights of powerful groups in society ("all men are pigs," "you can't say that in your position of white privilege"), the infringements are less likely to lead to harmful consequences.

7.4.2. The Epistemic and Institutional Power of the Speaker

I next propose three dimensions relating to the status of the speaker. These are particularly important in relation to institutional trust.

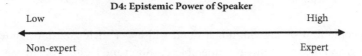

Knowledge is power, as Foucault (1980) argued, and significant asymmetries in that epistemic power can create vulnerabilities that lead to severe breaches. The role of the expert is particularly important here. Given the problem of discrimination, Socrates' old problem of how, lacking expert knowledge, we can distinguish an expert from a charlatan (Gentzler 1995), breaches of trust by experts can be very severe indeed. When the expert pediatrician Roy Meadow presented in several murder cases an extremely distorted statistic about the likelihood of two cases of sudden infant death syndrome in the same family, it may well have contributed to several tragic cases of miscarriage of justice (Colmez and Schneps 2013: 2–21). Jurors and judges blindly trusted Meadow because he was an extremely experienced expert doctor. What they failed to realize is that he was *not* an expert statistician and it was the statistics that he got horribly wrong.

The greater the institutional power of the speaker, the greater the breach of trust. There are at least four reasons for this. First, those in positions of power are able to exert their will over others and thus their interlocutors are put in a more vulnerable position. Second, people have a natural trust of authority (Milgram 1963) and many find it difficult to mistrust people in powerful positions. One of the main reasons for false confessions in the United States is that vulnerable suspects have trusted their police interrogator not to tell lies (Leo 2008). Third, with power comes responsibility and with responsibility comes blame if things go wrong. The moral buck stops with the leaders of companies and countries. Finally, breaches of trust by institutional leaders not only breach the interpersonal trust between leader and subjects, but also undermine people's trust in the institutions themselves. Trust in politicians and journalists in general has always been very low (Ipsos 2017). This must be because people's trust in the political and media institutions is low. Many of the examples in this book refer to political leaders, who tend to combine supreme institutional and epistemic (through access to security services) power. On the other hand, in cases where the speaker has very little institutional power, as in the work trainee in the case study described earlier, the breach will be considerably attenuated.

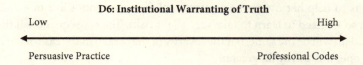

In many institutional contexts (e.g., the law, business, the media), there can be professional codes of conduct that heighten the warrant of truth and thus aggravate the breach of trust. Expert witnesses who lie breach trust to a far greater extent than defendants because the former are engaged as impartial experts while the latter are understood to be trying to avoid self-incrimination. Similarly, although witnesses take an oath, the highly adversarial nature of cross-examination means that there is lesser expectation of truth than in examination-in-chief.

7.4.3. Potential Harm, Reprehensibility of Motive, and Information Importance

The last three dimensions I propose concern the nature of the breach itself, rather than the status of the speaker or hearer.

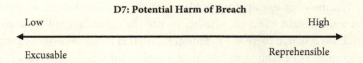

The key here is not the actual direct or indirect consequences of the untruthfulness, but the predictable *potential* harm of the breach of trust. If I tell customers it is safe to ride on a Ferris wheel when I have serious doubts about its current safety, this is an extremely severe breach of trust irrespective of whether or not an accident occurs. On the other hand, if I am trying to convince my timid daughter to ride on the wheel and I bullshit that there has never been an accident on a Ferris wheel, the fact that an accident then occurs does not worsen the severity of my breach of trust.

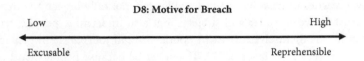

This is the ethical factor that was picked up in the Coleman and Kay (1981) study, and it is clearly very important. There are clear overlaps with dimension 4. My motive in telling customers that the faulty Ferris wheel is perfectly safe is that I am putting my earnings ahead of their safety, which is clearly reprehensible. My motive in telling my daughter that there has never been an accident on a Ferris wheel is to help her overcome an irrational fear: we cannot live in a risk-free world, so we need to learn to take very slight risks. The consequences if there is an accident will be the same, but the severity of the breach in the case of the Ferris wheel operator will be far greater.

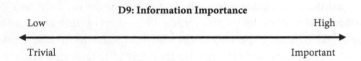

The importance of the message being conveyed is considered fundamental to perceptions of deceitfulness (McCornack and Levine 1990). Levine et al. note that

> We would expect evaluations of information importance and moral condemnation to be strongly and positively correlated. Generally, deceiving others about important information is more likely to result in moral condemnation. (Levine et al. 2003: 211)

In most cases, information importance will strongly correlate with potential harm. Withholding exculpatory evidence from the defense can be predicted to have a significant effect on whether or not the defendant will be convicted. However, even where there is a potential harm, this is not necessarily perceived by the speaker. For example, withholding a significant source of personal income from one's tax return might be construed as a significant breach of institutional trust, whereas withholding a small gift from the same return might be considered fairly trivial. Many tax evaders would consider their withholding as a tiny drop in the ocean of the treasury's finances and so might think that there is little, if any, potential harm arising from their deceit. They are, in fact, wrong because if everyone were to do the same, there would be a very significant harm to the economy. Nevertheless, it is perhaps useful to retain "information importance" as a separate dimension.

7.4.4. Weighting of Dimensions

The dimensions do not always hold the same weight, but it is very difficult to measure them in terms of gravity, particularly outside any specific context. Vulnerability of trustor might well be the most serious dimension. Potential harm and reprehensibility of motive are also clear candidates for seriousness in most contexts. But epistemic and institutional power and warranting can be particularly serious in the case of political or religious leaders. Furthermore, each context has particular sets of circumstances that can aggravate or mitigate the seriousness of the breach of trust beyond the specific breach itself.

7.5. Further Aggravating and Mitigating Circumstances

Given that unethical untruthfulness is so centrally concerned with trust, the primary determinant in assessing degree of culpability is the gravity of the breach of trust. High ratings on each of the preceding dimensions indicate aggravating circumstances. Low ratings on each of the dimensions indicate mitigating circumstances. However, cases can involve a further set of aggravating and mitigating circumstances that are not directly connected with these breach of trust dimensions. Some of these factors are briefly indicated in this section.

7.5.1. Further Aggravating Factors

As in criminal sentencing, **prior record** can be considered strongly aggravating. In contrast to those who claim that frequent breaches of trust lead to less reliance on the speaker and so, by implication, less blame (e.g., Wakeham 2017), habitual willful insincerity and epistemic negligence increase blameworthiness, just as previous convictions in criminal cases do. Certainly, if a speaker acquires a reputation for trustworthiness through being appropriately truthful and then abuses that trust on a given occasion, this might have more harmful effects than a single act of untruthfulness by a recognized untrustworthy speaker. However, it is seldom the case that *all* hearers recognize a speaker as untrustworthy. For example, however much some of us might have seen Donald Trump or Boris Johnson as "obviously" and "utterly" untrustworthy, there were evidently large parts of the US and UK electorates that felt they could trust these evidently dishonest politicians. Populist politicians like Trump and Johnson fabricate a world in which the lies and bullshit they emit can be construed as "the truth." Each new lie or bullshit claim thus substantiates a fake world and so aggravates the original untruthfulness.

Another aggravating factor is **deliberate targeting** of a victim, in which the accumulation of willful insincerities about a person compounds the harm of any individual act of insincerity. We see this most commonly now in trolling (Aiken 2016). Trolling does not necessarily involve insincerity, but it often does. In these cases, such as the trolling of figures who have said something controversial, each individual act of willful insincerity, or even epistemic negligence, aggravates the overall targeting of the victim, even if it is the first posting by a particular user. Deliberate targeting can also occur with respect to minority groups as a whole. We see this commonly in Islamophobic and anti-Semitic remarks on social media, which show hostility toward a minority group as a whole even when targeting an individual victim.

7.5.2. Further Mitigating Factors

There are a number of mitigating factors that do not fall on the breach of trust dimensions. As in criminal law, **provocation** is a significant factor. If you are being trolled on the internet, it is difficult to keep the moral high ground, even if one ought to do so. Various forms of **incapacity** might also be mitigating. Pathological lying/bullshit, as seen in Chapter 4, is a condonable suspension. Other forms of incapacity, such as being intoxicated, suffering from mental illness, or being under immense stress, will not *excuse* the culpable untruthfulness but will probably mitigate it. **Youth** can also mitigate culpable untruthfulness on the grounds that a young person is not yet fully cognizant of the consequences of his actions. Finally, **apology** will generally mitigate after the act and is often sufficient to resolve feelings of offense and betrayal. The extent of mitigation engendered by apology will generally depend on both the time lag between the act of culpable untruthfulness and the emission of the apology and the perception of whether or not the apology is "heartfelt" and thus suggesting remorse.

This is not intended to be a definitive list of further aggravating and mitigating circumstances but can give some idea of the types of factors involved.

7.6. An Analysis of Degree of Culpability

The breach of trust dimensions and further aggravating and mitigating circumstances can now be used to explain the intuitive feeling that the trainee in the opening scenario, though being willfully insincere, was doing so in a very attenuated form. First, the trustor (the boss) is not vulnerable (**D1**), the trainee and boss do not know each other well (**D2**), and no rights are infringed (**D3**). The trainee is not claiming expertise (**D4**) and she is not endowed with institutional power (**D5**), particularly in relation to her boss. Nor is she subject to particular institutional warranting of the truth beyond a normal professional duty of epistemic care (**D6**). The boss, in a position of great institutional power, should know that she will need to supervise the trainee closely, and she should not have created an atmosphere in which the trainee felt that she had to lie to cover for her mistake. The trainee might justifiably believe that the potential harm ensuing from her lie will not be great (**D7**): she can send the email straightaway and thus immediately "solve" the issue that generated the lie. Certainly, if the trainee starts to make such lies on a regular basis then this will undermine the (probably limited) trust the employer has in her, but if it is a "one-off" it is difficult to imagine that much harm could be done. The trainee's motive in producing the lie is not reprehensible (**D8**). She felt in that instant that she could not admit her mistake for fear of losing her job (or receiving a severe reprimand). We must all produce such lies at one time or another, and they are clearly self-protective rather than malicious. Finally, the email was not of huge importance (**D9**). Accordingly, while the trainee was willfully insincere, her level of culpability was low.

7.7. Conclusion

Like the analysis of epistemic responsibility, this analysis of culpability is exploratory. I have suggested that we can be culpable even if we are not aware of doing wrong, and I have argued that culpability hinges on a breach of interactional trust by the speaker. I have further argued that we can judge to some extent the degree of culpability by assessing a number of dimensions relating to the gravity of the breach of trust, and by considering further aggravating and mitigating circumstances.

This chapter completes the exploration of the various elements of the TRUST framework. In Chapter 8 I indicate how the various analytical components can be put together into an analytical procedure to produce full analyses of putative untruthful claims.

PART III
CASE STUDIES

Having outlined the components of the TRUST frameworks in Part II, Part III applies the framework to a number of cases studies of public discourse. Chapter 8 first summarizes the main analytical moves in the TRUST heuristic for analyzing untruthfulness. It then applies the heuristic to three short texts that have been widely called out as lies. Chapter 9 demonstrates an alternative "holistic" method of TRUST analysis in which the focus is not on individual claims or short sections of text with a few related claims, but on the general manifestation of untruthfulness with respect to a particular case. The chapter provides an extensive analysis of multiple claims regarding the poisoning of the Russian spy Sergei Skripal and his daughter Yulia in Salisbury, England, in March 2018.

8
Discourse and Democracy
The TRUST Heuristic and Sample Analyses

8.1. Introduction

In this and the following chapter, I shall apply the TRUST framework to four key cases of consequential untruthfulness in public discourse. It should be stressed once again that the TRUST framework can be applied to *any* case of putative untruthfulness and we have seen examples from, among others, workplace communication, cross-cultural communication, and everyday conversation. However, the examples in these chapters connect strongly with the timely theme of epistemic partisanship introduced in the Preface. In each case, extreme partisanship has led to either deliberate or unwitting distortion of reality with grave societal consequences. The common analytical thread in the three cases discussed in this chapter is that each was called out by a large section of the population as being an "obvious" case of lying. Through the TRUST analyses, I shall trouble this automatic assumption of lying and suggest that while each is a clear case of unethical untruthfulness, it is not necessarily a case of lying. Furthermore, I shall argue that whether or not these are cases of lying is not necessarily relevant to the question of culpability. My claim is that the TRUST framework can provide a fuller picture of the untruthfulness and its ethical import in each case.

The three cases in this chapter also share a common theme: the capacity of untruthful public discourse to undermine democratic legitimacy. Among the factors contributing to democratic legitimacy (Held 2006) are the integrity of electoral procedures (Norris 2014), the honesty of political communication, and the rationality of leaders' deliberation (Floridia 2017). The chapter begins by setting out the TRUST heuristic and summarizing the main analytical moves (8.2). It then starts the case studies with an analysis of Donald Trump's already noted tweet about large-scale voter fraud just before the US presidential elections in November 2016 (8.3). This is followed by an analysis of the "Brexit Battle Bus" claim during the EU Referendum that the United Kingdom sent £350 million per week to the European Union (8.4). Finally, I consider Tony Blair's 2002 statement about weapons of mass destruction in his Iraq Dossier delivered to Parliament, which was evaluated in the Iraq Inquiry Report (Chilcot 2016) (8.5). I supplement this analysis with very similar examples from the George W. Bush administration in the United States. The case studies are based on three short texts (a tweet, a campaign slogan, a statement to Parliament), and the analysis in each case teases apart these texts by working systematically through the TRUST heuristic. In these three cases we have incontrovertible evidence that the writers were being untruthful (either insincere or irresponsible or both), so the focus is on the *ways* in which they are being untruthful and on how we should judge them ethically.

8.2. The TRUST Heuristic

The heuristic outlined in Table 8.1 presents the main steps and sub-steps in a TRUST analysis.

There are six main steps in the heuristic leading to a final judgment on the ethics of the untruthful claim. Each of these steps includes two sub-steps. The third column of Table 8.1 indicates prompts for each of the sub-steps. In the final columns, I list the primary and (most of the) secondary analytical categories associated with the TRUST framework.

Each of the main steps in the analysis is represented by a single keyword to aid analytical memory: CLAIMS, EVIDENCE, SUSPENSIONS, SINCERITY, RESPONSIBILITY, CULPABILITY, JUDGMENT. The sequencing here is desirable rather than necessary. First, one identifies the CLAIMS (asserted, implied, or presupposed) that are open to a TRUST analysis. Next one explores the available EVIDENCE supporting a claim of untruthfulness. It is possible to continue the analysis without clear evidence of untruthfulness (indeed, often clear evidence will be hard to come by), but lack of such evidence will reduce confidence in the subsequent analysis. Then the heuristic suggests considering possible discursive SUSPENSIONS of the speaker's presumed commitment to truthfulness. If the speaker is clearly justified in not being truthful, then the untruthfulness cannot be unethical. This does not preclude continuing the analysis since TRUST is also concerned with the categorization of forms of untruthfulness. An early analysis of suspensions can help pick up conventional and condonable suspensions that might render further analysis unnecessary. However, consequential suspensions are seldom clear-cut, and it can be useful to loop back to this step after analyzing the claims in terms of sincerity and responsibility. The heuristic then suggests one passes to the analysis of SINCERITY. It can often make sense in practice to analyze sincerity before responsibility because when there is insufficient evidence to establish insincerity (which is often the case because of the mind-reading issue), there is often still evidence of epistemic responsibility. The analysis of RESPONSIBILITY, then, can either be a useful addition to the judgments of insincerity or it can be a "fall-back" option when one suspects insincerity but does

Table 8.1 The TRUST Heuristic

Steps	Type of Analysis	Prompt	Primary Analytical Categories	Secondary Analytical Categories
1	CLAIMS			
1A	Assertibility of claim	What is being directly or indirectly asserted?	ASSERTION	*Stated, Implied, Presupposed, Withheld*
1B	Falsifiability of claim	Is the claim falsifiable?	FACTUAL SIGNIFICANCE	*"Salty-like," "Tasty-like"*
2	EVIDENCE			
2A	Evidence for falsity	Is there evidence that the claim is false or groundless?	FACT-CHECKING	*Searches: Internet, Archival, Media*
2B	Reliability of sources	How reliable is the evidence for falsity/false belief?	SOURCE QUALITY	*Authoritativeness, Corroboration*
3	SUSPENSIONS			
3A	Justifiable suspensions	Is the suspension of truthfulness justifiable in principle?	CONVENTIONAL SUSPENSIONS CONSEQUENTIAL SUSPENSIONS	*Prescribed, Performed Private, Polite, Protective*
3B	Justified suspensions	Is the suspension justified in this discursive context?	CONDONABLE SUSPENSIONS	*Playful, Pathological*
4	SINCERITY			
4A	Insincere discourse strategies	Are insincere discourse strategies being used? If so, which strategies and pragmatic tactics?	WITHHOLDING MISLEADING → LYING	*Omitting, Evading, Blocking Falsely Implicating, Equivocating, etc. Deceptive, Bald-faced, Degree, Fabricating*
4B	Willfulness	Is the claim *willfully* insincere?	WILLFULNESS CONDITIONS	*Breach of trust, Not justifiably suspended*

(*continued*)

Table 8.1 Continued

Steps	Type of Analysis	Prompt	Primary Analytical Categories	Secondary Analytical Categories
5	**RESPONSIBILITY**			
5A	Epistemic pathologies	Is there evidence of epistemically irresponsible discourse pathologies? If so, which pathologies and symptoms are there?	DOGMA DISTORTION → BULLSHIT	*Confirmatory Selection, Rude Dismissal, etc. Overstatement, Miscitation, etc. Gobbledygook, Claptrap, Pseudo-poppycock*
5B	Negligence	Is the claim epistemically *negligent*?	NEGLIGENCE CONDITIONS	*Duty of Epistemic Care, Failure to Investigate Sufficiently or Hedge Commitment*
6	**CULPABILITY**			
6A	Breach of trust dimensions	Where does the claim fall on each of the breach of trust ethical dimensions?	BREACH OF TRUST CLINES	*1: Vulnerability of Trustor; 2: Mutual Attachment; 3: Infringement of Rights; 4/5: Epistemic/Institutional Power of Speaker; 6: Institutional Warranting; 7: Potential Harm; 8: Reprehensibleness of Motive; 9: Importance of Information*
6B	Mitigation/ Aggravation	What other mitigating and aggravating circumstances might come into play?		
7	**JUDGMENT**	What is the overall ethical judgment of untruthfulness?		

not have sufficient evidence to make a cognitive appraisal about the speaker's belief. Finally, if the discursive act of untruthfulness does appear to be unethical, we pass to considering the relative CULPABILITY of the breach of trust that has occurred. This leads us to make a final JUDGMENT of the act of untruthfulness.

The heuristic aids in making a full TRUST analysis. However, it should be stressed that any of the steps may be undertaken on their own, as I have done in previous chapters. It is certainly *not* the case, for example, that identification of a putative suspension curtails the analysis or is indicative of a "failed" analysis. Indeed, one of the potential applications of the TRUST framework is in the analysis of cross-cultural and intracultural politeness, as exemplified in the example at the end of Chapter 4.

The following provides a brief summary of each of the steps as noted (and numbered) in Table 8.1.

1. The CLAIMS Analysis

The putatively untruthful claims in the discourse need to be identified and recognized as falsifiable (see Chapter 3).

1A. Assertibility of Claim
The analyst needs to ask what is being directly or indirectly asserted. The untruthfulness may be in the form of a claim that is stated, implied, or presupposed over one or more utterances or in the form of a fact that is deliberately or irresponsibly omitted.

1B. Falsifiability of Claim
Generally, the claim is open to a TRUST analysis only if it can be potentially falsified or if it has been posited as falsifiable when it is not.

2. The Analysis of EVIDENCE

Having identified falsifiable claims, the evidence for the claim being false or groundless and the reliability of that evidence need to be established (see Chapter 3).

2A. Evidence for Falsity
In most cases the analyst needs to check whether the stated, implied, or presupposed claim is *factually false*. Established non-partisan fact-checking

sites, such as the Pulitzer Prize–winning PolitiFact (politifact.com) and Snopes (snopes.com) in the United States, and Full Fact (fullfact.org) in the United Kingdom, are a good starting point for public discourse. Searches in archives, databases, dictionaries, encyclopedias, government websites, academic networks, and even Dr. Google can all reveal evidence for falsity. Fact-checking should also be able to establish whether, in cases of putative bullshitting, a claim asserted categorically cannot actually be falsified. In a few cases, contradiction and serious testimonial inconsistencies can provide circumstantial evidence of insincerity.

2B. Reliability of Sources

One then needs to consider the reliability of the evidence for falsity or false belief. This step can be subsumed by 2A if one searches only in reliable sources. However, in practice, one often has to rely on media sources, the reliability of which may not be obvious. Media Bias/Fact Check (MBFC) rates publications for both bias and factual reporting and, as indicated in Chapter 3, is a useful source for this sub-step.

3. The Analysis of SUSPENSIONS

The third main step is to consider whether there is a suspension of the speaker's commitment to truthfulness that is both justifiable in principle and justified in discursive practice.

3A. Justifiable Suspensions

As discussed in Chapter 4, there are three primary categories of ethically *justifiable* suspensions of epistemic commitment: *conventional, consequential,* and *condonable*. Sometimes all three can come into play, so it is worth considering each in turn. Regarding *conventional* suspensions, analysts should look for metadiscursive cues to *prescribed* suspensions (e.g., the labels "comedy," "fiction," "satire," "joke") and implicature or marked intonation that typically suggest *performed* suspensions such as irony and hyperbole. Regarding *consequential* suspensions, analysts should consider carefully questions of privacy, particularly in relation to withholding, and look for politeness strategies (Brown and Levinson 1987) and any other standard discursive cues that the speaker's commitment to truthfulness is overridden by the greater good of saving the interlocutor's face (self-esteem) or showing warmth and friendliness. They also need to consider the complex issues relating to *protective* and *self-protective* suspensions. With regard to *condonable* suspensions, analysts should look for evidence of a lack of intentionality (*pathological*) or a good-humored resolution of the initial deception (*playful*).

3B. Justified Suspensions
Suspensions that are typically or normally justifiable in a certain *type* of context in a certain discourse community are not necessarily justified in the *specific* context. For a suspension to be *justified* in a given discursive context, the hearer should reasonably be expected to be aware of the suspension (if conventional) or unharmed by it (unless the hearer, such as a murderer, is himself the source of harm triggering the speaker's suspension) if consequential or condonable. Analysts need to consider the cultural norms and individual sensibilities in play and to be sensitive to local contingencies. They also need to be careful to avoid cultural stereotyping when considering, for example, whether a polite suspension is justified or not.

4. The Analysis of SINCERITY

If not *all* the identified untruthfulness can be explained simply in terms of justified suspensions of sincerity or epistemic responsibility, one passes to the fourth step: an analysis of discursive SINCERITY. As explored in Chapter 5, this involves both identifying insincere discourse strategies and considering whether they are willful in the context.

4A. Insincere Discourse Strategies
The TRUST framework identifies three hierarchically related discourse strategies:

(1) *Withholding* (without misleading);
(2) *Misleading* (without lying);
(3) *Lying*.

Withholding (without misleading) is marked by textual omission (the truthful assertion is not voiced) and is discursively accomplished through such substrategies as *omitting* material information, *evading* incriminating questions, and *blocking* others from revealing the truth. There are many different pragmatic evading tactics and several blocking tactics. *Misleading* (without lying) involves implicitly *suggesting* through language what you do not believe. One can mislead through *wording*, using such pragmatic tactics as *equivocating* or *obfuscating*, by triggering inferences in the hearer, as in *falsely implicating*, or by *reframing*

240   CASE STUDIES

the context as in *faking* or *taking words out of context*. *Lying*, or asserting what you believe to be false, can be *deceptive* or *bald-faced*; it might only be with respect to *degree*, or it can be a complete fabrication. Analysts should check putative categories of insincerity against the four tests indicated in Chapter 5 and the definitions of each of the categories. The main categories are indicated on the left of the diagram in Figure 8.1, duplicated from Figure 6.1.

4B. Willfulness

Having identified insincere discourse strategies, we need to assess whether the speaker is not only withholding the truth but also doing so *willfully* and thus unethically. This requires checking whether the speaker (1) is breaching trust by deliberately trying to disrupt the inquiry, and (2) is not justified in suspending her commitment to sincerity. Both conditions are required because while most consequential suspensions are deceptive, and thus breach interactional trust, they would not be considered willful if the suspension is justified. While an ethical judgment of willful insincerity might be desired, it cannot always be delivered on the balance of probabilities. This is partly why the analysis of epistemic responsibility is so important.

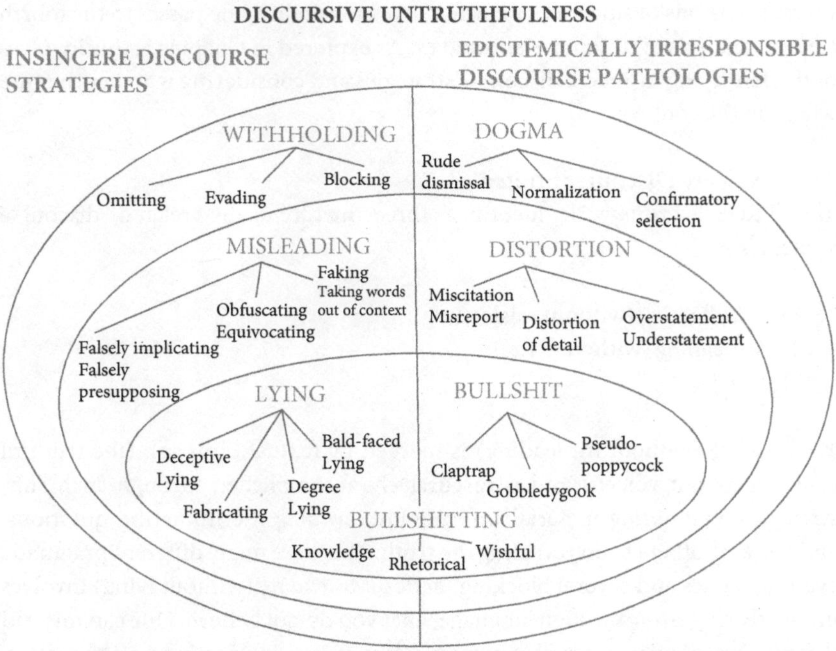

DISCURSIVE UNTRUTHFULNESS

INSINCERE DISCOURSE STRATEGIES

EPISTEMICALLY IRRESPONSIBLE DISCOURSE PATHOLOGIES

WITHHOLDING — Omitting, Evading, Blocking

DOGMA — Rude dismissal, Normalization, Confirmatory selection

MISLEADING — Faking, Taking words out of context, Obfuscating, Equivocating, Falsely implicating, Falsely presupposing

DISTORTION — Miscitation, Misreport, Distortion of detail, Overstatement, Understatement

LYING — Deceptive Lying, Bald-faced Lying, Degree Lying, Fabricating

BULLSHIT — Claptrap, Gobbledygook, Pseudo-poppycock

BULLSHITTING — Knowledge, Rhetorical, Wishful

Figure 8.1. Discourse strategies and pathologies of discursive untruthfulness.

5. Analysis of Responsibility

Whether or not evidence of insincere discourse strategies has been found, one can then pass to the fifth main step: an analysis of epistemic RESPONSIBILITY. This involves both identifying epistemically irresponsible discourse pathologies and considering whether they are negligent in the context.

5A. Epistemic Pathologies

An epistemically responsible speaker is one who *cares about* getting things right. As indicated in Chapter 6, TRUST proposes three main hierarchically related categories of epistemically irresponsible discourse pathologies:

(1) *Dogma* (without explicit linguistic distortion);
(2) *Distortion* (without bullshit);
(3) *Bullshit*.

The analyst will be looking not only for these three main types, but also for specific subtypes or discursive symptoms; the main ones are indicated on the right-hand side of the diagram in Figure 8.1. Thus, *dogma*, or closed-minded discourse that disregards counter-evidence, can be manifested in discursive evidence of *confirmatory selection, rude dismissal*, or the *normalization* of unwarranted claims. *Distortion*, or the unintentional linguistic misrepresentation of evidence, can be manifested in such discursive symptoms as *miscitation/misreport, over/understatement*, or *detail distortion*. Finally, *bullshit*, or recklessly disregarding evidential grounding, can be manifested in such discourse types as *claptrap, gobbledygook* and *pseudo-poppycock*. Analysts should also watch for the hybrid category of *bullshitting*.

5B. Negligence

After identifying relevant discourse pathologies, the analyst then needs to ask whether the claim is epistemically negligent. This involves checking the three negligence conditions: (1) duty of epistemic care; (2) insufficient investigative investment; and (3) a failure to hedge one's commitment. The duty of epistemic care can be established by the general discursive context: the speaker's established or claimed role. Failure to investigate sufficiently can be established by the co-text (the previous and subsequent discourse) and the intertexts (other discourse related to the case). What constitutes "sufficient" investment will depend on the context, the availability of evidence, and the gravity of the potential consequences. Failure to hedge one's commitment can usually be established through the lack of linguistic hedges.

6. Analysis of CULPABILITY

If the speaker is judged to have been willfully insincere or epistemically negligent, the analysis passes to the question of how culpable the speaker is. This analysis is based on the conditions of trust that hold in the specific discourse context and any further mitigating and aggravating circumstances particular to that context.

6A. Breach of Trust Dimensions

First, one needs to consider where the willfully insincere or epistemically negligent claim falls on each of the nine breach of trust dimensions (see Chapter 7). In each case, it is proposed that, all things being equal, a high value on the dimension provokes or aggravates the breach, while a low value avoids or attenuates the breach. So, for example, withholding information that a medical procedure is known to be unsafe (Potential Harm) and doing so to protect one's own interests (Reprehensibility of Motive) are serious ethical breaches, while bullshitting to your elderly mother that the operation is completely safe (Harm) and doing so to reassure her (Motive) might even be considered consequential suspensions. Furthermore, if it is the surgeon who is withholding the safety information, then there are high values on epistemic power (expertise), institutional power (the surgeon's institutional status), and institutional warranting (the doctor's codes of conduct), all of which considerably aggravate the breach.

6B. Mitigation and Aggravation

The breach of trust dimensions are a practical "way in" to the question of culpability, but it is unlikely they will be exhaustive. As with assessment criteria in the marking of academic essays, it is not possible to weight the breach of trust dimensions, assign measurable values along each dimension, and then simply tot up a result. The dimensions help in the ethical processing and in explaining one's judgment, but assessment of ethical gravity, like the assessment of essay quality, is ultimately a gestalt phenomenon. We thus need to ask whether there are other mitigating and aggravating circumstances that might come into play in the specific context.

7. Ethical JUDGMENT

This final step is there simply to remind the analyst to make an overall ethical judgment of untruthfulness in the context bearing in mind all the analytical steps.

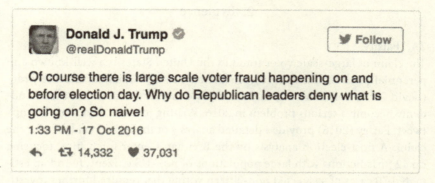

Figure 8.2. Trump's voter fraud tweet.

8.3. Voter Fraud

The first case study explored in the chapter is Donald Trump's "voter fraud" tweet. Long before he became president of the United States, Donald Trump was shunning the mainstream media in favor of direct communication with his voters through Twitter. Just a few weeks before election day, he posted the tweet in Figure 8.2:

1. Claims

1A. Assertibility
There are two assertible claims here:[1]

> C1. *Stated:* "There is large scale voter fraud happening on and before election day."
> C2. *Presupposed*: Republican leaders deny this.

1B. Falsifiability
Since C2 is presupposed within a rhetorical question, it functions, along with the "tasty" exclamation "So naive!", primarily to rhetorically reinforce C1. Accordingly, I shall focus the analysis of evidence on the falsifiable C1, with C2 and the exclamation supporting the analysis.

---

[1] Sub-steps in the TRUST heuristic are numbered according to Table 8.1.

2. Evidence

2A. Falsity
The claim of large-scale voter fraud in the United States is a well-known and perennial myth (Minnite 2010). Historically, election fraud is extremely rare (Levitt 2007) and there was no reliable evidence at the time that it had suddenly become a serious problem in 2016. Writing just two days after Trump's tweet, Farley (2016) provided detailed analysis of the lack of evidence for the claim. A post-election analysis by the Brennan Center for Justice, focusing on 42 jurisdictions with large populations of non-US citizens, found an estimated 30 cases of suspected non-citizen voting that required further investigation out of 23.5 million votes surveyed, or 0.0001% of votes cast (Famighetti et al. 2017).

2B. Reliability
The falsity of large-scale voter fraud is confirmed both historically through authoritative academic sources (e.g., Levitt 2007) and, in terms of the 2016 elections, through a number of reputable fact-checking sites such as PolitiFact and FactCheck.Org. PolitiFact, for example, classifies the statement as "Pants-on-fire" (Qiu 2016), by which they mean very clearly untrue.

3. Suspensions

3A. Justifiable in Principle
Trump might try to claim a conventional suspension on the grounds that tweets are not truth-warranting. As we saw in Chapter 4, though, while Twitter was originally conceived as an ephemeral activity, tweeting has entered the mainstream social media and is an integral part of media strategy in most large organizations. It can no longer be considered ephemeral in such contexts and certainly not in the context of a presidential campaign. One could imagine a left-wing comedian performing this statement ironically, but given Trump's discursive history and the views of his supporters, a performed suspension is untenable. Consequential suspension could only be in such form as Trump claiming that he is lying to protect America from the evils of Obamacare, but such a suspension could never be justified in a democracy. Furthermore, there can be nothing condonable about this tweet: it could never be justified for him to say just after the elections, "By the way, I was just kidding about voter fraud," and the world is in serious trouble if Trump is a pathological bullshitter unable to control the bullshit he produces.

3B. Justified in Practice

The discursive context of a tweet from a presidential candidate just before the elections cannot possibly mean that any putative suspension of truthfulness might have been justified in practice.

4. Sincerity

4A. Insincere Discourse Strategies

This may well be a deceptive lie, or a "Pants-on-fire" claim, as PolitiFact describes it. In that case Trump withholds the truth that there is no large-scale voter fraud and he misleads the reader by lying. However, as indicated in the Introduction, to make a grounded attribution of lying here we would need evidence that Trump actually *believed* that there was *no* large-scale voter fraud. It is common for supporters of populist movements to believe that the establishment will do what it takes to block them (Müller 2016). A poll just before the EU Referendum in the United Kingdom, for example, found that 64% of UK Independence Party supporters believed the Referendum would be rigged (despite, as in the United States, there being no historical evidence of large-scale voter fraud in the United Kingdom) (Stone 2016).

4B. Willfulness

If Trump *is* lying, it is most certainly willful: it would constitute a very serious breach of trust with the voters, and one where a suspension of epistemic commitment could not possibly be justified.

5. Responsibility

5A. Epistemic Pathologies

There is both external and internal evidence that Trump's tweet might be irresponsible rather than insincere. In terms of external evidence, it seems unlikely (though not impossible) that Trump would go to the length of setting up a Voter Fraud Commission, the Presidential Advisory Committee on Election Integrity (PACEI 2017), in May 2017 if he knew full well that there was no issue with large-scale voter fraud. While the Commission was disbanded in January 2018, that was primarily because States refused to cooperate in providing the personal details of voters. Trump did not abandon the investigation, but transferred it to the Department of Homeland Security. There are also indications that he may have grossly misinterpreted the available evidence. Pew Research published a report in 2012 indicating that there were approximately 24 million voter registration inaccuracies, including that "[m]ore than 1.8 million deceased individuals are listed as voters" (Pew 2012: 1). However, the report is about inaccuracies and inefficiencies rather than irregularities: the stem *inaccura** occurs 31 times in the report, *inefficien** 26 times, and *irregular** 0 times. There is no suggestion in the report that any of these registration inaccuracies have led to voter fraud. The word "fraud" is mentioned once in the report in the following context:

> The inability of this paper-based process to keep up with voters as they move or die can lead to problems with the rolls, including the *perception* that they lack integrity or could be susceptible to fraud. (Pew 2012: 3)[2]

Yet Trump either misreported or deliberately took Pew's words completely out of context in a campaign speech in Wisconsin delivered on the same day as his voter fraud tweet:

> [00:20:43] So many cities are corrupt and voter fraud is very, very common. The following information comes straight from Pew Research, quote, "Approximately 24 million people, one of every eight, voter registrations in the United States are no longer valid or significantly inaccurate." One in eight. More than *1.8* million deceased individuals right now are listed as voters. Oh, that's wonderful. [00:21:21] Well, if they're going to vote for me, we'll think about it, right? But I have a feeling they're not going to vote for me. Of the *1.8* million, *1.8* million is voting for somebody else. (Trump 2016; original emphasis in transcript)

When contextualized as I have done here, this reformulation of "inaccurate" as "fraudulent" seems preposterous, but, as will be seen in Chapter 9, this is precisely the type of shift from fact to fantasy that occurs in conspiracy discourse.

There is also internal evidence that Trump's tweet might be pathological rather than willful. As indicated in Chapter 2, the tweet follows directly Christensen's template for a question-begging dogmatic argument. The tweet opens with a *normalization* ("Of course"), indicating a *dogmatic* frame of mind that simply takes things as given and not open to question. Ironically, the use of Twitter by politicians has been found (at least in South Korea) to correspond to a perception of open-mindedness: "When politicians actively share their candid opinions through the open public sphere of Twitter, this can cultivate an open-minded image that leads members of the public to perceive politician users as sincere

---

[2] As in previous chapters, all graphic emphases (italics, bold, underlining) in quotes in this chapter and the next are mine unless "original emphasis" is explicitly indicated.

and reliable" (Hwang 2013: 254). However, there is nothing open-minded about Trump's use of Twitter, as is demonstrated by his failure to admit to any of the glaring mistakes/lies he has made. The tweet then *distorts* the evidence by grossly *overstating* ("large scale") the likely extent of voter fraud. But what raises the tweet definitively to the level of *bullshit* is that Trump *presupposes* his false claim through the presuppositional verb *deny*: "Why do Republican leaders deny what is going on?" This renders the voter fraud unquestionable. Trump even goes so far as to assess the factually correct stance (that there is *no* large-scale voter fraud) with an evaluative exclamative: "So naive!" Yet he has no empirical grounds for making his claim in the first place.

5B. Negligence
The claim easily fulfills the three conditions for epistemic negligence. First, as a presidential candidate, Trump has a strong *duty of epistemic care*. He carries the weight of the Republican campaign behind him and he knows his tweets are very widely read and believed by his supporters. Second, he *fails to investigate sufficiently* in accordance with his epistemic duty. As with many of his tweets, he provides no evidence for the reckless claim he is making. He *does* provide "evidence" in his campaign speech the same day but, as indicated earlier, he completely misconstrues the nature of the statistical data he is reporting. On another occasion, when challenged about a widely publicized and grossly inaccurate graphic suggesting that most whites are killed by blacks, he responded that it was not his tweet and that he had merely retweeted it, and he tellingly asked rhetorically, "Am I gonna check every statistic?" (Borchers 2015). Finally, he *fails to hedge his commitment* to his claim in accordance with the available evidence (e.g., Levitt 2007). Indeed, he simply presupposes its factual status and then chastises his fellow Republicans for not believing it. In conclusion, whether or not Trump lied in this tweet, he is clearly demonstrating epistemic negligence.

6. Culpability

6A. Breach of Trust
How serious an ethical breach of trust is this tweet? Well, first, many of Trump's supporters are poorly educated and thus *vulnerable* to manipulation (D1), and while one cannot really talk of strong *mutual attachment* (D2) between Trump and his fans, if Hwang's observations in Korea apply to the US context too, and tweeting is associated with openness in a politician, then this does raise the emotional attachment and aggravate the breach. Trump is arguably *infringing the rights* of ordinary voters (D3) by effectively suggesting that their votes may not count. He has strong *epistemic power* (D4) partly because supporters might

erroneously believe that he has access to privileged knowledge about voter fraud, but also because Twitter is now becoming the first port of call for breaking news (it was the biggest source of it on election day; Isaac and Ember 2016) and this raises the stakes because there is strong evidence that false information once accepted is very difficult to correct (Ecker et al. 2011). He was in a position of great *institutional power* (D5) as the Republican presidential candidate. Although politicians have very low trust ratings (Ipsos 2017), they have a clear duty of epistemic care that puts them in a position of trust with respect to the electorate, and the fact that politicians regularly abuse sincerity and epistemic responsibility does not make their breaches of trust any less serious. However, the breach is most seriously aggravated because of its *potential harm* (D7) in undermining democratic institutions and leading to the wrong candidate gaining power. Furthermore, Trump's only *motive* appears to have been to win the presidential elections at all costs (D8). Finally, the information was vitally important (D9) as it undermined the legitimacy of the election itself.

6B. Mitigation/Aggravation

It is difficult to find mitigating factors in this case since the breach of trust is about as aggravated as one can get. In terms of aggravation, Trump's track record of mendacity makes the breach of trust worse rather than better. In terms of overall culpability, it would appear to make little difference whether one manages to establish the claim as a lie or not: it was, in any case, an extremely dangerous piece of bullshit.

7. Judgment

Sent out just three weeks before the US presidential elections, Trump's tweet fed directly into a populist post-factual narrative of the establishment rigging elections. In so doing, it untruthfully undermined trust in US electoral integrity. This may well have led to a feeling among Trump voters that their vote did not really count and so they may as well just use it to protest the establishment, or the "swamp" in Reagan's and Trump's term. If voters feel their vote does not really count, this clearly undermines the quality of their consent in the federal government and thus democratic legitimacy itself. This was all predictable when Trump sent the tweet, and his motive in doing so was clearly reprehensible. Furthermore, he has continued to make this false claim: after winning the election, he claimed falsely on many occasions that he had also won the popular vote if one discounted the "fraudulent" votes.

8.4. The Brexit Battle Bus

Just a few months before Trump's tweet, the EU Referendum campaign was in full swing in the United Kingdom and the Vote Leave leaders, led by Boris Johnson, were traveling around the country in a campaign bus nicknamed the "Brexit Battle Bus." The message on this bus was considered by so-called Remainers to be one of the most egregious examples of Vote Leave's dishonest campaign strategy (see Figure 8.3).

1. Claim

1A. Assertibility
There are a number of factually significant claims here:

> C1: *Stated*: We send the EU £350 million a week.
> C2: *Implied*: This money could be spent on the NHS (National Health Service) instead.
> C3: *Implied*: We have lost control.

1B. Falsifiability
C3, however strongly one might disagree, is too "tasty" a claim to analyze with TRUST. C2, as an assertion, rather than the false promise of "let's fund," is dependent on the analysis of C1. So, I shall focus here on the falsifiable claim C1.

Figure 8.3. The Brexit Battle Bus.

2. Evidence

2A. Falsity
The indisputable facts here are that the United Kingdom received a discount on their gross contributions to the European Union (the so-called rebate) that reduced them in 2015 to about £250 million per week. Subsidies from the EU then reduced the *net* contribution to around £160 million per week. This figure was further reduced in practice by direct income, such as competitive EU research funding of which the United Kingdom was the second largest beneficiary (Royal 2015: 14). Furthermore, the implication that the putative £350 million saved would be spent on the NHS was immediately retracted on the morning after the vote and was removed (along with many other false promises) from Vote Leave's official website (Griffin 2016).

2B. Reliability
These facts about how much money the EU actually cost the United Kingdom were confirmed by the *Daily Telegraph* (Kirk and Dunford 2016), a passionately Leave-supporting broadsheet newspaper rated by Media Bias/Fact Check as "Right Biased" and whose factual reporting at the time was rated as "High Quality," though this has now slipped to "Mixed Quality" (MBFC 2019).

3. Suspensions

3A. Justifiable in Principle
In terms of prescribed conventional suspensions, the genre here is campaign advertising. Since 1999, non-broadcast political advertising in the United Kingdom has not been subject to the Advertising Code, so technically one might claim that it is not subject to a commitment to truthfulness. However, that would be to confuse morality with legality. The law draws on morality but is certainly not a surrogate for it, and the law tends to be very cautious in terms of enforcing moral principles. Carson makes a similar point in relation to the US Federal Trade Commission rules on deceptive advertising: "Although they are permitted and tolerated by the law, such ads can be deceptive and morally wrong" (2010: 186–188). In the United Kingdom, the Non-Broadcast Advertising Code provides an idea of what is ethically prescribed for non-political advertising (and arguably should be reapplied to political advertising). The Code allows for a degree of "puffery," or "obvious exaggerations ... that the average consumer ... is unlikely to take literally" (CAP 2014: 3.2), such as "Cleans whiter than white." Political puffery might extend to what might be called ideological "emomemes" (emotive memes) such as "Let's take back control" or Reagan's (and subsequently Trump's)

"Let's make America great again," with their presuppositions that we (in the United Kingdom) have in fact lost control and that America is in fact no longer great. While many of us may feel that such presuppositions are "false," they are simply not "salty" enough to verify. On the other hand, commercial, but also political, puffery cannot extend to verifiable facts: "marketers must hold documentary evidence to prove claims that consumers are likely to regard as objective and that are capable of objective substantiation" (CAP 2014: 3.7). The £350 million claim is clearly conveyed as an objective fact requiring substantiation and so cannot be a justifiably prescribed suspension even in principle.

We can also dismiss consequential suspension as it would be tantamount to accepting a Platonic "noble" lie: Brexiters are justified in lying because they are making Britain *Great* again. No democracy could accept such a premise. Furthermore, there is nothing condonable about this campaign slogan: it is hardly playful, and we would need an improbable psychiatric assessment to confirm my "tasty" belief that Boris Johnson is a pathological bullshitter.

3B. Justified in Practice

Given the strong likelihood of the claim deceiving voters, it cannot possibly be justified in practice as a conventional or consequential suspension.

4. Sincerity

4A. Insincere Discourse Strategies

Claim C1, "We send the EU £350 million a week," has clearly omitted material information about the EU rebate and the subsidies. This would contravene the Advertising Code if it were bound by it:

> 3.3. Marketing communications must not mislead the consumer by omitting material information. . . . Material information is information that the consumer needs to make informed decisions in relation to a product. (CAP 2014: 3.3)

Information about rebates and subsidies is needed by the voter to make an informed decision in relation to the cost of Britain's membership in the European Union. Given that this is a carefully designed piece of campaign advertising that will have been seen by many people before arriving at the point of being posted on buses, it is hard to imagine that an accidental omission would not have been picked up. Furthermore, if the TV Movie *Brexit: The Uncivil War* is accurate on this point, it appears that Dominic Cummins, the director of the Vote Leave campaign, tasked his workers to come up with the highest figure possible for UK payments to the EU. Cummins must have queried how that figure was arrived at, and therefore it could not be a simple mistake. This would appear then to be a clear case, at the very least, of *withholding*. Furthermore, the statement "Let's fund our NHS instead" is *misleading* since it carries, through "instead," the false conventional implicature that the "£350 million" not sent to the EU will be spent on the NHS (which was apparently never envisaged). More than this, though, "We send the EU £350 million a week" must be a *deceptive lie* unless, quite remarkably, no one in the Vote Leave campaign team was aware of the UK rebate. If it had been worded as "We *owe* the EU £350 million a week" that might have been "merely," though highly, misleading ("we owe x before the rebate is taken into consideration") but *send* is a definitive material process (either we send that money or we do not).

4B. Willfulness
The withholding, misleading, and lying displayed here are clearly willful because they are not justifiably suspended and they clearly breach the trust of the voters.

5. Responsibility

5A. Epistemic Pathologies
In the unlikely case that there was no insincerity involved, this is a clear case of epistemic irresponsibility. It is a gross *overstatement* of the amount of money sent to the EU per week. But the complete disregard of the facts would also make this a clear case of *bullshit* if it is not a case of lying.

5B. Negligence
Furthermore, the claim, if it is not willfully insincere, is certainly epistemically negligent. The campaign team had a duty of epistemic care not to mislead the electorate, they clearly failed to invest sufficiently in investigating the truth if they did not bother to check the figure, and the statement is absolutely categorical with no hedging whatsoever.

6. Culpability

6A. Breach of Trust
Although the truth is technically not *institutionally warranted* (**D6**) in non-broadcast campaign advertising in the United Kingdom, and although most of us are on our guard with respect to political advertising, we do not expect straight deceptive lies, which are categorically prohibited in commercial

advertising. Furthermore, as with Trump, the average supporter of Brexit was less well educated and thus more *vulnerable* to emotional manipulation (D1). There was considerable *institutional power* behind the Brexit bus (D5) and the electorate might have been forgiven for thinking that the campaign team would have the *epistemic power* to make such a claim (D4) with its obvious *potential harm* (D7). Finally, the information conveyed was clearly crucial in terms of the Leave campaign (D9).

6B. Mitigation/Aggravation
A considerable further aggravating factor is that the Referendum was described by Prime Minister David Cameron as a "once-in-a-generation" opportunity to affect the future of the United Kingdom.

7. Judgment

While this campaign ad was almost certainly insincere, the breach of trust involved is so great that it matters little from an ethical perspective whether we ultimately classify the Brexit Battle Bus claim as lying or bullshit. It was, in short, an egregious piece of unethical untruthfulness that should have been prohibited by a Code. As with the Trump tweet, though, the greatest harm of this ad is caused not by the misleading of specific voters about the cost of EU membership but the damage such insincere advertising does to trust in the democratic process itself. If the evidential ground on which rational citizens build their opinions is unstable because campaigners have been dishonest, then the edifice of belief those voters construct will also be unstable and will lead to poor democratic choices. Once again, then, the quality of people's consent in government will be diminished, thus challenging its democratic legitimacy.

8.5. "Bliar" and Weapons of Mass Deception

Soon after the Brexit result, the Iraq Inquiry, which had been set up by Prime Minister Gordon Brown in 2009 to investigate Britain's involvement in Iraq before, during, and after the Iraq War in 2003, finally released its report. The so-called Chilcot Report (named after its chairman, Sir John Chilcot) was damning of then Prime Minister Tony Blair's actions leading up to the war but it fell short of calling him a liar (Chilcot 2016). A crucial piece of evidence in the 3.5-million-word report is what Blair wrote on weapons of mass destruction (WMD) in his Foreword to the Iraq Dossier that he presented to Parliament in September 2002 when he was trying to convince a resistant House to vote for war:

> What I believe the assessed intelligence has established beyond doubt is that Saddam has continued to produce chemical and biological weapons, that he continues in his efforts to develop nuclear weapons, and that he has been able to extend the range of his ballistic missile programme.... I am in no doubt that the threat is serious and current, that he has made progress on WMD, and that he has to be stopped. (Tony Blair, Foreword to Iraq Dossier, September 2002)

Most of the Left saw this claim as a very clear case of lying. Chilcot implied that it was misleading but did not question Blair's "belief" and thus did not accuse him of lying.

In analyzing this statement, I shall also draw on Corn's journalistic account of George W. Bush's lies (Corn 2003) and Carson's philosophical analysis of "lying and deception" by the Bush administration at around the same time as Blair's statement (Carson 2010: 212–218). It should be noted that Carson draws on the traditional philosophical distinction between "lying" and "deception short of lying" (the latter corresponding to misleading and withholding in TRUST terms), so he does not recognize the major categories of discourse pathology: dogma, distortion, and bullshit.

1. Claim

1A. Assertibility
There are a number of interconnected factually significant *stated* claims here:

C1: Saddam has continued to produce chemical and biological weapons, etc.
C2: The assessed intelligence has established this beyond doubt.
C3: The threat is serious and current ... and Saddam has to be stopped.

1B. Falsifiability
The falsifiable claims C1 and C2 will be the principal focus as C3 depends on them for the claim that the threat is "serious and current," while the need to stop Saddam is opinion rather than falsifiable fact.

2. Evidence

2A. Falsity
The facts as established by the Report of the Iraq Inquiry (Chilcot 2016) are that:

C1a: There were no WMD at the time. Intensive searching of Iraq for years after the war revealed no WMD.

C2a: The Iraq Dossier was informed by unreliable security sources.

C2b: The Joint Intelligence Committee (JIC) that put together the Dossier considerably qualified their claims about the evidence for WMD, but these qualifications were dropped in Blair's Preface.

Similar evidence of unreliable security information combined with the concealment of doubt can be found in the US context. Gompert et al. (2014) note that the CIA's original draft National Intelligence Estimate (NIE) on Iraq and WMD, which was equivalent to the JIC's Iraq Dossier, "contained several qualifiers that were dropped":

> As the draft NIE went up the intelligence chain of command, the conclusions were treated increasingly definitively. Only the summary of the NIE was partially declassified, and it omitted most of the reservations and nonconforming evidence. . . . A year later, a Senate Select Committee on Intelligence report found that the NIE was wrong, that it overstated the case, that statements in it were not supported, and that intelligence was mischaracterized. (Gompert et al. 2014: 169)

2B. Reliability

The facts are established comprehensively and reliably by the 3.5 million word Report of the Iraq Inquiry (Chilcot 2016), which was the result of a seven-year investigation. In the US context, the Senate Report on Iraqi WMD Intelligence (Senate 2004), as indicated earlier, provided a similarly authoritative critique of the handling of intelligence before the war.

3. Suspensions

3A. Justifiable in Principle

Justifiable suspensions can be rapidly dismissed. In terms of a putative prescribed conventional suspension, the Foreword to a vitally important Dossier of crucial evidence on WMD can only be a highly truth-warranting discursive context. Carson makes the same point in relation to claims made by Bush about Iraq acquiring nuclear weapons: "On a solemn occasion, such as the State of the Union Address, a democratically elected leader warrants the truth of what he says to a very high degree" (210: 217). Carson adds, "especially if the statements are used as a basis for starting a war that will kill thousands of people," but I would see this as concerning the degree of culpability (potential harm) rather than the prescribed convention of the presidential speech. As for consequential suspensions, in some cases, as we shall see with the Skripal poisoning, a government might need to keep highly sensitive material confidential to protect the lives of spies or ensure security, but the Chilcot Report established conclusively that was not the case here. In any case, Blair was ostensibly only drawing on evidence already published in the Dossier.

3B. Justified in Practice

Blair may well have believed that he was making a consequential protective suspension that was justified in the particular circumstances: in his mind (and Bush's), it was vital to rid the world of the monstrous dictator Saddam Hussein and, if convincing Parliament that Iraq had WMD was the only way of achieving that, then so be it. However, such consequential reasoning is highly dangerous and very seldom justified in a democracy. There is a serious risk of the *post hoc* fallacy operating here: had Saddam really had stockpiles of WMD and had regime change led to a fledgling democracy rather than the type of chaos that led to the rise of ISIS, would that justify deception by Blair and Bush on this issue? Rather than considering such warmongering deceptions as justified suspensions, it might be better to see them as mitigating the degree of culpability. Nevertheless, actual good consequences are not in play in this case, and the clear unreliability of the evidence could not have justified a consequential suspension.

4. Sincerity

4A. Insincere Discourse Strategies

Blair probably *withheld* vital information about the JIC's reservations in the Iraq Dossier, just as Bush probably withheld reservations in the NIE. The Chilcot Report also provides clear evidence that Bush and Blair had already decided on regime change. This intent was concealed from Parliament and knowledge of this intent might have been material in the MPs' final decision on whether or not to go to war.

Blair also probably *misled* Parliament. He arguably *equivocated* in framing his judgment in terms of personal conviction. *Equivocation* is the deliberate use of ambiguous language with the aim of leading the hearers to believe what they know is not the case. Blair framed his statements as follows:

- "What *I believe* the assessed intelligence has established beyond doubt..."
- "*I am in no doubt* that the threat is serious and current..."

The equivocation here is a pragmatic one. Subjective positioning of this sort is most often a form of hedging ("This is just my opinion, but..."). However, when the speaker is in a position of great authority, the subjective "authorized voice" can come across as authoritative. For example, when the Lord Chief Justice in Australia opined, "I think jurors understand 'beyond reasonable doubt,'" that subjectively positioned statement became the authoritative precedent on the issue for decades, irrespective of a plethora of empirical studies demonstrating that jurors did *not* understand the criminal standard of proof (Heffer 2013a). So, when delivered by an authorized voice, what in other contexts might provide a subjective frame becomes an authoritative frame: "I'm powerful and authoritative so you can take what I believe as true." Blair, then, tries to lead Parliament to believe that the presence of WMD is *authoritatively* beyond doubt when it is (as Blair knows) only *subjectively* beyond doubt. Defense Secretary Donald Rumsfeld made a similar subjectively framed claim when he said, on January 7, 2003, "There is *no doubt in my mind* but that [the Iraqis] currently have chemical and biological weapons" (Corn 2003: 211).

The focus of most discussion has been on Bush and Blair's "lies." Carson (2010: 212–221) goes to great lengths to demonstrate that some of the claims made by the Bush administration are lies rather than "merely" deception. He is helped by the fact that many of the statements made are not subjectively framed. Vice President Dick Cheney said in August 2002, "*Simply stated, there is no doubt that Saddam Hussein now has weapons of mass destruction. There is no doubt he is amassing them to use against our friends, our allies, and against us*" (Corn 2003: 208). Bush claimed in March 2003 that "[i]ntelligence gathered by this and other governments leaves *no doubt* that the Iraq regime continues to possess and conceal some of the most lethal weapons ever devised" (Alterman 2004: 298). Rumsfeld was even less cautious when he spoke in September 2002: "*There's no debate in the world* as to whether they have those weapons.... *We all know* that. *A trained ape knows* that" (Corn 2003: 211). Carson argues that Bush and company lied about their level of certainty (i.e., they exaggerated in TRUST terms): they must have known there were doubts about the veracity of their claims. Yet, as Carson himself notes, "it is possible that [Bush] dismissed all of the counter-evidence presented to him as completely unfounded and did not think that it was a serious basis for questioning the truth of the claims he made" (2010: 217). As with my own analyses of insincerity, Carson's are often couched in a series of conditionals. For example, with regard to a Defense Intelligence Agency report which concluded that two well-publicized images of trailers were not in fact mobile biological weapons labs, Carson writes:

> *If they were aware of this report* when they made their claims about the biological weapons labs, *it is nearly certain* that Bush and Cheney lied. However, *we do not know whether* Bush and Cheney actually saw or heard about this report. *It seems likely that* they were aware of the report as it contained important newsworthy intelligence. *Even if he was not aware* of this report on May 29, it

is reasonable to suppose that someone who knew about the report *would have brought* this to the attention of Bush and Cheney after Bush's initial false claims on May 29. *This is a reasonable assumption, though far from certain.* (Carson 2010: 220–221)

As the final sentence makes clear, Carson makes reasonable assumptions and draws very reasonable conclusions from those assumptions but, as found so often in analyzing insincerity, it is very difficult to come to definitive conclusions.

Returning to Blair's statement, despite the utter conviction of most on the Left that Blair must have been lying, there is no incontrovertible evidence that Blair did *not* believe what he was saying. In fact, precisely because he seems to have been intent on going to war by this stage, he was likely to be self-deceived. Indeed, the framing equivocation that points to misleading also detracts from a judgment of lying. As Chilcot concluded (rightly in my view):

> The Inquiry is not questioning Mr Blair's **belief**. . . . But the deliberate selection of a formulation which grounded the statement in what Mr Blair **believed**, rather than in the *judgements* which the JIC had *actually reached* in the assessment of its intelligence, indicates a distinction between his **beliefs** and the JIC's *actual judgements*. (Chilcot 2016: 73–74)

What Chilcot appears to be pointing to here is precisely a contrast between personal sincerity ("Mr Blair's belief"), indicated in bold, and the epistemic responsibility to refer to "the JIC's actual judgements," indicated in italics, while recognizing the underlined willful misleading ("deliberate selection of a formulation").

4B. Willfulness
Blair's misleading is clearly willful because it is not justifiably suspended and it breaches the trust of Parliament.

5. Responsibility

5A. Epistemic Pathologies
Turning to epistemic responsibility, there are clear signs of *dogma*. Blair was clearly guilty of *confirmatory selection*, of choosing only those aspects of the JIC report that confirmed his preexisting views and ignoring the qualifications that conveyed doubt about the conclusions. He was also guilty of *rude dismissal* in not listening to critical friends in his Cabinet like Foreign Secretary Robin Cook, who consequently resigned. As with the Bush administration, he emphatically

distorted the truth by considerably *overstating* the likelihood of WMD ("established beyond doubt," "in no doubt") with respect to the Iraq Dossier. Whether he shows a complete disregard for evidential grounding (*bullshit*) is less clear. On the one hand it is likely that he was focused on convincing the audience (the MPs) rather than respecting the facts, which is a characteristic of claptrap bullshit. On the other hand, there *was* some consensus at the time that Saddam *probably* had WMD and Blair did frame his statements carefully in terms of his own subjectivity ("I believe," "I am in"), however misleading this framing was.

Considering a similar presidential cognitive state, Carson is determined to keep things within the realm of (intentional) insincerity by describing Bush as being "intellectually dishonest":

> [H]e was *willful* in believing what he wanted to believe (believing what was consistent with his case for going to war) and not giving credence for evidence for things he did not want to believe (not believing or giving credence to what was inconsistent with his case for going to war). On the best construction possible, Bush was *intellectually dishonest*. (Carson 2010: 217)

What Carson describes here is a dangerously dogmatic attitude but not necessarily a dishonest one. There seem to be two different uses of the term "intellectually dishonest." The first clearly relates to sincerity and is found in such forms as arguing a case you do not genuinely believe in order to win an argument. This is a case of misleading through faking. However, the term is also used in a sense that is very close to epistemic irresponsibility. Thus one contributor to the question-and-answer website Quora gave the following answer to a question asking for concrete examples of intellectual dishonesty: "I know of very few people who are *intentionally* intellectually dishonest, but when it occurs it is typically the result of an ideology that *blinds one to his or her own inconsistency*" (Johnson 2015: n.p.). In TRUST terms, though, it is simply not possible for intellectual dishonesty to be unintentional: being *blinded* to one's own inconsistency is necessarily pathological dogma rather than an intentional discourse strategy.

5B. Negligence

Blair satisfies the three conditions for epistemic negligence. First, as prime minister, he had a very strong *duty of epistemic care*. We have seen that Blair, Bush, and company were all speaking in prescribed conventional contexts where the truth was strongly warranted. But the duty of epistemic care is about the speaker's *role* responsibility: it is about his duty not to betray the trust of the audience. Second, as Chilcot makes clear, Blair failed to *invest sufficiently* in investigating the truth, an extremely charitable reading of his statement being that he failed to read the Iraq Dossier carefully. Similarly, Carson notes that Bush "conveniently ignored the fact that many intelligence reports available to the administration before the war contradicted what the administration had so confidently claimed" (2010: 221). Finally, Blair failed to *hedge his commitment* to his assertion in accordance with the available evidence (e.g., in the Iraq Dossier). Similarly, members of the Bush administration were only too keen to *boost* their conviction rather than hedge it in any way.

Despite focusing solely on intentional insincerity, Carson, in the conclusion to his section on lying and deception with regard to WMD, finds himself having to fall back on the notions of negligence and recklessness:

> On the most charitable construction possible, Bush and other members of his administration were *negligent and reckless in forming and acting on their views* about Saddam Hussein's regime. They *ignored* a great deal of intelligence that pointed to different conclusions than those that they drew. (Carson 2010: 218)

This conclusion is a clear indication that what is required is an analysis of epistemic irresponsibility and particularly the ethically loaded concept of epistemic negligence.

6. Culpability

The fact that Blair's statements on WMD are probably neither lying nor bullshit in no way exonerates him. He was in a position of ultimate *institutional power* (**D5**) and thus trust with respect to the nation. He was also in a position of great *epistemic power* (**D4**) because he had access to privileged security documents while Parliament had access only to the Iraq Dossier, and Blair's Foreword framed that document in an extremely biased way. A Foreword, unlike a parliamentary speech, is not an adversarial genre but an introductory one where readers will not necessarily be on their guard and Parliament may have let its resistance break down and become more *vulnerable* (**D1**). Immediately after the release of the Chilcot Report, Tony Blair issued a press statement saying that it "should lay to rest allegations of bad faith, lies or deceit" (Kettle 2016). However, there was clearly bad faith because by this stage (as the Chilcot Report shows) he was intent on going to war come what may. This in itself is a *reprehensible motive* for the breach of trust (**D8**). The false information conveyed was of immense importance (**D9**) and the *potential harm* of the breach (**D7**) was both enormous and easily predictable because it is well known that going to war will lead to serious loss of life.

7. Judgment

Categorially, Blair's statement about WMD seems to be a case of *misleading distortion*, with elements of both insincerity (withholding, equivocation) and epistemic irresponsibility (confirmatory selection, rude dismissal, and gross overstatement). Even if there is insufficient evidence to prove willful misleading or lying beyond reasonable doubt, in such a context of high trust, Blair's distortion of the weight of the evidence for WMD was extremely negligent. More gravely still, it undermined citizens' trust in the rational deliberation of their leader. As citizens, we consent to our leaders governing by means of rational deliberation with respect to the available evidence. If we cannot trust them to deliberate rationally and responsibly, then the quality of our consent is diminished and democratic legitimacy is once again undermined.

8.6. Conclusion

This chapter has shown how the different elements of the TRUST framework can come together to produce a detailed analysis of attested cases of untruthfulness in a particular domain. The framework does not provide categorical answers, particularly with respect to the analysis of sincerity, but it scaffolds a rich analysis of sincerity and epistemic responsibility that can lead to an informed decision about ethical breach. Taken together, the three case studies demonstrate how untruthfulness in public discourse can damage democratic legitimacy. Trump's tweet on voter fraud undermined voters' trust in the integrity of US electoral procedures and devalued each citizen's vote. The Brexit Battle Bus slogan undermined the quality of evidence available for voters to use when deliberating on the life-changing decision of whether or not to leave the European Union. Blair's statement on WMD, on the other hand, undermined citizens' trust in the ability of UK leaders to deliberate rationally and responsibly in the case of international crises. This damaging of trust could be seen in reactions to May's response to the Skripal poisoning, which will be discussed in Chapter 9. Overall, these cases of untruthfulness not only negatively affected the quality of information in the public domain, but also undermined our confidence in the legitimacy of our democratically elected governments.

9
Poisoning and Partisanship
An Analysis of the Salisbury Nerve Agent Attack

9.1. Introduction

In this second analytical chapter, I demonstrate an alternative "holistic" method of TRUST analysis in which the focus is not on individual claims or short sections of text with a few related claims, but on the general manifestation of untruthfulness with respect to a particular case. Here I provide an extensive analysis of multiple claims regarding the poisoning of the Russian spy Sergei Skripal and his daughter Yulia in Salisbury, England, in March 2018. I start with a short statement to Parliament, which superficially reminds us of Blair's Preface, but I use that as a springboard for exploring various types of untruthful discourse that have emerged in relation to this international crisis. The framework thus becomes a way of structuring a much broader analysis of untruthfulness in international discourse. This analysis was also intended to test out the TRUST framework in real time as events unfolded and where, at least at first, there was still a great deal of uncertainty. Whereas the "Bliar" analysis benefited from sixteen years of distance and seven years of investigation, resulting in the extremely long and detailed Iraq Inquiry Report, I began analyzing the Skripal poisoning from Day 1 (March 4, 2018) and the first draft of this analysis was written just a month after the event.[1]

Thematically, this chapter extends the discussion of public discourse in the previous chapter, but here I deal with another factor that can affect democratic legitimacy: the overall quality of information about a subject in the public domain. In particular, I am concerned with epistemic partisanship, as discussed in the Preface and Introduction, and how this can poison our rational understanding of the world. The analysis is still structured according to the TRUST heuristic.

---

[1] That draft focused specifically on May's statement to Parliament eight days after the event. I explicitly recognized the risk that subsequent evidence might make some of the analysis seem naïve at best, or wrong at worst, but I predicted (correctly) that the core of the analysis would remain secure and that, post publication, my much better informed readers would be able to recognize that. What I did *not* anticipate, as one can never predict the future, was that the case would be more or less resolved, bar the impossibility of arresting the suspects, within about eight months, and thus long before publication of the book.

I begin by introducing some background to the Skripal poisoning case and what we now know with some confidence, more than one year after the incident (9.2). I then examine the CLAIMS made by the British Prime Minister Theresa May in her "Salisbury Statement" to Parliament just eight days after the poisoning, and particularly the putative EVIDENCE for falsity (9.3). This provides an evidential bedrock for subsequent discussion. First, I consider some possible SUSPENSIONS to journalists' and politicians' commitment to truthfulness in such cases (9.4). Then I consider the contrasting approaches to SINCERITY of the UK and Russian governments (9.5). This leads to a discussion of RESPONSIBILITY, particularly in relation to the promotion of conspiracy theories (9.6). Finally, I consider degrees of CULPABILITY and make final JUDGMENTS in relation to the case (9.7).

9.2. The Skripal Poisoning: What We Know

Sergei Skripal is a former officer in Russia's GRU (Glavnoye Razvedyvatel'noye Upravleniye, or "Main Intelligence Directorate") military intelligence agency who sold details about fellow spies to British intelligence before he was caught and convicted of high treason in 2006. He benefited from a spy swap in 2010 and settled in the small English town of Salisbury (Urban 2018). On March 4, 2018, he and his daughter Yulia were found in a semi-comatose state on a park bench in the center of Salisbury.[2] Public Health England soon recognized the symptoms as those of a nerve agent, but it took about a week for the nearby Porton Down defense laboratory to identify the poison as the rare nerve agent Novichok A234, developed by the Soviet Union. On March 12, Prime Minister Theresa May delivered a statement to Parliament attributing direct or indirect responsibility to Russia and giving Putin a 24-hour ultimatum to explain what had happened. The Russians dismissed the accusation as nonsense and accused the British government of either fabricating or perpetrating the attack. The United Kingdom and its Western allies, convinced by confidential evidence, expelled over 150 Russian diplomats/spies. The Russians responded in kind. By March 28, the police had established that the Skripals had been poisoned through liquid Novichok applied to the door handle of Sergei's house. On April 12, the Organization for the Prohibition of Chemical Weapons (OPCW) confirmed the

---

[2] By extraordinary coincidence, they were found by the British Army's Chief Nursing Officer Colonel Alison McCourt and her teenage daughter. This, combined with the fact that McCourt insisted on maintaining anonymity until she recommended her daughter for a bravery award in January 2019, inevitably fueled existing conspiracy theories about the Skripal poisoning being a false-flag operation (e.g., Murray 2019). Though unusual, it was not an "impossible" coincidence given that McCourt and her family live just outside Salisbury, a small town of 45,000 inhabitants. McCourt was clearly off duty (and with her family) at the time. If she had suspected a nerve agent, she would not have allowed her sixteen-year-old daughter to be the first to attend to the Skripals.

UK analysis of the "very pure" nerve agent; it was subsequently revealed that two GRU agents caught in the Netherlands had hacked into the Swiss laboratory where the samples were being tested (Wintour 2018). On June 30, the accidental Novichok poisoning of Dawn Sturgess and Charlie Rowley led to the discovery of the adapted perfume bottle that was probably used to spray the Novichok onto the Skripals' door handle.[3] On August 6, the British government declared that, thanks to the work of "super recognizers" scouring thousands of hours of CCTV video, they had identified the two suspects, who were subsequently revealed on September 5 under their aliases "Ruslan Boshirov" and "Alexander Petrov." The Counter Terrorism Command also released the detailed itinerary of the two agents' forty-eight hours in the United Kingdom, including the hotel they stayed at in East London, where traces of Novichok were found, their two trips to Salisbury on March 3 and 4, video evidence of their passing close to Skripal's home in the time window where the poisoning could have taken place, and the booking of two separate return flights (presumably in case unforeseen circumstances in Salisbury led to them missing the first one). On September 26 and October 8, the investigative website Bellingcat revealed that "Boshirov" and "Petrov" were the senior and highly decorated GRU agents Colonel Anatoliy Chepiga and Dr. Alexander Mishkin (BIT 2018b; BIT 2018a).[4] Furthermore, leaks from the secretive Russian passport authority 777001 led to the discovery that Chepiga and Mishkin's cover passports were only a few numbers apart and very close to those of other known GRU agents, some of whom had their address listed as the Moscow headquarters of the GRU (Roth 2018). These passport blunders, combined with confidential information seized from the two GRU hackers caught in the Netherlands, appear to have led to numerous other GRU agents being identified across the world and, by early January 2019, the British intelligence community, according to one confidential source, were confident not only that they knew "everything we need to know about Salisbury" but that they had dismantled the entire GRU network in the United Kingdom (Mendick 2019).[5]

9.3. Claims, Evidence, and the Salisbury Statement

While we now have overwhelming evidence of Russian responsibility,[6] most of the evidence indicated in the preceding was not available at the time of May's

---

[3] What happened to that bottle between March 4 and June 30 remains a mystery.

[4] It is quite probable that this information was already known to British intelligence and it may even have been indirectly leaked to Bellingcat.

[5] This last claim should be taken as hearsay, as I can find no independent verification.

[6] There are still many unanswered questions (Dejevsky 2019), but these are unknown details in an otherwise compelling narrative.

statement to Parliament (hereafter the Salisbury Statement) on March 12. At the time, parallels with Blair's statement on WMD seemed striking. As in Tony Blair's case sixteen years earlier, Theresa May was politically motivated to take decisive action. Just as Iraq did in 2002, Russia in 2018 posed a considerable threat to international peace and stability and there was a strong sense that they had "gone too far." Furthermore, many in the United Kingdom felt that the government's response to the Alexander Litvinenko poisoning in 2006 was far too weak. In that case, it was almost ten years before a public inquest found that there was a "high probability" that Andrey Lugovoi (now a deputy of the Duma) and the businessman Dmitry Kovtun were responsible for the poisoning of Litvinenko by radioactive polonium 210 (Harding 2016). At the same time, the danger of a rush to judgment in the light of Iraq seemed evident and explains the Labour Party leader Jeremy Corbyn's understandable calls for caution in taking action against Russia (Stewart 2018a). On the far left, the putative link between Blair's and May's statements has been a call to arms. The influential far left activist Craig Murray wrote an article entitled "The Novichok Story Is Indeed Another Iraqi WMD Scam" (Murray 2018). Among other claims, he argued that the nerve agent Novichok did not exist, just as Iraqi WMD did not exist.

Analysis of the Salisbury Statement on March 12, 2018 shows, however, that both the context and the content were different. For a start, unlike Blair's personal Preface, the Salisbury Statement was carefully crafted by the Cobra emergency committee,[7] which was chaired by the Home Secretary Amber Rudd but included both Cabinet members and intelligence leaders. It thus provided the official script for the Government narrative on the case,[8] rather than the prime minister's expression of personal conviction, and was designed to be as watertight as possible (the specific claims made have been numbered for ease of analysis):

[1] It is now clear that Mr Skripal and his daughter were poisoned [2] with a military-grade nerve agent [3] of a type developed by Russia. [4] This is part of a group of nerve agents known as "Novichok." [5] Based on the positive identification of this chemical agent by world-leading experts at the Defense Science and Technology Laboratory at Porton Down; [6] our knowledge that Russia has previously produced this agent and would still be capable of doing so; [7] Russia's record of conducting state-sponsored assassinations; and [8] our assessment that Russia views some defectors as legitimate targets for

---

[7] "Cobra" is an acronym for Cabinet Office Briefing Room A, a bunker room where crises are discussed.

[8] An example of following the script can be seen in the speech of the UK's deputy permanent representative to the United Nations, Jonathan Allen, to the UN Security Council two days later (UNSC 2018).

assassinations; [9] the Government has concluded that it is highly likely that Russia was responsible for the act against Sergei and Yulia Skripal. [10] Mr Speaker, there are therefore only two plausible explanations for what happened in Salisbury on the 4th of March. Either this was a direct act by the Russian State against our country. Or the Russian government lost control of this potentially catastrophically damaging nerve agent and allowed it to get into the hands of others. (Gov.UK 2018)

The ten claims made in the Salisbury Statement are explicitly asserted, factually significant, and thus potentially falsifiable. Each of them has been challenged extensively, though we should perhaps begin rather than end with the reliability of sources. Partly as a result of the secretive involvement of intelligence agencies, this is precisely the type of incident that naturally generates conspiracy theories. Sites rated as "Conspiracy" or "Questionable" by MFBC are the main sources of "falsifying" or conspiracy evidence about the Skripal case in the West. In Russia, though, government and the state media have been making claims that are qualitatively of the same sort as the conspiracy theories published on highly questionable Western sites. While this is well understood by students of Putin's Russia (e.g., Ostrovsky 2017), the combination of a deliberate Russian disinformation campaign (see later discussion), and an understandable skepticism of the UK government after the Iraq WMD fiasco seems to have resulted in an alarming number of people who believe implausible or even conspiracy theories on the Skripal poisoning.

For the sake of brevity, the enormous putative evidence for falsity of the Salisbury Statement's ten claims has been condensed into three types: the contemporary claims for the Skripals being poisoned by Novichok [claims 1–5]; the historical claims of capacity, precedent, and motive [6–8]; and the likelihood of Russian responsibility [9–10]. Given that many of the counterclaims are clearly false, I shall give brief indications of how they are, in turn, untruthful.

Claims [1–5]: *The Skripals were clearly poisoned with "Russian" military-grade Novichok.*

With regard to Claim 1 that the Skripals were indeed poisoned, many far right and far left news sources disturbingly consider the entire incident to be a media hoax. A typical headline in the alt-right US publication *The Duran* presupposes that it is all a hoax, even giving the "Hoax" titular status: "Guardian fake news. UK media tries to keep Skripal Poisoning Hoax alive" (Christoforou 2018a, n.p.). Many Russian officials have also claimed that the whole affair is a hoax. The Russian ambassador to the UN, pointing out the "hundreds of very clever ways of killing someone" in comparison to the "risky, dangerous" nature of a nerve agent attack, asked, "Couldn't you come up with a better fake story?" (York 2018). The massive clean-up operation in Salisbury alone confirms that the poisoning must have taken place and that such claims of the incident being a hoax are either clear lies or bullshit without any evidential grounding.

With regard to Claim 2, Putin announced on his first reaction to the tragedy two weeks after the event that "if it had been a military grade nerve agent, the people would have died on the spot" (Luhn 2018). This claim, which immediately gained around 250,000 impressions and was massively retweeted (Urban 2018: 276), is predicated on the unlikely scenario that both Porton Down and (subsequently) the OPCW were either wrong in their chemical analyses or were lying. The imputation of lying was fueled by the Russian Foreign Minister Sergei Lavrov, who maintained that he had received confidential information from the Spiez Laboratory in Switzerland (possibly via the GRU hacking mentioned earlier) that the agent was actually the much less toxic poison BZ. But the OPCW pointed out that BZ had only been used in a control sample and the Spiez lab responded in a tweet that "[w]e have no doubt that Porton Down was right in identifying Novichok as the poisoning agent" (Urban 2018: 279). Furthermore, the claim of dying on the spot does not take into account at least the following: the very low dosage designed for assassination of an individual rather than destruction of a community; the much slower process of absorption through the skin rather than inhalation; and loss of potency due to the cold damp weather conditions and probable hand washing (Kaszeta 2018). The subsequent tragic death of Dawn Sturgess shows how lethal the agent was. The modifier "military-grade," though, was arguably misleading and some have claimed is meaningless (Urban 2018: 277). The Soviets developed a number of variants of Novichok, including A234, specifically for military use under their secret Foliant program (Tucker 2006: 233). Furthermore, the term "military grade" was used by Porton Down rather than being government spin. But Porton Down might simply have been indicating what the OPCW subsequently described as "pure," with the implication that it could only be produced in extremely sophisticated laboratories.

With regard to Claims 3 and 4, though, Russian officials deny the very existence of the Novichok program. For example, the deputy foreign minister declared with a notable lack of hedging: "I want to state *with all possible certainty* that the Soviet Union or Russia had no programs to develop a toxic agent called Novichok" (Williams 2018). Some have rightly claimed that, as in the Iraq WMD case, our intelligence depends mainly on just one defector, in this case Vil Mirzayanov. However, whereas in the Iraq case the intelligence was based mostly on hearsay, Mirzayanov not only published the formulas for variants of Novichok in Russia before he defected, but he was also tried for revealing those "state secrets" (McCarthy 2018). It is possible that Russia is willfully misleading rather than lying in this case. Russian scientist Leonid Rink claimed in an interview with *RIA Novosti* on March 20 that:

> Novichok is not a substance [but] the whole system of chemical weapons. The chemical-weapons system adopted by the Soviet Union was called "Novichok 5." The title was not used without numbers. (Wesolowsky 2018)

If Rink is correct, the Russians might be relying on the misleading equivocation that "Novichok" refers to the "newcomer" program rather than the nerve agents themselves and that the program was, in any case, called "Novichok 5" rather than "Novichok." Notably, however, Rink's interview, which seems to confirm the existence of a Novichok program of some sort, was subsequently redacted to bring it back to the official Russian script:

> As a matter of fact, in the Soviet Union and Russia there was no program for the development of chemical weapons that was called "Novichok." Programs for the development of chemical weapons existed, but not with that title. (Wesolowsky 2018)

It is difficult to see how the Russian government could not be at the very least willfully misleading in this case. There is very strong evidence that a Novichok program existed.

Finally, with regard to Claim 5 (Porton Down's confirmation of Novichok), many believe that May lied about the source of the sample being Russia when Porton Down did not confirm this. But the Salisbury Statement does *not* claim that the poison used on the Skripals was manufactured in Russia. There is a case that "of a type developed by" [3] is misleading and this will be discussed further, but there is no direct lie here. Urban (2018: 281–282) speculates that Porton Down might actually have identified the specific place of manufacture by comparing the Salisbury sample with one secretly held in their lab. In that case, rather than falsely implying that the source of the particular sample was Russia, the government would be withholding the fact that they *knew* it was Russia to maintain the confidentiality of the secretly held sample.

Claims [6–8]: *The Russians had the capacity, record, and motive to carry out the attack.*

On capacity [6], the Russians point out that the OPCW, just five months before the poisoning, had verified the destruction of their entire chemical weapons stockpile (OPCW 2017; Ahmed 2018). However, under the Chemical Weapons

Convention, declarations are voluntary, and Russia never declared the Novichok program to the OPCW, so the OPCW could not verify its destruction. It is difficult to see how this "evidence of destruction" could not be a willful lie. On record [7], Russia has always denied its *mokroye delo* ("[blood] wet affairs"), but during Putin's presidency there have been a number of suspected state-sponsored attempted assassinations using poison, in addition to the highly publicized Litvinenko murder (Lomas 2018).[9] The UK police are currently examining fourteen cases of possible Russian state-sponsored assassinations on British soil (Dearden 2018), and while none of these cases has been proved yet, there is clear evidential grounding for making such a claim about Russia's historical record. Denial of state-sponsored assassinations from the top is most likely to be willful lying.

On motive [8], Russia clearly denies that defectors are seen as legitimate targets for assassinations. However, legislation passed by the Russian Parliament in 2006 granted Russia's president expanded powers to use force against opponents living in other countries, and in 2010 President Putin warned on Russian television:

> [T]raitors will kick the bucket, believe me. Those other folks betrayed their friends, their brother in arms. Whatever they got in exchange for it, those 30 pieces of silver they were given, they will choke on them. (Khan 2018)

Furthermore, the use of a poison that points directly to Russia seems to underline a clear message to would-be traitors like Skripal that "treason against the Russian state would be punished severely" (Urban 2018: 301); that traitors would literally choke on their betrayal.[10] Others have argued that Russia could not have targeted Skripal because he was the beneficiary of a spy swap and a presidential pardon, but there is little evidence that Putin has felt constrained to remain within the rule of law (Ostrovsky 2017) and, unlike more attractive targets, Skripal was an easy one because he was living openly under his own name. Finally, while Putin and others claimed that Russia would not have carried out such an attack just before the presidential elections and the World Cup, the killing of a "despicable traitor" could only boost Putin's popularity in Russia: his campaign spokesman Andrei Kondrashov said after his victory that "[t]he Skripal scandal has mobilized the

---

[9] The Chechen rebel Khattab was assassinated through a letter containing sarin in 2002; Viktor Yushchenko was poisoned through dioxin when he was running for the Ukrainian presidency in 2004 (he survived to become president); Anna Politkovskaya drank a poisoned cup of tea in 2006 (two years later she was murdered in an elevator); her lawyer Karinna Moskalenko was poisoned (probably through mercury) in 2008; traces of the toxic flower gelsimium were found in Alexander Perepilichny's stomach when he died suddenly in 2012; and opposition politician Vladimir Kara-Murza has survived not one but two cases of poisoning.

[10] I am allowing myself a slight performative suspension with my figurative "choke": technically, nerve agents are not "choking agents" like chlorine and phosgene (OPCW 2019b).

nation, increased turnout, and has consolidated citizens around Vladimir Putin" (Carroll 2018). Once again, then, there is ample evidence to support a claim about motive and it is most likely that Putin and other top officials are lying. However, most Putin sympathizers in the West are likely to believe these claims and thus be epistemically irresponsible rather than willfully insincere.

Claims [9–10]: *It is highly likely that Russia was either directly or indirectly responsible.*

Most pro-Kremlin media simply dismiss the claim of responsibility as nonsense and, as we shall see, have proffered a wide variety of "more likely" conspiracy theories. These are clearly bullshit claims where they are not willful lying. At the time of the Salisbury Statement, one could not rule out a third-party actor wanting to put the blame on Russia (Ahmed 2018), or even a rogue part of the Russian secret services wanting to enact revenge. A balanced assessment, though, would see these theories as far less likely given the overwhelming evidence on capacity, record, and motive. With regard to probability ("highly likely"), this depends considerably on the strength of the intelligence that had been withheld from the public at the time. Britain's briefings to EU diplomats were said to divulge "unprecedented levels of intelligence" (Sengupta 2018). Furthermore, when compared with Blair's "established beyond doubt" and Rumsfeld's "a trained ape knows that," "highly likely" seems relatively measured, particularly in the light of claim 10, which allows for indirect responsibility. In any case, while one might argue over the exact measurement of likelihood, there was far from sufficient evidence, even in March 2018, that claims 9 and 10 were false or unfounded.

While the Salisbury Statement was, then, broadly truthful and, unlike Blair's Preface, showed evidence of careful deliberation, the Skripal case has generated a plethora of untruthful claims, muddying the quality of information in the public domain, and it is to these that we now turn.

9.4. SUSPENSIONS: Satire, Fake News, and Consequential Withholding

Given the gravity of the incident, most claims made in public discourse in the West have been truth-warranting. However, all news is open to satire and thus conventional suspension. The German satirical website *The Postillon*, for example, ran the headline "British police find Putin's passport at scene of Salisbury poison attack" (Postillon 2018), along with a fake picture of the police picking up Putin's passport from the scene with tweezers. In satirical publications like *The Postillon* or *The Onion* (US), writers do not attempt to deceive the reader but to perform the untruthfulness of their stories. Thus, the Putin passport story says that "the passport was only now found in another search of the scene, as it had been hidden under a fallen leaf," which mocks the assiduousness of the specialist search teams who were to "leave no stone unturned." *Postillon* makes explicit in their FAQs that "everything you can read here is satire and therefore all made-up" (https://www.the-postillon.com/p/faq.html) so even an extremely gullible but epistemically responsible reader would know not to take its stories seriously. However, when such texts are removed from their suspended contexts and posted on social media, they are often framed as truth-warranting "news." It is at this point that satire or fiction becomes fake news that can poison public discourse. Thus Snopes.com felt the need to fact-check the Putin Passport claim (Emery 2018). More disturbingly, an explicitly "fictional dramatization" apparently showing a BBC reporter announcing the effective outbreak of nuclear war between NATO and Russia went viral on WhatsApp (with the truth-suspending disclaimer removed) in the aftermath of the Skripal poisoning and led to the BBC having to explicitly deny that nuclear war had broken out (Baynes 2018).

One disinformation strategy of the Russian response has been to turn the Skripal poisoning into a joke. For example, by disseminating the hashtags #HighlyLikely and #HighlyLikelyRussia (Urban 2018: 276), the government has "tried to turn the English phrase "highly likely" into a mocking catchphrase that implies Russia is being blamed for everything with the flimsiest of evidence" (Robinson 2018). And on March 18, the Russian Embassy in the United Kingdom tweeted a photo of Detective Poirot with the caption "*In absence of evidence*, we *definitely* need Poirot in Salisbury!" (Robinson 2018). This is a clear case of a potentially *justifiable* suspension (humor) not being *justified* in the circumstances; here it is a case of weaponizing humor as a disinformation strategy to deflect blame for a grave international incident. As in many of Trump's tweets and so many official Russian tweets, a clearly false claim ("absence of evidence") is *presupposed* in the message. It is this presupposition that can be construed as truth-warranting even if the explicit message ("we need Poirot") might fall into an admittedly weak category of humor. One litmus test for the justifiability of state humor is accepting being the target of humor, i.e., tolerating political satire. Putin does not have a good record in this respect. When he came to power, the most popular program on Russian TV, inspired by the 1980s British show *Spitting Image*, was the satirical puppet show *Kukly*, which ran on the independent TV station NTV. However, Putin was so infuriated by his puppet version that when NTV refused to remove it, he had the state-controlled Gazprom Media take over the company and remove the puppet from the show (Bennetts 2016). Some of the fabricated stories about the Skripal case broadcast by the Russian state media *ought to be* satirical, but they are framed as "news" and so are not justifiable suspensions.

A more justifiable form of putative suspension, and of major importance in this case, is the *consequential* withholding of information held by the secret services. The claim is always that this is a *protective* suspension because the security of the state would be compromised if the information were made public. The UK government claimed at the time of the Salisbury Statement that it had security information that pointed more definitively to Russia than the evidence they had made public, and the UK's allies seem to have been convinced by that evidence. One possibility, for example, is that Porton Down was actually able to identify the place of manufacture because, as indicated earlier, it already held a sample of the A234 variant from a specific lab in Russia. The CEO said, in response to Russian claims that the Novichok used in Salisbury could have come from his laboratory, that "there is no way anything like that could have come from us *or left the four walls of our facility*" (Williams 2018, n.p.). In terms of Grice's Cooperative Principle, this sentence seems to flout the maxim of Quantity, since if they held no samples of Novichok it is superfluous to add that they could not have left the facility, so it conveys the implicature that they hold samples securely. One should not read too much into this: the chief executive might simply be saying that even if they *had* held samples, they would not have escaped the facility, or he may want to withhold from the Russians the fact that the facility *did not* hold samples by implicating that they did. However, given the knowledge of Novichok development in Russia, experts believe it is not implausible that Western powers would develop their own samples in order to develop antidotes or even that, like the German secret services with respect to another Novichok variant, they had managed to obtain a clandestine sample (Williams 2018). If Porton Down did hold samples, the Skripal poisoning itself probably justifies the withholding of that information from the Russians. Furthermore, although the OPCW requires countries to declare their samples of chemical weapons, they also allow states to keep those declarations confidential under certain circumstances (OPCW 2019a). It is undoubtedly true that revealing state secrets can compromise the safety of spies or even the security of the state as a whole. At the same time, we return to the Iraq problem: can we trust the intelligence services to get it right and the government to assess it correctly (both of which failed in the case of WMD)? At the time of the first draft of this analysis, I concluded that we simply had to accept that we would not be able to arrive at definitive answers to these questions. Now it seems fairly clear that, in contrast to Iraq WMD, the intelligence services did more or less get things right in this case.

Later in the investigation, we know that the suspects' names were withheld for several months in the hope that Chepiga and Mishkin would travel to

Europe again so that they could be caught and extradited (this being constitutionally impossible from Russia). When the Press Association tweeted in mid-July that suspects had been identified, Security Minister Ben Wallace responded that "this story belongs in the 'ill-informed and wild speculation folder'" (Morris 2018, n.p.). Given that the police released the news about the identification of the suspects just over two weeks later and admitted that they had withheld this information for some time, it seems highly unlikely that Wallace was unaware of the identification. He might have hoped that the double linguistic distancing—the scare quotes and the "folder" category—might have dropped his statement from outright lying to the level of misleading. However, at the time, the public reaction could be summed up in the following tweeted reply: "So who's lying now, you or the #BBC?" To my knowledge, though, while the pro-Kremlin media made much of this insincerity, there were no subsequent accusations of lying in the mainstream UK media (e.g., in left-wing publications like *The Guardian*) because it is generally recognized that the police have a right to withhold crucial information in such cases and it is accordingly justifiable for a security minister to be insincere to protect that confidentiality in the case of leaks.

9.5. SINCERITY, Inflation, and Disinformation

The different approaches of UK and Russian officials to sincerity might be summed up as a distinction between a strategy of *inflation* of evidentially grounded claims and a strategy of *disinformation* involving deliberately fabricated claims.

9.5.1. British Inflation

With respect to the Salisbury Statement, we see a clash between the measured approach of the Home Secretary Amber Rudd and the reckless approach of the Foreign Secretary Boris Johnson, whom the government had tried to sideline in developing the Statement itself (Urban 2018: 235). While Rudd was very careful in the days after the attack not to accuse Putin directly of the assassination, Johnson was quick to inflate the claims, saying just four days later:

> Our quarrel is with Putin's Kremlin, and with his decision—and we think it *overwhelmingly likely* that it was his decision—to direct the use of a nerve agent on the streets of the UK, on the streets of Europe, for the first time since the Second World War. (Kentish 2018)

It is quite plausible that there was tension between what the UK government would have liked Porton Down to say and what the scientists were willing to say. As scientists, they could not say that the nerve agent was definitely produced in Russia[11] and the CEO made this clear. The formulation "of a type developed by Russia" [3] is designed to point to Russia while avoiding making a clear source claim. However, Johnson here is clearly *inflating* the Salisbury Statement claims in terms of both agency and probability. The Statement attributed responsibility directly *or indirectly* to "Russia." Here, Johnson attributes responsibility directly to Putin himself. Furthermore, while the Statement considered Russian responsibility of some sort "highly likely," Johnson declares it "overwhelmingly likely" that Putin gave the order directly. The Litvinenko Inquiry Report (Litvinenko 2016) gave different likelihoods for the FSB (Federal'naya Sluzhba Bezopasnosti, or "State Security Agency") being responsible ("strong probability," s10.15) and Putin giving the order ("probably", s10.16), and one would expect the same type of difference in probability in the Skripal case. So, while it may have been "highly likely" that Russia was responsible either directly or indirectly, it was perhaps only "quite likely" at the time that Putin himself gave the order. It is not clear here whether Johnson is willfully lying by degree or being epistemically negligent.

Johnson exacerbated matters in an interview with German television station Deutsche Welle. He had been referring to the fact that he had already accused Putin directly of ordering the attack. Then the following occurred:

INTERVIEWER: You argue that the *source* of this nerve agent, Novichok, is Russia. How did you manage to *find it out* so quickly? Does Britain possess *samples of it*?
JOHNSON: Let me be clear with you.... When I look at the evidence, I mean the people from Porton Down, the laboratory....
INTERVIEWER: So they have the samples...
JOHNSON: They do. And *they were absolutely categorical* and I asked the guy myself, *I said, "Are you sure?" And he said there's no doubt*. We have very little alternative but to take the action that we have taken. (Stone 2018, n.p.)

The YouTube video clip of this excerpt is entitled "Boris Johnson blatantly lies to Deutsche Welle and says Porton Down lab were absolutely categorical" (Stone 2018), and it was taken for granted by many that Johnson was lying. Johnson's reputation does not help in this case: he has openly admitted to lying on several occasions and, like Trump, he is a politician generally unhampered by considerations of sincerity or epistemic responsibility. However, Johnson does not

---

[11] Unless the hypothesis of them holding a clandestine sample from a Russian lab is true.

actually state explicitly in this extract that Porton Down gave the origin of the particular sample as Russia.

There is a major equivocation here based on the distinction between *type* and *token*. The Salisbury Statement makes a claim about *type* ("of a type developed in Russia") but not about the particular *token* (the sample retrieved from the Salisbury attack). The interviewer's comment about "the *source* of this nerve agent Novichok" does not make clear whether she is talking about the source of this *type* of nerve agent (known to be Russia) or the source of the particular sample used in Salisbury (then unknown). In the following question, the referent *it* in "find it out" is also ambiguous: the identification of the nerve agent Novichok? the source of the Novichok type? or the place of manufacture of the sample? Accordingly, the predicates of Johnson's "they were absolutely categorical [that . . .]", and "he said there's no doubt [that . . .]" are not at all clear. Porton Down may well have been categorical that they had identified Novichok, but they were equally categorical that they could not identify the source of the particular sample, as the CEO Gary Aitkenhead felt compelled to reaffirm publicly when Johnson's words were misconstrued:

> It is our job to provide the scientific evidence of what this particular nerve agent is, we identified that it is from this particular family and that it is a military grade, but it is not our job to say where it was manufactured. (Bond 2018)

When set in the context of Johnson's direct accusation of Putin and his talk of having to take action against Russia, Johnson sets up a cause-effect relation that has led many listeners/readers to the conclusion that he was saying that "the guy" had identified the place of manufacture of the sample.[12]

The problem was exacerbated when the Foreign Office, already embarrassed by Johnson's remarks, deleted a tweet which indicated that "this was a military-grade Novichok nerve agent *produced in Russia*" (Heffer 2018). It is quite plausible, as the Foreign Office claims, that this was an error made by a press officer trying to squeeze a message into a tweet: it is easy to see how a hurried assistant might think that "produced in" is roughly synonymous with "of a type developed by." However, the act of deletion was picked up by the Russian Embassy, who repackaged it as an act of deliberate withholding to cover a blatant lie. So, Johnson's legendary loose tongue and the Foreign Office's lack of care gave the wrong impression that the government were not only lying on this point but that they had lied in the Salisbury Statement too. It is not clear whether Johnson was

---

[12] If the theory about Porton Down actually possessing a clandestine sample is true, then Johnson is uncharacteristically guilty of being too truthful when he should have been following an insincere script.

willfully lying or negligently *distorting* the evidence in the days following the poisoning, but it is undoubtedly the case that his statements unnecessarily damaged the credibility of the government in the early stages of this case and gave fuel to the Russian propaganda machine.

9.5.2. Russian Disinformation

While it could be argued that the British were still working within an economy of truth (however economical), the bulk of the official Russian reaction to the case has involved concerted disinformation. The term "disinformation" comes from the Russian *dezinformatsiya*, which was the name of a department of black propaganda in Stalinist Russia. The main aim of disinformation is to sow doubt, disunity, and, above all, distrust (Pacepa and Rychlak 2013). Ostrovsky points out that "[a]t the height of the cold war some fifteen thousand officers were working on psychological and disinformation warfare" (Ostrovsky 2017: 12). So mass disinformation is hardly new to Russia: what has changed is simply the technology by means of which it is conveyed. One known "troll factory," the ironically named Internet Research Agency based in St. Petersburg, intervened heavily in the US presidential elections in 2016 (NIC 2017) and was active in the aftermath of the Skripal case. The overall strategy of disinformation is closer to insincere *bullshitting* than to lying. The focus is on achieving the rhetorical goals of doubt, disunity, and distrust, rather than conveying a specific alternative narrative that must be believed by the recipient (Pomerantsev 2015). This explains why Russian officials have been happy to *fabricate* over twenty different explanations for the poisoning (York 2018). These range from the plausible (samples of Novichok may well have been produced outside Russia) to the patently absurd (the Skripals were poisoned by the UK government to distract from Brexit or even the Telford child grooming scandal): "[I]t doesn't matter whether the Skripals were intentionally poisoned for the sake of the subsequent media campaign or if it was 'just pure luck'" that the poisoning served this purpose (Danilov 2018, n.p.). The EU vs Disinformation site had compiled over 150 cases of Russian disinformation on the Skripal case by March 2019 (EUvsDisinfo 2019). While many of the stories themselves appear to show epistemic negligence, where they are emanating from official Russian sources, they are likely to be willfully insincere rather than naively negligent.

One reaction of the Russians to the accusation, as seen earlier, is to meet it with (humorous) derision, thus demoting it from the realm of truthfulness. Another common reaction is to meet it with the label *provokatsiia* ("provocation"). *Provokatsiia* does two things: it switches the blame and often accuses the other side of a false flag operation:

> While conspiracy theories typically posit a powerful and secret cabal that pulls the strings of a complex plot, provocation has a pedestrian he-said-she-said dynamic that simply pins the tail of blame on the other donkey. (Patyk 2018, n.p.)

For example, Dmitry Kovtun, the co-murderer of Litvinenko, reacted as follows to news of the poisoning on *Interfax*:

> If someone really poisoned Skripal—if it wasn't an accident—then *of course it's a provocation* [провокация/*provokatsiia*] by British intelligence, designed foremost to discredit the Russian authorities ahead of the presidential election. (Anon 2018, n.p.)

There is a remarkable linguistic similarity between this comment and Trump's tweet on voter fraud discussed in the previous chapter. In both cases there is a groundless conspiracy-level claim combined with the powerful normalization marker "of course" (конечно in Russian). *Provokatsiia* was equally used as an official explanation for the murder of Putin's main opponent Boris Nemtsov, which Putin himself claimed "bears all the hallmarks of a provocation" (Shuster 2015). Closely related to *provokatsiia* is simply dismissing the accusation as nonsense deriving from pure Russophobia. Russian Foreign Ministry Spokesperson Maria Zakharova (one of the main sources of disinformation in this case) described it as "just some sort of *insufferable absurdity*" (RT 2018), while Russian Foreign Minister Sergei Lavrov said that it was "*all nonsense*": "We have nothing to do with it. Everyone seems to be so *brainwashed* that our blogosphere is already full of comments that *turn things upside down*" (Lavrov 2018). Putin himself, in his first comments on the poisoning two weeks after the event, said "It's complete *drivel, rubbish, nonsense* that somebody in Russia would allow themselves to do such a thing ahead of elections and the World Cup" (TWP 2018). Once again, there are parallels with Trump and doublespeak. Mainstream news becomes "fake news," information becomes "disinformation," the truth becomes "lies."

While Johnson's statements to Deutsche Welle might have been misconstrued, there is no question that both his overall strategy of claim inflation and the Russian government's strategy of disinformation are willfully insincere and damaging to the quality of public discourse.

9.6. RESPONSIBILITY: Epistemic Negligence and the Promotion of Conspiracy Theories

While disinformation was actively pursued by the Russian state, there were many commentators both in Russia and the West who seemed genuinely to believe the

Russian disinformation and conspiracy theories. Extreme epistemic partisanship can lead to almost any incident being made to fit into any conspiracy theory. For example, *The Duran* ran the headline "The poisoning of Sergei Skripal leads right to Hillary Clinton and the DNC [the Democratic National Committee]" and asked "Was Skripal the latest victim of the Clinton mafia's murder machine?" (Christoforou 2018b, n.p.). A branch of the UK Independence Party, whose former charismatic leader Nigel Farage was both the main driver behind Brexit and a keen admirer of Putin, tweeted that the culprit could be "a third party *such as the EU* trying to interfere in UK Russian relations" (@UKIP High Wycombe, March 8, 2018).

However, the most influential form of epistemic irresponsibility has come from those British and other Western tweeters and bloggers who uncritically relay Russian disinformation. Indeed, it may well be the case, as Mark Galeotti argues, that these radical social media users not only relay Russian propaganda but might actually generate it:

> This is one of the ways in which the Russians often work—they get to enjoy the rich buffet of nonsense that Western lunatics come up with and simply pick which ones they're going to offer to a wider audience. (York 2018, n.p.)

For example, the state-owned channel Russia 1 relayed Christoforou's fanciful connection of the poisoning with the Steele Dossier and the "Clinton mafia" (York 2018). Unlike Russian officials or Internet Research Agency employees, Western bloggers do not seem to be deliberately setting out to willfully mislead the public. Indeed, they seem to be convinced that they are telling nothing but the truth. It is simply that they are arriving at that truth in an irresponsible fashion.

There is space here to consider just one example of this phenomenon: a tweeter known as Ian56. Ian56 is extremely influential. He had around 32,000 followers at the time of the Skripal poisoning and over two days (March 19–20, 2018) his was one of the ten most retweeted accounts mentioning "Skripal" (Nimmo 2018). The contents of his tweets were so unerringly pro-Kremlin that he came to be mistaken for a Russian troll or even bot. Ben Nimmo of the Digital Forensic Research Lab of the Atlantic Council concluded quite reasonably about the @Ian56789 account:

> It remains unclear whether it is merely a pro-Kremlin troll, linked in an informal network with like-minded accounts, or whether it was part of a more organized effort, such as the "troll factory" in St. Petersburg. . . . What is clear is that its profile picture was not its own, its biographical claims are inconsistent and its content systematically promoted Russian government narratives. (Nimmo 2018, n.p.)

Although Nimmo does not directly accuse Ian56 of being a professional Russian troll, there is an implication, particularly in the second sentence, that there is willful deception taking place. There is some evidence of a correlation between user anonymity and sensitive content (Peddinti et al. 2014). Yet use of a false profile picture in itself is not indicative of willful deception: use of a significantly more attractive avatar (in this case an English male model) on Internet fora is common. There is a murky line between false avatars and false accounts. Nimmo's conclusions are not epistemically negligent: he draws on sufficient evidence, gives two possible options, and, crucially, hedges his conclusion with "it remains unclear." The political editor of *The Guardian*, though, arguably went one step further and became epistemically negligent when she reported unspecified "Whitehall sources" who supposedly claimed that the account was a Russian "bot" (Stewart 2018b). It was a significant propaganda victory for the Kremlin, then, when Ian56 was interviewed on Sky News not as a Russian *bot* but as an English *being* (Bunkall 2018).

Analysis of Ian56's twitter activity, though, demonstrates an extreme form of epistemic partisanship in which anything pro-Kremlin or pro-Trump, however fanciful, is taken categorically as true, and anything that emanates from the Western "MSM" (the mainstream media) is treated as categorically false. Nimmo seems to have missed that Ian56 had already been flagged by the BBC in early January 2017 as the most influential account in the spreading of the "Queen is dead" conspiracy hoax under the hashtag #mediablackout (BBCTrending 2017). Crucially, Ian56's contribution did not concern the putative death of the Queen but the untrustworthiness of any Western media (Figure 9.1).

The irrelevance of the post to the thread and the aggressive ad hominem attack on the reader ("congratulations ... you haven't the faintest idea") are classic trolling behaviors. The BBC article then notes that his tweets were liked and retweeted by known "'sockpuppets'—fake or duplicate accounts designed to magnify a message online" (BBCTrending 2017, n.p.). This is precisely what happened in the case of Ian56's Skripal tweets: they were amplified so much by sockpuppets, bots, and known Russian trolls that it became impossible to distinguish the tweets of this account from those emanating from the Internet Research Agency (IRA) "troll factory."[13] This is not a question of political partisanship: it is about epistemic responsibility. In his short interview on Sky, Ian56 (he does not give his surname) claims in a remarkable overstatement: "I am speaking for the vast majority of British people, *59-point-9 million out of 60-million* English people" (Bunkall 2018).

---

[13] Massive retweeting of ideologically favorable tweets is a known strategy in cyberwarfare, in which the United States and the United Kingdom are now investing heavily to counteract Russian and Chinese cyberwarfare.

Figure 9.1. Ian56's contribution to the "Queen is Dead" media hoax.

The issue that Ian56 raises for TRUST is with regard to the "negligence" condition "duty of epistemic care." From his brief appearance on Sky News, Ian56 appears to be retired and with no institutional affiliation. However, his account is extremely influential, perhaps even influencing the professional Russian trolls. Twitter accounts arguably become ethically *accountable*, and thus automatically have a duty of epistemic care, when they have this level of potential influence on public opinion. Ian56 is therefore being not just epistemically irresponsible as a private citizen, but epistemically negligent as a social media personality.

9.7. Degrees of CULPABILITY and Final JUDGMENTS

The stakes are extremely grave in this case. On the British side, we have a government making claims which, if they proved to be willfully insincere or epistemically negligent, could lead to irrevocable damage to international relations. As we saw in the case of WMD, we have speakers with great epistemic and institutional power (D4/5). As citizens, we are vulnerable trustees because we are not party to withheld intelligence information (D1). And it is not difficult to see that great harm could come from either willful insincerity or epistemic negligence on the part of the government (D7). On the Russian side, their responsibility for the crime is aggravated by their institutional warranting of the truth (D6) and their knowledge of the facts that they are concealing so blatantly from their own people (D4/5). In their disinformation campaign, they are hoodwinking both their own people and Western sympathizers. Clearly, the motive for hiding their actions is utterly reprehensible (D8) and there is potential grave harm in the covering up of their misdeeds (D7). Indeed, there is an aggravating circumstance here (6B) in that they are destabilizing our trust in evidence and truth. For example, Nimmo (2018) analyzes a poll posted by a moderate left-wing tweeter "@Rachael_Swindon" who asked the Twittersphere quite reasonably: "Are you satisfied that Theresa May has supplied enough evidence for us to be able to confidently point the finger of blame towards Russia?" 77% of respondents to her poll said "No," but the underlying assumption of such a poll is that most of the respondents will be British. Yet Nimmo found that most of the retweets of the poll (and thus probably votes) were from either Russian-language or pro-Kremlin accounts (Nimmo 2018). Yet @Rachael concludes from the results of the poll that "[t]he mood of the British public is starting to shift." Not only has she been deceived by the poll, but then the poll itself becomes "evidence" of a mood shift. The damage to trust is potentially enormous, then, making these discursive acts of unethical untruthfulness utterly reprehensible.

In terms of JUDGMENT, when taken in the overall context of the discourse surrounding this case and in light of the evidence that has emerged, the Salisbury Statement seems fairly measured. While one can question the assessment of "highly likely" so early in the investigation, we are not privy to the confidential information held by the UK government at the time, and there is no clear evidence that any of the claims made were false. In terms of suspensions, some withholding of confidential security information was probably justifiable as a consequential protective suspension, and satire is a justifiable conventional suspension provided it is explicitly cued. However, the Russians used performative humor as a weapon in their information war, and the false presuppositions conveyed through that humor cannot be justified suspensions. In terms of Sincerity, Boris Johnson inflated the Salisbury Statement claims, but it is not clear to what extent this was willful misleading or lying, on the one hand, or a combination of an epistemically reckless straying from the official script and careless speech, on the other. In either case, it damaged the credibility of the government. The Russians engaged in a willful strategy of disinformation designed to instill distrust in Western information and thus distract from the clear evidence of their own responsibility. They were assisted in this by pro-Kremlin Western bloggers and tweeters who demonstrated extreme epistemic irresponsibility that became negligent in cases where they had established a standing in social media.

9.8. Conclusion

My epistemic journey in this case took me from an initial degree of doubt and suspicion, fueled by the Iraq WMD case, to utter conviction of specific Russian responsibility as I processed the accumulating weight of the evidence against Russia. What was extraordinary, though, in tracking the daily progress of the case, was how little effect the growing evidence had on those buying in to the Russian narrative of innocence. A poll by the Levada Centre at the end of October 2018, by which time most details of the case were known, revealed that only 3% of Russian citizens believed the Russian intelligence services (Российские спецслужбы) were responsible for the poisoning, while 28% believed it was perpetrated by British intelligence (Levada 2018). Large numbers of people in the West were also convinced that Russia could not be responsible or at least that there was reasonable doubt. On April 20, after Novichok had been confirmed by the OPCW and police had identified the method of delivery, less than half of Labour Party supporters believed that the Russian state was responsible for the poisoning (BMG 2018), and one or two high-profile mainstream journalists still remain unconvinced (e.g., Dejevsky 2019).

The discursive evidence in this chapter seems to suggest three possible interconnected reasons for this: disinformation, distrust, and dogma. Disinformation willfully muddies the waters and is deliberately designed to lead to distrust in the victim's national political and media institutions. We saw the effect of Russian disinformation on the US presidential elections in 2016, and it is likely that it had an effect on perceptions of the Skripal case in the West. Such disinformation can work so well in the West, though, partly because there is already very low trust in both the politicians and the professional journalists who communicate to the public in such a case. As we saw with the reactions to statements by May, Johnson, and Wallace, the public are very quick to call willful "lies" where there might be subtleties, ambiguities, or suspensions. Such discursive misdemeanors are then placed on the same level as outright Kremlin fabrication. For the Ian56s of this world, *any* news we are receiving from the "MSM" is all lies because the "MSM" simply cannot be trusted. Yet these people tend to conflate two different phenomena: bias and unreliability. Most media sources are biased toward the ideological leanings of their outlet, and we have seen in previous chapters how this can cloud judgement of the evidence. However, this is very different from being unreliable in reporting the facts. In comparison with alternative media, the mainstream media as a whole are considerably more reliable in reporting the facts because journalists are trained to do this: they have professional expertise in factual reporting, even if they then overlay an ideological orientation. Many alternative media journalists and social media personalities lack the journalistic expertise to guarantee a basic level of factual reporting.

As Kruger and Dunning (1999) noted, there seems to be an inversely proportional relationship between lack of knowledge or expertise and the confidence with which claims are made. This Dunning-Kruger effect can be seen in the way untrained and inexperienced reporters, bloggers, tweeters, and commenters discuss the Skripal case with utter conviction and with supposed expertise in nerve agents, police investigations, security services, and the workings of government. The problem is that such supreme confidence, or intellectual arrogance, is highly dogmatic, shutting out evidence and alternative views. Instead of *weighing up* the evidence, Dunning-Kruger dogmatists are *weighed down* by their convictions, so they latch on to elements of doubt or even conspiracies rather than face the cognitively dissonant possibility of their being wrong. This is what leads to dangerous epistemic partisanship, which in turn poisons the quality of public discourse and thus the quality of citizens' deliberation on fundamental issues. Countering these forms of discursive pathology is as important as tackling deliberate disinformation if we are to defend democratic legitimacy.

Conclusion

C.1. Introduction

The TRUST framework represents a radical challenge both to existing notions of untruthfulness and to the relevance of this topic to language research. In this conclusion, I return to the three central propositions of the TRUST framework concerning the *scope* (S), *ethical import* (E), and *discursive analysis* (D) of untruthfulness, and tease out some of their implications, limitations, and possible future directions. I then briefly take up the challenge of the relevance of this topic to language research and consider the possibility of an interdisciplinary Ethical Discourse Analysis. Finally, I discuss the potential impact of the framework in terms of the fightback against epistemic partisanship.

C.2. TRUSTed: The Scope of Untruthfulness

With regard to the extension of insincerity from utterance to discourse (S1), most insincerity in situated discourse does not involve explicitly stating a false belief, but using strategies or pragmatic tactics to hide what we do not want our interlocutor to know. The TRUST framework enables us to account for those forms of untruthfulness rather than simply indicating whether a claim is an example of lying or not. Further, extending insincerity from utterance to discourse reveals that the overriding category of insincerity is actually not lying but withholding. At that point, misleading becomes a subcategory of withholding and lying a subcategory of misleading. This discursive nesting has powerful implications for the analysis of untruthfulness in situated discourse because, as seen in the case studies, it permits us not simply to assign a single category of untruthfulness, but to consider in what ways a single claim of untruthfulness might withhold, mislead, and lie (if it does all three) at the same time. This considerably enriches the analysis and increases our understanding of the different types of untruthfulness at work in discourse. It seems not unreasonable to assume that insincere speakers worldwide have available to them the major discourse strategies of withholding, misleading, and lying. But how those strategies are realized pragmatically and linguistically is likely to vary considerably across communities and cultures, and this opens up an extensive research program for intercultural and intracultural pragmatics.

There are naturally some limitations with regard to the analysis of insincerity. In some respects, the main categories might seem too broad. The umbrella use of "withholding" is a term of art. The narrower use to cover "withholding without misleading" is closer to ordinary language, though I also incorporate concealing sub-strategies (*evading* and *blocking*) within that category. The term "misleading," as detailed in Chapter 5, is not entirely satisfactory, but it functions better than "deception" and the figurative sense of "mis-leading" seems effective. In other respects, though, my construal of insincerity is narrow from a critical theoretical perspective (Rousseau, Gide, Benjamin) and semioticians might object to my focusing on the verbal to the exclusion of the non-verbal or visual. These were methodological rather than ideological choices: going beyond the verbal (and the withheld) would have made an already large project unmanageable. Where I have introduced new categories, such as my sub-strategies of withholding, my categories of plagiarism, or the dogmatic discursive symptoms of *confirmatory selection* and *rude dismissal*, I am aware that these need to be explored in greater depth. But my focus has been on the big picture and in trying to develop a comprehensive framework that can be applied in practice. When practice is in play, things become messy.

Regarding the more radical proposition that untruthfulness should also include non-intentional epistemic irresponsibility (S2), removing the requirement for intentionality again has powerful implications. In the first place, it opens up the analysis to the many cases in our post-factual world in which speakers appear sincerely to believe their bullshit. But, perhaps more importantly, it opens up the analysis to the even more frequent cases where we simply cannot know whether or not the speakers believe what they are saying. Unfortunately, as noted with regard to Politifact's category of "Pants-on-fire," making a "ridiculous claim" does not guarantee that the speaker does not believe it. The inclusion of epistemic irresponsibility in our account of untruthfulness allows us to analyze these innumerable cases. Constructing categories for epistemic irresponsibility is, however, uncharted territory, so I have relied, to some extent, on drawing parallels with the categories of insincerity. *Dogma* results from closed-mindedness as *withholding* is discursive closure and both tend to be represented by discursive absence (lack of counter evidence, lack of revelation). *Distortion*, like *misleading*, involves linguistic realization and leading the hearer astray (though unwittingly in the case of distortion). Just as *lying* is uncompromising with respect to insincerity, *bullshit* is uncompromising with respect to responsibility. However, the discourse pathologies are not operationalized to the same degree as the insincere discourse strategies and there is work to be done in this respect. The bridge category of *bullshitting* sits somewhat awkwardly in the middle of the map of discursive untruthfulness but it does not sit well on either side of the map.

The question of agency is undoubtedly problematic with respect to the irresponsible discourse pathologies. At what point does the unconscious bias of *confirmatory selection* become deliberate *omission*? At what point does sincere indignant *rude dismissal* become deliberate *blocking*? At what point does careless *distorting* become deliberate *lying*? Intentionality is not a binary phenomenon but ranges from barely conscious awareness of acting to careful deliberation. It *might* be possible to operationalize the distinction between discourse strategies and pathologies a little more rigorously, and that is certainly a conceivable future direction, but these are questions that ultimately cannot be answered analytically through clear tests but must be answered through *in situ* careful deliberation and judgement. They are questions for the jury rather than the expert witness.

C.3. TRUSTworthy: Ethical Value and Linguistics

My fundamental claim with regard to ethical value is that it lies in the discursive *context* rather than in the linguistic form, or lack of it. Specifically, the ethical value of untruthfulness lies in relations of trust deriving from a presumption of truthfulness in discourse (E). I am indebted in particular to Williams (2002), Faulkner (2007), and Pettit (2015) for this account of the connection between truthfulness and trust. What is particularly original in TRUST, though, is the way these relations of trust have been systematized within the framework. The TRUST framework focuses on three specific ways in which trust relations are manifested in discursive untruthfulness.

First, I argued through proposition E1 that the potential negative ethical value of untruthfulness is neutralized when the speaker is *justified* in *suspending* her presumed epistemic commitment. In this case, either there is no breach of trust because there is a mutual understanding between speaker and hearer that truth is not in play in that particular moment in the interaction, or there is an interactional breach of trust that is considered to be overridden for some greater good. The analysis of justifiable and justified suspensions can help provide a more dynamic and nuanced account of the economy of truthfulness. Sociocultural discourse conventions, whether in the form of speech acts, genres, or strategies, can provide us with a set of presumptions about the likely value of discursive insincerity and epistemic irresponsibility in a given speech event, but these presumptions can be overturned in the local discourse dynamics. In a sense, Wittgenstein's (2009) notion of language games is misleading when applied to discourse because games come with fixed rules. The more general and dynamic notion of "play" is perhaps more useful (Cook 2000).

The second proposition about the nexus between truthfulness and trust (E2) is that where an act of discursive insincerity or epistemic irresponsibility leads to an *unjustified breach of trust*, we can say it is *willful* or *negligent*, respectively (and thus morally blameworthy). While the concept of willful insincerity does not seem to be problematic for linguists and philosophers, I have met some resistance to accepting the culpable ignorance at the heart of epistemic negligence. What is certainly recognized in TRUST is that most cases of epistemic irresponsibility in everyday interaction could not be classed as "negligent." It could be argued that we *all* have a duty of epistemic care when we are not in a justified suspended context and thus are warranting the truth of what we are saying. But that would put too much of an investigative burden on us. We all make factual mistakes all the time: it would be too much to expect us not to in everyday encounters where our mistakes will have very limited damage. In this case, strategic trust does come into play: we should not trust everything everyone says on every occasion, and we generally do not do so.

My final proposition about the nexus between ethical untruthfulness and trust (E3) is that the conditions of trust in place in a given context help determine the *degree of culpability* of the breach of trust. It would seem clear that if we are going to make any form of ethical statement about an act of discursive untruthfulness, this statement should say something about the gravity of the breach of trust. As indicated in Chapter 7, we might talk about "high trust" (strong asymmetry of institutional or epistemic power and high vulnerability of the trustor) or "low trust" (symmetrical power relations and low vulnerability) discursive contexts, but it is difficult to operationalize this in practice. The choice of introducing nine breach of trust dimensions, then, is primarily for the purpose of practical analysis. Most of these dimensions are not new in themselves. Vulnerability (**D1**), Potential Harm (**D7**), Reprehensibility (**D8**), and Information Importance (**D9**) in particular have been much discussed. What is new is the attempt to integrate them into a single framework. The dimensions have proved very useful in analysis so far. I have made no attempt to measure points along each dimension, let alone weight the dimensions in an overall assessment. The point is simply to make the analyst aware of different factors to be borne in mind when making an ethical evaluation of the specific act of untruthfulness. However, it would not be impossible to make the process more rigorous, and even measurable to some extent, through the standard qualitative research method of inter-rater reliability.

C.4. TRUSTing: Situated Discourse Analysis of Unethical Communication

TRUST is unique in providing a systematic framework for analyzing both the discursive form and ethical value of untruthfulness in situated discourse (D). It is also unique in mapping out a complete categorization system for both faces of untruthfulness (discursive insincerity and epistemic irresponsibility) and seeing these categories in terms of their discursive manifestation as insincere strategies and irresponsible pathologies. It provides a systematic account of "suspensions" of a speaker's commitment to truthfulness that can accommodate the complex variations in epistemic context that can occur in situated discursive practice and that can further accommodate not only sociocultural and sociolinguistic variation but also the oft-forgotten individual differences between speakers. And it views the ethics of untruthfulness within a broader understanding of trust, in which both the ethical value itself and the degree of culpability depend not on the *form* of untruthfulness, but on the interpersonal relations and the conditions of trust that hold in the particular discursive context.

One of my major aims in developing this framework has been to move analytical discussion of lying, insincerity, and untruthfulness from words, speech acts, or pragmatic devices to more general discourse strategies and pathologies. This provides a rich map of categories through which one can navigate. I have tried to provide rigorous operational grounds for distinguishing between withholding, misleading, and lying in terms of false contribution to the QUD, expression of the believed-false *p*, options to change epistemic stance, and plausible deniability. On the other hand, the sub-strategies and pragmatic tactics described here are not intended to be exhaustive, and there is scope for proposing new sub-strategies and tactics. However, I would urge being parsimonious in categorization since otherwise the framework becomes too unwieldy in terms of application. There are literally hundreds of existing terms for forms of insincerity, and there is an analytical need to recognize where these fall in terms of broader categories of insincerity. Some (e.g., intentional omitting, equivocation, and fabricating) fall fairly easily into the categories of withholding, misleading, and lying. Others, such as spin and bluffing, describe super-strategies that hold in particular domains such as political discourse and negotiation.

The TRUST heuristic outlined in this book has been developed in dialectic with discursive practice. Hypotheses were tested on text and helped shape the framework.[1] In its emerging forms, the TRUST heuristic has been applied to around two hundred cases of putative untruthfulness, and this engagement with

---

[1] I am grateful to both undergraduate and postgraduate research students for helping me with this testing.

discursive practice is ongoing. The framework emerged through much trial and more error. One of the errors came when I became convinced that it was possible to develop a formal heuristic (a decision chart) that would lead the analyst to the "correct" categorization of untruthfulness. However, when I applied my complex decision chart, I realized that I did not actually want to arrive at a single answer. Yes, it was possible to take the analyst systematically through the different types of suspension and the different strategies and sub-strategies of insincerity, but the journey was much more informative and valuable than the destination, and I do not want analysts to construe the TRUST framework in purely decisional terms. My hope is that the framework actually troubles rather than facilitates simple categorization. It is not as simple as many think to call a lie or bullshit.

As for trial, perhaps the most important development that came through testing was the realization that the discursive categories of epistemic responsibility must be discourse pathologies rather than discourse strategies (D2). The notion of "discourse pathology" is likely to draw fire from linguists because, as indicated earlier, it is mostly not possible to distinguish *linguistically* between, say, a conscious discourse strategy of *bullshitting* and a pathology of *bullshit*. But, equally, it is mostly not possible to distinguish *linguistically* between *lying* and sincere assertion. Analyses of untruthfulness *must* involve more than text. Another development that came through testing, and this time from my research students, was the temporary addition of a universal duty of epistemic care with regard to human rights. However, I had to row back on this one because I found that some of my millennial and iGen students were using it to make quite dogmatic judgments about truthfulness based on opinion rather than factual falsity. The current wording with respect to the first negligence condition (duty of epistemic care) includes "with respect to another's reputation," which keeps it within the safer scope of defamation law. One area that emerged in testing but has been put on hold is the recognition that some aspects of untruthfulness can only be seen and understood over extensive stretches of discourse. The Skripal poisoning case study is a move to extend the analysis beyond individual texts. However, this is still only part of the story, and there is certainly scope for exploring how the steps can be extended to much larger stretches of discourse.

One common contemporary critique of any attempt to propose a model or framework is that it will be culture-bound. As a discourse analyst, I am very wary of claims of universality, such as Habermas's notion of "universal pragmatics" (1998). At the same time, it does seem unlikely that there are societies where discursive sincerity and epistemic responsibility do not play an important role in the ethics of discourse. Claimed cultural differences often turn out to be misconceptions on closer inspection: confusing culture with ontogenetic development (children take time to develop our adult conception of lying); mistaking self-protective suspensions for willful lying; construing "cheap" communication

(Haiman 1998) as consequential. The discursive virtues of truthfulness are undoubtedly economically regulated at the local level, but are also not necessarily stable even within discourse communities. My informal surveys with students on false implicature and false invitation demonstrated quite remarkably that there is no "community" consensus on the boundaries between lying and not lying or between politeness and dishonesty. More work needs to be done on the ethical tensions *within* communities, rather than just supposed differences *across* communities.

Finally, when constructing a model or framework, a difficult compromise always has to be made between theoretical clarity and oversimplification. Categories almost certainly underdetermine the phenomena they are meant to describe, and they come with the distinct danger of forcing interpretations or reifying concepts that do not correspond well with the facts. But this is where the intellectual virtue of critical openness comes into play. Models are ultimately constructed to be deconstructed in the open play of academic discussion.

C.5. EDA: Ethical Discourse Analysis

Implicit to the argument in this book, given that it is coming from a linguist rather than a philosopher, is the claim that the analysis of discursive untruthfulness and communication ethics more broadly should be considered a legitimate topic within language and communication. However, it is necessarily an interdisciplinary topic. My theoretical point of departure, in contrast to the mainstream Saussurean linguistic tradition, was that language and communication do not exist in an ethical vacuum. Language matters not just in what is said (reference), what is meant (semantics and pragmatics), or what is constructed (identity and ideology), but also in the ethical import of its saying or not being said. This ethical dimension to language is recognized by the US National Communication Association (NCA) in their *Credo for Ethical Communication*:

> Questions of right and wrong arise whenever people communicate. Ethical communication is fundamental to responsible thinking, decision making, and the development of relationships and communities within and across contexts, cultures, channels, and media. . . . We believe that unethical communication threatens the quality of all communication and consequently the well-being of individuals and the society in which we live. (NCA 2004: ix)

Untruthful discourse, when it is also unethical, can lead the hearers astray (mislead) and deny them what they have a right to know, but it can also breach a trust between interlocutors that can damage relationships in the long term.

At one level, then, this book might be seen as an exploration of a new form of interdisciplinary engagement between discourse analysis and ethics. We might call this Ethical Discourse Analysis (EDA). Just as Critical Discourse Analysis (Wodak and Meyer 2009; Fairclough 2010) focuses on the ideological dimension of discourse, Ethical Discourse Analysis focuses on the ethical dimension of discourse. So, we are interested in not only how, say, to distinguish between lying and misleading, but also how to assess the discursive conditions under which lying and misleading can be construed as ethical or unethical. Ethical Discourse Analysis has both a descriptive and a normative dimension. Descriptively, it works toward developing tools for analyzing the ethical dimension in discourse, and this book works on developing such tools for analyzing untruthful discourse. But, as in Critical Discourse Analysis in linguistics and virtue ethics and epistemology in philosophy (Battaly 2015), there is also a normative dimension to EDA. If, as the NCA claims, unethical communication adversely affects "the well-being of individuals and the society in which we live" (NCA 2004: ix), it is incumbent on us as academics to promote ethical communication, and, in the specific case of this book, epistemically virtuous discourse.

It is vital to stress for the linguistic reader that EDA is not a form of prescriptive linguistics as ordinarily understood. Prescriptive linguistics generally lays down rules about how to use linguistic *forms* ("ending sentences with a preposition is something up with which I will not put"). Ethical Discourse Analysis, on the other hand, is concerned with interactional well-being. Virtuous discourse is truthful when it is appropriate to be so, as this promotes understanding and trust. The quality of being truthful, though, resides in the speaker, not the speech. A text may be truthful in the sense that it is accurate, but it will not be virtuous unless a *commitment* has been made to its accuracy. If a politician cynically reads a speech written by his speechwriter for strategic effect but is not epistemically committed to the content, as true as that content is, the speech itself cannot be ethically truthful. The speech is virtuous only if it is accompanied by the requisite intellectual/affective properties of truthfulness.

C.6. IMPACT: Fighting Back against Epistemic Partisanship

In the Preface, I motivated this book in terms of the danger of epistemic partisanship, the judgment of knowledge on purely partisan grounds. So, I should conclude with some indication of how the TRUST framework might help in the fight-back against epistemic partisanship. There are three major areas of potential impact: education, training, and regulation.

First and foremost, there is a need to instill through education a greater awareness in the population of the full economy of untruthfulness. The framework can be used wherever critical thinking is being developed to train our epistemic sensibility: our awareness of the complex issues involved with truthfulness and untruthfulness and how we might go about making reasoned judgments of untruthfulness in everyday life. Thanks to our natural psychological biases, we are often far too quick in accusing others of lying, and this might be causing damage at the levels of both interpersonal and international trust. Children need to be explicitly taught, perhaps through the Golden Rule, that to be accused of lying when you know you are not (and know that only you can know whether you have lied or not) can be particularly damaging to relations of trust. Even if we subsequently discover that we did indeed get things wrong, it does not remove the hurt from the false accusation of lying. The TRUST framework makes one think very carefully before making a potentially trust-damaging accusation of lying. At the same time, the framework makes clear that just because one has not lied, this does not absolve us of moral responsibility. Just because one has not lied or been otherwise insincere, it does not absolve us of moral responsibility for being epistemically negligent. If we have a duty of epistemic care and we fail to fulfill that duty, we are, in one sense, just as responsible as if we had performed our duty, discovered the facts, and then lied about them: the real-world damage will be the same. Such fundamental tenets of rational civic discourse tend to find no outlet at school. Furthermore, a focus on SAT scores and school league tables and the measurement of educational achievement can come at the expense of the development of critical thinking, which is the best insurance against dogma. Critical thinking and civic discourse need to be built into the school curriculum so that all citizens become aware of the dangers of both epistemic negligence and the indiscriminate calling out of lying.

Critical thinking as an antidote to dogma is also fundamental in the education or training of advocacy. TRUST can be used to train for "testimonial sensibility" (Fricker 2007). Fricker is concerned with the intellectual vice of "epistemic injustice," which "wrongs someone in their capacity as the subject of knowledge" (2007: 5), for example by assigning too little credibility to someone's testimony on the basis of who they are (e.g., class, gender, ethnicity) rather than what they know. Epistemic injustice is countered by "critical openness" (2007: 66), or preventing your prejudices from influencing your assessment of others' testimony, and this can be developed by training in "testimonial sensibility": "An appropriately trained testimonial sensibility enables the hearer to respond to the word of another with the sort of critical openness that is required for a thoroughly effortless sharing of knowledge" (2007: 84). Greater awareness of the discursive dynamics of dogma and distortion, as developed in TRUST, can contribute to training in critical openness, which might help obviate the dogmatic attitude that I have argued here underlies all forms of epistemic irresponsibility.

Epistemic partisanship is not a preserve of the Right. The Left is just as likely to succumb to it, as indicated by the sexual harassment example in Chapter 6. If we avoid dogma in all its forms, we should be able to avoid testimonial insensibility.

The critical awareness developed through training in TRUST might also inform journalistic practice. First, the fact-checker's proof of a false claim is our *point of departure*, not our destination, in an analysis of untruthfulness. In itself, the false claim tells us nothing about the speaker's untruthfulness, only that he has gotten his facts objectively wrong. The framework ensures that the rich complexity of untruthfulness in situated context can be explored. I would like to see fact-checking sites such as PolitiFact either accept a purely fact-checking role or adopt a more sophisticated account of the conceptual leap from "mostly false" to "Pants on Fire." TRUST, particularly in the form of its heuristic, provides a ready-made account of that move. Following the TRUST heuristic might lead to the exposure of fewer pants on fire but should lead to the identification of more bulls in shit. Second, journalists in general need a more sophisticated analytical account of untruthfulness with regard to the voluminous media discussion of our "post-truth" or "post-factual" world. Many journalists are aware of Frankfurt's (2005) work, but do not realize he covers only a small part of the domain of epistemic irresponsibility. The TRUST framework is able to provide an analytical sophistication that would improve journalistic discussion of post-factuality and epistemic partisanship. Third, the TRUST framework demonstrates how an approach to news reporting as either *salty*-like or *tasty*-like can have real practical consequences. If the reporting of news is conceived as *salty*-like, journalists should *investigate the truth* and report the results of that investigation impartially. This may or may not concur with interested parties' beliefs or opinions and it may challenge received wisdom. But if news is held to be *tasty*-like, the focus will shift from investigating the truth to *sampling public opinion*. No matter how well-informed or evidence-based the opinions are, "balance" will mean giving equal time and weight to the different opinions and then measuring how "popular" those opinions are. But where, as with climate change, the MMR vaccination scare, or, more controversially, the EU Referendum, the facts and expert (i.e., evidence-based) opinions are overwhelmingly on one side, superficial presentational balance leads to radical epistemic imbalance. Where a news organization like the BBC is highly trusted, presentational "balance" can give the misleading impression that the two sides of an argument are equally weighted in terms of evidence so that the viewer can make a free choice without being constrained by that evidence. It is equivalent to a university biology professor giving equal weight in her lessons to evolution and intelligent design.

The TRUST framework might also be part of a focus on the educational development of character, an area that has been out of focus for many decades. The

Oxford Character Project based at Oxford University, for example, "seeks to help talented students develop key virtues of character which will prepare them to be the wise thinkers and good leaders the world so desperately needs" (https://oxfordcharacter.org/). Truthfulness is a key virtue for "wise thinkers and good leaders," and the TRUST framework can explicitly help develop that virtue in such character development programs. It can also help in training in cross-cultural communication. The analysis of suspensions in particular provides a nuanced way of exploring both cross-cultural and intercultural variation in politeness and the judgment of untruthfulness in general.

While education and training are the best means of avoiding epistemic partisanship in the first place, regulation can help protect civic discourse from its pernicious effects. This can come through such institutional agencies as advertising authorities, ethics committees, public account committees, professional codes of conduct, and legislation. The TRUST framework can usefully inform those working in such regulatory bodies. This is all the more important when certain organizations are paradoxically using science precisely to encourage epistemic partisanship. It now appears that both the Trump election campaign and the Brexit referendum campaign made use of a British company, Cambridge Analytica, which is specialized in "military disinformation campaigns and 'election management'" and which "claims to use cutting-edge technology to build intimate psychometric profiles of voters to find and target their emotional triggers" (Cadwalladr 2017). The Trump campaign paid the company over $6 million to target swing voters in this way and thereby short-circuit any attempt to engage rationally with the issues. Freedom of speech is a freedom to express opinion, not a freedom to lie, mislead, persecute, provoke emotional triggers, or spread hate. For this reason, it is wrong to shy away from regulating political discourse in the name of freedom of speech, as occurred in the United Kingdom when political advertising was removed from the Advertising Code in 1999. TRUST is needed to make sure such regulation is fair. In terms of advertising authorities, ethics committees, and public account committees actually evaluating cases that come before them, there is an urgent need for a more careful and considered approach. The systematic steps in analysis represented by the TRUST heuristic provide a straightforward procedure for investigating actual cases of discursive untruthfulness in situated contexts.

There is undoubtedly a current tension in society between those who care and those who do not care about the facts. But there is a growing determination among those who care to develop tools to counteract untruthfulness in society. The TRUST framework is a tool that goes beyond the simple identification of factual falsity to a more thorough ethical analysis of discursive untruthfulness. The hope is that the framework will help develop a greater discursive and ethical sensibility to truthfulness that will eventually protect against the current malaise of epistemic partisanship. If this fight is successful, if the public as a whole develops keener critical skills to distinguish fake from "fair"[2] news, if bullshit in high places is no longer tolerated and it becomes impossible for a confirmed liar or bullshit artist to gain power, if companies like Facebook and Google that wield huge informational power are more carefully regulated and in turn regulate their platforms more carefully, and if advertising of all sorts (including political campaigns) requires higher ethical standards, then the issue of untruthfulness may fall back to one of timeless importance, but would no longer be of such political moment.

---

[2] By "fair" news, I do not necessarily mean impartial, but grounded in evidence. Mainstream news outlets (e.g., the *New York Times* or *Wall Street Journal* in the United States or the *Guardian* or *The Times* in the United Kingdom) present evidence from an ideological angle but they will make some effort to establish the facts. Fake news is not grounded in evidence, whether deliberately (fabricating) or unintentionally (bullshit).

References

Abelard, P. (1976[1121–1132]) *Sic et Non*. Edited by B. B. Boyer and R. McKeon. Chicago: University of Chicago Press.

Adler, J. E. (1997) Lying, misleading, or falsely implicating. *Journal of Philosophy* 94(9): 435–452.

Adler, J. E. (2002) *Belief's Own Ethics*. Cambridge, MA: MIT Press.

Agar, M. (1996) *Language Shock: Understanding the Culture of Conversation*. New York: William Morrow.

Ahmed, N. (2018) The UK Government is manufacturing its nerve agent case for "action" on Russia. *Insurge Intelligence*. March 13. https://medium.com/insurge-intelligence/the-british-governments-russia-nerve-agent-claims-are-bullshit-a69b4ee484ce.

Aiken, M. (2016) *The Cyber Effect*. London: John Murray.

Aikhenvald, A. Y. (2004) *Evidentiality*. Oxford: Oxford University Press.

Allan, K. (2013) What is common ground? In A. Capone, F. Lo Piparo, and M. Carapezza (eds.), *Perspectives on Linguistic Pragmatics*. Cham, Switzerland: Springer. 285–310.

Alston, W. P. (1991) *Perceiving God: The Epistemology of Religious Experience*. Ithaca, NY: Cornell University Press.

Alston, W. P. (2000) *Illocutionary Acts and Sentence Meaning*. Ithaca, NY: Cornell University Press.

Alterman, E. (2004) *When Presidents Lie*. New York: Viking.

Anderson, B. (2016[1983]) *Imagined Communities: Reflections on the Origin and Spread of Nationalism*. Rev. ed. London: Verso.

Anon. (2018) Dmitry Kovtun announces possible speculation about the incident with Skripal. *Interfax*. March 6. https://www.interfax.ru/russia/602593.

Anon. (2019) Gavin Williamson is sacked as defence secretary for leaking Britain's Huawei plans. *Economist*. May 2. https://www.economist.com/britain/2019/05/02/gavin-williamson-is-sacked-as-defence-secretary-for-leaking-britains-huawei-plans.

Anscombe, G. E. M. (1979) What is it to believe someone? In C. F. Delaney (ed.), *Rationality and Religious Belief*. Notre Dame, IN: University of Notre Dame Press. 141–151.

Aquinas, T. (1989) *St Thomas Aquinas, Summa Theologiae: A Concise Translation*. Edited by T. McDermott. London: Eyre and Spottiswoode.

Arico, A. J., and D. Fallis. (2013) Lies, damned lies, and statistics: An empirical investigation of the concept of lying. *Philosophical Psychology* 26(6): 790–816.

Aristotle. (2007) *On Rhetoric: A Theory of Civic Discourse*. 2nd ed. Translated by G. A. Kennedy. Oxford: Oxford University Press.

Arlinger, S., T. Lunner, B. Lyxell, and K. Pichora-Fuller. (2009) The emergence of cognitive hearing science: Background and basic processes. *Scandinavian Journal of Psychology* 50(5): 371–384.

Armstrong, D. M. (1973) *Belief, Truth, and Knowledge*. Cambridge: Cambridge University Press.

Ashworth, A. (2010) *Sentencing and Criminal Justice*. Cambridge: Cambridge University Press.
Atkinson, J. M. (1984) *Our Masters' Voices*. London: Methuen.
Augustine. (1950) Christian Instruction. In *Saint Augustine: Fathers of the Church, Vol. II*. Washington, DC: Catholic University of America Press. 3–235.
Augustine. (1961) *Enchiridion*. Translated by J. F. Shaw. Washington, DC: Regnery Gateway.
Austin, J. L. (1962) *How to Do Things with Words*. Oxford: Oxford University Press.
Austin, J. L. (1970) A plea for excuses. In J. L. Austin (ed.), *Philosophical Papers*. Oxford: Clarendon Press. 175–204.
Avilés, L. (2002) Solving the freeloaders paradox: Genetic associations and frequency-dependent selection in the evolution of cooperation among nonrelatives. *Proceedings of the National Academy of Sciences* 99(22): 14268–14273.
Ayer, A. J. (1946) *Language, Truth and Logic*. New York: Dover Publications.
Bach, K. (2006) The top 10 misconceptions about implicature. In L. R. Horn, B. J. Birner, and G. L. Ward (eds.), *Drawing the Boundaries of Meaning: Neo-Gricean Studies in Pragmatics and Semantics in Honor of Laurence R. Horn*. Amsterdam: John Benjamins. 21–30.
Baddeley, A. (2007) *Working Memory, Thought and Action*. Oxford: Oxford University Press.
Baier, A. C. (1986) Trust and antitrust. *Ethics* 96: 231–260.
Bakhtin, M. (1981) *The Dialogic Imagination*. Austin: University of Texas Press.
Bakhtin, M. (1986) *Speech Genres and Other Late Essays*. Austin: University of Texas Press.
Barbe, K. (1995) *Irony in Context*. Amsterdam: John Benjamins.
Barnes, J. A. (1994) *A Pack of Lies: Towards a Sociology of Lying*. Cambridge: Cambridge University Press.
Baron, J. (2007) *Thinking and Deciding*. 4th ed. Cambridge: Cambridge University Press.
Baron-Cohen, S. (1992) Out of sight or out of mind? Another look at deception in autism. *Journal of Child Psychology and Psychiatry* 33(7): 1141–1155.
Baron-Cohen, S., H. Tager-Flusberg, and M. Lombardo (eds.). (2013) *Understanding Other Minds: Perspectives from Developmental Social Neuroscience*. 3rd ed. New York: Oxford University Press.
Bartlett, F. C. (1932) *Remembering: A Study in Experimental and Social Psychology*. Cambridge: Cambridge University Press.
Bartlett, R. C., and S. D. Collins. (2011) *Aristotle's Nicomachean Ethics*. Chicago: Chicago University Press.
Battaly, H. (2015) *Virtue*. Cambridge: Polity.
Batty, D., S. Weale, and C. Bannock. (2017) Sexual harassment "at epidemic levels" in UK universities. *The Guardian*. March 5. https://www.theguardian.com/education/2017/mar/05/students-staff-uk-universities-sexual-harassment-epidemic.
Bauman, R. (1984) *Let Your Words Be Few: Symbolism and Silence among Seventeenth-Century Quakers*. Cambridge: Cambridge University Press.
Bauman, R., and C. L. Briggs. (1990) Poetics and performance as critical perspectives on language and social life. *Annual Review of Anthropology* 19: 59–88.
Bavelas, J. B., A. Black, N. Chovil, and J. Mullett. (1990) *Equivocal Communication*. Newbury Park, CA: Sage.
Baynes, C. (2018) BBC forced to deny outbreak of nuclear war after fake news clip goes viral. *The Independent*. April 20. https://www.independent.co.uk/news/media/bbc-forced-deny-fake-news-nuclear-war-viral-video-russia-nato-a8313896.html.

Bazerman, C. (1988) *Shaping Written Knowledge: The Genre and Activity of the Experimental Article in Science*. Madison: University of Wisconsin Press.

BBC. (1957) *Spaghetti Harvest. Panorama*. April 1. https://www.youtube.com/watch?v=MEqp0x6ajGE.

BBC. (2017) Quebec mosque attack: Fox News deletes tweet after Canada complains. *BBC News*. February 1. https://www.bbc.co.uk/news/world-us-canada-38821804.

BBCTrending. (2017) Who was behind "Queen is dead" conspiracy hoax? January 5. https://www.bbc.co.uk/news/blogs-trending-38510353.

Becker, L. C. (1996) Trust as noncognitive security about motives. *Ethics* 107(1): 43–61.

Bednarek, M. (2006) Epistemological positioning and evidentiality in English news discourse: A text-driven approach. *Text & Talk* 26(6): 635–660.

Bell, A. (1984) Language style as audience design. *Language in Society* 13: 145–204.

Bennetts, M. (2016) The rise—and risks—of political satire in Putin's Russia. *The Independent*. May 10. https://www.independent.co.uk/arts-entertainment/the-rise-and-risks-of-political-satire-in-putins-russia-a7022436.html.

Billig, M. (1996) *Arguing and Thinking: A Rhetorical Approach to Social Psychology*. 2nd ed. Cambridge: Cambridge University Press.

BIT. (2018a) Full report: Skripal poisoning suspect Dr. Alexander Mishkin, Hero of Russia. *Bellingcat*. October 9. https://www.bellingcat.com/news/uk-and-europe/2018/10/09/full-report-skripal-poisoning-suspect-dr-alexander-mishkin-hero-russia/.

BIT. (2018b) Skripal suspect Boshirov identified as GRU Colonel Anatoliy Chepiga. *Bellingcat*. September 26. https://www.bellingcat.com/news/uk-and-europe/2018/09/26/skripal-suspect-boshirov-identified-gru-colonel-anatoliy-chepiga/.

Black, M. (1983) *The Prevalence of Humbug and Other Essays*. Ithaca, NY: Cornell University Press.

Blackburn, S. (2005) *Truth: A Guide for the Perplexed*. London: Allen Lane.

BMG. (2018) *The Independent/BMG Poll: Almost Half of Brits Back Theresa May's Handling of Salisbury Novichok Incident*. BMG Research. April 20. https://www.bmgresearch.co.uk/independent-bmg-poll-almost-half-brits-back-theresa-mays-handling-salisbury-novichok-incident/.

BNC. (2007) *The British National Corpus*. Version 3 (BNC XML Edition). BNC Consortium: University of Oxford. http://www.natcorp.ox.ac.uk/.

Boghossian, P. A. (2001) What is social construction? *Times Literary Supplement*. February 23. http://as.nyu.edu/docs/IO/1153/socialconstruction.pdf.

Bok, S. (1978) *Lying: Moral Choice in Public and Private Life*. New York: Vintage.

Bolinger, D. (1973) Truth is a linguistic question. *Language* 49(3): 539–550.

Bond, C. F., and B. M. DePaulo. (2006) Accuracy of deception judgements. *Personality and Social Psychology Review* 10: 214–234.

Bond, D. (2018) Lab chief unable to confirm Russia was "precise source" of nerve agent. *Financial Times*. April 3. https://www.ft.com/content/2428cef8-3757-11e8-8b98-2f31af407cc8.

Boon, S. D., and J. G. Holmes. (2008) The dynamics of interpersonal trust: Resolving uncertainty in the face of risk. In R. A. Hinde and J. Groebel (eds.), *Cooperation and Prosocial Behaviour*. Cambridge: Cambridge University Press. 190–211.

Booth, R., A. Travis, and A. Gentleman. (2016) Leave donor plans new party to replace Ukip—possibly without Farage in charge. *The Guardian*. June 29. https://www.theguardian.com/politics/2016/jun/29/leave-donor-plans-new-party-to-replace-ukip-without-farage.

Booth, W. C. (1974) *Modern Dogma and the Rhetoric of Assent*. London: University of Notre Dame Press.

Borchers, C. (2015) Donald Trump actually admitted that he doesn't check his facts. Seriously. *Washington Post*. November 24. https://www.washingtonpost.com/news/the-fix/wp/2015/11/24/donald-trump-actually-admitted-that-he-doesnt-check-his-facts-seriously/?utm_term=.e8d42dec24a7.

boyd, d. (2010) Social network sites as networked publics: Affordances, dynamics, and implications. In Z. Papacharissi (ed.), *Networked Self: Identity, Community, and Culture on Social Network Sites*. London: Routledge. 39–58.

Bradac, J. J. (1983) The language of lovers, flovers, and friends: Communicating in social and personal relationships. *Journal of Language and Social Psychology* 2: 141–162.

Brandom, R. (1994) *Making It Explicit*. Cambridge, MA: Harvard University Press.

Brown, P., and S. C. Levinson. (1987) *Politeness: Some Universals in Language Usage*. Cambridge: Cambridge University Press.

Buekens, F., and M. Boudry. (2015) The dark side of the long: Explaining the temptations of obscurantism. *Theoria* 81: 126–142.

Bull, P. (2003) *The Microanalysis of Political Communication: Claptrap and Ambiguity*. London: Routledge.

Bull, P. (2016) Claps and claptrap: The analysis of speaker-audience interaction in political speeches. *Journal of Social and Political Psychology* 4(1): 473–492.

Buller, D. B., and J. K. Burgoon. (1996) Interpersonal Deception Theory. *Communication Theory* 6(3): 203–242.

Bunkall, A. (2018) Russian bots behind "4,000% rise" in spread of lies after Salisbury and Syria attacks—Govt analysis. *Sky News*. https://news.sky.com/story/russian-bots-behind-4-000-rise-in-spread-of-lies-after-salisbury-and-syria-attacks-11338466.

Burgoon, J. K., D. B. Buller, L. K. Guerrero, W. A. Afifi, and C. M. Feldman. (1996) Interpersonal deception: XII. Information management dimensions underlying deceptive and truthful messages. *Communication Monographs* 63(1): 50–69.

Burke, E. (1999[1795]) *Select Works of Edmund Burke. Vol. 3: Notes on a Regicide Peace*. A New Imprint of the Payne Edition. Foreword and Biographical Note by Francis Canavan. Indianapolis: Liberty Fund.

Burke, K. (1969) *A Grammar of Motives*. Berkeley: University of California Press.

Burton-Roberts, N. (2013) Cancellation and intention. *Journal of Pragmatics* 48(1): 17–28.

Butler, J. (1990) *Gender Trouble: Feminism and the Subversion of Identity*. New York: Routledge.

Cadwalladr, C. (2017) Revealed: How US billionaire helped to back Brexit. *The Guardian*. February 26. https://www.theguardian.com/politics/2017/feb/26/us-billionaire-mercer-helped-back-brexit.

Cameron, D. (2015) PM speech on opportunity. June 22. https://www.gov.uk/government/speeches/pm-speech-on-opportunity.

Campbell, J. (2001) *The Liar's Tale: A History of Falsehood*. 1st ed. New York: Norton.

Candlin, C., and J. Crichton. (2013) *Discourses of Trust*. Basingstoke: Palgrave Macmillan.

Cane, P. (2002) *Responsibility in Law and Morality*. Oxford: Hart.

CAP. (2014) *The CAP Code: The UK Code of Non-broadcast Advertising, Sales Promotion and Direct & Promotional Marketing*. 12th ed. London: Committee of Advertising Practice. https://www.asa.org.uk/codes-and-rulings/advertising-codes/non-broadcast-code.html.

Carroll, O. (2018) Russia election: Putin's team says Skripal scandal "mobilised nation and increased turnout." *Independent*. March 19. https://www.independent.co.uk/news/world/europe/russia-election-latest-putin-victory-skripal-attack-link-increase-citizen-turnout-uk-salisbury-spy-a8262996.html.

Carson, T. L. (2006) The definition of lying. *Noûs* 40(2): 284–306.

Carson, T. L. (2010) *Lying and Deception: Theory and Practice*. Oxford: Oxford University Press.

Carson, T. L., R. E. Wokutch, and K. F. Murrmann. (1982) Bluffing in labor negotiations: Legal and ethical issues. *Journal of Business Ethics* 1: 13–22.

Cassam, Q. (2019) *Vices of the Mind*. Oxford: Oxford University Press.

Castelfranchi, C., and I. Poggi. (1994) Lying as pretending to give information. In H. Parret (ed.), *Pretending to Communicate*. New York: De Gruyter. 276–290.

CED. (2003) *Collins English Dictionary*. 6th ed. Glasgow: HarperCollins.

Cheney, G., S. May, and D. Munshi (eds.). (2011) *The Handbook of Communication Ethics*. International Communication Association (ICA) Handbook. New York: Routledge.

Chilcot, S. J. (2016) *The Report of the Iraq Inquiry*. http://www.iraqinquiry.org.uk/the-report/.

Chisholm, R. M., and T. D. Feehan. (1977) The intent to deceive. *Journal of Philosophy* 74: 143–159.

Christensen, D. (2011) Disagreement, question-begging and epistemic self-criticism. *Philosophers' Imprint* 11(6): 1–22.

Christians, C. G., and M. Traber (eds.). (1997) *Communication Ethics and Universal Values*. London: Sage.

Christoforou, A. (2018a) Guardian fake news: UK media tries to keep Skripal Poisoning Hoax alive. *The Duran*. May 18. http://theduran.com/guardian-fake-news-uk-media-tries-to-keep-skripal-poisoning-hoax-alive-video/.

Christoforou, A. (2018b) The poisoning of Sergei Skripal leads right to Hillary Clinton and the DNC. *The Duran*. March 10. http://theduran.com/the-poisoning-of-sergei-skripal-reads-right-to-hillary-clinton-and-the-dnc/.

Church, I. M., and P. L. Samuelson. (2011) *Intellectual Humility: An Introduction to the Philosophy and Science*. London: Bloomsbury.

Claridge, C. (2011) *Hyperbole in English*. Cambridge: Cambridge University Press.

Clayman, S., and J. Heritage. (2002) *The News Interview: Journalists and Public Figures on the Air*. Cambridge: Cambridge University Press.

Coady, C. A. J. (2006) Pathologies of testimony. In J. Lackey and E. Sosa (eds.), *The Epistemology of Testimony*. Oxford: Clarendon. 253–271.

Code, L. (1987) *Epistemic Responsibility*. Hanover, NH: Brown University Press.

Code, L. (2013) Doubt and denial: Epistemic responsibility meets climate change scepticism. *Oñati Socio-Legal Series* 3(5): 838–853.

Cohen, G. A. (2002) Deeper into bullshit. In S. Buss and L. Overton (eds.), *Contours of Agency: Essays on Themes from Harry Frankfurt*. Cambridge, MA: MIT Press. 321–339.

Cole, S. A. N. (1997) Semantic prototypes and the pragmatics of "lie" across cultures. *The LACUS Forum* 23: 475–483.

Coleman, L., and P. Kay. (1981) Prototype semantics: The English word *lie*. *Language* 57(1): 26–44.

Collins. (2013) *Collins English Dictionary Online*. Glasgow: Collins.

Collins, H. M., and R. Evans. (2007) *Rethinking Expertise*. Chicago: University of Chicago Press.
Collis, R. (2017) Why it's so difficult to tell real news from fake news. *From Our Own Correspondent*. January 14. https://www.bbc.co.uk/programmes/p04pntvt.
Colmez, C., and L. Schneps. (2013) *Math on Trial: How Numbers Get Used and Abused in the Courtroom*. New York: Basic Books.
Cook, G. (2000) *Language Play, Language Learning*. Oxford: Oxford University Press.
Corn, D. (2003) *The Lies of George W. Bush*. New York: Crown.
Coyne, J. A. (2009) *Why Evolution Is True*. Oxford: Oxford University Press.
Coyne, J. A. (2015) *Faith v. Fact*. New York: Viking Press.
Craswell, R. (2009) When is a willful breach "willful"? The link between definitions and damages. *Michigan Law Review* 107(8): 1501–1515.
Cross, S. (2008) Hippoglossus hippoglossus and chips: Twice please love? Adventures in the underbelly of Euromyths. In R. Keeble (ed.), *Communication Ethics Now*. Leicester: Troubador. 53–57.
D'Ancona, M. (2017) *Post-Truth: The New War on Truth and How to Fight Back*. London: Ebury.
Damphousse, K. R., L. Pointon, D. Upchurch, and R. K. Moore. (2007) *Assessing the Validity of Voice Stress Analysis Tools in a Jail Setting*. US Department of Justice. Report No. 219031.
Danilov, I. (2018) A shameful secret: For Skripal, Britain hides paedophile-killers. *RIA Novosti*. March 14. https://ria.ru/20180314/1516309854.html.
Danziger, E. (2010) On trying and lying: Cultural configurations of Grice's Maxim of Quality. *Intercultural Pragmatics* 7(2): 199–219.
Danziger, K. (2008) *Marking the Mind: A History of Memory*. Cambridge: Cambridge University Press.
Dapía, S. G. (2016) *Jorge Luis Borges, Post-analytic Philosophy, and Representation*. London: Routledge.
Davies, C. (2014) Jacintha Saldanha "took blame" for Duchess of Cambridge prank call. *The Guardian*. September 11. https://www.theguardian.com/world/2014/sep/11/jacintha-saldanha-took-blame-prank-call-duchess-cambridge-australian-djs-inquest.
Davis, W. A. (2007) How normative is implicature? *Journal of Pragmatics* 39: 1655–1672.
Davis, W. A. (2014) Implicature. In E. N. Zalta (ed.), *The Stanford Encyclopedia of Philosophy*, Fall 2014 Edition. https://plato.stanford.edu/archives/fall2014/entries/implicature/.
Dawson, M. M., and J. A. Overfield. (2006) Plagiarism: Do students know what it is? *Bioscience Education* 8(1): 1–15.
Day, L., C. Bryson, C. White, S. Purdon, H. Bewley, et al. (2016) *National Evaluation of the Troubled Families Programme*. Department for Communities and Local Government. London: Her Majesty's Stationery Office.
De Waal, C. (2006) The importance of being earnest: A pragmatic approach to bullshitting. In G. L. Hardcastle and G. A. Reisch (eds.), *Bullshit and Philosophy*. Chicago: Open Court. 99–114.
Dearden, L. (2018) British police to investigate potential Russian state involvement in up to 14 deaths in UK. *The Independent*. March 13. https://www.independent.co.uk/news/uk/crime/russia-uk-deaths-british-police-investigation-state-involvement-putin-latest-news-a8253336.html.

Dejevsky, M. (2019) One year on, the Skripal poisoning case is still riddled with questions that no one wants to answer. *The Independent.* March 4. https://www.independent.co.uk/voices/skripal-poisoning-salisbury-attack-yulia-russia-novichok-putin-a8807191.html.

DePaul, M., and L. Zagzebski (eds.). (2003) *Intellectual Virtue: Perspectives from Ethics and Epistemology.* Oxford: Oxford University Press.

DePaulo, B. M., D. A. Kashy, S. E. Kirkendol, M. M. Wyer, and J. A. Epstein. (1996) Lying in everyday life. *Journal of Personality and Social Psychology* 70(5): 979–995.

DePaulo, B. M., W. L. Morris, and R. W. Sternglanz. (2009) When the truth hurts: Deception in the name of kindness. In A. L. Vangelisti (ed.), *Feeling Hurt in Close Relationships.* Cambridge: Cambridge University Press. 167–190.

DePaulo, P. J., and B. M. DePaulo. (1989) Can deception by salespersons and customers be detected through nonverbal behavioral cues? *Journal of Applied Social Psychology* 19: 1552–1577.

Descartes, R. (1996) *Meditations on First Philosophy.* Edited by J. Cottingham. Cambridge: Cambridge University Press.

Dickson, D. (2017) Seven lies Satan wants you to believe. *The Church of Jesus Christ of Latter Day Saints.* https://www.churchofjesuschrist.org/study/new-era/2017/01/seven-lies-satan-wants-you-to-believe?lang=eng.

Dietz, S. (2019) White and prosocial lies. In J. Meibauer (ed.), *The Oxford Handbook of Lying.* Oxford: Oxford University Press. 288–299.

Dike, C. C., M. Baranoski, and E. E. Griffith, (2005) Pathological lying revisited. *Journal of the American Academy of Psychiatry and Law* 33(3): 342–349.

Douglas, J. (1976) *Investigative Social Research: Individual and Team Field Research.* Beverly Hills: Sage.

Drabold, W. (2016) Watch Melania Trump's speech at the Republican Convention. *Time.* July 19. http://time.com/4412008/republican-convention-melania-trump-2/.

Drobnic Holan, A., and L. Qiu. (2015) 2015 Lie of the Year: The campaign misstatements of Donald Trump. *Politifact.* December 21. http://www.politifact.com/truth-o-meter/article/2015/dec/21/2015-lie-year-donald-trump-campaign-misstatements/.

Drury, N. (2004) *The New Age: Searching for the Spiritual Self.* London: Thames and Hudson.

du Boulay, J. (1976) Lies, mockery and family integrity. In J. G. Peristiany (ed.), *Mediterranean Family Structures.* Cambridge: Cambridge University Press. 389–406.

Duff, D. (2009) *Romanticism and the Uses of Genre.* Oxford: Oxford University Press.

Dummett, M. (1978) *Truth and Other Enigmas.* London: Duckworth.

Dynel, M. (2010) On "Revolutionary Road": A proposal for extending the Gricean model of communication to cover multiple hearers. *Lodz Papers in Pragmatics* 6: 283–304.

Dynel, M. (2011a) Revisiting Goffman's postulates on participant statuses in verbal interaction. *Language and Linguistics Compass* 5: 454–465.

Dynel, M. (2011b) A web of deceit: A neo-Gricean view on types of verbal deception. *International Review of Pragmatics* 3: 139–167.

Dynel, M. (2015) Intention to deceive, bald-faced lies, and deceptive implicature: Insights into lying at the semantics-pragmatics interface. *Intercultural Pragmatics* 12(3): 309–332.

Dynel, M. (2018) *Irony, Deception and Humour: Seeking the Truth about Overt and Covert Untruthfulness.* Mouton Series in Pragmatics. Berlin: Mouton de Gruyter.

Ecker, U. K. H., S. Lewandowsky, and J. Apai. (2011) Terrorists brought down the plane!— No, actually it was a technical fault: Processing corrections of emotive information. *Quarterly Journal of Experimental Psychology* 64(2): 283–310.

Eco, U. (1994) *Six Walks in the Fictional Woods*. Cambridge, MA: Harvard University Press.

Edmonds, D., and J. Eidinow. (2001) *Wittgenstein's Poker: The Story of a Ten-Minute Argument between Two Great Philosophers*. London: Faber.

Ekman, P. (2009) *Telling Lies: Clues to Deceit in the Marketplace, Politics, and Marriage*. 3rd ed. New York: W. W. Norton.

El Guindi, F. (1998) *Veil: Modesty, Privacy and Resistance*. Oxford: Berg.

Emery, D. (2018) Did British police find Putin's passport at the scene of the Salisbury poison attack? *Snopes.com*. March 19. https://www.snopes.com/fact-check/putin-passport-salisbury-poison-attack/.

Eriksson, A., and F. Lacerda. (2007) Charlantry in forensic speech science: A problem to be taken seriously. *The International Journal of Speech, Language and the Law* 14(2): 169–193.

EU Commission. (2018) Euro myths A–Z. https://blogs.ec.europa.eu/ECintheUK/euromyths-a-z-index/.

EUvsDisinfo. (2019) Conspiracy mania marks one-year anniversary of the Skripal poisoning. *Disinformation Review*. March 7. https://euvsdisinfo.eu/conspiracy-mania-marks-one-year-anniversary-of-the-skripal-poisoning/.

Evans, M. (2006) The republic of bullshit. In G. L. Hardcastle and G. A. Reisch (eds.), *Bullshit and Philosophy*. Chicago: Open Court. 185–202.

Fairclough, N. (2010) *Critical Discourse Analysis: The Critical Study of Language*. 2nd ed. Harlow: Longman.

Falkenberg, G. (1988) Insincerity and disloyalty. *Argumentation* 2(1): 89–97.

Fallis, D. (2009) What is lying? *Journal of Philosophy* 106: 29–56.

Fallis, D. (2010) Lying and deception. *Philosophers' Imprint* 10: 1–22.

Fallis, D. (2012) Lying as a violation of Grice's First Maxim of Quality. *Dialectica* 66: 563–581.

Fallis, D. (2015a) Are bald-faced lies deceptive after all? *Ratio* 28(1): 81–96.

Fallis, D. (2015b) Frankfurt wasn't bullshitting! *Southwest Philosophical Studies* 37: 11–20.

Fallis, D. (2019) Lying and omissions. In J. Meibauer (ed.), *The Oxford Handbook of Lying*. Oxford: Oxford University Press. 183–192.

Famighetti, C., D. Keith, and M. Pérez. (2017) *Noncitizen Voting: The Missing Millions* Brennan Center for Justice. https://www.brennancenter.org/publication/noncitizen-voting-missing-millions.

Farley, R. (2016) Trump's bogus voter fraud claims. *FactCheck.Org*. October 19. https://www.factcheck.org/2016/10/trumps-bogus-voter-fraud-claims/.

Faulkner, P. (2007) What is wrong with lying? *Philosophy and Phenomenological Research* 75(3): 535–557.

Faulkner, P. (2014a) The moral obligations of trust. *Philosophical Explorations* 17(3): 332–345.

Faulkner, P. (2014b) A virtue theory of testimony. *Proceedings of the Aristotelian Society* CXIV(2): 189–211.

Feldman, R. S., J. A. Forrest, and B. R. Happ. (2002) Self-presentation and verbal deception: Do self-presenters lie more? *Basic and Applied Social Psychology* 24: 163–170.

Fernandez-Armesto, F. (1997) *Truth: A History and a Guide for the Perplexed*. London: Bantam.

Fish, S. (1989) *Doing What Comes Naturally: Change, Rhetoric and the Practice of Theory in Legal and Literary Studies*. Oxford: Clarendon Press.

Fisherman, M. (2015) CNN's most embarrassing flub ever? The ISIS dildo gay pride flag, explained. *Vox*. June 29. https://www.vox.com/2015/6/28/8857415/cnn-isis-dildo-gay-pride-flag.

FitzPatrick, W. J. (2008) Moral responsibility and normative ignorance: Answering a new skeptical challenge. *Ethics* 118(4): 589–613.

Floridia, A. (2017) *From Participation to Deliberation: A Critical Genealogy of Deliberative Democracy*. Colchester: ECPR Press.

Foucault, M. (1977) *Discipline and Punish: The Birth of the Prison*. London: Allen Lane.

Foucault, M. (1980) *Power/Knowledge*. Translated by C. Gordon, L. Marshall, J. Mepham, and K. Soper. New York: Pantheon.

Fowler, R. (1979) *Language and Control*. London: Routledge and Kegan Paul.

Fox, B. A. (2001) Evidentiality: Authority, responsiblity, and entitlement in English conversation. *Journal of Linguistic Anthropology* 11(2): 167–192.

Frankfurt, H. G. (1986) On bullshit. *Raritan* 6(2): 81–100.

Frankfurt, H. G. (1988) *The Importance of What We Care About*. Cambridge: Cambridge University Press.

Frankfurt, H. G. (2002) Reply to G. A. Cohen. In S. Buss and L. Overton (eds.), *Contours of Agency*. Cambridge, MA: MIT Press. 340–344.

Frankfurt, H. G. (2005) *On Bullshit*. Princeton, NJ: Princeton University Press.

Franklin, B. (1996) *The Autobiography of Bennjamin Franklin*. Mineola, NY: Dover.

Fraser, B. (1980) Conversational mitigation. *Journal of Pragmatics* 4: 341–350.

Fraser, B. (1994) No conversation without misrepresentation. In H. Parret (ed.), *Pretending to Communicate*. New York: De Gruyter. 143–153.

Fricker, M. (2007) *Epistemic Injustice: Power and the Ethics of Knowing*. Oxford: Oxford University Press.

Fried, C. (1968) Privacy. *Yale Law Journal* 77(3): 475–493.

Fried, C. (1978) *Right and Wrong*. Cambridge, MA: Harvard University Press.

Fuller, S. (2006) Just bullshit. In G. L. Hardcastle and G. A. Reisch (eds.), *Bullshit and Philosophy*. Chicago: Open Court. 241–257.

Gaber, I. (2000) Lies, damn lies . . . and political spin. *British Journalism Review* 11(1): 60–70.

Gächter, S., and J. F. Schulz. (2016) Intrinsic honesty and the prevalence of rule violations across societies. *Nature* 531: 496–499.

Galasiński, D. (2000) *The Language of Deception: A Discourse Analytical Study*. London: Sage.

Galasiński, D. (2019) Lying and discourse analysis. In J. Meibauer (ed.), *The Oxford Handbook of Lying*. Oxford: Oxford University Press. 517–528.

Galasiński, D., and J. Ziółkowska. (2013) Managing information: Misrepresentation in the patient's notes. *Qualitative Inquiry* 19: 589–599.

Ganis, G. (2019) Lying and neuroscience. In J. Meibauer (ed.), *The Oxford Handbook of Lying*. Oxford: Oxford University Press. 456–468.

Garfinkel, H. (1963) A conception of, and experiments with, "trust" as a condition of stable concerted actions. In O. J. Harvey (ed.), *Motivation and Social Interaction: Cognitive Approaches*. New York: Ronald Press. 187–238.

Garner, B. (ed.). (2009) *Black's Law Dictionary*. 9th ed. St. Paul, MN: West.

Geach, P. T. (1977) *The Virtues*. The Stanton Lectures, 1973–74. Cambridge: Cambridge University Press.

Gensler, H. J. (1998) *Ethics: A Contemporary Introduction*. London: Routledge.
Gentzler, J. (1995) How to discriminate between experts and frauds: Some problems for Socratic peirastic. *History of Philosophy Quarterly* 12(3): 227–246.
Gettier, E. L. (1963) Is justified true belief knowledge? *Analysis* 23(6): 121–123.
Giddens, A. (1991) *Modernity and Self-identity*. Cambridge: Polity.
Gilbert, D. T. (1991) How mental systems believe. *American Psychologist* 46: 107–119.
Gilovich, T., D. Griffin, and D. Kahneman. (2002) *Heuristics and Biases: The Psychology of Intuitive Judgment* Cambridge: Cambridge University Press.
Gilsenan, M. (1976) Lying, honor and contradiction. In B. Kapferer (ed.), *Transaction and Meaning: Directions in the Anthropology of Exchange and Symbolic Behavior*. Philadelphia: Institute for the Study of Human Issues. 191–219.
Ginzburg, J. (2012) *The Interactive Stance: Meaning for Conversation*. Oxford: Oxford University Press.
Glenn Paton, J. (1991) *26 Italian Songs and Arias*. Van Nuys: Alfred.
Goffman, E. (1955) On face-work: An analysis of ritual elements in social interaction. *Psychiatry: Journal for the Study of Interpersonal Processes* 18: 213–231.
Goffman, E. (1959) *The Presentation of Self in Everyday Life*. London: Penguin.
Goffman, E. (1963) *Behavior in Public Places*. New York: Free Press.
Goffman, E. (1969) *Strategic Interaction*. Philadelphia: University of Pennsylvania Press.
Goffman, E. (1974) *Frame Analysis: An Essay on the Organization of Experience*. New York: Harper and Row.
Goffman, E. (1981) *Forms of Talk*. Philadelphia: University of Pennsylvania Press.
Goldberg, S. (2012) *Relying on Others: An Essay in Epistemology*. Oxford: Oxford University Press.
Goldberg, S. (2013) Anonymous assertion. *Episteme* 10: 135–151.
Gompert, D. C., H. Binnendijk, and B. Lin. (2014) *Blinders, Blunders, and Wars: What America and China Can Learn*. Santa Monica, CA: RAND.
Goodwin, C. (1994) Professional vision. *American Anthropologist* 96(3): 606–633.
Gov.UK. (2015) PM praises Troubled Families programme success. Ministry of Housing, Communities and Local Government. June 22. https://www.gov.uk/government/news/pm-praises-troubled-families-programme-success.
Gov.UK. (2018) PM Commons Statement on Salisbury incident: 12 March 2018. Government of the United Kingdom. https://www.gov.uk/government/speeches/pm-commons-statement-on-salisbury-incident-12-march-2018.
Gow, A. S. F. (1936) *A. E. Housman: A Sketch*. Cambridge: Cambridge University Press.
Gramsci, A. (1971) *Selections from the Prison Notebooks of Antonio Gramsci*. Edited by Q. Hoare and G. N. Smith. London: Lawrence and Wishart.
Granhag, P. A., L. A. Strömwall, R. M. Willén and M. Hartwig. (2013) Eliciting cues to deception by tactical disclosure of evidence: The first test of the Evidence Framing Matrix. *Legal and Criminological Psychology* 18(2): 341–355.
Granhag, P. A., A. Vrij, and B. Verschuere. (2015) *Detecting Deception: Current Challenges and Cognitive Approaches*. Chichester: Wiley.
Greco, J. (2003) Knowledge as credit for true belief. In M. DePaul and L. Zagzebski (eds.), *Intellectual Virtue: Perspectives from Ethics and Epistemology*. Oxford: Oxford University Press. 111–134.
Green, R. F. (1999) *A Crisis of Truth: Literature and Law in Ricardian England*. Philadelphia: University of Pennsylvania Press.
Green, S. P. (2001) Lying, misleading, and falsely denying: How moral concepts inform the law of perjury, fraud, and false statements. *Hastings Law Journal* 53: 157–212.

Green, S. P. (2006) *Lying, Cheating, and Stealing: A Moral Theory of White-Collar Crime.* Oxford: Oxford University Press.

Grice, H. P. (1975) Logic and conversation. In P. Cole and J. Morgan (eds.), *Syntax and Semantics 3: Speech Acts.* New York: Academic Press. 41–58.

Grice, H. P. (1989) *Studies in the Way of Words.* Cambridge, MA: Harvard University Press.

Griffin, A. (2016) Brexit: Vote Leave wipes NHS £350m claim and rest of its website after EU referendum. *The Independent.* June 27. https://www.independent.co.uk/news/uk/home-news/brexit-vote-leave-wipes-nhs-350m-claim-and-rest-of-its-website-after-eu-referendum-a7105546.html.

Griffin, D. (forthcoming) *Lexomancy: Law and Magic in the Pseudolegal Writings of the Sovereign Citizen Movement.* PhD Dissertation. Cardiff University.

Gumperz, J. J. (1982) *Discourse Strategies.* Cambridge: Cambridge University Press.

Gupta, S., K. Sakamoto, and A. Ortony. (2013) Telling it like it isn't: A comprehensive approach to analyzing verbal deception. In F. Paglieri, L. Tummolini, R. Falcone, and M. Miceli (eds.), *The Goals of Cognition: Essays in Honor of Cristiano Castelfranchi.* London: College Publications. https://www.researchgate.net/publication/286264813_Telling_it_like_it_isn't_a_comprehensive_approach_to_analyzing_verbal_deception.

Habermas, J. (1998) *On the Pragmatics of Communication.* Cambridge: Polity.

Hacking, I. (1999) *The Social Construction of What?* Cambridge, MA: Harvard University Press.

Haiman, J. (1998) *Talk Is Cheap: Sarcasm, Alienation, and the Evolution of Language.* Oxford: Oxford University Press.

Hall, O. M. (1994) *The Art and Craft of Novel Writing.* Cincinnati, OH: Story Press.

Hanks, W. (1996) *Language and Communicative Practices.* Boulder, CO: Westview Press.

Happe, F. G. E. (1995) Understanding minds and metaphors: Insights from the study of figurative language in autism. *Metaphor Symbolic Activity* 10: 275–295.

Hardin, K. J. (2010) The Spanish notion of Lie: Revisiting Coleman and Kay. *Journal of Pragmatics* 42(12): 3199–3213.

Hardin, R. (2002) *Trust and Trustworthiness.* New York: Russell Sage Foundation.

Harding, L. (2016) *A Very Expensive Poison: The Definitive Story of the Murder of Litvinenko and Russia's War with the West.* London: Guardian Faber.

Harris, S. (2017) What is true? *Making Sense with Sam Harris.* https://itunes.apple.com/podcast/id733163012.

Hart, H. L. A. (1949) The ascription of responsibility and rights. *Proceedings of the Aristotelian Society* 49: 171–194.

Hart, H. L. A. (2008) *Punishment and Responsibility: Essays in the Philosophy of Law.* 2nd ed. Oxford: Oxford University Press.

Hartwig, M,. and C. F. Bond. (2011) Why do lie-catchers fail? A lens model meta-analysis of human lie judgments. *Psychological Bulletin* 137: 643–659.

Harwood, J. (2014) Easy lies. *Journal of Language and Social Psychology* 33(4): 405–410.

Heffer, C. (2013a) Communication and magic: Authorized voice, legal-linguistic habitus and the recontextualization of "beyond reasonable doubt." In, C. Heffer, F. Rock and J. Conley (eds.), *Legal-Lay Communication: Textual Travels in the Law.* New York: Oxford University Press. 206–225.

Heffer, C. (2013b) Projecting voice: Towards an agentive understanding of a critical capacity. *Cardiff Papers in Language and Literature.* Cardiff: Cardiff University Press.

Heffer, C. (2013c) Revelation and rhetoric: A critical model of forensic discourse. *International Journal for the Semiotics of Law* 26(2): 459–485.

Heffer, C. (2017) When voices fail to carry: Voice projection and the case of the "dumb" jury. In J. Leung and A. Durant (eds.), *Meaning and Power in the Language of Law*. Cambridge: Cambridge University Press. 207–235.

Heffer, G. (2018) Foreign Office deletes tweet claiming Salisbury nerve agent made in Russia. *Sky News*. April 4. https://news.sky.com/story/foreign-office-deletes-tweet-claiming-salisbury-nerve-agent-made-in-russia-11316445.

Held, D. (2006) *Models of Democracy*. 3rd ed. Cambridge: Polity.

Herlihy, J., L. Jobson, and S. Turner. (2012) Just tell us what happened to you: Autobiographical memory and seeking asylum. *Applied Cognitive Psychology* 26(5): 661–676.

Herman, B. (1993) *The Practice of Moral Judgment*. Cambridge, MA: Harvard University Press.

Herrmann, T. (1983) *Speech and Situation: A Psychological Conception of Situated Speaking*. Berlin: Springer-Verlag.

Hertzberg, L. (1988) On the attitude of trust. *Inquiry* 31(3): 307–322.

Hertzberg, L. (2010) On being trusted. In A. Grøn, A. M. Pahuus, and C. Welz (eds.), *Trust, Sociality, Selfhood*. Tubingen: Mohr Siebeck. 193–204.

Hickman, L. A., and T. M. Alexander. (1998) *The Essential Dewey*. Vol. 2, *Ethics, Logic, Psychology*. Bloomington: Indiana University Press.

Horn, L. R. (2004) Implicature. In L. R. Horn and G. Ward (eds.), *The Handbook of Pragmatics*. Oxford: Blackwell. 3–28.

Humberstone, L. (1992) Direction of fit. *Mind* 101(401): 59–83.

Hume, D. (2007) *An Enquiry Concerning Human Understanding*. Edited by P. F. Millican. Oxford: Oxford University Press.

Hursthouse, R., and G. Pettigrove. (2016) Virtue ethics. In E. N. Zalta (ed.), *The Stanford Encyclopedia of Philosophy*. https://plato.stanford.edu/archives/win2016/entries/ethics-virtue/.

Hwang, S. (2013) The effect of Twitter use on politicians' credibility and attitudes toward politicians. *Journal of Public Relations Research* 25(3): 246–258.

Hymes, D. (1974) *Foundations in Sociolinguistics: An Ethnographic Approach*. Philadelphia: University of Pennsylvania Press.

Inbau, F., J. Reid, J. Buckley, and B. Jayne. (2001) *Criminal Interrogations and Confessions*. 4th ed. Gaithersburg, MD: Aspen.

Ipsos. (2017) *Ipsos MORI Veracity Index 2017*. Ipsos MORI Social Research Institute. https://www.ipsos-mori.com/Assets/Docs/Polls/ipsos-mori-veracity-index-2016-charts.pdf.

Irwin, H. J. (2009) *The Psychology of Paranormal Belief: A Researcher's Handbook*. Hatfield: University of Hertfordshire Press.

Isaac, M., and S. Ember. (2016) For election day influence, Twitter ruled social media. *New York Times*. November 8. https://www.nytimes.com/2016/11/09/technology/for-election-day-chatter-twitter-ruled-social-media.html.

Isenberg, A. (1964) Deontology and the ethics of lying. *Philosophy and Phenomenological Research* 24(4): 463–480.

Jakobson, R. O. (1957) *Shifters, Verbal Categories, and the Russian Verb*. Cambridge, MA: Harvard University Press.

Jamieson, K. H., and J. N. Cappella. (2008) *Echo Chamber: Rush Limbaugh and the Conservative Media Establishment*. Oxford: Oxford University Press.

Johnson, T. L. (2015) Thomas L. Johnson's answer to "What is a concrete example of intellectual dishonesty?" https://www.quora.com/What-is-a-concrete-example-of-intellectual-dishonesty/answer/Thomas-L-Johnson-1.

Jordan, A. E. (2003) Implications of academic dishonesty for teaching in psychology. *Psychology of Teaching* 30: 216–219.

Kahneman, D. (2013) *Thinking, Fast and Slow*. New York: Farrar, Straus and Giroux.

Kahneman, D., P. Slovic, and A. Tversky. (1982) *Judgement under Uncertainty: Heuristics and Biases*. Cambridge: Cambridge University Press.

Kalenböck, G., W. Mihatsch, and S. Schneider (eds.). (2010) *New Approaches to Hedging*. Bingley, UK: Emerald Group.

Kant, I. (2012) *Groundwork of the Metaphysics of Morals*. Rev. ed.; translation revised by Jens Timmermann. Edited by M. J. Gregor and J. Timmermann. Cambridge: Cambridge University Press.

Kareem, R. (2017) The case for fictional Islam. *Critical Muslim*. https://www.criticalmuslim.io/the-case-for-fictional-islam.

Karlsen, Ø. (2015) *Dag*. Norwegian Film Institute. Norway. http://www.imdb.com/title/tt1711386/.

Kassin, S. M. (2008) False confessions: Causes, consequences, and implications for reform. *Current Directions in Psychological Science* 17(4): 249–253.

Kassin, S. M., C. A. Meissner, and R. J. Norwick. (2005) "I'd know a false confession if I saw one": A comparative study of college students and police investigators. *Law and Human Behavior* 29: 211–227.

Kaszeta, D. (2018) Myth busting: Why didn't the Skripals die on the spot? *Politico*. April 6. https://www.politics.co.uk/comment-analysis/2018/04/06/myth-busting-why-didn-t-the-skripals-die-on-the-spot.

Keane, A. L. L. B., and P. McKeown. (2016) *The Modern Law of Evidence*. 11th ed. Oxford: Oxford University Press.

Keating, C. F., and K. R. Heltman. (1994) Dominance and deception in children and adults: Are leaders the best misleaders? *Personality and Social Psychology Bulletin* 20: 312–321.

Kecskes, I. (2013) *Intercultural Pragmatics*. Oxford: Oxford University Press.

Keeble, R. (ed.). (2008) *Communication Ethics Now*. Leicester: Troubador.

Kelley, D. (2013) *The Art of Reasoning: An Introduction to Logic and Critical Thinking*. 4th ed. New York: W. W. Norton.

Kennedy, M. (2017) Jack Monroe wins Twitter libel case against Katie Hopkins. *The Guardian*. March 10. https://www.theguardian.com/media/2017/mar/10/jack-monroe-wins-twitter-libel-case-against-katie-hopkins.

Kentish, B. (2018) Boris Johnson says it is "overwhelmingly likely" Vladimir Putin ordered nerve agent attack on British soil. March 16. https://www.independent.co.uk/news/uk/politics/boris-johnson-putin-order-salisbury-nerve-agent-attack-russia-spy-poisoning-sergei-skripal-a8259086.html.

Kettle, M. (2016) Tony Blair's statement on Chilcot – what he said and what he meant. *The Guardian*. 6 July. https://www.theguardian.com/uk-news/ng-interactive/2016/jul/06/tony-blair-statement-on-chilcot-iraq-what-he-said-and-what-he-meant.

Khan, S. (2018) Video re-emerges of Putin threat that "traitors will kick the bucket." March 7. https://www.independent.co.uk/news/world/europe/vladimir-putin-traitors-kick-bucket-sergei-skripal-latest-video-30-pieces-silver-a8243206.html.

Khlentzos, D. (2016) Challenges to metaphysical realism. In E. N. Zalta (ed.), *The Stanford Encyclopedia of Philosophy*. Winter 2016. https://plato.stanford.edu/archives/win2016/entries/realism-sem-challenge/.

Khoury, A. C. (2011) Blameworthiness and wrongness. *Journal of Value Inquiry* 45: 135–146.

Kimbrough, S. (2006) On letting it slide. In G. L. Hardcastle and G. A. Reisch (eds.), *Bullshit and Philosophy*. Chicago: Open Court. 3–18.

Kirk, A., and D. Dunford. (2016) EU referendum: The claims that won it for Brexit, fact checked. *The Daily Telegraph*. June 29. https://www.telegraph.co.uk/politics/0/eu-referendum-claims-won-brexit-fact-checked/.

Kirkpatrick, B. (ed.) (2000) *Roget's Thesaurus of English Words and Phrases*. London: Penguin.

Kissine, M. (2013) *From Utterances to Speech Acts*. Cambridge: Cambridge University Press.

Kruger, J., and D. Dunning. (1999) Unskilled and unaware of it: How difficulties in recognizing one's own incompetence lead to inflated self-assessments. *Journal of Personality and Social Psychology* 77(6): 1121–1134.

Labov, W. (1972) *Language in the Inner City*. Philadelphia: University of Pennsylvania Press.

Lackey, J. (2013) Lies and deception: An unhappy divorce. *Analysis* 73: 236–248.

Lackey, J. (2019) Group lies. In A. Stokke and E. Michaelson (eds.), *Lying: Language, Knowledge, Ethics, Politics*. Oxford: Oxford University Press. 262–284.

Lagerspetz, O. (2015) *Trust, Ethics and Human Reason*. London: Bloomsbury.

Lavrov. (2018) Foreign Minister Sergey Lavrov's answers to media questions, March 13, 2018. http://www.mid.ru/en/foreign_policy/news/-/asset_publisher/cKNonkJE02Bw/content/id/3118300.

Leech, G. N. (1983) *Principles of Pragmatics*. London: Longman.

Leo, R. A. (2008) *Police Interrogation and American Justice*. Cambridge, MA: Harvard University Press.

Levada. (2018) The case of the Skripals. The Levada Center. October 25. https://www.levada.ru/2018/10/25/delo-skripalej/.

Levine, T. R. (2001) Dichotomous and continuous views of deception: A reexamination of deception ratings in information manipulation theory. *Communication Research Reports* 18: 230–240.

Levine, T. R. (2014) Truth-Default Theory (TDT): A theory of human deception and deception detection. *Journal of Language and Social Psychology* 33(4): 378–392.

Levine, T. R., K. J. K. Asada, and L. L. Massi Lindsey. (2003) The relative impact of violation type and lie severity on judgments of message deceitfulness. *Communication Research Reports* 20(3): 208–218.

Levine, T. R., R. K. Kima, and L. M. Hamela. (2010) People lie for a reason: Three experiments documenting the Principle of Veracity. *Communication Research Reports* 4: 271–285.

Levinson, P. (2017) *Fake News in Real Context*. New York: Connected Editions.

Levitt, J. (2007) *The Truth about Voter Fraud*. New York: Brennan Center for Justice.

Lewis, D. K. (1969) *Convention*. Cambridge, MA: Harvard University Press.

Lewis, D. K. (1983) Languages and language. In *Philosophical Papers*, Vol. I. Oxford: Oxford University Press. 163–189.

Lewis, D. K. (2002) *Convention: A Philosophical Study*. Oxford: Blackwell.

Littlefield, M. (2008) Constructing the organ of deceit: The rhetoric of fMRI and brain fingerprinting in post-9/11 America. *Science, Technology & Human Values* 34(3): 365–392.

Litvinenko. (2016) *Report into the Death of Alexander Litvinenko. Chairman: Sir Robert Owen*. https://assets.publishing.service.gov.uk/government/uploads/system/uploads/attachment_data/file/493855/The-Litvinenko-Inquiry-H-C-695.pdf.

Livingston, E. (2017) When will universities wake up to this epidemic of sexual harassment? *The Guardian*. March 7. https://www.theguardian.com/commentisfree/2017/mar/07/when-will-universities-wake-up-to-sexual-harassment.

Loeb, E. (1947) Social organization and the long house in Southeast Asia and Micronesia. *The Far Eastern Quarterly* 6(2): 168–172.

Loeser, C. E. (2015) From Paper Terrorists to Cop Killers: The Sovereign Citizen Threat. *North Carolina Law Review* 93(4): 1106–1139.

Loftus, E. (1979) *Eyewitness Testimony*. Cambridge, MA: Harvard University Press.

Loftus, E. (1992) *Witness for the Defence*. New York: St. Martin's Press.

Løgstrup, K. E. (1997) *The Ethical Demand*. Notre Dame, IN: University of Notre Dame Press.

Lomas, D. (2018) Sergei Skripal and the long history of assassination attempts abroad. *The Conversation*. March 12. https://theconversation.com/sergei-skripal-and-the-long-history-of-assassination-attempts-abroad-93021.

Lord, C., L. Ross, and M. Lepper. (1979) Biased assimilation and attitude polarization: The effects of prior theories on subsequently considered evidence. *Journal of Personality and Social Psychology Bulletin* 37(11): 2098–2109.

Luhmann, N. (1979) *Trust and Power*. Chichester: Wiley.

Luhn, A. (2018) Putin says "not possible" Skripals were poisoned with military nerve agent. 25 May. https://www.telegraph.co.uk/news/2018/05/25/putin-says-not-possible-skripals-poisoned-military-nerve-agent/.

Luscombe, D. E. (1969) *The School of Peter Abelard*. Cambridge: Cambridge University Press.

Lynch, M. P. (2004) *True to Life: Why Truth Matters*. Cambridge, MA: MIT Press.

MacFarlane, J. (2014) *Assessment Sensitivity: Relative Truth and Its Applications*. Oxford: Oxford University Press.

Maes, H., and K. Schaubroeck. (2006) Different kinds and aspects of bullshit. In G. L. Hardcastle and G. A. Reisch (eds.), *Bullshit and Philosophy*. Chicago: Open Court. 171–181.

Mahon, J. E. (2008) Two definitions of lying. *International Journal of Applied Philosophy* 22: 211–230.

Mahon, J. E. (2016) The definition of lying and deception. In E. N. Zalta (ed.), *The Stanford Encyclopedia of Philosophy*. Winter 2016. https://plato.stanford.edu/archives/win2016/entries/lying-definition/.

Mahon, J. E. (2019) Contemporary approaches to the philosophy of lying. In J. Meibauer (ed.), *The Oxford Handbook of Lying*. Oxford: Oxford University Press. 32–55.

Maier, E. (2019) Lying and fiction. In J. Meibauer (ed.), *The Oxford Handbook of Lying*. Oxford: Oxford University Press. 303–314.

Mance, H. (2016) Britain has had enough of experts, says Gove. *The Financial Times*. June 3. https://www.ft.com/content/3be49734-29cb-11e6-83e4-abc22d5d108c.

Manson, A. (2011) The search for principles of mitigation: Integrating cultural demands. In J. V. Roberts (ed.), *Mitigation and Aggravation at Sentencing*. Cambridge: Cambridge University Press. 40–59.

Mantel, H. (2017) Can These Bones Live? *The BBC Reith Lectures* [Podcast]. https://www.bbc.co.uk/programmes/b08wp3g3.

Marsili, N. (2019) Lying and certainty. In J. Meibauer (ed.), *The Oxford Handbook of Lying*. Oxford: Oxford University Press. 170–182.

Maverick, M. (1944) The case against "Gobbledygook." *New York Times*. May 21. https://www.nytimes.com/1944/05/21/archives/the-case-against-gobbledygook-maury-maverick-assails-vague-pompous.html.

MBFC. (2019) Media Bias/Fact Check. https://mediabiasfactcheck.com/.

McCarthy, T. (2018) Russian spy poisoning: Chemist says non-state actor couldn't carry out attack. 16 March. https://www.theguardian.com/uk-news/2018/mar/16/russian-spy-poisoning-attack-novichok-chemist.

McCornack, S. A. (1992) Information Manipulation Theory. *Communication Monographs* 59: 1–16.

McCornack, S. A., T. A. Levine, K. A. Solowczuk, H. I. Torres, and D. M. Campbell. (1992) When the alteration of information is viewed as deception: An empirical test of information manipulation theory. *Communication Monographs* 59: 17–29.

McCornack, S. A., and T. R. Levine. (1990) When lies are uncovered: Emotional and relational outcomes of discovered deception. *Communication Monographs* 57: 119–138.

McCornack, S. A., K. Morrison, J. E. Paik, A. M. Wisner, and X. Zhu. (2014) Information Manipulation Theory 2: A propositional theory of deceptive discourse production. *Journal of Language and Social Psychology* 33(4): 348–377.

McLeod, C. (2015) Trust. In E. N. Zalta (ed.), *Stanford Encyclopedia of Philosophy*. Fall 2015 Edition. https://plato.stanford.edu/archives/fall2015/entries/trust/.

Meibauer, J. (2005) Lying and falsely implicating. *Journal of Pragmatics* 37(9): 1373–1399.

Meibauer, J. (2014a) Bald-faced lies as acts of verbal aggression. *Journal of Language Aggression and Conflict* 2(1): 127–149.

Meibauer, J. (2014b) *Lying at the Semantics-Pragmatics Interface*. Mouton Series in Pragmatics. Boston: De Gruyter Mouton.

Meibauer, J. (2016a) Aspects of a theory of bullshit. *Pragmatics & Cognition* 23(1): 68–91.

Meibauer, J. (2016b) Understanding bald-faced lies: An empirical approach. *International Review of Pragmatics* 8(2): 247–270.

Meibauer, J. (2018) The linguistics of lying. *Annual Review of Linguistics* 4: 357–375.

Meibauer, J. (ed.). (2019) *The Oxford Handbook of Lying*. Oxford: Oxford University Press.

Memon, A. (2012) Credibility of asylum claims: Consistency and accuracy of autobiographical memory reports following trauma. *Applied Cognitive Psychology* 26(5): 677–679.

Mendick, R. (2019) How the UK joined the dots from Salisbury Novichok attack to Vladimir Putin. *The Daily Telegraph*. 6 January. https://www.telegraph.co.uk/news/2019/01/06/uk-joined-dots-salisbury-novichok-attack-vladimir-putin/.

Metts, S. (1989) An exploratory investigation of deception in close relationships. *Journal of Social and Personal Relationships* 6: 159–179.

Milgram, S. (1963) Behavioral study of obedience. *Journal of Abnormal and Social Psychology* 67(4): 371–378.

Minnite, L. (2010) *The Myth of Voter Fraud*. Ithaca, NY: Cornell University Press.

Minsky, M. (1977) Frame-system theory. In P. N. Johnson-Laird and P. C. Wason (eds.), *Thinking: Readings in Cognitive Science*. Cambridge: Cambridge University Press. 355–376.

Montmarquet, J. (1987) Epistemic virtue. *Mind* 96: 482–497.

Montmarquet, J. (1993) *Epistemic Virtue and Doxastic Responsibility*. Lanham, MD: Rowman & Littlefield.

Montmarquet, J. (1995) Culpable ignorance and excuses. *Philosophical Studies* 80(1): 41–49.

Montmarquet, J. (1999) Zimmerman on culpable ignorance. *Ethics* 109(4): 842–845.

Moore, M. (1998) *Placing Blame*. Oxford: Clarendon Press.

Morison, B. (2014) Sextus Empiricus. In E. N. Zalta (ed.), *The Stanford Encyclopedia of Philosophy* (Spring 2014 Edition). https://plato.stanford.edu/archives/spr2014/entries/sextus-empiricus/.

Morris, S. (2018) Novichok poisoning: Police identify Skripal suspects—report. *The Guardian*. July 19. https://www.theguardian.com/uk-news/2018/jul/19/police-identify-skripal-novichok-salisbury-poisoning-suspects.

Müller, J.-W. (2016) *What Is Populism?* Philadelphia: University of Pennsylvania Press.

Mulligan, K., and F. Correia. (2013) Facts. In E. N. Zalta (ed.), *The Stanford Encyclopedia of Philosophy*. http://plato.stanford.edu/archives/spr2013/entries/facts/.

Murray, C. (2018) The Novichok story is indeed another Iraqi WMD scam. *Craig Murray*. March 14. www.craigmurray.org.uk/archives/2018/03/the-novichok-story-is-indeed-another-iraqi-wmd-scam/.

Murray, C. (2019) Pure: Ten points I just can't believe about the official Skripal narrative. *Craig Murray*. March 7. https://www.craigmurray.org.uk/archives/2019/03/pure-ten-points-i-just-cant-believe-about-the-official-skripal-narrative/.

Naftulin, D. H., J. E. Ware, and F. A. Donnelly. (1973) The Doctor Fox lecture: A paradigm of educational seduction. *Journal of Medical Education* 48: 630–635.

Nagel, T. (2002) *Concealment and Exposure*. Oxford: Oxford University Press.

NCA. (2004) Credo for Ethical Communication. *Free Speech Yearbook* 41(1): ix.

NIC. (2017) *Assessing Russian Activities and Intentions in Recent US Elections*. National Intelligence Council. ICA 2017-01D. January 6. https://en.wikisource.org/wiki/Assessing_Russian_Activities_and_Intentions_in_Recent_US_Elections.

Nimmo, B. (2018) #PutinAtWar: Trolls on Twitter. Battles on Twitter over the Skripal poisoning case. *Digital Forensic Research Lab*. March 23. https://medium.com/dfrlab/putinatwar-trolls-on-twitter-5d0bb3dc30ae.

Norris, C. (1996) *Reclaiming Truth: Contribution to a Critique of Cultural Relativism*. London: Lawrence & Wishart.

Norris, P. (2014) *Why Electoral Integrity Matters*. Cambridge: Cambridge University Press.

NPR. (2012) *Michelle Obama's Convention Speech*. National Public Radio. September 4. https://www.npr.org/2012/09/04/160578836/transcript-michelle-obamas-convention-speech.

O'Neill, O. (2002) *A Question of Trust: The BBC Reith Lectures 2002*. Cambridge: Cambridge University Press.

Olekalns, M., and P. L. Smith. (2009) Mutually dependent: Power, trust, affect and the use of deception in negotiation. *Journal of Business Ethics* 85(3): 347–365.

OPCW. (2017) Director-general commends major milestone as Russia completes destruction of chemical weapons stockpile under OPCW verification. Organization for the Prohibition of Chemical Weapons. https://www.opcw.org/media-centre/news/2017/09/opcw-director-general-commends-major-milestone-russia-completes.

OPCW. (2019a) *Annex on the Protection of Confidential Information*. Organization for the Prevention of Chemical Weapons. https://www.opcw.org/chemical-weapons-convention/annexes/confidentiality-annex.

OPCW. (2019b) What is a chemical weapon? Organization for the Prevention of Chemical Weapons. https://www.opcw.org/our-work/what-chemical-weapon.
Ortony, A., and S. Gupta. (2019) Lying and deception. In J. Meibauer (ed.), *The Oxford Handbook of Lying*. Oxford: Oxford University Press. 149–169.
Orwell, G. (1946) *Politics and the English Language*. London: Horizon.
Ostrovsky, A. (2017) *The Invention of Russia: The Rise of Putin and the Age of Fake News*. London: Atlantic Books.
Oswald, M., and S. Grosjean. (2004) Confirmation bias. In R. Pohl (ed.), *Cognitive Illusions*. Hove and New York: Psychology Press. 79–96.
PAC. (2016) *Troubled Families: Progress Review*. Public Accounts Committee. December 16. https://publications.parliament.uk/pa/cm201617/cmselect/cmpubacc/711/71102.htm.
PACEI. (2017) *Presidential Advisory Commission on Election Integrity*. https://www.whitehouse.gov/articles/presidential-advisory-commission-election-integrity/.
Pacepa, I. M., and R. J. Rychlak. (2013) *Disinformation*. Washington, DC: WND Books.
Pagin, P. (2016) Assertion. In E. N. Zalta (ed.), *The Stanford Encyclopedia of Philosophy*. (Winter 2016 Edition). https://plato.stanford.edu/archives/win2016/entries/assertion/.
Pariser, E. (2011) *The Filter Bubble: What the Internet Is Hiding from You*. London: Viking.
Parret, H. (1993) *Pretending to Communicate*. Berlin: W. de Gruyter.
Patyk, L. E. (2018) The real reason Russia blames Britain for the Skripal poisonings. *Washington Post*. April 2. https://www.washingtonpost.com/news/made-by-history/wp/2018/04/02/the-real-reason-russia-blames-britain-for-the-skripal-poisonings/?noredirect=on&utm_term=.2e2bd90ad198.
Peck, T. (2019) Goodbye Gavin Williamson, we should never have seen your like in the first place. *The Independent*. May 1. https://www.independent.co.uk/voices/gavin-williamson-leak-huawei-brexit-theresa-may-sacked-penny-mordaunt-a8895556.html.
Pecorari, D. (2008) *Academic Writing and Plagiarism: A Linguistic Analysis*. New York: Continuum.
Peddinti, S., K. Ross, and J. Cappos. (2014) On the internet, nobody knows you're a dog: A Twitter case study of anonymity in social networks. In *Proceedings of the Second ACM Conference on Online Social Networks COSN '14*. Dublin: Association for Computing Machinery. 83–94.
Peirce, C. S. (1960[1935]) *Collected Papers of Charles Sanders Peirce*. Vols. V and VI: *Pragmatism and Pragmaticism and Scientific Metaphysics*. Edited by C. Hartshorne and P. Weiss. Cambridge, MA: Harvard University Press.
Pennycook, G., J. A. Cheyne, N. Barr, D. J. Koehler, and J. A. Fugelsang. (2015) On the reception and detection of pseudo-profound bullshit. *Judgment and Decision Making* 10(6): 549–563.
Perillo, J. T., and S. M. Kassin. (2011) Inside interrogation: The lie, the bluff, and false confessions. *Law and Human Behavior* 35(4): 327–337.
Peterson, C., J. L. Peterson, and D. Seeto. (1983) Developmental changes in ideas about lying. *Child Development* 54: 1529–1535.
Pettit, P. (2001) *A Theory of Freedom: From the Psychology to the Politics of Agency*. Cambridge: Polity.
Pettit, P. (2015) *The Birth of Ethics*. The Tanner Lectures in Human Values. Berkeley: University of California.

Pew. (2012) Inaccurate, costly, and inefficient: Evidence that America's voter registration system needs an upgrade. Pew Center for the States. https://www.pewtrusts.org/~/media/legacy/uploadedfiles/pcs_assets/2012/pewupgradingvoterregistrationpdf.pdf.
Plato. (1992) *Republic*. Edited by G. M. A. Grube and C. D. C. Reeve. Indianapolis: Hackett.
Plato. (2004) *Theaetetus*. Translated by R. Waterfield. London: Penguin.
Pohl, R. F. (2007) Ways to assess hindsight bias. *Social Cognition* 25: 14–31.
Pomerantsev, P. (2015) *Nothing Is True and Everything Is Possible: Adventures in Modern Russia*. London: Faber & Faber.
Popper, K. (1945) *The Open Society and Its Enemies*. London: G. Routledge & Sons.
Popper, K. (1959) *The Logic of Scientific Discovery*. London: Hutchinson.
Postillon. (2018) British police find Putin's passport at scene of Salisbury poison attack 16 March. https://www.the-postillon.com/2018/03/salisbury-putin.html.
Press-Association. (2016) Government misled public with 99% success rate claim on troubled families, say MPs. *The Guardian*. December 20. https://www.theguardian.com/society/2016/dec/20/troubled-families-government-misled-public-99-success-claim-say-mps.
Price, D., N. Cain, and K. Duodu. (2009) *Defamation: Law, Procedure and Practice*. 4th ed. London: Sweet and Maxwell.
Pruss, A. (2012) Sincerely asserting what you do not believe. *Australasian Journal of Philosophy* 90: 541–546.
Putnam, H. (1981) *Reason, Truth and History*. Cambridge: Cambridge University Press.
Putnam, H. (1983) *Philosophical Papers*. Vol. 3, *Realism and Reason*. Cambridge: Cambridge University Press.
Qiu, L. (2016) Donald Trump's Pants on Fire claim of "large scale voter fraud." *Politifact*. October 17. https://www.politifact.com/factchecks/2016/oct/17/donald-trump/donald-trumps-pants-fire-claim-large-scale-voter-f/.
Rabaté, J.-M. (2005) *The Ethics of the Lie*. Translated by S. Verderber. New York: Other Press.
Rainey, B., E. Wicks, and C. Ovey. (2017) *The European Convention on Human Rights*. 7th ed. Oxford: Oxford University Press.
Rampton, B. (1995) *Crossing: Language and Ethnicity among Adolescents*. London: Longman.
Rawls, J. (1955) Two concepts of rules. *The Philosophical Review* 64: 3–32.
Rawls, J. (1972) *A Theory of Justice*. Oxford: Clarendon.
Reuters. (2015) Donald Trump: I was "100% right" about Muslims cheering 9/11 attacks. *The Guardian*. November 29. https://www.theguardian.com/us-news/2015/nov/29/donald-trump-muslims-cheering-911-attacks.
Riggio, R. E., J. Tucker, and B. Throckmorton. (1988) Social skills and deception ability. *Personality and Social Psychology Bulletin* 13: 568–577.
Rini, R. (2017) Fake news and partisan epistemology. *Kennedy Institute of Ethics Journal* 27(2): 43–64.
Roberts, C. (2004) Context in dynamic interpretation. In L. R. Horn and G. L. Ward (eds.), *The Handbook of Pragmatics*. Oxford: Blackwell. 197–220.
Roberts, C. (2012) Information structure in discourse: Towards an integrated formal theory of pragmatics. *Semantics and Pragmatics* 5: 1–69.
Roberts, D. (2017) Donald Trump and the rise of tribal epistemology. *Vox*. May 19. https://www.vox.com/policy-and-politics/2017/3/22/14762030/donald-trump-tribal-epistemology.

Robertson, J. P. S., and S. J. Shamsie. (1959) A systematic examination of gibberish in a multilingual schizophrenic patient. *Language and Speech* 2(1): 1–8.

Robinson, O. (2018) How Putin's Russia turned humour into a weapon. *BBC News.* December 15. https://www.bbc.co.uk/news/world-europe-46567364.

Rogers, T., and M. I. Norton. (2011) The artful dodger: Answering the wrong question the right way. *Journal of Experimental Psychology: Applied* 17(2): 139–147.

Rorty, R. (1979) *Philosophy and the Mirror of Nature.* Princeton, NJ: Princeton University Press.

Rorty, R. (1991) *Objectivity, Relativism and Truth.* Cambridge: Cambridge University Press.

Rosen, G. (2004) Skepticism about moral responsibility. *Philosophical Perspectives* 18: 295–313.

Ross, L. (1977) The intuitive psychologist and his shortcomings: Distortions in the attribution process. In L. Berkowitz (ed.), *Advances in Experimental Social Psychology.* New York: Academic Press. 173–220.

Roth, A. (2018) Russian passport leak after Salisbury may reveal spy methods. September 23. https://www.theguardian.com/world/2018/sep/23/russian-passport-leak-after-salisbury-may-reveal-spy-methods.

Royal. (2015) *UK Research and the European Union: The Role of the EU in Funding UK Research.* The Royal Society. https://royalsociety.org/-/media/policy/projects/eu-uk-funding/uk-membership-of-eu.pdf.

RT. (2018) "Absurdity": Moscow slams Boris Johnson's insinuations over Russian ex-spy incident. *Russia Today.* March 6. https://www.rt.com/news/420659-russian-double-agent-johnson-moscow/.

Rudy-Hiller, F. (2018) The epistemic condition for moral responsibility. In E. N. Zalta (ed.), *Stanford Encyclopedia of Philosophy.* (Fall 2018). https://plato.stanford.edu/archives/fall2018/entries/moral-responsibility-epistemic/.

Russell, B. (2004[1928]) *Sceptical Essays.* London: Routledge.

Rutschmann, R., and A. Wiegmann. (2017) No need for an intention to deceive: Challenging the traditional definition of lying. *Philosophical Psychology* 30(4): 434–453.

Sack, R. D. (2017) *Sack on Defamation: Libel, Slander, and Related Problems.* 5th ed. New York: Practising Law Institute.

Sacks, H. (1975) Everyone has to lie. In B. B. Blount and M. Sanches (eds.), *Sociocultural Dimensions of Language Use.* New York: Academic Press. 57–80.

Sacks, H., E. Schegloff, and G. Jefferson. (1974) A simplest systematics for the organization of turn-taking in conversation. *Language* 50: 696–735.

Sarno, D. (2009) Twitter creator Jack Dorsey illuminates the site's founding document.... *Los Angeles Times.* February 18. http://latimesblogs.latimes.com/technology/2009/02/twitter-creator.html.

Saul, J. M. (2002) Speaker meaning, what is said, and what is implicated. *Noûs* 36: 228–248.

Saul, J. M. (2012) *Lying, Misleading, and What Is Said: An Exploration in Philosophy of Language and in Ethics.* Oxford: Oxford University Press.

Saul, J. M. (2018) Negligent falsehood, white ignorance, and false news. In E. Michaelson and A. Stokke (eds.), *Lying: Language, Knowledge, Ethics, and Politics.* Oxford: Oxford University Press. 246–261.

Saussure, F. de. (1983[1916]) *Course in General Linguistics.* Translated by R. Harris. London: Duckworth.

Schank, R. C., and R. P. Abelson. (1977) *Scripts, Plans, Goals and Understanding: An Inquiry into Human Knowledge Structures.* Hillsdale, NJ: Erlbaum.

Schauer, F. (1978) Fear, risk and the First Amendment: Unraveling the chilling effect. *Boston University Law Review* 58(5): 685–732.

Schiffer, S. (1972) *Meaning.* Oxford: Clarendon Press.

Schlick, M. (1936) Meaning and verification. *Philosophical Review* 45(4): 339–369.

Schroeter, M., and C. Taylor (eds.). (2018) *Exploring Silence and Absence in Discourse.* Basingstoke: Palgrave Macmillan.

Scollon, R., S. W. Scollon, and R. H. Jones. (2012) *Intercultural Communication: A Discourse Approach.* 3rd ed. Oxford: Wiley-Blackwell.

Scott, G. G. (2010) *Playing the Lying Game.* Santa Barbara, CA: Praeger.

Searle, J. R. (1964) How to derive ought from is. *The Philosophical Review* 73: 43–58.

Searle, J. R. (1969) *Speech Acts: An Essay in the Philosophy of Language.* Cambridge: Cambridge University Press.

Searle, J. R. (1979) *Expression and Meaning: Studies in the Theory of Speech Acts.* Cambridge: Cambridge University Press.

Searle, J. R. (1983) *Intentionality: An Essay in the Philosophy of Mind.* Cambridge: Cambridge University Press.

Searle, J. R. (2018) Constitutive rules. *Argumenta* 4(1): 51–54.

Sears, R., L. Rau, and R. Alpert. (1965) *Identification and Child Rearing.* New York: John Wiley.

Seierstad, A. (2003) *A Hundred and One Days: A Baghdad Journal.* Translated by I. Christophersen. New York: Basic Books.

Senate. (2004) *Report on the U.S. Intelligence Community's Prewar Intelligence Assessments on Iraq.* US Senate Select Committee on Intelligence. http://intelligence.senate.gov/.

Seneca, L. A. (2014) *Letters from a Stoic: Epistulae Morales AD Lucilium.* Translated by R. M. Gummere. Scotts Valley, CA: CreateSpace.

Sengupta, K. (2018) Britain divulged "unprecedented levels of intelligence" to convince countries Russia was behind nerve agent attack. March 27. https://www.independent.co.uk/news/uk/home-news/salisbury-nerve-agent-attack-spy-intelligence-information-russia-a8276776.html.

Sextus Empiricus. (2000) *Outlines of Scepticism.* Edited by J. Annas and J. Barnes. Cambridge: Cambridge University Press.

Sher, G. (2009) *Who Knew? Responsibility without Awareness.* New York: Oxford University Press.

Shiffrin, S. V. (2014) *Speech Matters: On Lying, Morality, and the Law.* Carl G. Hempel Lecture Series. Princeton, NJ: Princeton University Press.

Shuster, S. (2015) Why the Kremlin is blaming Putin critic's murder on a "provocation." February 28. http://time.com/3727379/putin-boris-nemtsov-kremlin-provocation/.

Shuy, R. (2017) *The Deceptive Ambiguity of Institutionally Powerful Police, Prosecutors and Undercover Agents.* New York: Oxford University Press.

Sidnell, J., and T. Stivers (eds.). (2014) *The Handbook of Conversation Analysis.* Chichester: Wiley Blackwell.

Simpson, D. (1992) Lying, liars and language. *Philosophy and Phenomenological Research* 52: 623–639.

Simpson, J. A. (2007) Foundations of interpersonal trust. In A. W. Kruglanski and E. T. Higgins (eds.), *Social Psychology: Handbook of Basic Principles.* New York: Guilford. 587–607.

Singh, S., and E. Ernst. (2008) *Trick or Treatment? Alternative Medicine on Trial.* London: Bantam.

Slote, S. (2013) *Joyce's Nietzschean Ethics.* 1st ed. New York: Palgrave Macmillan.

Smith, D. L. (2004) *Why We Lie: The Evolutionary Roots of Deception and the Unconscious Mind.* New York, NY: St. Martin's Press.

Smith, H. M. (1983) Culpable ignorance. *Philosophical Review* 92(4): 543–571.

Smith, M., and J. Randerson. (2014) Jeremy Paxman's top 10 Newsnight moments—in videos. *The Guardian.* June 18. https://www.theguardian.com/media/2014/apr/30/jeremy-paxmans-top-10-newsnight-moments.

Smith, N. (2017) Oscars 2017: Truth behind "Envelopegate" emerges. *BBC News.* February 28. http://www.bbc.co.uk/news/entertainment-arts-39112851.

Snyder, J. R. (2009) *Dissimulation and the Culture of Secrecy in Early Modern Europe.* Berkeley: University of California Press.

Sokal, A. (1996) Transgressing the boundaries: Toward a transformative hermeneutics of quantum gravity. *Social Text* 46/47: 217–252.

Solan, L. M. (2004) Pernicious ambiguity in contracts and statutes. *Chicago-Kent Law Review* 79: 859–888.

Solan, L. M., and P. M. Tiersma. (2005) *Speaking of Crime: The Language of Criminal Justice.* Chicago: University of Chicago Press.

Solender, A. (2018) How one website sets out to classify news, expose "fake news." *Inside Sources.* June 11. https://www.insidesources.com/one-website-sets-classify-news-expose-fake-news/.

Solon, O. (2016) Barack Obama on fake news: "We have problems" if we can't tell the difference. *The Guardian.* November 18. https://www.theguardian.com/media/2016/nov/17/barack-obama-fake-news-facebook-social-media.

Sorensen, R. O. Y. (2007) Bald-faced lies! Lying without the intent to deceive. *Pacific Philosophical Quarterly* 88(2): 251–264.

Sorensen, R. O. Y. (2010) Knowledge-lies. *Analysis* 70: 608–615.

Spender, D. (1980) *Man Made Language.* London: Routledge & Kegan Paul.

Sperber, D., F. Clement, C. Heintz, O. Mascaro, H. Mercier, et al. (2010) Epistemic vigilance. *Mind & Language* 25(4): 359–393.

Sporer, S. L., and B. Schwandt. (2006) Paraverbal indicators of deception: A meta-analytic synthesis. *Applied Cognitive Psychology* 20: 421–446.

Stalnaker, R. (1984) *Inquiry.* Cambridge, MA: MIT Press.

Stalnaker, R. (2002) Common ground. *Linguistics and Philosophy* 25: 701–721.

Steiner, G. (1998) *After Babel: Aspects of Language and Translation.* 3rd ed. Oxford: Oxford University Press.

Stenner, K. (2010) *The Authoritarian Dynamic.* Cambridge: Cambridge University Press.

Stewart, H. (2018a) Corbyn under fire from own MPs over response to PM's Russia statement. March 14. https://www.theguardian.com/uk-news/2018/mar/14/jeremy-corbyn-under-fire-over-response-to-pms-russia-statement.

Stewart, H. (2018b) Russia spread fake news via Twitter bots after Salisbury poisoning—analysis. *The Guardian.* https://www.theguardian.com/world/2018/apr/19/russia-fake-news-salisbury-poisoning-twitter-bots-uk.

Stokke, A. (2013) Lying and asserting. *Journal of Philosophy* 110: 33–60.

Stokke, A. (2014) Insincerity. *Noûs* 48(3): 496–520.

Stokke, A. (2018) *Lying and Insincerity.* Oxford: Oxford University Press.

Stokke, A. (2019a) Bullshitting. In J. Meibauer (ed.), *The Oxford Handbook of Lying.* Oxford: Oxford University Press. 264–276.

Stokke, A. (2019b) Lying, sincerity and quality. In J. Meibauer (ed.), *The Oxford Handbook of Lying*. Oxford: Oxford University Press. 134–148.

Stokke, A., and D. Fallis. (2017) Bullshitting, lying and indifference toward truth. *Ergo* 4(10): 277–309.

Stone, J. (2016) Ukip voters worried that MI5 will rig EU referendum, new poll finds. *The Independent*. June 21. http://www.independent.co.uk/news/uk/politics/eu-referendum-rigged-poll-mi5-ukip-nigel-farage-vote-leave-remain-a7093536.html.

Stone, P. (2018) Boris Johnson blatantly lies to Deutsche Welle and says Porton Down lab were absolutely categorical. https://www.youtube.com/watch?v=D89rfg-kQuQ.

Strudler, A. (2010) The distinctive wrong in lying. *Ethical Theory and Moral Practice* 13(2): 171–179.

Swales, J. (1990) *Genre Analysis*. Cambridge: Cambridge University Press.

Sweetser, E. (1987) The definition of lie: An examination of the folk models underlying a semantic prototype. In D. Holland (ed.), *Cultural Models in Language and Thought*. New York: Cambridge University Press. 43–66.

Taleb, N. N. (2007) *The Black Swan: The Impact of the Highly Improbable*. London: Allen Lane.

Talwar, V., and K. Lee. (2002) Development of lying to conceal a transgression: Children's control of expressive behavior during verbal deception. *International Journal of Behavioral Development* 26: 436–444.

Terkourafi, M. (2019) Lying and politeness. In J. Meibauer (ed.), *The Oxford Handbook of Lying*. Oxford: Oxford University Press. 382–396.

Thijsse, E. (2000) The doxastic-epistemic force of declarative utterances. In H. C. Bunt and W. J. Black (eds.), *Abduction, Belief and Context in Dialogue: Studies in Computational Pragmatics*. Amsterdam: John Benjamins. 327–352.

Tiersma, P. M. (1990) The language of perjury: "Literal truth," ambiguity, and the false statement requirement. *Southern California Law Review* 63(2): 373–432.

Toulmin, S. (2003) *The Uses of Argument*. 2nd ed. Cambridge: Cambridge University Press.

Trilling, L. (1972) *Sincerity and Authenticity*. Cambridge, MA: Harvard University Press.

Trivers, R. L. (1971) The evolution of reciprocal altruism. *The Quarterly Review of Biology* 46(1): 35–57.

Trivers, R. L. (2011) *Deceit and Self-deception: Fooling Yourself the Better to Fool Others*. London: Allen Lane.

Trump, D. (2016) *Donald Trump Campaign Event in Green Bay, Wisconsin*. C-Span. October 17. https://www.c-span.org/video/?417019-1/donald-trump-campaigns-green-bay-wisconsin.

Tucker, J. B. (2006) *War of Nerves*. New York: Anchor Books.

Turner, R. E., C. Edgley, and G. Olmstead. (1975) Information control in conversations: Honesty is not always the best policy. *Kansas Journal of Sociology* 11(1): 69–89.

Turri, J. (2014) Knowledge and suberogatory assertion. *Philosophical Studies* 167: 557–567.

Turri, J., M. Alfano, and J. Greco. (2009) Virtue epistemology. In E. N. Zalta (ed.), *The Stanford Encyclopedia of Philosophy*. (Spring 2009 Edition). https://plato.stanford.edu/archives/spr2009/entries/epistemology-virtue/.

Turri, J., and A. Turri. (2015) The truth about lying. *Cognition* 138(1): 161–168.

Twain, M. (2013[1895]) *Fenimore Cooper's Literary Offenses*. Auckland, NZ: The Floating Press.

TWP. (2018) Russia's frantic parade of lies. *Washington Post.* April 16. https://www.washingtonpost.com/opinions/russias-frantic-parade-of-lies/2018/04/16/5895d86a-4199-11e8-ad8f-27a8c409298b_story.html?noredirect=on&utm_term=.1b6a7a5fb6d4.

UNSC. (2018) *8203rd Meeting of the UN Security Council.* March 15. https://undocs.org/en/S/PV.8203.

Urban, M. (2018) *The Skripal Files.* London: Macmillan.

UUK. (2018) *Higher Education in Numbers.* Universities UK. http://www.universitiesuk.ac.uk/facts-and-stats/Pages/higher-education-data.aspx.

van der Geest, S. (2018) Privacy from an anthropological perspective. In A. de Groot and B. van der Sloot (eds.), *Handbook of Privacy Studies.* Amsterdam: Amsterdam University Press. 413–443.

Vickers, H. (2017) *The Crown: Truth and Fiction.* London: Zuleika.

Vincent, J., and C. Castelfranchi. (1981) On the art of deception: How to lie while saying the truth. In H. Parret, M. Sbisà, and J. Verschueren (eds.), *Possibilities and Limitations of Pragmatics: Proceedings of the Conference on Pragmatics, Urbino, July 8–14.* Amsterdam: Benjamins. 749–777.

Vincent Marrelli, J. (2004) *Words in the Way of Truth: Truthfulness, Deception, Lying across Cultures and Disciplines.* Naples: Edizioni Scientifiche Italiane.

Vincent Marrelli, J. (2006) Truthfulness. In J.-O. Östman, J. Verschueren, and E. Versluys (eds.), *Handbook of Pragmatics.* Amsterdam: Benjamins. 1–72.

Vrij, A. (2008) *Detecting Lies and Deceit: Pitfalls and Opportunities.* 2nd ed. Hoboken, NJ: Wiley.

Vrij, A., P. A. Granhag, and S. Porter. (2010) Pitfalls and opportunities in nonverbal and verbal lie detection. *Psychological Science in the Public Interest* 11: 89–121.

Wakeham, J. (2017) Bullshit as a problem of social epistemology. *Sociological Theory* 35(1): 15–58.

Walczyk, J. J., L. L. Harris, T. K. Duck, and D. Mulay. (2014) A social-cognitive framework for understanding serious lies: Activation-Decision-Construction-Action Theory. *New Ideas in Psychology* 34: 22–36.

Walton, D. N. (2014) *Burden of Proof, Presumption and Argumentation.* New York: Cambridge University Press.

Wattles, J. (1996) *The Golden Rule.* New York: Oxford University Press.

Wautischer, H. (ed.). (1998) *Tribal Epistemologies: Essays in the Philosophy of Anthropology.* Burlington, VT: Ashgate.

Weale, S., and D. Batty. (2017) Calls for action by universities on "epidemic" of harassment on campus. *The Guardian.* March 6. https://www.theguardian.com/education/2017/mar/06/calls-for-review-into-how-universities-handle-sexual-harassment-allegations.

Weatherall, A. (2011) I don't know as a prepositioned epistemic hedge. *Research on Language & Social Interaction* 44(4): 317–337.

Webber, J. (2013) Liar! *Analysis* 73(4): 651–659.

Weinrich, H. (2005[1965]) *The Linguistics of Lying and Other Essays.* Seattle: University of Washington Press.

Wesolowsky, T. (2018) A timeline of Russia's changing story on Skripal Poisoning. *Radio Free Europe/Radio Liberty.* March 21. https://www.rferl.org/a/timeline-deny-distort-novichok-russia-changing-stories-poisoning/29113561.html.

Wiegmann, A., J. Jana Samland, and M. R. Waldmann. (2016) Lying despite telling the truth. *Cognition* 150: 37–42.

Williams, B. (2002) *Truth and Truthfulness: An Essay in Genealogy*. Princeton, NJ: Princeton University Press.

Williams, M. (2018) Fact Check long read: Does the UK's case against Russia stack up? *Channel 4 News*. March 26. https://www.channel4.com/news/factcheck/long-read-does-the-uks-case-against-russia-stack-up.

Wilson, D., and D. Sperber. (1992) On verbal irony. *Lingua* 87: 53–76.

Wilson, D., and D. Sperber. (2002) Truthfulness and relevance. *Mind* 111(443): 583–632.

Wilson, N. L. (1959) Substances without substrata. *Review of Metaphysics* 12: 521–539.

Wintour, P. (2018) Dutch expelled Russians over alleged Novichok lab hacking plot. September 14. https://www.theguardian.com/uk-news/2018/sep/14/dutch-expelled-russians-over-alleged-novichok-laboratory-hacking-plot.

Wittgenstein, L. (1998) *Culture and Value*. Rev. 2nd ed. Translated by P. Winch. Edited by A. Pichler and G. H. v. Wright. Oxford: Blackwell.

Wittgenstein, L. (2009) *Philosophical Investigations*. 4th ed. Edited and translated by P. M. S. Hacker and J. Schulte. Oxford: Wiley-Blackwell.

WND. (2017) Phoney baloney: The 9 fakest fake-news checkers. *WND*. February 19. https://www.wnd.com/2017/02/phony-baloney-the-9-fakest-fake-news-checkers/.

Wodak, R., and M. Meyer. (2009) *Methods of Critical Discourse Analysis*. 2nd ed. London: Sage.

Wolfensberger, W., and S. Tullman. (1982) A brief outline of the principle of normalization. *Rehabilitation Psychology* 27(3): 131–145.

Woodward, K. (1999) Statistical panic. *Differences: A Journal of Feminist Cultural Studies in History and Philosophy of Science* 11(2): 177–203.

Woodward, K. (2009) *Statistical Panic: Cultural Politics and Poetics of the Emotions*. Durham, NC: Duke University Press.

Wreen, M. (2013) A P.S. on B.S.: Some remarks on humbug and bullshit. *Metaphilosophy* 44: 105–115.

Yeung, L. N. T., T. R. Levine, and K. Nishiyama. (1999) Information Manipulation Theory and perceptions of deception in Hong Kong. *Communication Reports* 12: 1–11.

York, C. (2018) Why does Russia have more than 20 explanations for the Salisbury poisoning? *Huffington Post UK*. April 7. https://www.huffingtonpost.co.uk/entry/russia-skripal-explanations_uk.

Zimmerman, M. J. (1997) Moral responsibility and ignorance. *Ethics* 107: 410–426.

Zushi, Y. (2017) Are freedom of information requests poisoning us against the public sector? *The New Statesman*. March 9. https://www.newstatesman.com/2017/03/foi-culture-public-sector-sexual-harrassment-universities.

Index

Tables and figures are indicated by *t* and *f* following the page number

For the benefit of digital users, indexed terms that span two pages (e.g., 52–53) may, on occasion, appear on only one of those pages.

accuracy, and epistemic responsibility, 63–65
advertising
    Advertising Code, and claims in Brexit Battle Bus message, 250–51
    and deception, 12, 173, 250, 253
    political advertising, 250–52, 294–95
    and puffery, 13, 172–73, 250–51
advocacy, link between epistemic responsibility and, 61–62
agency, 16, 116, 274, 286
altruism, reciprocal, 29–31, 36–37, 116–17
ambiguity, 160–61. *See also* equivocating
apology, 228
Aquinas, Thomas, 57, 125
Aristotle, 62, 96–7, 213
artful dodging, 4, 154–55. *See also* evasion
assertion
    assertibility of claims, 237
    and bullshitting, 65
    and defining lying, 165–66
    and epistemic responsibility, 58–59
    and false implicature, 47
    falsifiability and, 99–100
    falsity as unwarranted assertibility, 104–5
    indifference toward, 65–68
    "negligent false assertion," 82
    sincere versus insincere, 65–66
    and sincerity, 43–45
assessment sensitivity, 98–100, 104
Augustine, 27, 94
authenticity, 50n.20

balance, journalistic 293
bald-faced evasion, 36
bald-faced lies, 33–35, 36–37, 42, 50, 167–68, 172–73
bald-faced truth, 50
banter, 11, 119, 141, 218
belief(s)
    dogma and making world fit, 75–78
    questioned, 31

benign bullshit, 179–80
betrayed trust, 31
bias, 184–85, 282
Blair, Tony, 253–61
Blake, William, 105–6
blameworthiness, 212–13, 214
blocking, 152, 157–58
bluffing, 170
Bolinger, Dwight 15–17
Boshirov, Ruslan, 263–64
brazen lies, 37
Brexit, 97–98, 249–53
"Bronston" case (*Bronston v. United States*), 147–49
brute facts, 96
bullshit
    benign bullshit, 179–80
    in Blair's Foreword to Iraq Dossier claims, 258–59
    and categories of insincerity, 285–86
    claptrap, 196–97, 199–200
    confession as motivation for calling out, 90
    contextualized, 8, 218–19
    defined, 195
    detection as motivation for calling out, 91–92
    as disregarding evidential grounding, 195–202
    and dogma, 78, 80
    as epistemically irresponsible discourse pathology, 182
    evasive bullshit, 178–79
    falsification as motivation for calling out, 93–94
    gobbledygook, 196–99
    and inquiry, 71–75
    miscalling, 88–89
    versus negligent falsehood, 82
    as pathological discourse, 195–97
    Plato accuses poets of, 122
    pseudo-poppycock, 196–97, 201–2
    and responsibility in TRUST heuristic, 241
    self-contradiction as motivation for calling out, 92–93

bullshitting
    and categories of insincerity, 285–86
    cognitive core of, 68
    defined, 179
    and disinformation, 276
    and epistemic responsibility, 57–58
    and ethical value of untruthfulness, 8
    evasive bullshitting, 157
    Frankfurt on, 5, 65–68, 71, 124, 178, 180, 198–200
    and indifference, 65–71
    as insincere and irresponsible, 178–80
    knowledge bullshitting, 180
    link between Evidence maxim and, 69–71
    versus negligent falsehood, 82
    non-deceptive, and fitting world to beliefs, 76–77
    pathological bullshitting, 132
    rhetorical bullshitting, 180
    types of insincere, 180–81
    wishful bullshitting, 181
Bush, George W., 257, 259

Cambridge Analytica, 294
Cameron, David, 253
    Carson, Thomas L. 12, 28–29, 33–34, 44, 114–15, 117–19, 151–52, 159–60, 254, 255–56, 257, 259–60
caveat auditor, 10
character, educational development of, 293–94
"Charlie the Gambler" case, 34–37
"Cheating Student" case, 33–37, 41–42, 54
Cheney, Dick, 257–58
Chepiga, Anatoliy, 263–64, 272–73
"cherry picking," 164
Chilcot Report, 253
children, development of lying strategies in, 91–92, 111
Chisholm, Roderick M. and Thomas D. Feehan, 32, 44, 143, 150
claims of untruthfulness, 87–88, 109–10
    calling out lies and bullshit, 88–94
    and factually falsifiable claims, 95–100
    and falsity, pragmatism, and relativism, 103–9
    and source reliability, 100–3
claptrap, 182, 196–97, 199–200, 258–59
Clinton, Bill, 160–61
CNN, 82, 83, 100–1
cognitive biases, 184–85
cognitive trust, 216–19
Coleman, Linda and Paul Kay, 8, 34, 46–47, 50, 94, 113, 129, 226

common ground
    and bullshitting, 68–69
    discursive insincerity and, 53
    implicature and, 45–46
Communication Ethics, 13–14
communicative goals, and insincerity, 143–45
communicative trust, 216–19
concealing, 4, 19, 143, 151–52
condonable suspension of truthfulness, 238–39
confession, as motivation for calling out lies and bullshit, 90
confirmation bias, 184–85
confirmatory selection, 184–85, 258–59, 285, 286
consensus theory of truth, 106
consequential suspension of truthfulness, 125–30, 132–33, 238–39
conspiracy theories, 5–6, 214, 263–64n.2, 266, 270, 277–80
constitutive rules of assertion, 43–44
context, taking words out of, 16, 164
contextualized bullshit, 8, 218–19
contrived distraction, 142
conventional suspension of truthfulness, 120–24, 238–39
cooperation. *See also* Maxims of Conversation
    and Golden Rule, 12, 116–20, 132–33
    implicature and, 40–41
    trust and, 27–28
Cooperative Principle, 27–28, 162
counterfeit, 200
Credulous Leader, 5–6
critical openness, 80, 292–93
critical thinking, 291–93
culpability, 211. *See also* gravity of breach of trust
    analysis of degree of, 215–16, 229
    and analyzing untruthfulness in situated discourse, 13
    of claims in Blair's Foreword to Iraq Dossier, 260
    of claims in Brexit Battle Bus message, 252–53
    and epistemic irresponsibility, 212–15
    and ethical value of untruthfulness, 287
    of Skripal poisoning claims, 280–81
    and strategic and communicative trust, 216–19
    of Trump's voter fraud tweet, 247–48
    in TRUST heuristic, 234–37, 235*t*, 242
culpable ignorance, 213–15
cultural relativity, 121–23, 289–90
culture, consequentialism and, 130–31

INDEX

Cummins, Dominic, 251–52
cyberwarfare, 279

deception
  categories similar to withholding, misleading, and lying, 150t
  and discursive insincerity, 50–53, 143–45
  and epistemic irresponsibility, 38
  and evolutionary and child development, 111
  intention to deceive, 6, 17, 34–35
  and location of ethical value of untruthfulness, 9
  versus misleading, 159–60
  as not involved in all cases of insincerity, 33–36
  as not requisite for breach of trust, 36–37
  and social adeptness, 32
  trust and, 27–28, 32–33
  types of, 14, 16
  as violation of Grice's maxims, 139–43
deceptionists/non-deceptionists, 33–34, 36
deceptive lying, 166–67, 189–90
defamation, 204–5
definition of lie/lying. *See* lying
degree lying, 168–70
deliberate targeting of victim, 228
denial and deniability, 89, 148–49
detail distortion, 182, 194–95
detection, as motivation for calling out lies and bullshit, 91–92
discourse
  dogma as underlying epistemically irresponsible, 78
  epistemically irresponsible, 75–83
  insincere discourse strategies, 20
  justifiable suspensions of truthfulness in, 133t
  monologic, 80
discourse ethics, 13–14
discourse pathologies, 80–81, 181–82, 195–97, 240f, 289. *See also* epistemically irresponsible discourse pathologies
discourse strategy, 144–45, 146f, 147t, 151–52, 174t
discursive insincerity, 27–28, 50–55, 138–39, 176
  analysis of, 20
  and bullshitting, 178
  categories of, 4, 240f
  and deception as violation of Grice's maxims, 139–43
  defined, 53
  epistemic irresponsibility and, 14
  link between TRUST categories and other taxonomies, 149
  lying as self-contradiction, 165–70
  misleading as discursively leading astray, 158–64
  in practice, 50–53
  sketch of, 53–54
  and speaker intentions and strategic goals, 143–45
  summary and sample sincerity analysis, 173–76
  tests for insincere discourse strategies, 147t
  of Trump's voter fraud tweet, 245
  in TRUST heuristic, 234–37, 235t, 239–40
  willful insincerity, 170–73
  withholding and, 52–53, 54–55, 145–46, 150–58
dishonesty, 10, 131, 135, 153, 218–19
  institutional, 218–19
  intellectual, 259
  professional, 10, 153
disinformation, 276–77, 278, 282
dismissal, rude, 186, 258–59, 285
dissimulation, 153
distortion
  versus bullshit, 196
  and categories of insincerity, 285–86
  in claims in Blair's Foreword to Iraq Dossier, 258–59, 261
  and deception, 16
  defined, 190
  as epistemically irresponsible discourse pathology, 181–82, 188–95
  and responsibility in TRUST heuristic, 241
  taking words out of context as, 164
  by Trump's voter fraud tweet, 246–47
distraction, contrived, 142
distrust, and miscalling of lies and bullshit, 89
dogma
  and categories of insincerity, 285–86
  and claims in Blair's Foreword to Iraq Dossier, 258–59
  as closing off inquiry, 78–80
  critical thinking as antidote to, 292–93
  and direction of fit, 75–78
  and discourse pathologies, 80–81
  as epistemically irresponsible discourse pathology, 181–82, 183–88
  and miscalling of lies and bullshit, 88–89
  and negligent falsehood, 81–83
  pathological dogma defined, 183–84
  and responsibility in TRUST heuristic, 241
doxastic justification, 58–59, 60–62, 70–71

Dunning-Kruger effect, 283
Dynel, Marta 34, 46, 52, 69–70, 74, 123, 140, 151, 153

echo chambers, 186–87, 188
economy of truthfulness, 111–16
empathy, 119
epistemically irresponsible discourse pathologies, 177–78
  bullshit as disregarding evidential grounding, 195–202
  and bullshitting, 178–82
  categories of, 181–82
  and distortion, 188–95
  and dogma, 183–88
  epistemic negligence, 202–7
  summary and sample analysis of, 207–10
epistemic care, duty of, 203–5, 247, 259–60, 280, 287
epistemic injustice, 292–93
epistemic irresponsibility, 57–58, 84–85. *See also* bullshit; bullshitting; discourse pathologies; distortion; dogma; epistemic negligence; epistemic responsibility
  and bullshitting, 65
  categories of insincerity and, 285–86
  culpability and, 212–15
  discourse pathologies, 240f
  discursive insincerity and, 14
  dogma and, 75–83
  and factual falsity, 95
  falsifiability and, 98
  inquiry disrupted by, 104
  and negligent falsehood, 83
  as not involving deception, 38
  and scope of untruthfulness, 5–6
  of Skripal poisoning claims, 277–80
epistemic negligence, 19, 177, 202–7
  of claims in Blair's Foreword to Iraq Dossier, 259–60
  of claims in Brexit Battle Bus message, 252
  and ethical value of untruthfulness, 287
  key conditions for, 17
  of politicians as breach of trust, 217
  and responsibility in TRUST heuristic, 241
  of Trump's voter fraud tweet, 247
epistemic partisanship, 103, 262–63, 291–95
epistemic power of speaker, 224–25, 260
epistemic responsibility, 5–6, 10. *See also* epistemic irresponsibility
  accuracy and, 63–65
  and analyzing untruthfulness in situated discourse, 13

assertion and, 58–59
  as intellectual and moral virtue, 61–63
  justifiable suspensions of, 124
  and justification, 58–61
  playful suspensions of, 131–32
  suspension of commitment to, 132–33
  and trust, 58–65
  in TRUST heuristic, 234–37, 235t, 241
epistemic vigilance, 10, 218
epistemological relativity, 105–7
equivocating, 160–61, 175–76, 256–57
Essential Rule of Assertion, 43–44
Ethical Discourse Analysis (EDA), 290–91
ethical value of untruthfulness, 1, 7–11, 19–20, 286–87
evading/evasion, 4, 152, 154–58, 164, 174t, 179
  bald-faced, 36
  versus blocking, 158
  withholding and, 152, 154–57
evasive bullshit, 178–79
evidence for falsity, 87–88, 109–10
  calling out lies and bullshit, 88–94
  and factually falsifiable claims, 95–100
  falsity, pragmatism, and relativism, 103–9
  and source reliability, 100–3
  in TRUST heuristic, 234–38, 235t
exaggerating, 168–70, 172–73, 175–76, 182, 192
experience, and source reliability, 100–1
expertise, and source reliability, 101–2

fabricating/fabrication, 168, 174t, 193, 263, 276
benign fabrication, 107
false news, 168
face
  boosting, 114, 135, 179
  face-saving, 19, 113–14, 125–27, 133, 173, 238
  and reputation, 204
fact checks, 293. *See also* evidence for falsity
facts, brute versus institutional, 96
factual falsity, 14–15, 87, 93, 95–96
factually falsifiable claims, 95–100
factually significant claims, 96
factual reporting, 102–3
fake news, 168, 186
faking, 163
Fallis, Don 34, 36, 42, 68–70, 115
falsehood
  justified evidence of, 95–96
  negligent, 81–83
false implicature/falsely implicating, 46–48, 142, 145, 150t, 162, 164, 174t
false invitations, 134–36
falsely presupposing, and misleading, 163
false news, 168, 186

falsifiability, 97–100, 109–10, 237, 243, 249, 254
falsifications, 16, 19, 93–94, 166–67.
    See also lying
falsity. See also evidence for falsity
    and epistemological relativity, 105–7
    factual, 14–15, 87, 93, 95–96
    as unwarranted assertibility, 104–5
Faulkner, Paul 31, 33, 61, 89, 219, 286
fiction, 121–22
filter bubbles, and dogma, 185
Fox News, 208–10
Frankfurt, Harry G., 5, 65–67, 71, 124, 198, 200
freedom of speech, 205, 294
freeloaders, 30–31
full plagiarism, 153–54, 154t, 154n.3

Galasiński, Dariusz, 16–17, 155, 164, 193
genre, and conventional suspension of
    commitment to truthfulness, 120–24
gobbledygook, 182, 196–99
Goffman, Erving 30, 126, 153–54, 204
Golden Rule, 12, 116–20, 132–33
gravity of breach of trust, 220–21
    dimensions for analyzing, 221–27, 242, 287
    and ethical value of untruthfulness, 287
    further aggravating and mitigating
        circumstances concerning, 227–28
greetings, ritualized, 113–14
Grice, Paul, 3–4, 27–28, 73–75. See also
    Cooperative Principle; Maxims of
    Conversation
group lies, 167

half-truth, 153. See also omission
hedging claims, 60–61, 206–7, 247, 256–57.
    See also epistemic negligence
hindsight lying, 75–76
hoaxes, 131–32, 266–67
hot air, versus bullshit, 71
Howard, Michael, 155–57
human inquiry, 71
humbug, 198
humor, 270–72
hyperbole, 6, 119, 121, 175

@Ian56, 278–80
ideational plagiarism, 153–54, 154t, 172
ignorance
    culpable, 213–15
    justifiable, 212
impartiality, and source reliability, 102
implicature, 40–41
    and common ground between
        speakers, 45–46

false implicature as violation of Grice's
    maxims, 142
false implicature and misleading, 145, 162
false implicature and Questions under
    Discussion, 46–48
incapacity, 228
indifference
    bullshitting and, 65–71
    toward assertions, 65–68
indifferent lies, 33–34
indigenous knowledge, 109n.8
information importance, 226–27
Information Manipulation Theory (IMT),
    139–40, 142
inquiry, 38
    and bullshit, 71–75
    disrupted by insincerity, 104, 143
    dogma as closing off, 78–80
    and insincerity, 43–50
    withholding as disrupting, 54–55
insincerity. See also bullshitting; discursive
        insincerity; epistemic irresponsibility;
        lying; misleading; sincerity; withholding
    and analyzing untruthfulness in situated
        discourse, 13
    and bullshitting, 69–71
    categories and typologies of, 139–49
    communicative nesting of, 145f
    as covert, 112–13
    and deception as violation of Grice's
        maxims, 139–43
    defined, 48
    and ethical value of untruthfulness, 11
    and factual falsity, 95
    and inquiry, 43–50, 104
    as not rooted in intent to deceive, 29–38
    and scope of untruthfulness, 3–4, 19, 284–85
    as subjective, 138
    utterance, 4, 19
    willful, 11, 19, 138, 170–73, 240, 245, 258, 287
institutional dishonesty, 218–19
institutional facts, 96
institutional power of speaker, 22, 224–25, 260
intellectual dishonesty, 259
intellectual vices, 202–3
intention, 16, 17, 143–45, 285–86.
    See also willful insincerity
intention to deceive, 6, 17, 34–35
intentional misrepresentation, 6
interactional inquiry, 71
interdependence, and vulnerability, 223
Interpersonal Deception Theory (IDT), 139–40
investigation, sufficient, 205–6, 247
investigative investment, 79

Iraq Dossier, Foreword to, 253–61
Iraq Inquiry, 253, 254–55
irony, 45–46, 123–24
irresponsibility. *See* epistemic irresponsibility
"ISIS dildo flag" case, 82, 83, 100–1

Johnson, Boris, 96, 102, 228, 249–53, 273–75, 281
joking, 131–32
judgment
  Golden Rule and, 119–20
  and presumption of truthfulness, 29
  in TRUST heuristic, 234–37, 235*t*, 242
justifiable suspensions of truthfulness
  and ethical value of untruthfulness, 286–87
  as not justified, 271–72
  in TRUST heuristic, 238–39
justification
  and bullshitting, 70–71
  and epistemic responsibility, 58–61
  in evasion, 155
  evidence of falsehood, 95–96
  and suspension of commitment to truthfulness, 116
justified suspended context, 115–16
justified untruthfulness, 111–12, 136–37
  and condonable suspension of truthfulness, 131–32
  and consequential suspension of truthfulness, 125–30
  and conventional suspension of truthfulness, 120–24
  in discourse, 133*t*
  and economy of truthfulness, 112–16
  and ethical responsibility, 10
  and ethical value of untruthfulness, 286–87
  Golden Rule and, 116–20
  in TRUST heuristic, 239
  and trust-related untruthfulness, 9

Kant, Immanuel, 9, 39, 44, 117–18, 125, 129–30
kidding, 131–32
knowledge, indigenous, 109n.8
knowledge bullshitting, 180
knowledge lies, 33–34

language, ethical dimension to, 290
learned nonsense, 198
LGBT Pride march, mistaken news regarding terrorist flag at, 82, 83, 100–1
lie detection, 2, 50, 77, 91–92

lies. *See also* lying
  bald-faced, 33–35, 36–37, 42, 50, 167–68, 172–73
  of Boris Johnson, 274–76
  of Bush administration, 257
  confession as motivation for calling out, 90
  detection as motivation for calling out, 91–92
  falsification as motivation for calling out, 93–94
  group lies, 167
  linking of fiction and, 121–22
  miscalling, 88–89
  noble lies, 172–73
  pathological lies, 132
  self-contradiction as motivation for calling out, 92–93
"likes, truth-by-," 105–6
linguistic plagiarism, 153–54, 154*t*, 154n.3, 172
lying. *See also* falsifications; lies
  accusations of, 291–92
  acquisition of, 111
  assertion and, 44
  versus bullshitting, 66
  as category in TRUST framework, 2–3
  as covert, 112–13
  and deception as not requisite for breach of trust, 36–37
  deception categories similar to, 149, 150*t*
  deceptive, 166–67, 189–90
  defined, 165–67
  degree, 168–70
  and evolutionary and child development, 111
  false implicature as, 47
  hindsight lying, 75–76
  indirect lying, 159
  insincerity conflated with, 3–4
  and intent to deceive, 32
  and Maxim of Sincerity, 41–42
  miscalls of, 88–89
  versus misleading, 44–45, 125, 145–49
  misleading as, 49, 54–55, 159
  misleading without, 159
  versus negligent falsehood, 81
  non-deceptive, 33–34
  by omission, 151
  and polite suspensions of sincerity, 128–29
  as self-contradiction, 165–70
  versus suspension of sincerity, 125
  in TRUST framework, 239–40
  willfulness in, 172–73
  and Word-Mind-World problem of untruthfulness, 15–16

malapropism, 121, 143, 165
Maxims of Conversation, 39–42, 40*t*
   deception as violation of, 139–43
   flouting of, 41–42, 46–47, 113, 115,140–42, 141*f*
   Maxim of Evidence, 69–71
   Maxim of Manner, 220–21
   Maxim of Quality, 73–74, 112–13, 142, 220–21
   Maxim of Quantity, 151, 220–21
   Maxim of Relation, 220–21
   Maxim of Sincerity, 41–42, 74, 75, 123–24
   revised maxim of truthfulness, 73–75
May, Theresa, 263–64. *See also* Skripal poisoning
McCornack, Steven, 50–52, 92, 140, 142, 162, 221, 226
Meadow, Roy, 224
Media Bias/Fact Check (MBFC), 102–3
Meibauer, Jörg, 34–35, 37, 159–60, 162, 163
meiosis, 169, 190
mendacity, 57, 74
mental reservation, 9
metaphor, 113, 119, 121, 141*t*
metaphysical realism, 104–5
minimizing, 168–70, 182
Mirzayanov, Vil, 267–68
miscitation, 182, 193
Mishkin, Alexander, 263–64, 272–73
misleading
   in Blair's Foreword to Iraq Dossier, 261
   in Brexit Battle Bus message, 251–52
   conceptions of, 159–60
   versus deception, 159–60
   deception categories similar to, 149, 150*t*
   and discursive insincerity, 54–55
   as discursively leading astray, 158–64
   as disrupting inquiry, 48–50
   evasion and, 155
   and false implicature, 145
   forms of, 49
   insincerity and, 4
   and limitations to analysis of sincerity, 285
   versus lying, 44–45, 125, 145–49
   lying as form of, 49, 54–55
   and spin, 164
   versus suspension of sincerity, 125
   through inference, 162–63
   through reframing, 163–64
   through semantics, 160–61
misreport, 182, 193–94
misrepresentation, 6, 19
monologic discourse, 80
Montmarquet, James 59, 64, 214

moral reasoning, Golden Rule and, 116–19
motivation
   for calling out lying, 88–94
   for breach of trust, 225–27
"murderer at the door" case, 9, 119, 129–30
mutual knowledge and implicature, 45–46
myth, 81, 89, 108, 168, 201

nation, as socially constructed community, 107, 108
negligence, epistemic. *See* epistemic negligence
negligent falsehood, 81–83
noble lies, 172–73
nonsense, 72–73
   learned, 198
non-verbal untruthfulness, 45, 91, 166, 285
normalization, as discursive symptom of dogma, 187–88
not intentional misrepresentation, 6
Novichok, 263–64, 266–68, 272, 275–76.
   See also Skripal poisoning

Obama, Michelle, 199–200
obfuscating/obfuscation, 160
obscurantism, 198
omission, 151–52, 153–54
overstatement, 169, 182, 191–92, 258–59.
   See also exaggerating
overtly untruthful speech acts, 112–13

partisanship, epistemic, 103, 262–63, 291–95
paternalistic suspensions of sincerity, 130
pathological discourse, 80–81, 181–82, 195–97, 240*f*, 289. *See also* epistemically irresponsible discourse pathologies
pathological suspensions of truthfulness, 132
Paxman, Jeremy, 155–57
performed suspension of commitment to truthfulness, 123–24, 132–33
perjury, 148, 159, 172
persecution lie, 35
Petrov, Alexander, 263–64
plagiarism, 153–54, 154*t*, 172
Plato, 122
playful suspensions of sincerity or epistemic responsibility, 131–32
poetry, 122
politeness
   and untruthfulness, 32, 114, 120, 144, 204, 237, 239, 290, 294
   polite suspensions of sincerity, 32, 34–35, 127–29, 132–33

political interviews, evasion in, 154–57
polygraph, 91, 170
Popper, Karl 79–80, 97, 105n
pragmatics, 2, 14, 17, 38, 136, 284–85
pragmatism, 104–5
pranking, 131–32
prescribed conventional suspensions of truthfulness, 120–23
prescribed suspension of commitment to truthfulness, 121–23, 132–33
presumption, 27, 39, 80, 143, 286.
 See also truthfulness
presupposing, falsely, 163
pretending, 4, 66, 113, 144, 150*t*, 153, 163, 166
Principle of Charity, 190
prior record, 227–28
private suspensions of sincerity, 126–27, 132–33
professional dishonesty, 218–19
promise, 36–37, 89, 249
propaganda, 15, 103, 276–79
propositional justification, 58–59
prosocial lie, 34–35
protective suspensions of sincerity, 129–30, 132–33
provocation/*provokatsiia*, 228, 276–77
pseudo-poppycock, 182, 196–97, 201–2
pseudo-profound bullshit, 198
pseudoscientific poppycock, 202
puffery, 172–73
Putin, Vladimir, 267, 269, 271–72, 274, 277

Quebec mosque terrorist attack, 208–10

realism, metaphysical, 104–5
reciprocal altruism, 29–31, 36–37, 116–17
relativity
 falsity and epistemological, 105–7
 prescribed conventional suspensions of truthfulness and cultural, 121–23
 socially constructed, 107–8
 truth-irrelevant contexts, 113–14
reliability, 100–3, 238, 244, 250, 255
Republic (Plato), 122
reputation, 203–205
responsibility. *See also* epistemic responsibility
 and scope of truthfulness, 27–28
 in TRUST heuristic, 234–37, 235*t*, 241
rhetorical bullshitting, 180
ritualized greetings, 113–14
Roberts, Craige, 48, 68, 71
role responsibility, 83, 203, 259
Rorty, Richard, 106
rude dismissal, 186, 258–59, 285, 286

Rumsfeld, Donald, 256–57
Russian disinformation, 276–77, 278

salience, in communication, 51–53
Salisbury Statement. *See* Skripal poisoning
satire, 270–71
Saul, Jennifer, 81–83, 120–21, 125, 165–66, 172
scope of truthfulness, 27–28
scope of untruthfulness, 1, 2–7, 18–19, 284–86
Searle, John R., 4, 43–44, 74, 76, 96
self-contradiction, 92–93, 165–70
self-deception, 91, 111
self-protective suspensions of sincerity, 130, 215–16
simple reversal, 186
sincerity. *See also* insincerity
 assertion and, 43–45
 as confused with authenticity, 50n.20
 defined, 48, 49–50
 insincere performances of, 90
 lying/misleading versus suspension of, 125
 maxim of, 41–42, 74, 75, 123–24
 paternalistic suspensions of, 130
 playful suspensions of, 131–32
 polite suspensions of, 127–29, 132–33
 private suspensions of, 126–27, 132–33
 protective suspensions of, 129–30, 132–33
 and scope of truthfulness, 27–28
 self-protective suspensions of, 130, 215–16
 in TRUST heuristic, 234–37, 235*t*, 239–40
Sincerity Rule of Assertion, 43–44
situated context of acts of untruthfulness, 1, 288–90
skepticism, 79
Skripal poisoning, 282–83
 British inflation of claims, 273–76
 culpability and judgment of claims, 280–81
 epistemic irresponsibility of claims, 277–80
 Russian disinformation, 276–77
 suspension of commitment to truthfulness regarding, 270–73
social constructionism, 107–8
Socrates, 79–80, 101, 105, 122, 224
source evaluators, 102–3
source reliability, 100–3, 238, 244, 250, 255
Sovereign Citizen documents, 201
"Spartacus" case 34, 35
speaker, epistemic and institutional power of, 224–25
speech, freedom of, 205, 294
speech acts, 4, 9, 14, 43–44, 74–75, 97, 112–13, 115, 144, 166
spin, 164, 170, 172–73

Stalnaker, Robert, 38, 45, 48
Stokke, Andreas, 4, 42, 48–50, 68
strategic goal, in communication, 51
strategic trust, 216–19
sufficient investigation, 205–6, 247
supermaxim of Truthfulness, 73–75, 123–24
super-strategies, 164
Suspensions Analysis, 134–36
suspensions of truthfulness
    condonable, 131–33
    consequential, 125–30, 132–33
    conventional, 120–24
    as justifiable and justified, 136
    performed, 123–24, 132–33
    prescribed, 121–23, 132–33
    summary and sample analysis of, 132–36
    in TRUST heuristic, 234–37, 235t, 238–39
    warranting the truth and, 114–16
Sweetser, Eve, 5, 9, 29, 93, 113–14, 127, 207

taking words out of context, 16, 164
taqiyya, 129, 133
temptation resistance paradigm 91
testimony, 10, 81, 90, 92–93, 100, 292
    testimonial sensibility, 292–93
third party, vulnerability of, 222–24
token, versus type, 275
torture, 130–31
trolling, 204, 228, 276, 278–79
Troubled Families Programme, 158, 161
Trump, Donald
    and aggravation of untruthfulness, 227–28
    Cambridge Analytica used in election campaign of, 294
    and discursive insincerity, 174–76
    and distortion, 189–90
    and false news, 168, 186
    as lying, 15
    and normalization, 187–88
    track record of, 102
    and truth as subjective perception, 87
    voter fraud tweet of, 78, 243–48, 277
Trump, Melania, 200
trust. *See also* gravity of breach of trust
    betrayed, 31
    connection between truthfulness and, 286–87
    cooperation and, 27–28
    deception as not requisite for breach of, 36–37
    epistemic responsibility and, 58–65
    and ethical commitment to truthfulness, 30–32
    ethical dimensions of, 222t
    and ethical value of untruthfulness, 19
    and Grice's Cooperative Principle, 38–39
    and intent to deceive, 32–33
    and location of ethical value of untruthfulness, 9–10, 19
    motive of breach of, 226
    and presumption of truthfulness, 28–30
    strategic and communicative, 216–19
    unjustified breach of, 287
    willful insincerity and breaches of, 171
TRUST framework
    applied to sample analyses, 233–34
    and calling out lies and bullshit, 88
    central theoretical propositions of, 18–20
    and counteracting untruthfulness, 294–95
    critical awareness developed in, 293
    and fighting against epistemic partisanship, 291–95
    link between, categories and other taxonomies, 149
    and negligent falsehood, 82–83
    overview of, 20–23
    and regulation of civic discourse, 294
    tools for analyzing untruthfulness in situated discourse in, 11–18
TRUST heuristic, 234–42
    applied to Blair's Foreword to Iraq Dossier, 253–61
    applied to Brexit Battle Bus message, 249–53
    applied to Trump's voter fraud tweet, 243–48
trustor, vulnerability of, 222–24
trustworthiness
    and culpability, 217–19, 227–28
    of source, 100–103
    of speaker, 29–31
truth
    "by-likes," 105–6
    consensus theory of, 106
    dogma and distortion of, 80
    epistemic responsibility as caring for, 62–63
    ethical evaluation of, 111–12
    half-truth, 153. *See also* omission
    as relative to discourse/interpretative community, 105–7
    and social constructionism, 107–8
    as subjective, 87
    "telling the," 7
    as valued by insincere speakers, 145–46
    warranting, 114–16
    withholding, 54–55

truthfulness. *See also* justifiable suspensions of truthfulness
  analysis of suspension of, in TRUST heuristic, 234–37, 235t, 238–39
  condonable suspension of commitment to, 131–33, 238–39
  connection between trust and, 286–87
  consequential suspension of commitment to, 125–30, 132–33, 238–39
  conventional suspension of commitment to, 120–24, 238–39
  economy of, 111–16
  ethical commitment to, 30–32
  ethical value of untruthfulness and speaker's commitment to, 10
  Golden Rule and exemption from, 119–20
  justifiable suspensions of, 133t, 238–39
  maxim of, 73–75
  pathological suspensions of, 132
  performed suspension of commitment to, 123–24, 132–33
  prescribed suspension of commitment to, 121–23, 132–33
  presumption of, 28–30, 93, 112, 115, 117, 119, 217, 286
  relevance of, 113–14
  revised maxim of, 73–75
  scope of, 27–28
  standard of, 212
  as subjective, 18, 87
  summary and sample analysis of suspension of commitment to, 132–36
  supermaxim of, 73–75, 123–24
  suspending commitment to, 114–16
  suspension of, 83
  trust and presumption of, 28–30
  as virtue, 30–31
  willful insincerity and suspension of commitment to, 172
  Williams's conception of, 63–64
truth-irrelevant contexts, 113–14
turnaround, 161
Twitter
  Fox News's tweet on Quebec mosque terrorist attack, 208–10
  and prescribed suspension of commitment to truthfulness, 123
  Trump tweets on voter fraud, 78, 243–48, 277
  tweets on Skripal poisoning, 278–81
type, versus token, 275

uncertainty, 58, 64, 207, 217, 257, 267
understatement, 169, 182, 191–92
universality, claims of, 289–90

unreliability, 282
untruthfulness, as best starting point for TRUST framework, 6–7. *See also* claims of untruthfulness; ethical value of untruthfulness; justified untruthfulness
utterance insincerity, 4, 19

van der Geest, Sjaak, 126–27
victim, deliberate targeting of, 228
video evidence, 100–1
Vincent Marrelli, Jocelyn, 6, 113, 123, 144, 149, 160, 163
virtue
  epistemic responsibility as intellectual and moral, 61–63
  truthfulness as, 30–31
voter fraud, 78, 243–48, 277
Voter Fraud Commission, 245–46

warranted assertibility, 104
warranting context, 120–22, 165, 166, 172, 179, 216
warranting the truth, 5, 13, 47, 51, 106, 109, 114–15, 222t, 225, 271
weapons of mass destruction, 253–61
Weinrich, Harald 15–17
willful insincerity, 11, 19, 138, 170–73, 240, 245, 258, 287. *See also* intentionality
Williams, Bernard, 30–31, 44–45, 49–50, 62–64
Williamson, Gavin, 37
wishful bullshitting, 181
withholding. *See also* equivocating; evasion; false implicature; misleading; obfuscating; omission
  and analysis of Trump's discursive sincerity, 175–76
  blocking and, 152, 157–58
  of claims in Brexit Battle Bus message, 251–52
  as concealing relevant information, 150–58
  deception categories similar to, 149, 150t
  and discursive insincerity, 4, 52–53, 54–55, 145–46, 150–58
  evasion as, 155
  and limitations to analysis of sincerity, 285
  versus misleading and lying, 145–49
  as omission, 151–52
  sub-strategies of, 151–52, 152f
  willfulness in, 172–73
Wittgenstein, Ludwig 79, 111, 124
Word-Mind-World problem of untruthfulness, 14–17
working memory, 51–52
wronged, feeling, 31
wrongness, 212–13